HOLDING THEIR GROUND

Class, Locality and Culture in 19th and 20th Century South Africa

History Workshop 4

HOLDING
THEIR
GROUND

Class, Locality and Culture
in 19th and 20th Century South Africa

Edited by Philip Bonner, Isabel Hofmeyr,
Deborah James and Tom Lodge

 Witwatersrand University Press

Ravan Press

Published by

Ravan Press (Pty) Ltd
PO Box 31134, Braamfontein, Johannesburg, 2017 , South Africa

and

Witwatersrand University Press
1 Jan Smuts Avenue, Johannesburg, 2001, South Africa

First published in 1989

ISBN 0 86975 398 3

Cover design by Nicholas W Combrinck and Diaset (Pty) Ltd
Set in 11/12 point Garamond by GraphicSet, Blairgowrie, Randburg
Printed and bound by Sigma Press (Pty) Ltd

CONTENTS

ii

Preface

Although this book's main purpose is to provide readers with a collection of the papers which were presented at the academic conference of the 1987 History Workshop, it would be incomplete without a description of the other main event for which many will remember the 1987 Workshop — the Open Day, this year entitled the Festival of History and Culture. As in previous years, the purpose of this event was to present to audiences from a wide range of backgrounds a selection of films, plays, videos, slide shows and exhibitions depicting the history and struggles of local communities.

Attracting an audience to the Open Day always poses a number of difficulties. Careful planning is needed if the Workshop is to reach all strata of a society as deeply divided as that of South Africa. One factor is the geographical distance between white suburban dwellers — who are well placed to attend functions at the University campus — and black township inhabitants who would not automatically regard cultural events at this venue as theirs to attend. Mere press publicity, on its own, would not be sufficient to counteract this problem. At the last Open Day, our solution was to spend a large proportion of the budget on providing buses for trade unionists and other groups. This tended, however, to limit somewhat the range of people who attended the Open Day. On this occasion, we decided to cut down on bussing and rather to concentrate on working through a broader range of organisations including the Commercial, Catering and Allied Workers Union of South Africa (CCAWUSA), the Metal and Allied Workers Union (MAWU), the Congress of South African Trade Unions (COSATU), the Council of Unions of South Africa (CUSA), and the National Education Union of South Africa (NEUSA). Additional people were reached through newspaper advertisements and through sending a programme of events to those on our substantial mailing list.

When the audience finally arrived on Saturday 14 February, it was as large and as varied in interest and affiliation as we could have hoped. While the enthusiasm matched that of previous Open Day audiences, this was now tempered by a degree of seriousness. Euphoric and celebratory culture seemed to have given way to new purposefulness and determination.

While some of the cultural and media presentations came from the broader community of artists, actors, film-makers and journalists, a number were made by members of the Workshop itself. The display of these items at the Open Day at once provided an opportunity to make known the Workshop's projects to the wider public, while allowing audience responses to feed back into the development of new projects or the refinement of existing ones. Of all these projects, perhaps the most demanding and challenging had been the making — with the expert help and guidance of the members of the American Social History Project (ASHP) — of the slide/tape show *Fight Where We Stand*. The script had been written in consultation with groups of potential users, and this had revealed much about what preoccupied those we were attempting to reach. When it was shown at the Open Day, the great interest shown by audiences in its form and content suggested that this had, indeed, been a fruitful approach. Especially successful — and greeted by applause — was the suggestion that the story of the characters in the show was not merely a remote piece of history, but that it continued into the present through their current struggles against demands for rent by township authorities. The enthusiastic response from a wide range of groups also indicated to Workshop members who had compiled the show that they had been wise to resist pressure, exerted earlier by some political groupings, to present particular, organisation-bound versions of events.

Also drawing an interested response from audiences were several of the ASHP slide shows, and their film *1877*. Two slide/tape shows made by participants in the History Workshop training workshops in September 1986 were presented as well. *Mr Big Beaten by History*, made by the Swaziland Oral History Project, depicted the role of oral traditions in the present, and *In Search of Roots: Beginnings of the SA Chinese* was made by the Transvaal Chinese Assocation.

Besides slide/tape shows there were other presentations, too, which provided dramatic and immediate illustration of historical experiences and events. *Factory Vrouens* was a play compiled from plays and poetry written by Afrikaner women garment workers during the 1930s and 1940s, collected and researched by Elsabe Brink, a history Masters student from the University of the Witwatersrand. Watching this play, which was enthusiastically received by worker audiences, we asked ourselves whether the Workshop is destined never to expand its interest in the white working class beyond the only segment of it which adopted a less than hard-line racist ideology. Should not our commitment to research with an independent agenda lead us to look at the rest of this working class, and to confront our audiences with its peculiar and unpalatable character as well as its role in our struggle?

As well as providing a forum for the presentation of Workshop- or University-linked projects, the day allowed for cultural expressions by a large number of groups with cultural wares to show. Some of these treated the opportunity to perform at the Open Day as a public statement of their commitment; as a means of informing outsiders sympathetic to their cause of their struggles and histories.

Among these were a number of worker-orientated productions. *Qonda* — 'a play about attempts to disorganise workers in the context of township violence' — was initiated by the Dunlop Workers who had appeared at the previous open day. *The Long March* explored the plight of the community in the light of a strike at BTR Sarmcol; a working-class choir called the 'K Team' sang worker songs; and *Death is Part of the Process* was an exploration by Granada TV of the recent mining tragedy at the Kinross Mine. The National Union of Mineworkers sent a large contingent of workers to see the show, where they participated in style. *Night Shift* explored the experiences of a woman shift worker, while *Women without Men* examined the experiences of the families of migrant workers in the Transkei.

One of the most moving displays was that by a delegation of people from Mogopa, a removed community engaged in an ongoing struggle to retain ownership of their land against the efforts of the state to remove them to a designated black area. Their appearance at the Open Day was prompted by the fact that a video of their history and experience of resistance to removal was being shown. Their way of participating, however, brought its own particular spirit to the day. A group of about one hundred elderly rural people arrived by bus, after a long journey. They were dressed in colourful hand-made clothing (some intricately and skilfully fashioned from woven strips of discarded plastic bags) and carried banners protesting against their removal. After assembling in the Great Hall foyer holding their banners aloft, they began to sing, walking slowly through the University corridors towards the place where their video was being shown. The vividness and immediacy of this group's expression of resistance reminded many among the crowds attending the Open Day of the Sofasonke party's participation in the 1984 Workshop. The Mogopa people seemed, indeed, to be trying to create their own history in the present, before our eyes.

That a similar spirit pervaded much of the Open Day was indicated by some newspaper reviews. The *Star* reported:

> The open day was intended, say the organisers, to involve people in reinterpreting their past. That may be so in terms of the film and photographic contributions and a production like 'Factory Vrouens'... But in the majority of performances, drawn from townships in the Transvaal and Natal, the past was hijacked for the present.

And according to the *Weekly Mail*,

> You could hardly walk 20 paces without coming upon another group of people dancing in a huddle and singing freedom songs... The campus at Wits was transformed. The casual visitor might have been forgiven for thinking that the revolution had already happened... Surprising, to say the least, for the open day at an academic conference. But the History Workshop is no ordinary academic conference, and far more importantly, this is no ordinary point in history. What charged the air on Saturday, what transfixed the proceedings, was an inescapable sense that, far from merely dealing with history, this actually *was* history.

The day was packed with so many events that many found it difficult to choose between them. The musical event that finally drew it to a close, however, seemed to be a unanimous choice, and people began to pack into the Great Hall to listen to the *mbube* singing of the Soshanguve Black Tycoons. Inspired by Ladysmith Black Mambazo, but with a repertoire of entirely original songs written by their leader David Ndaba, this group of high-school students enthralled the audience with their perfectly co-ordinated dance movements and their witty and topical lyrics.

But just when it seemed that the day's events had finally ended, a crowd of youths and children streamed on to the stage. These were members and friends of the Soshanguve Youth Group. The entirely unexpected and unscheduled performance they gave, in which large segments of the audience were caught up and participated with vigour and excitement, seemed to be final proof that people from the broader community had finally appropriated the Open Day, its events and its meanings, for themselves.

We would like to thank the many people and organisations whose help and co-operation made the 1987 History Workshop — the Open Day, the Popular History Day, and the academic conference — so successful.

Outstanding planning and organisation, as well as a great deal of unpaid and out of hours labour, was given by our administrative secretary Betsy Coville, by Open Day organiser Anne Mullins, and by administrative assistant Roshnie Moonsammy. We are grateful to the Ford Foundation for their generous financial support, both for *Fight Where we Stand* and for the Open Day; and to the University of the Witwatersrand for its overall funding of the Workshop, and for its more specific support and co-operation for the conference and Open Day of 1987. Numerous university departments and administrative units helped us in a variety of ways, and we thank them for this.

There were many who supported the Workshop by their attendance and enthusiastic participation, and who are too numerous to be thanked by name. Presenters and audiences at the Open Day, researchers and writers attending the academic conference, and popularisers involved in the session on popularising history; all through their participation helped to make the Workshop what it was.

Philip Bonner   Belinda Bozzoli   Luli Callinicos
Peter Delius   Ahmed Essop   Isabel Hofmeyr
Jonathan Hyslop   Georgina Jaffee   Deborah James
Paul la Hausse   Tom Lodge   Andy Manson
Charles van Onselin   Eddie Webster   Leslie Witz

Acknowledgements

The photograph of the Ndebele bride in her cloak was taken by Constance Stuart Larrabee who was kind enough to send us several of her pictures for us to choose from. © Constance Stuart Larrabee 1989. The archival picture of Chief Nyabela Mahlangu is lodged in the University of Pretoria and was brought to our attention in the Master's Dissertation by Albert van Jaarsveld, Department of History, University of Zululand. The publishers extend their thanks for this material and for any material whose copyright holders have inadvertently been overlooked in spite of careful research.

FULL LIST OF CONFERENCE PAPERS

Besides those included in this book, the following papers were presented to the Conference. A full set of papers is available in the University of the Witwatersrand Africana Library.

VIVIAN BICKFORD-SMITH: Cape Town at the Advent of the Mineral Revolution, c. 1875: Economic Activity and Social Structure.

G. BLOCH: Popularising History: Some Reflections and Experiences.

PHILIP BONNER: Family, Crime and Political Consciousness on the East Rand, 1939-1955.

DEBBY BONNIN: Two Generations of Worker Leadership: The Histories and Traditions of the Sarmcol Workers.

J. BOTTOMLEY: Political Resurgence in the Orange River Colony, and the Brandfort Congress of 1904.

E. BRINK: 'Only Decent Girls Are Employed': The Respectability, Decency and Virtue of the Garment Workers on the Witwatersrand during the Thirties.

DAVID BROWN: The Basements of Babylon: English Literacy and the Division of Labour on the South African Gold Mines.

COLIN BUNDY: Street Sociology and Pavement Politics: Aspects of Youth/Student Resistance in Cape Town, 1985.

G. CAMPBELL: Labour and the Problem of Class in Nineteenth-Century Imerina (Madagascar).

J.T. CAMPBELL: T.D. Mweli Skota and the Making and Unmaking of a Black Elite.

MATTHEW CHASKALSON, KAREN JOCHELSON AND SEBASTIAN JEREMY: Rent Boycotts and the Urban Political Economy.

LINDA CHISHOLM: Crime, Class and Nationalism: The Criminology of Jacob de Villiers Roos, 1869-1918.

STEPHEN CLINGMAN: Biography and Representation: Some Analogies from Fiction.

TIM CLYNICK: Chiefs, Concessionaires and Reserve Politics on the Tlaping Alluvial Diamond Diggings at Taung, 1919-1921: A

LIST OF CONTRIBUTORS

PHILIP BONNER is Associate Professor in the Department of History, University of the Witwatersrand. He is author of *Kings, Commoners and Concessionaires: The Evolution and Dissolution of the 19th Century Swazi State* (Cambridge and Johannesburg, 1983), and editor of *Working Papers in Southern African Studies*, Vol. I (Johannesburg, 1977) and Vol. II (Johannesburg, 1981). He has published on black urbanisation and politics on the Rand, South African labour history, and contemporary trade unionism in South Africa.

PETER DELIUS is a Senior Lecturer in the Department of History, University of the Witwatersrand. He is the author of *The Land Belongs to Us* (Johannesburg, 1983; London, 1984), *The Conversion* (Johannesburg, 1984), and co-editor of *Putting a Plough to the Ground* (Johannesburg, 1986).

KATHY EALES is completing an MA in History which explores the significance of gender in the administration of African women in Johannesburg before 1940. She works as a publications officer at the Centre for Applied Legal Studies, University of the Witwatersrand.

IAIN EDWARDS is a Research Fellow in the Centre for Social and Development Studies, University of Natal, Durban. His PhD is concerned with African shackland society in Durban in the nineteen-thirties and forties.

ISABEL HOFMEYR is a Lecturer in African Literature at the University of the Witwatersrand. She has published in the field of South African literature and culture.

DEBORAH JAMES is a Lecturer in the Department of Social Anthropology, University of the Witwatersrand. Her MA, completed in 1987, is concerned with household structure, land tenure and ethnicity in a mixed Pedi/Ndebele community in Lebowa.

PAUL LA HAUSSE is a Research Officer in the African Studies Institute, University of the Witwatersrand. In 1984 he completed his MA on 'The Struggle for the City: Alcohol, the Ematsheni and Popular Culture in Durban, 1902-36'. He is the author of *Brewers, Beerhalls and Boycotts: A History of Liquor in South Africa* (Johannesburg, 1988), and is presently doing research on black politics and culture in Natal.

TOM LODGE lectured in the Department of Political Science, University of the Witwatersrand, from 1978 to 1988. He is now Director of the Africa Program at the Social Science Research Council, New York. He is the author of *Black Politics in South Africa since 1945* (London and Johannesburg, 1983).

BILL NASSON is a Lecturer in Economic History at the University of Cape Town. He is co-editor of *Education: From Poverty to Liberty* (Cape Town and New York, 1989), and author of *Abraham Esau's War: The Making of a Black South African War in the Cape Colony*, 1899-1902, which is forthcoming.

PAUL RICH is a lecturer in Politics at the University of Bristol. He is the author of *White Power and the Liberal Conscience* (London and Johannesburg, 1984), *Race and Empire in British Politics* (Cambridge, 1986), and co-editor of *Race, Government and Politics in Britain* (London, 1986). He is currently working on a study of political ideologies in South Africa entitled *The Apartheid Mind and its Enemies*.

HILARY SAPIRE is a researcher at the Centre for Policy Studies, University of the Witwatersrand. She has recently completed a PhD on 'African Urbanisation and Struggles against Municipal Controls in Brakpan, 1920-1958'.

Introduction

Philip Bonner and Tom Lodge

The papers brought together in this volume are a selection from those presented to the fourth History Workshop Conference held at the University of the Witwatersrand in February 1987. As with previous History Workshop Conferences, the proceedings divided themselves into two related parts — the sessions at which academic papers were presented, and a Festival of History and Culture. The Festival of History and Culture is described in the Preface to this collection. The academic section of the conference, and more specifically the papers included in this volume, are the subject of this introduction.

The theme of the conference was 'The Making of Class'. Altogether ninety-two papers were presented on topics related to this theme. The eight papers selected for this volume thus represent only a tiny fraction of the academic labour expended on the conference. Papers relating to two distinct sub-themes of the conference have however been published elsewhere. Vol. 13, No. 2, 1988 of *Social Dynamics* is devoted to a selection of five papers presented to the conference on the theme of 'exploring experiential testimonies', while *Perspectives on Education*, Vol. 10, No. 2, Summer 1989, includes three papers presented at the day of the conference which focused on People's History.

The papers presented to the 1987 conference were exceptionally rich and wide ranging. Contributions on pre-colonial and nineteenth-century South African history were far more numerous than before, and there was a much more even spread of contributions across all regions of South Africa. In addition, sixteen papers dealt with contemporary politics, culture, work-place and society, demonstrating a welcome new vigour in the field of contemporary studies. Across the whole spectrum of contributions the issues of community, class, culture and consciousness figured prominently, and there was a marked continuity with and progression from the 1984 Conference and the selection of papers from it published under the title *Class, Community and Conflict*. It is on these issues that this introduction primarily focuses.

Community, Space and Class

'Social life is inscribed in space and time', writes P.Clavel.[1] Frederick Cooper expands on this theme. 'Marxist theory,' he contends, 'has to confront the fact that social relations exist in space; even as society shapes space, space shapes society.' Elsewhere in the same chapter Cooper adds that 'much space in African cities is illegal space'.[2] Cooper's remarks are especially pertinent to South Africa where the policy of segregation has made the contestation of space one of the central political struggles. In the towns this battle was fully joined in the early twentieth century. On the Rand, after a brief hiatus of indecision in the early 1900s, when both capital and the state chose to countenance the establishment of uncontrolled black urban communities in informal locations on mine ground and in the freehold townships in the western areas of Johannesburg and Alexandra, the state took decisive steps to prevent this recurring and to close all remaining spaces down.[3] A central theme in the history of black urban communities in South Africa was thereafter their attempts to create and defend illegal space. A central thrust of state urban policy was equally to close down such communities and to quarantine them in localities selected by the state where they could be more effectively regimented and controlled.

The protracted battle of attrition was joined when the central features of segregation hardened into fixed form. A vast thicket of state and municipal influx control regulations and interlocking permits was built up to try and stem the flow, but this proved incapable of checking the repeated surges of black immigration to the towns. These continued to seep into every unpoliced or unprotected pocket of illegal space, engendering fears among white working-class and middle-class urban dwellers that they were being swamped in an engulfing black tide.

A number of contributors to this collection discuss different aspects of this process. Sapire's paper examines an early phase of black urbanisation on the Rand to which scant attention is normally given. She indicates how white working- and middle-class fears about the economic, social and political threat of black immigration were cast in the form of the social metaphors of the 'sanitation syndrome' and 'black peril' scares over black molestation of white women, and provided an early impulse to urban segregation. Parts of this story are familiar from the work of Koch among others.[4] A particularly important area of contested terrain to which Sapire draws our attention, however, is settlement or 'squatting' in peri-urban areas. This was especially pronounced on the Rand. In 1919 the South African Party made provision for the sub-division of farms in the peri-urban areas into smallholdings on which white pensioners and phthisis sufferers might settle. The move was intended to defuse white worker militancy, particularly among miners.[5] In certain respects it fulfilled the government's expectations, but not in the way it had intended. Smallholdings became important centres of capital accumulation as the holders proceeded to rack-rent black tenants.

These dispersed informal settlements proved exceptionally difficult to police and were soon soaking up illegal occupants like a sponge. As with the diamond diggings for white workers, where a whole range of informal and illegal economic activities also flourished, they often acted as a net which the newly dispossessed could catch in the free fall towards full proletarianisation.[6] A highly heterogeneous set of communities established themselves on these semi-rural grey areas next to Brakpan and other Reef towns. Share-cropping families, the wives of miners who were working on neighbouring mines, single male workers in town, and a host of others engaged in petty commodity production and criminal activities clustered in these zones. Little is known of the culture, or of the family and other social relationships of this increasingly important component of the urban proletariat in the making. Isabel Hofmeyr, in her paper in this collection, cites Raymond Williams as suggesting that places have to be made both materially and imaginatively. We have no idea of how these groups imagined themselves or even if they imagined themselves collectively as a community or communities. Clearly, therefore, a rich new area of research beckons, which is pointed to by the work of Sapire and others in this volume.

The same theme of illegal space and peri-urban settlement runs through the papers of Edwards and La Hausse. La Hausse shows how, as early as the mid-1920s, 22 000 people lived in shacks on the fringes of Durban's municipal area. Edwards calculates that at Mkhumbane (Cato Manor), again on the periphery of Durban, a population of 24 000 squatters had congregated by 1949. La Hausse says comparatively little about the shape and structures of these groups, and is concerned more with the political dynamics of the varied and transitional urban cultures that they helped spawn. Here workers could 'create cultural alternatives to everyday coercion and control', centring on the shebeen and other illegal or informal income-generating activities. It was the creation of an alternative cultural milieu, of 'a rich and subversive language of protest', and of a passively or actively oppositional culture in such areas which gave urban authorities in Durban such cause for concern. Identical fears, as Eales shows, were expressed on the Rand. Citing Fred Cooper, she argues that such illegal space 'did little to socialise people into a rigid labour discipline' but rather helped forge a subversive ethos of non-work and non-accommodation. It was within this illegal space, in La Hausse's argument, that 'the autonomy of the beer brewers, the self-assertion of the amalaita and the restlessness of the *abaqhafi*' could mingle together, in a potentially highly combustible combination.

Edwards tells us less about culture, but says more of composition and form. Like the Rand peri-urban settlements, the 1940s squatter encampment of Mkhumbane enclosed a varied and diverse population, 60 per cent of whom were recent arrivals to the town. Unlike earlier, more dispersed and amorphous peri-urban settlements, it had a clear structure and form. Mkhumbane was clearly 'made', both materially and imaginatively. It existed in a defined and circumscribed place and, according to Edwards, it had a sense of unity and community based on the circulation of money, commodities, and services, and the interdependencies forged by the complexity of shack ownership and sub-tenancy as well as by co-operatives and stokvels. It was informed by and distilled a vision and philosophy of 'New Africa' which, if perhaps not completely pieced together in this paper, obviously spoke powerfully to racist and populist sentiments. The community also generated its own political structures, although these remain in the background, and somewhat obscured behind the vision of New Africa. These were civilian guards and 'self-elected leaders' — charismatic, undemocratic, often uneducated shack-owning petty entrepreneurs. The latter themes are among the most interesting and least researched of this period of urbanisation and of other attempts at other times to seize illegal space. To the issue of leadership we will return later in this introduction.

Among the senses that are most powerfully conveyed in Edwards's paper is the buoyancy and bustle of this community. Like so many other black urban communities between the 1920s and the 1940s, Mkhumbane adopted a largely defensive culture, defending the uncontrolled space it had won. But this did not imply a cramped, apprehensive and apathetic collective cast of mind. Rather what comes through clearly in Edwards's account is the vigour, the self-confidence, and the multiple initiatives of these inhabitants of the shacks — their brash energy and self-reliance, which found its characteristic expressions in the shackland's vast informal economy, and in its multitude of co-operatives and stokvels. Edwards's focus on co-operatives is indeed both timely and suggestive. The role of stokvels in black urban communities is relatively well known; that of co-operatives is considerably more opaque. A number of other contributions to this collection touch on this issue of co-operatives where they emerge as an important and under-researched area of black activity and initiative in the inter-war years. Edwards's treatment suggests that we have yet to gain a sufficiently rounded and differentiated understanding of their activities, and that their operations may in instances extend beyond the manipulations of a failed or frustrated African petty bourgeoisie.

Some of the themes developed by Edwards and La Hausse find echoes in Bill Nasson's paper on Cape Town's District Six. Nasson's rich, evocative and nuanced study of daily life in District Six in the 1930s and 1940s depicts an equally robust and boisterous working class to that described by Edwards and La Hausse. By virtue of its deeper historical roots, it was also infinitely more cohesive and stable. Like Mkhumbane, Nasson portrays District Six as exhibiting a basically defensive culture. However, in a way only matched by Sophiatown on the Rand — so Nasson argues — it had a powerful sense of its own coherence, identity and place: in Williams's terms, it was in a much fuller sense imaginatively constructed. A pervasive feature of practically every aspect of popular culture and leisure time in District Six was that it was 'neighbourly and shared'. Leisure consumption was not 'private and anonymous' but boisterous and communal. Neither church leaders nor middle-class cultural entrepreneurs succeeded in directing or sanitising this culture: to the end it remained autonomous — as Nasson puts it, 'worker-organised and worker-led'. Partly structuring these relationships was another dimension of space. There was simply too little room for a private encapsulated family life. Even schools did not have yards big enough for the schoolchildren to play games. Constricted space thus drove leisure on to the streets. Not surprisingly perhaps, in the Coon Carnival, 'the ritual climax of the recreational year', the whole population took to the streets, storming — as Pinnock reminded us in a contribution to a previous History Workshop volume — the city centres, avenues and arcades.[7]

One key to the creation and preservation of this identity was the way in which it placed its own construction on leisure time and leisure activity. Nasson's paper takes us into that leisure realm and reveals the dense world of meanings, styles, symbols and signs that constituted District Six's sense of place and culture. Importantly, he shows this culture to be something constantly made, created, fashioned and imagined from what he calls 'the indigenous resources of the locality'. These resources could be any detail of everyday life that anyone with a sharp eye or a quick wit could transform into an occasion or street performance. The detail could be anything like a physical deformity, and unusual colour of hair, or, importantly, a movie — ever a crucial resource from which stories and selves could be crafted.

One of the central impulses behind these quixotic cultural forms was a very particular verbal style and sense of humour. These patterns of narration highlight the important area of everyday storytelling and narrative that 'enables' the expression of people's experience. Without a sensitivity to particular narrative forms, insights into popular wisdom and common sense whose cognition generally occurs in and through narrative will always be partial.[8] Hofmeyr's paper begins to broach some of these issues by examining the role that narrative played in shaping the historical sense of identity of a group of settlers in the north-western Transvaal.

These narrative questions spill over, too, into issues of oral testimony, used in most of the papers here. In recounting the past, informants often glamourise it or imagine it as they would like to have lived it.[9] Thabane comments on this problem in a paper, presented to the History Workshop in 1987, which dealt with the collection of oral tradition in Lesotho. Even where other internal and external evidence points to the opposite, he writes,

> This message comes out very vividly in the informant's descriptions of the social fabric: in the olden days people loved, helped, and had mercy towards one another.[10]

The same problem is apparent in Nasson's testimonies from District Six. Apart from two passing allusions about not being able to court a girl from another neighbourhood, and about the way gangs reserved rows of seats in cinemas for themselves, any sense of real conflict is missing from Nasson's account of District Six. In some ways this presents itself as a problem peculiarly Sou!th African, where the dispossession and relocation of subordinated communities has been less the exception than the rule. Here an even more powerful impulse exists to romanticise certain periods or places in the past. District Six and Sophiatown stand as classic examples of this process.

However, in other ways these omissions can be seen as rich *cultural* evidence concerning popular consciousness. Why do informants repress memories of conflict? Furthermore, how do people negotiate this repression in their testimony? All these seem vital questions to grapple with in attempting to understand popular culture. They are also questions that all seem to require narrative answers.

Culture, Class and Political Mobilisation

Two linked themes run through a number of the contributions to this volume. These are, to use La Hausse's words, 'the extent to which leaders [of popular political movements (eds)] had their own class agendas, and the way in which 'the common-sense ideas and the culture of [the] labouring poor set important limits' to these leaders' freedom of action, forcing them to 'negotiate within a particular [and usually regionally centred (eds)] cultural universe', if they wished to succeed. A third concern of a number of papers that can be linked to the foregoing is the type of interventions that could be accomplished and the degree of leverage acquired by white liberal bodies on the middle-class leadership of such black urban communities. This will be dealt with in a later section.

A fascinating discussion of the former two issues is provided by La Hausse, who along with Nasson gives us perhaps the most subtle and sensitive insights into popular culture in this volume. La Hausse suggests that there existed highly variegated, sometimes divided, but somehow at root working-class cultures and communities in Durban in the late 1920s. These were responsive to whichever organisation resonated best with their proletarian needs and complex transitional culture. The tiny conservative middle-class leadership of the Natal Native Congress was conspicuously incapable of making this appeal. The leader of the Industrial and Commercial Workers' Union (ICU), A.W.G. Champion, though vacillating and self-servingly opportunistic, achieved considerably more success. A great deal of the political purchase he managed to achieve over Durban's black working class La Hausse attributes to his 'capturing' of membership through the ICU's cultural institutions (*ngoma* troupes, brass bands, etc.) and through invoking the symbols of Zulu nationalism and the Zulu past. His success in the former, La Hausse may be read as saying, was itself partly premised on the existence of 'illegal space' in the peri-urban areas. It was perhaps the dispersed nature of this settlement and the absence of large defined communities which allowed Champion the room he required for political manoeuvre. However, the oppositional forces nurtured in the illegal or weakly controlled spaces around Durban ultimately brushed him aside. When Champion was prepared to exchange the creation of privileged space in the form of a separate black middle-class township for the end of the beer boycott and the dismantling of the ICU, key components of Durban's labouring poor simply repudiated his leadership and began attuning themselves to other more radical tones such as those of the Communist Party of South Africa (CPSA). Among the most active and vociferous of those demanding and enforcing more radical action were the women's auxiliaries and the brigades of *amalaita* youth. Their centrality throughout these protests and confrontations prefigures much of the later history of working-class political action.

Even more critical perhaps was the switch of allegiance of another sub-stratum of the leadership of Durban's labouring poor. These have attracted increasing attention in recent writing, including a number of contributions to this volume (La Hausse, Rich, Edwards). Bradford speaks of them as craftsmen and small-scale producers, along with those with some secondary education.[11] Both Bozzoli, in the introduction to *Class, Community, and Conflict* and La Hausse in this volume label them radical artisans. To each of these writers they represented a group whose skills had been devalued, mainly as a result of the white labour policy of the 1920s.[12] In many instances, however, they included a wider and less easily definable cross-section of the community than this. La Hausse interestingly cites one informant who said that what separated the leaders from the rest was their ability to survive by their wits. Sometimes this meant education; more often it meant the ability to spot whatever opportunities for petty trading or petty producing or petty thieving existed. Equally, it could mean a sharp-eyed ability to spot cultural opportunities, as Nasson suggests, or a demotic capacity both to sense and then capitalise on a range of popular cultural notions and understandings as La Hausse illustrates. Edwards identifies a key element among this leadership in the 1940s as the sometimes not too scrupulous trade union secretaries, the more substantial shack renters, Zionist preachers and herbalists. Closer inspection would probably reveal taxi-drivers as well. Socially and geographically mobile, unconstrained by the need to work regular factory hours, facile and conversant with local cultural symbols and style, and able to insert themselves into numerous local social networks, these were the key political brokers in Mkhumbane and probably in many legal and illegal spaces elsewhere.

It was on these leaders in many cases that rested the fortunes of political organisations. Between the late 1920s and 1930 they seem to have swung their support first to the ICU and then to the CPSA. In the 1930s in the Orange Free State, as Rich shows in his paper in this volume, they helped to mobilise support for Rheinallt-Jones's election to the Senate, before switching their allegiance to Basner in 1942. In Mkhumbane in the late 1940s they chose to go it alone, spurning a jaded ICU, corrupt Advisory Boards, fragmented and ineffectual trade unions, and an untested African National Congress (ANC) Youth League. It is here that we see populist leadership in undiluted form — deeply antipathetic to the educated elite, and exhibiting profound racial antagonisms to Asians and whites. It is perhaps not coincidental that one of the worst racial riots in South Africa's history would almost immediately ensue.[13] If we are to get a fuller view from below it is probably to lower-level leaders like this that we should turn. Even then a problem would remain. On whose behalf do they speak?

Gender and Class

If important spaces in and around urban centres were able to remain largely outside official control, so too did a key section of the black population — urban women. As Sapire, Eales and other contributors to this volume show, women streamed into the cities and the peri-urban areas from the later 1910s. Their presence there soon presented the authorities with a host of social, economic and political problems. As the municipal authorities knew only too well, the settlement of women in the towns meant the emergence of a new generation of youth at least partly socialised in the illegal spaces of the cities or in areas that were not fully under official control. The process of settling in the towns seems also to have bred among this first generation of urban women a new independence and assertion that made them less amenable to any form of control. La Hausse documents the activities of the formidable phalanxes of the ICU women's brigade during the beer hall boycott, and further amplifies our understanding of the scope and character of

black women's militancy in Natal, first analysed by Bradford in the
previous History Workshop collection. Edwards's paper on
Mkhumbane provides at least some of the context for women's
participation in the Cato Manor riots of 1958, while Sapire
demonstrates the intractability of Brakpan's beer brewers when faced
with any form of official control. A great deal of emphasis is given in
these papers to the centrality of beer brewing to the survival of urban
African families, and this is assumed to explain the vehemence and
violence of women's actions in the beer hall boycotts in Natal and
elsewhere. What is also hinted at, but not fully developed in these
accounts, is the establishment by women of new and more independent
relationships with men. La Hausse, for example, talks of key women
leaders being unmarried; Edwards writes of the drift of many women
of broken marriages to the towns. Sapire and Eales document the large
number of single women on the Rand, a significant proportion of
whom engaged in informal or full-time prostitution. The existence of
large numbers of single women, or women in more informal unions
with men in the towns, may well give further insights into the vibrancy
and vigour of urban African communities at this time, for, in the
absence of fairly stable family unions, recourse to alternative and wider
networks of relationships would very likely have been necessary to
provide for both emotional and material support.

The central role played by women in the formation of a settled black
urban population, and in the life of the illegal spaces in the towns,
makes the lack of control over their ingress one of the most baffling
puzzles of black urbanisation. This is one of the questions addressed by
Eales in her contribution to this volume. Central to the authorities'
hesitation, she suggests, was fear on the part of the Department of
Native Affairs (although not, it should be said, of the municipal
administrations) of the explosion of opposition that might be
detonated by such a move. The alternative that the Johannesburg City
Council devised was to extend the city's curfew regulations to women,
and this it attempted to do in 1925 and 1931. African opposition was
vocal, but was divided, as Eales shows, on class and gender lines.
Christian and temperance-orientated middle-class African women
were only too keen to see beer brewers and prostitutes expelled or
brought under more effective control, and merely objected to the
regulation being applied to themselves. Many African men, middle-
class and others, were anxious to have greater control exerted over
their daughters, and were primarily concerned lest their authority be

usurped in their own homes. The limitations of the ANC and ICU in this period, which other contributors to this volume have documented elsewhere, further diminished the prospects of any large-scale mobilisation against the regulations. As a result, the first and only effective challenge that was mounted in 1925 was one that was characteristic of this decade — an appeal to the courts. When the curfew was re-imposed in 1931, even this fell away, a testament to the weakness of political organisation on the Rand at this time. As it turned out, neither this regulation nor successive amendments to the Urban Areas Act in 1930 and 1937 achieved the desired control over working-class women. Women only needed to state that they were married to a man who was living in the urban areas and they would be permitted to stay. And, as Eales points out, no check could be made as to the existence of such marriages, since Roman Dutch law refused to recognise customary unions, and no register of marriages could consequently be drawn up. The situation would not materially alter until the extension of passes to women in the mid-1950s.

Ethnicity, Region and Class

Ethnicity is a subject that is generally skirted round in South African studies. Despite a rapidly expanding corpus of writing on this topic elsewhere in the continent, the number of serious and substantial contributions to the South African literature can be counted on the fingers of one hand.[14] Such neglect can be attributed at least in part to the transparent and by now generally discredited efforts of the South African government to manipulate ethnic categories in its effort to entrench white domination. For some, this in itself serves as an explanation of ethnicity and the issue or problem disappears. Even those more aware of the materiality of ethnicity eschew analysis of the subject, for fear that this will indirectly legitimise or underwrite the Bantustan project. This is quite possibly one of the reasons for the decline in recent years of research into pre-colonial history. Such an attitude is in our view misconceived. Ethnic cultures and identities possess a reality in South Africa which it would be myopic to ignore. As the growing role of vigilantes at the present moment suggests, it can also be politically unwise. Ethnic identities, as can be seen from much of the rest of the African literature, need to be confronted and understood, both as instruments of manipulation from above and as modes of accommodation and adjustment from below. No serious study of popular culture or political action can afford to allow them to be ignored.

A whole underworld of research almost certainly awaits the researcher who explores the transformation and creation of ethnic identities on the mines on the Rand. Other sites of the manufacture or redefinition of ethnic identities are equally likely to be identified elsewhere as well. Several contributors to this volume touch on the persistence or transformation of ethnic identities (La Hausse and Edwards in particular), but it is only Delius's study of the Transvaal Ndzundza Ndebele that focuses squarely on the issue. Delius's paper permits the consideration both of the grotesque absurdity of the South African government's ethnic policy, *and* of the materiality of ethnicity. On the one hand, we find a chiefdom which was conquered, dispossessed of its land and had its inhabitants scattered as tied labourers across the length and breadth of the Transvaal in the late nineteenth century, being partly re-assembled in the 1970s in a location 150 kilometres from its original site, once the labour tenants were rendered superfluous by mechanisation. On the other hand, as Delius shows, these same labourers, in the course of their sufferings, developed a tenacious and conservative ethnic identity as a means of defence, which is presently being deployed at least in part to frustrate the government's plans.

Delius's paper is one of the few in this volume to link pre-colonial pre-conquest South African societies to twentieth-century developments. Delius's argument is that Ndebele society was more ethnically heterogeneous and diverse in its mid-nineteenth century heyday than later, and that much of the Ndzundza Ndebele's cohesive twentieth-century ethnicity was a product of subsequent subordination to white rule. To this extent Delius's analysis is at one with other recent analyses of African tribalism and ethnicity, which see them as essentially the products of colonial rule. Where he departs from this perspective, however, is when he sees the manufacture or redefinition of Ndbebele ethnicity as the product of a grass-roots response to conquest and dispossession. The Ndzundza Ndebele's experience was highly unusual in at least two separate respects. Firstly, they were entirely dispossessed of their land in the late nineteenth century and were indentured out on white farms. There, as a result of intense poverty and the absence of alternative places of refuge, they were obliged to remain. Their experience thus differs radically from most of the other tribalisms studied in Africa, which developed among societies which retained access to their land, and or among migrants from these societies competing with migrants from other areas for jobs, accommodation and social security in the towns. Secondly, and related to this difference, Ndzundza Ndebele ethnicity emerges in Delius's argument as a much more grass-roots response. Common to most other analyses of the manufacture of ethnicities is the idea that they were created from above. Two main agents are usually identified in this process: firstly, missionaries and colonial administrators who standardised 'tribal' languages and defined tribal units as a means of implementing the policy of indirect rule, and secondly, African intellectuals and 'progressive chiefs' who were 'inventing tradition' as a means of securing better terms in the colonial order and of buttressing their positions against any challenge from below.[15]

Chiefs were likewise among the main proponents and beneficiaries of Ndzundza Ndebele ethnicity. In contrast with most other students of these issues, however, Delius sees the manufacture of Ndzundza Ndebele ethnicity primarily as an act of popular resistance. Denied all other means of challenge or avenues of escape, save perhaps flight to the towns, the Ndebele cemented an ethnicity to hold their shattered society together, and to create a culture of consolation which would provide emotional and psychological support. Even here there was a category at the grass roots of Ndebele society with a greater interest in this process than the rest. These were homestead heads who used tradition to maintain a hold over the labour of their wives and their children. Not surprisingly, as Delius points out, Boer farmers, who were initially suspicious of this development, later lent their strong support.

Isabel Hofmeyr's paper, which is likewise set the in late nineteenth-century/early twentieth-century rural Transvaal takes us in a slightly different direction, and intersects in an unexpected way with some of the themes previously discussed in this introduction. As with other studies of African societies in alien urban surroundings, Hofmeyr's paper shows that white society in the frontier regions of the Transvaal also had to appropriate space and create a sense of community and identity. Ranger has spoken in passing of the way settler societies in central Africa attempted to 'take hold of the land'. A key element of this process was the domestication of parts of the veld into farms, the replacement of African by European names, the beaconing of boundaries, and the construction of urban centres and roads.[16] In the early days of settlement in the Waterberg, as Hofmeyr shows, much of this was absent, and a sense of settlement and community had to be constructed imaginatively and often in fictional form. This was a region 'constituted by narrative' and in part by the 'official imagination of the map'. At the centre of both of these fictions was the farm, replete with its connotations of gentility for the 'reconstruction' wave of English-speaking settlers. In both the fictions of narrative and the map, black people 'were removed imaginatively beyond the borders of the farm to merge with the landscape and its wildlife'. A central part of the identity of the region prior to effective settlement, so Hofmeyr tells us, was this story-telling which eventually found its way into prose. Here the recurrent designs were of the Waterberg mountain range as 'barrier frontier', as well as 'beacons and boundaries... cultural forms through which the land [was] structured and possessed'. Ironically, as Hofmeyr records, it was at precisely the moment that the Waterberg was more effectively settled and domesticated, and that such 'solvents' of local culture as motorcars and primary education began to have more effect, that this distinctive tradition of story-telling ended, only some time thereafter to be nostalgically reconstructed as prose.

Co-option and Class

The inter-war period, to which several of the contributors to this volume devote their attention, was the heyday of the Joint Councils, especially in respect of issues related to black urbanisation. The success of liberal initiatives in this field varied enormously, and depended in large measure on the vigour of the main African political movements, and on the self-organisation of the African labouring and 'dangerous' classes in the towns. In Natal, as a result of the high degree of mobilisation among the urban Africans, liberal endeavours were without much effect. On the Witwatersrand, and in the small Free State towns, however, more purchase was gained. As Eales indicates, the Joint Councils garnered at least some middle-class African support on the Rand to lend legitimacy to their proposals for reinforcing male authority over women in order to prevent single women migrating to the urban areas and married women switching their affections to other men in the towns. In the Free State, as Rich shows, Rheinallt-Jones was able to enlist enough support from ex-ICU stalwarts such as Sello, Binda and Mote to ensure his election as Native Representative to the Senate in 1937. His earlier championing of African trading rights in the Free State locations aside, it is unclear why he was able to secure this support. What Rich's paper hints at is that this may have resonated in some way with the movement towards co-operatives elsewhere. What his paper clearly exposes are the unchartered historical expanses of the Orange Free State's past.

A similar process and pattern can be discerned nearly two decades later in the Nationalist government's attempts to co-opt sections of black society into structures which, in Hyslop's words, would provide 'the illusion of self-determination' within a separate political framework organised on ethnic lines. Along with Urban Bantu Councils in the towns, school boards and school committees were designed to fulfil this task. Each of these structures was designed to break down earlier inner-city or squatter community solidarities which, although often composed of fairly self-conscious ethnic cultural networks, were not organised along ethnic lines. As Hyslop shows, the degree to which school committees and school boards could function in this regard depended directly on the strength or weakness of organised black political opposition. Initially, before the ANC was proscribed, school committees and school boards enjoyed minimal participation and almost no legitimacy within the main urban areas. In the rural areas they proved more successful, as they were quickly perceived as levers of power by chiefs and homeland politicians, and after the suppression of the popular political movements in the early 1960s, a greater measure of participation was also enjoyed in the towns. However, as Hyslop points out, the arbitrary and autocratic behaviour of the homeland authorities and of the Department of Bantu Education alienated potential supporters among teachers and parents in both the rural areas and the towns, so that their capacity for ideological incorporation was reduced if not removed. Worse still from the point of view of the authorities, was that the project of reshaping the partly ethnic, partly communal urban solidarities of the 1930s and 1940s was comprehensively discredited and destroyed. In their place emerged not mutually insulated ethnic cultures, but a more popular culture than ever before, united in its determination to overturn the same wider and collectively experienced structures of control. Thus, the moment the forces of popular opposition began to mobilise in the towns, the school boards and school committees became either isolated or discredited even as sites for opposition. Hyslop's paper therefore points us to some of the central failings of Bantu Education, and of the entire apartheid programme of the 1960s and 1970s. Together with several other contributions to this volume it shows how the prospects of co-option are dim unless they extend to grass-roots spokesmen of the labouring poor, and that the latter are unlikely to be available for co-option unless some of the key material and political problems of the popular masses are addressed.

Notes

1 **P. Clavel,** *Espace et Pouvoir* (Paris, 1978), p. 1. Cited in J. Amsden, 'Historians and Spatial Imagination', *Radical History Review*, 21 (March 1980)

2 F. Cooper, 'Urban Space, Industrial Time, and Wage Labor in Africa'. In F. Cooper (ed.), *Struggle for the City: Migrant Labor, Capital and the State in Urban Africa* (Beverley Hills, 1983), pp. 23, 31.

3 A. Potgieter, Die Swartes aan die Witwatersrand, 1900-1933, Ph.D. Thesis, Rand Afrikaans University, 1978, pp. 58-153.

4 E. Koch, Doornfontein and its African Working Class, 1914-1935, M.A. Dissertation, University of the Witwatersrand, 1983.

5 Union of South Africa, *Report of the Small Holdings Commission (Transvaal)* (UG 51 '13), pp. 4-30; *Report of the Commission on Small Holdings in the Peri-Urban Areas of the Union of South Africa*, (UG 37/1957), pp. 3-10.

6 See, for example, T. Clynick, 'Community Politics on the Lichtenburg Alluvial Diamond Fields, 1926-1929', in B. Bozzoli (ed.), *Class, Community and Conflict*, (Johannesburg, 1987), pp. 235-80, and draft chapters of his M.A. Dissertation, The Alluvial Diamond Diggers of the South Western Transvaal: 'Poor Whites' in the Countryside, 1901-37.

7 D. Pinnock, 'Stones, Boys and the Making of a Cape Flats Mafia', in B. Bozzoli (ed.), *Class, Community and Conflict* pp. 421-22.

8 Thanks to Isabel Hofmeyr for the comments on narrative.

9 L. Passerini, 'Italian Working Class Culture between the Wars: Consensus to Facism and Work Ideology', *International Journal of Oral History*, 1 (1980), 4-27.

10 M. Thabane, 'Africanist Historiography, Personal Reminiscences and Romanticisation of the Past', Paper presented to the History Workshop Conference on 'The Making of Class', 9-14 February, 1987, p. 3.

11 H. Bradford, 'Mass Movements and the Petty-bourgeoisie: The social origins of the I.C.U. Leadership 1924-1929', *Journal of African History*, 25, (1984), 295-310.

12 B. Bozzoli, 'Class, Community and Ideology in the Evolution of South African Society', in B. Bozzoli (ed.), *Class, Community and Conflict*, pp. 30-1.

13 S.L. Kirk, The 1949 Durban Riots: A Community in Conflict, M.A. Dissertation, University of Natal, Durban, 1983; E.C. Webster, 'The 1949 Durban Race Riots. A Study in Race and Class', in P.L. Bonner (ed.), *Working Papers in Southern African Studies* Vol. I (Johannesburg, 1977).

14 S. Marks, 'Natal, the Zulu Royal Family, and the Ideology of Segregation', *Journal of Southern African Studies*, 4 (April 1978), and *The Ambiguities of Dependence in South Africa* (Johannesburg, 1986); W. Beinart, 'Conflict in Qumbu: Rural Consciousness, Ethnicity and Violence in the Colonial Transkei, 1880-1913', *Journal of Southern African Studies*, 8 (October 1981); P. Harries 'The Roots of Ethnicity: Discourse and the Politics of Language Construction in South-East Africa, *African Affairs*, No. 346 (January 1988). Studies by Harries, Peires, Alverson and Marks are also due to be published in L. Vail (ed.), *The Growth of Tribalism in Southern Africa* (London and Los Angeles, forthcoming).

15 An excellent review of the literature and analyses of the subject is provided by T.O. Ranger in his essay, 'The Invention of Tradition in Colonial Africa', in E. Hobsbawm and T. Ranger (eds), *The Invention of Tradition* (Cambridge, 1983). See also L. Vail (ed.), *The Growth of Tribalism in Southern Africa*.

16 T.O. Ranger, 'Taking Hold of the Land: Holy Places and Pilgrimage in Twentieth Century Zimbabwe', *Past and Present*, 117 (Nov. 1987).

The Message of the Warriors

The ICU, the Labouring Poor and the Making of a Popular Political Culture in Durban, 1925-1930

Paul la Hausse

In 1925, six years after being established in Cape Town, the Industrial and Commercial Workers' Union (ICU) opened a branch in the port town of Durban. Three months later A.W.G. Champion, an ex-mine clerk and policeman, assumed control of the struggling Durban Branch and also became Natal Provincial Secretary. In March 1926 the General Secretary of the Union reported that the Durban Branch was 'progressing famously'.[1] By 1927, Champion could boast that Durban was a 'formidable fortress' of the ICU comprising 27 000 paid-up members.[2] Through a sustained and generally successful campaign of litigation aimed at a battery of repressive municipal by-laws, the ICU succeeded in capturing the imagination of Durban's labouring poor.[3]

By 1927 the ICU had opened offices in the smallest of South African towns. Over a large part of Natal, where the economic pressures on rural blacks sharpened with the introduction of extensive sheep and wattle farming, numerous branches of the ICU opened in rural towns stretching from Paulpietersburg in the north to Port Shepstone in the south.[4] The most powerful branch in the country was to be found in Durban. At the end of 1927, however, Champion was suspended from his position, pending investigation into financial irregularities in the Natal Union. Then, in June 1928, most of the Natal branches seceded from the national Union and formed the ICU *yase* Natal. Over the following two years, while the ICU experienced a sharp decline in support in Natal's countryside, the ICU *yase* Natal, under the leadership of Champion, continued in its attempts to organise African workers.

Memories of the spectacular rise and fall of the ICU are today preserved in the thinning ranks of elderly men and women. In some ways, historians have become accomplices in a process of forgetting. One notable exception is Helen Bradford, whose recent work on the ICU in the countryside explores the ways in which the Union *did* channel popular rural discontent and the complex relationship between Union leaders and their constituencies.[5] In general terms, as Bradford has noted, the ICU's leadership tended to be drawn from a racially oppressed lower middle-class grouping which was both fractured and susceptible to proletarianisation. It was this socially ambiguous nature of Union leaders which enabled them, at specific moments, to assume the role of radical spokesmen for the labouring classes in a way which the 'Black Englishmen' in the Congress movement could not.

The fierce populism which the Union succeeded in moulding tended to disguise the extent to which leaders had their own class agendas and the ways in which they used the Union to further them. Yet the common-sense ideas and the culture of Durban's labouring poor set important limits on leaders' attempts to carve out an urban constituency. And, at least in the short term, the success of Union mobilisation hinged on leadership's sensitivity to, and negotiations within, a particular cultural universe. Regional patterns of exploitation, domination and dispossession, as well as popular idioms and traditions of resistance, provided the basis for the development of a peculiar local political culture. Workers could thus appropriate and rework the language and tactics of leadership in the face of the flux of political struggles. It is in these terms that this study seeks to explore the ways in which the Union mobilised a local support-base, how it attempted to forge popular alliances and how, through political struggles, it ultimately lost the support of its volatile and often desperate constituency.

Urban Control, African Class Formation and Culture

In the early 1920s, while the South African state was making concerted attempts to formulate a 'native policy' more appropriate to conditions of capitalist economic growth, Durban could plausibly claim to possess a model for urban 'native administration' in the country.[6] In 1908 the Durban Town Council succeeded in its struggle to obtain legislation which enabled local authorities in Natal to monopolise the sale of sorghum beer (*utshwala*) to African workers in urban areas.[7] Between 1909 and 1928 the net profits from the town's municipal beerhalls amounted to at least £551 000, nearly all of which was used to build barracks for migrant workers, to erect more beerhalls and to finance a municipal Native Administration Department (NAD). Unlike other urban centres, Durban was in the unique position of having the administrative and financial capacity to support the reproduction of a cheap urban workforce at little cost to white taxpayers. Moreover, strict influx control laws attempted to limit the size of the town's African population to the labour needs of employers and simultaneously to undermine the formation of urban African households by policing the presence of women in the town.[8]

In 1928 the African population was conservatively estimated at 38 000, at least 33 000 of whom had known employment. As many as 15 000 black males might have been engaged as domestic servants, most of whom lived in *kias* on their employers' premises. This large service sector established youth as a significant social characteristic of Durban's labour market. The youngest 'houseboy' could be ten years old while most were not over the age of twenty. Their monthly wages, including food and accommodation, seldom exceeded £2. An older generation of over 5 000 men, lived fifteen to a room in the crowded Point municipal barracks which earned Zulu names such as *Umhlaguva* (trees with thorns which bite) or *Umfugwana* (a tightly-packed snuff-tin).[9] These men worked as *togt* (day) labourers on the docks. The *ozinyathi* (buffaloes), as they were popularly known, could claim a history of strike action extending back to the turn of the century.[10]

The arduous work of ricksha-pulling provided over 1 500 men from the countryside of Natal, Zululand and Pondoland with a potentially lucrative source of income. The ostensibly self-employed ricksha-pullers (*abawini*) lived in privately-owned or municipal barracks scattered through the town where, much to the dismay of white property-owners, they frequently sheltered their kin. The remainder of the African labour force worked in Durban's numerous small industrial, commercial and manufacturing concerns, or in the municipal or government service sector. By 1928 the ICU, in advertising its weekly meetings, could appeal to sections of the workforce whose self-consciousness, as their Zulu names suggest, was rooted in the new social solidarities of early industrial South Africa. *Abatshayelibezimoto* (car-drivers), *abamagalaji* (garage-workers) and *oweta* (waiters) took their place alongside dockworkers, ricksha-pullers and domestic servants as potential constituents of the ICU.

The wages of most male migrant workers, often referred to, perhaps

ironically, as the *izimpohlo* (bachelors), remained uniformly low, in
the region of £2.8s. Some workers, depending on their experience,
might be fortunate enough to earn £4 a month, whilst others, if
supplied with a daily ration of maize meal, could expect wages
sometimes as low as £1.10s a month.[11] Certainly, the £6 monthly wage
paid to compound *izinduna* (overseers) represented a level of wealth
which few could hope to enjoy. If some young workers, in a novel rite of
passage, braided coins into their hair,[12] workers in Durban ranked
amongst the worst-paid black workers in the country. Throughout the
twenties the wages of virtually all workers, even in real terms, had
barely risen and, in some cases, had actually declined.

Until at least the first decade of the century migrant workers in
Durban were drawn predominantly from Natal and Zululand. Yet by
the later twenties this pattern of labour migration had altered
dramatically. After 1926 the reproductive capacities of stressed African
rural economies were further undermined by a drought which seared
its way through large parts of the countryside. In Durban the
increasing number of blacks, particularly from Transkei and
Basutoland, travelled to the town in search of work.[13] In Natal rural
dispossession, combined with the desire by homestead heads to retain
access to land, compelled many blacks to enter into labour-tenant
relationships with white farmers. Wage labour in towns provided one
alternative to these punishing conditions in the countryside.

In general terms, specific groups constituted in terms of regional or
ethnic ties appear to have dominated particular occupations.[14] In the
late twenties, however, Durban's labour market was restructured, and
it is more than likely that the arrival of newly-proletarianised job-
seekers led to heightened competition over access to jobs. Certainly,
many Basotho and Xhosa were successful in joining the ranks of dock
and railway workers.[15] Yet as Durban entered the depression in late
1929, and as the size of Durban's reserve army of labour expanded, the
displacement of more vulnerable sections of the workforce (probably
inclusive of many non-Zulu-speakers) became a real possibility.

If age and regional origins served to define the social nature of
Durban's African workforce, so too did gender. In a labour market
dominated by young male workers, employment prospects for African
women were bleak. By 1930 only 4 per cent of the African workforce
was female. While several hundred women could hold down jobs as
domestic servants, other areas of employment previously available to
women were closed down.[16] Beer-brewing rapidly evolved as the single

main economic alternative to the absence of urban female employment opportunities. The economic marginalisation of women was reflected by the provision of only 250 beds in the Native Women's Hostel.[17] Similarly, only 120 houses were provided for African families in addition to temporary married quarters in the Depot Road location. These measured concessions to the urban African household were granted against the backdrop of the continuous expulsion of African women in terms of the Native Urban Areas Act of 1923. The convenient refusal to recognise the emergence of urban households and the common-law marriages of Durban's labouring poor had important consequences for the geography of family settlement. By 1925 over 22 000 Africans had settled, mostly in shacks, in the peri-urban areas of towns such as Mayville, Sydenham, Cato Manor and Clairwood.

It was frequently in the illegal space of these 'meanest quarters', as the Mayor put it, that workers were able to create cultural alternatives to everyday coercion and control. Shebeens, in particular, emerged as a central institution within an emerging proletarian culture. The establishment of Durban's beerhalls, and the consequent proscription of shebeens and the African drink trade, were rooted in a wider struggle by Durban's white rulers to forge a time and labour discipline appropriate to an urban capitalist social order. The battery of labour-coercive by-laws and penal sanctions anticipated the delivery of a suitably sober, submissive and disciplined workforce to local employers. The uneven realisation of this goal was as much due to the persistent evasion of work registration, pass-forgery and illegal entry into town, as to the more general creation of alternative sources of meaning and values by workers.

The experience of rural dispossession and proletarian life injected new content into older modes of social organisation and cultural expression. *Amalaita* gangs, for example, had their roots in the social solidarities of a pre-industrial past. In the town, however, they provided a basis for novel migrant youth networks and embodied patterns of ritual moulded by the experience of labour and penal discipline. Noted for their fondness for mouth-organs and fighting-sticks (*izinduku*), many 'houseboys' organised themselves into *amalaita* gangs, each of which established zones of informal control throughout the town.

In this world the magistrate and the policeman loomed large. The most common official response to the aggressive self-assertion and

petty theft of the *amalaita* was birching.[18] The prohibition on the
carrying of sticks by workers,[19] together with the arrest of youths found
playing mouth-organs in the street were also measures aimed at
depriving workers of the rituals and symbols associated with
dangerous patterns of behaviour. As the custodians of industrial labour
discipline, magistrates could also impose prison sentences on those
found selling or smoking *dagga*, yet the consumption of this drug
remained endemic amongst those engaged in manual work. In a town
where a red-trimmed calico uniform attempted to impose a rigid
identity on domestic workers and where African women found
wearing 'European' clothes could be arrested as prostitutes by young
white policemen, the language of dress could assume an alternative
symbolic power. The *abaqhafi* (drinkers of spirits)[20] signalled their
presence in the streets through their dress: wide-open shirts, coloured
scarves, large 'cowboy' hats and either Oxford bags or pants tied just
below the knee.

The sustained attempts to eradicate these potentially subversive
cultural formations, and to separate the 'dangerous classes' from
labourers, foundered not least because it was often precisely the hardworking domestic servant or dockworker who subscribed to these
alternative patterns of meaning. While some white observers noted
the danger of socially undifferentiated housing, processes of class
formation outstripped the provision of housing for the 'best elements
among the Native community'. Throughout the twenties the families
of clerks, teachers and traders could be found holed up in the single
rooms of private landlords, impinging on the defensive space of
shebeens, prostitutes and crowded workers' quarters.[21]

This is not to say that the culture of Durban's African population
was overtly political. On the contrary, the consciousness of workers
was infused with notions anchored in pre-capitalist ideologies, and at
times recreated imagined rights enjoyed in a collective historical past.
Ngoma dance, for example, could serve to affirm the kin or ethnic ties
of one group of workers in relation to others in competitive, and
sometimes violent, terms. Yet in no sense was the culture and
consciousness of workers fixed in a primordial universe. The
experience of exploitation and labour coercion continually wrought
transformations within consciousness. It was precisely the autonomy
of the beer brewer, the self-assertion of the *amalaita*, and the
restlessness of the *abaqhafi* which carried with them the potential for
mobilisation along political lines.

In the less easily illuminated interstices of Durban's labour-coercive environment numerous men and women carved out an even more tenuous existence through a network of activities such as prostitution, beer-brewing, dagga-selling, and the unlicensed hawking of second-hand clothes and medicines. For some, economic subsistence was squeezed out of the newly proletarianised through rigged gambling games or the sale of love-potions with the help of female accomplices.[22] Together with the unemployed and unemployable, they lived on the outer, and frequently criminal, fringes of the urban social order. A relatively small group of Africans managed to avoid the rigours of wage labour by renting trading stalls at municipal 'native' eating houses. By 1929 over 370 cobblers, butchers, skin-sellers, bicycle- and gramophone-menders, herbalists, tailors and general dealers offered their wares and services to Durban's labouring poor. Although a number of these traders employed black assistants, self-employment on the margins of proletarian existence was a difficult and tenuous enterprise, not least because whites regarded Africans as 'temporary sojourners' in the town. African petty traders had to fight a continual battle to improve their conditions of tenure at the eating houses, were frequently ejected from their positions, and continually faced competition from Indian traders.[23] Their insecure position found expression in the formation of the African Stall Owners' Association and their appeals to the ICU and the Natal Native Congress for support.[24] After 1928 many of these endemically undercapitalised entrepreneurs threw their weight behind the ICU *yase* Natal.

By and large, Champion's observation that there were 'no important [African] businesses when I arrived in Durban' was true of Durban during the late twenties.[25] It should not pass unnoticed, however, that for a small group of traders who were able to take out shopkeepers' licences, the profits from their business could be handsome. C. Ngcobo and E. Mngadi's Abantu Supply Butchery, for example, sold meat to Durban's poorer whites and incurred the wrath of white butchers whose prices they undercut.[26] Similarly, a handful of African-run eating houses such as 'Dube's', 'Cele's' and 'Cili's' secured their owners a relatively comfortable position within the ranks of Durban's black middle class. By 1930 at least thirty African taxi-owners could expect good returns from their initial outlay of capital. In general terms these entrepreneurs found their political home in the Natal Branch of the African National Congress (ANC), the Natal Native Congress (NNC).

The retreat of the Natal Congress movement into a preoccupation with issues pertinent to a small *kholwa* and propertied élite was to become particularly evident after 1924.[27] It was during this period that a radicalised section of the NNC under J.T. Gumede split from the more conservative section led by the Revd John Dube, a prominent landowner and proprietor of the Durban-based newspaper *Ilanga lase Natal*. In Durban the demand for differential treatment, in particular the establishment of housing for 'better class' Africans, found a central place on the generally parochial NNC agenda. Not surprisingly, more radical ICU leaders derided NNC members as *Ama-respectables* while ICU rank and file sometimes forcibly closed Congress meetings. Such experiences confirmed the distance between the NNC and the emergent urban underclasses, an alienation which Dube's journalism did little to heal.[28]

Union Leadership: Rural Refugees and Radical Artisans

The ravages of the Pact Government's 'civilised labour policy' were keenly felt by black South Africans. As the size of the new white petty bourgeoisie rapidly expanded after 1924, the threat of being edged down the short stairwell into the ranks of the labouring poor became increasingly real for those Africans in the lower reaches of the middle classes. Indeed, it was from the ranks of a 'disappointed class' of blacks, as Champion put it, that the ICU *yase* Natal tended to find its leadership.[29] J.H. London, for example, became Branch Secretary of the ICU in Durban after being 'discharged by Europeans who would no longer work with a Kaffir' and also after having given critical evidence to the Wages Board.[30] This shared sense of vulnerability is captured in a description of James Ngcobo, a member of the ICU *yase* Natal Governing Body, as 'the last pillar that was stripped by the Krantzkop Dutch, until he remained a beam without a brick'. Jacob Mkize, ensconced in the lower levels of leadership, would have spoken for more than one of his colleagues when he claimed 'there is no respect for skilled work in Durban'.[31]

The majority of ICU *yase* Natal leaders had skills which became increasingly devalued during the twenties. James Ngcobo was a builder and a painter as was Hamilton Msomi, a member of the ICU *yase* Natal Committee. Both Frances Mqwebu, Assistant Chairman of the ICU *yase* Natal Standing Committee and Jim London had worked as printers. As a teacher Bertha Mkize received a salary which might have compared unfavourably with labourers' wages. Having abandoned this profession, she established herself as a tailor prior to working for the Union. On the other hand, Champion and Abel Ngcobo had had long experience as clerks. Similarly, J.J. Macebo, Chairman of the Union's Governing Body, made the difficult transition from harness-maker to clerk during the 1920s.[32]

Charles Khumalo, a garage-worker during the twenties, recalls that what separated ICU leaders from workers was their ability to survive by their wits.[33] Yet not all ICU officials fell to one side of the mental/manual divide. David Sitshe, a member of the ICU *yase* Natal executive, was a semi-literate blacksmith's hand, and later a trader, while the illiterate Sam Mabaleka coupled his activities on the Union's Committee with manual labour at the Point. If Congress leaders ever needed confirmation of the 'unrespectable' nature of the ICU leadership they could find it in two early organisers, A.P. Maduna and Sam Dunn, both of whom had had convictions for theft.[34] Moreover, J.A. Duiker, one of Champion's chief 'lieutenants', had a string of convictions for theft in the Free State town of Lindley where he had been fired from his job as an interpreter prior to his arrival in Durban in 1924. Duiker might well have provided the Chief Constable with his model when he claimed that 'the ICU has no masters; in fact, quite half is made up of the riff-raff of the Union'.[35] Certainly, Dunn, Duiker and London, all of whom had served in the South African Native Contingent, helped to inject the ICU with the bitter-edged radicalism of the 'returned soldier'.[36]

It is likely, too, that the hardships of rural organisation which a surprising number of Durban's Union Officials had experienced,[37] even if they were at times cushioned by the comfort of a Buick, made them sensitive to the demands and experiences of Durban's migrant workforce. In other important ways the social backgrounds of Durban's ICU *yase* Natal officials distanced them from their constituency. One contemporary observer noted that Champion 'belong[ed] by birth to the category of landed proprietors in Natal'.[38] Not only was Champion, like a number of officials in the ICU *yase* Natal, an exempted African, but he had also inherited land at Groutville. Even so, it is likely that during the later twenties men like Champion found it increasingly difficult to maintain a secure economic base in the countryside. After selling his apanage in 1927, Champion came increasingly to rely on the ICU itself for his source of income. As

Detective Arnold noted: 'If the ICU ceased to function tomorrow [Champion] would have to work pretty hard to make a living.'[39] Macebo, as the third son of a Groutville farmer who owned 15 acres of land, abandoned the hope of retaining access to a rural income and sought work in Durban. Jim London, despite being the son of a wealthy landowner at Italeni, came to depend on work as a compositor and then as a compound *induna* in Durban for his income. If it was as refugees from the narrowing economic horizons of rural life that some of the key ICU *yase* Natal leaders entered Durban, it was often as frustrated semi-skilled and skilled wage-earners that they entered the Union.

The salaried positions of ICU *yase* Natal officials represented one way of retaining a brittle economic independence. An ICU official, depending on the state of Union funds, could earn at least £8 a month. In 1929 Champion himself was drawing a relatively handsome salary of £20 a month.[40] There were a variety of other ways in which ICU organisers in Durban could harness the Union to recoup for themselves more secure positions within the ranks of the middle classes. The clearest example of this is to be found in the establishment of the All-African Co-operative Society in 1927. The Co-operative Society, described as the 'greatest step to economic emancipation of the African Workers',[41] attempted to attract £1 subscriptions from workers. By June 1928 the Society, having been incorporated into the ICU *yase* Natal, had only 400 subscriptions and operated under the name of the Star Clothing and Shirt Factory. This enterprise provided work for over fifty men and women, including Bertha Mkize and her brother (one of Durban's first African tailors), who were supplied with an outlet for their downgraded skills.[42] It is small wonder that the ideology of this frustrated petty bourgeoisie should have taken the form of economic nationalism which owed more than a little to Garveyist notions of black self-improvement. Caleb Mtshali, for example, exhorted workers at a mass meeting to

> be independent, commence small stores yourselves, and make it a strict rule to deal no where but from your own colour... we have one sound trading concern now, that is a clothing factory... we will model our plans on the system of the American Negroes.[43]

The African Workers' Club set up by Champion in 1925 was, in spite of its name, inspired by the desire to create a sense of community amongst this aspirant middle class. Certainly the philosophy behind the Club — 'Ask for what you want, Take what you can get, Use what you have' — would have struck a chord amongst its members who were drawn predominantly from the ranks of the 'shoemakers, bicycle menders and stall holders'.[44]

Whereas the first Branch Secretary came to rely on the sale of chickens to supplement his income, Champion proved more ambitious in this regard. By 1928 he had established two businesses: a general dealer's store and the Natal Boot and Shoe Repairing Hospital. The name of Champion's store, *Vuka Afrika* (Africa Awake), was certainly a symbolic acknowledgement of Union officials' indebtedness to the separatist vision of black Americans.[45] It seems that Champion was not averse to financing these businesses, both of which collapsed in 1929, with Union funds. Furthermore, Union members were increasingly exhorted to underwrite a constellation of Union-based ventures such as the African Workers' Club and the local ICU paper, *Udibi lwase Afrika*, with subcriptions from their meagre wages.

Perhaps it was the uneven reception of these appeals which encouraged more peremptory forms of Union recruitment. As Charles Khumalo recalls, organisers fostered the belief amongst the more credulous migrant workers that Union membership was a prerequisite for obtaining employment.[46] Yet high-handed leadership styles might have resonated with workers' experience of an older political culture which assigned individuals particular places within an hierarchical social order. The generation gap between prominent Durban unionists (many of whom had been born during the 1880s) and younger workers could have strengthened rather than diminished leadership's authority. Certainly Jacob Cele, a young harness-maker at the time and later Ladysmith Branch Secretary, saw nothing wrong in the fact that 'because we were juniors [in the Union] we never knew what was being discussed in the Cabinet'.[47] Undemocratic leadership styles did, however, have important implications for the Union in wider political terms. Accusations of corruption, initially directed at Sam Dunn, led to Champion's suspension in 1927 and the secession of the Natal ICU in 1928.[48] It is hardly surprising, then, that the relationship between Union leaders and their constituency was mutable and dynamic. For example, only a few months prior to secession workers had attempted to force the Union into organising a general strike, but had been told by leadership to 'approach the proper authorities'.[49] Worker support for the Union thus remained conditional. Political action was to test this support to the full.

Secession: The Creation of a 'Zulu' Trade Union

During the first part of 1928 the future of the ICU in Natal looked anything but rosy. In the countryside the Union suffered setbacks at the hands of the state and of white farmers, while a number of organisers found themselves without jobs, either because of accusations of corruption or because pleas for salaries from the Durban headquarters went unheeded.[50] In Durban itself, in the absence of funds and faced with large debts, officials were living from hand to mouth. Champion sold *Vuka Afrika* and membership apparently declined. Yet ironically Champion's suspension in April 1928 seems to have been greeted with anger and a sense of betrayal by many workers in Durban. Even in Johannesburg 'hundreds of Zulus... handed in their tickets and refused to have anything further to do with the Organisation'.[51] In an impressive show of defiance, the ICU in Durban organised a rally on 5 May 1928. Over 2 400 of the several thousand men and women attended in ICU-manufactured khaki uniforms, red twill tunics or sported exuberant red sashes and rosettes. In a display notable for its capacity to syncretise 'idioms of the masters' with those of an heroic Zulu past, the members of this parade marched in military formation, under 'duly appointed leaders', through the streets of Durban.[52]

In a number of ways the parades, more or less timed to coincide with May Day, capture the underlying significance of the Natal ICU's secession a few weeks later. In a region of South Africa where the disbanding of the *amabutho* (Zulu regiments) in the late nineteenth century and the Bambatha rebellion of 1906 were both firmly embedded in popular consciousness, it is not surprising that ethnic and racial identity in Durban were closely interwoven. While it is debatable whether the negligible successes of the first ICU Natal Provincial Secretary, the Xhosa-speaking A.P. Maduna, can be ascribed to the fact of his birth, there is no doubt that he was transferred from Durban for this reason.[53] Both David Sitshe and Champion were well known for their capacity to deliver rousing speeches in the Zulu language, while the coloured organiser Sam Dunn was popularly known as *Zulu kwa Malandela*, 'for he always used this expression when in the course of his great oratory he appealed to the inner feelings of the Zulu people'.[54] In a town where members of *amalaita* gangs sometimes adorned themselves with the *umshokobezi* (a decoration comprising ox-tails bound round the head which was worn by rebels in 1906), where *utshwala* was self-consciously referred to as 'Zulu beer', and where some Zulu workers were prepared to countenance the dipping of Pondo-speakers,[55] Dunn's manipulation of his own identity in relation to the past was not inappropriate.

Clearly, the Union leadership helped to mobilise and channel the ethnic identity of migrant workers in Durban. The Zulu articles in *Udibi lwase Afrika* frequently appealed to a sense of Zulu nationhood, especially where those derided in its pages were non-Zulu-speakers.[56] The formation of the Independent ICU (IICU) in early 1929 was part of a broader process of fragmentation in the national Union. In Durban, however, the establishment of an IICU Branch was also precipitated by local conditions of struggle. It appears that men such as George Lenono, resentful of being labelled 'foreigners',[57] retreated to the outskirts of the town and formed a small, predominantly Basotho Branch of the IICU. If Champion's suspension suggested a form of betrayal of Zulu-speaking workers by 'foreign natives', then the founding of the ICU *yase* Natal was a formal manifestation of the relative autonomy of local patterns of opposition at a time when regional political economies underpinned the receptivity of the underclasses to exclusivist appeals.

In order to embed itself in popular assumptions, the Union's leadership had to develop a language resonant with Durban's labouring classes.[58] Yet if Zulu nationalism came to represent an increasingly important ideological tendency within the Union, it was tempered by a range of other ideological elements. These ranged from Garveyism, infused with anti-white, anti-Indian and anti-clerical ideas, through to a broader African nationalism and, in some instances, socialism. These discrete elements were moulded into a remarkably syncretic ideology of popular protest, overlaid with Zulu nationalism, and continually modified by pre-capitalist ideologies and the less-structured ideas of Durban's labouring poor.

For most of 1928 the main concern of the ICU *yase* Natal leadership was to keep the Union afloat and to defend itself, sometimes violently, against the 'meddling' of the National ICU organisers in its affairs. Having been forced to abandon its tactics of litigation due to financial constraints, the leaders reverted to petitioning the Town Council. These petitions, in the main, were concerned with the restrictions on petty trade and took precedence over the demands of workers for higher wages and improved living conditions, even though Champion had guaranteed thousands of workers in May that within three months of their joining the new Union they would be 'getting better wages'.[59]

Towards the end of 1928 Detective Arnold, a seasoned observer of ICU activities in the town, could claim with confidence that the ICU *yase* Natal was a 'spent force' which would 'never recover its former power'.[60] Two developments, however, served to alter the position of the Union in the town. The first was the decision of the Sydenham Local Administration and Health Board to erect a beerhall in its peri-urban area of jurisdiction. The second was the arrival of Communist Party of South Africa (CPSA) organisers in Durban in January 1929.

The establishment of a branch of the CPSA in Durban by S.P. Bunting and Douglas Wolton at the beginning of 1929 coincided with the attempts of the Party to implement a political programme which called for a 'South African Native Republic' to be achieved through a national and democratic revolution.[61] In a series of mass meetings, some of which were held under the auspices of the ICU *yase* Natal, the white Party organisers articulated the United Front politics which underlay the 'Native Republic' programme.[62] Their fiery speeches undoubtedly found some resonance with local idioms of resistance, as the large numbers of workers who attended their meetings suggest. The response of Union leadership to the CPSA was ambiguous. Although Champion and Union officials had frequent dealings with Party organisers, the leader of the ICU *yase* Natal publicly denigrated the CPSA since he had 'never held with white men leading [blacks]'. Perhaps more to the point was Champion's claim, a short while later, that he repudiated Communism on the grounds that it would dispossess 'men like myself who hold landed properties'.[63]

The reservations which Champion expressed were not wholly shared by other Union leaders and rank and file. At least one member of the ICU *yase* Natal's governing body joined the Party along with other Union members. The concerted attempts to spread the Party message to dock and railway workers was greeted with alarm by local police informers, one of whom noted that 'it is open talk that Natives will join up in the Communist Movement, in their hundreds'.[64] In a situation where there was no necessary correlation between the interests of ICU *yase* Natal leadership and those whom they claimed to represent, it is likely that the activities of Party organisers encouraged increasing downward identification by this leadership with rank and file. In many ways the economic hardships experienced by most Africans in Durban during the late twenties gave impetus to the process.

The peri-urban areas of Durban supported increasing numbers of

landless Africans. In Sydenham, where at least 10 000 Africans had
settled, eviction by local authority proved 'an impossible task'. The
majority of African male inhabitants in this area worked in Durban
itself, while an increasing number of women brewed *isitshimiyane* to
supplement household incomes. It was in this area that the Local
Health Board obtained permission to erect a beerhall in March 1929.
This move would have effectively enforced prohibition in the area and
paved the way for the destruction of a resilient shebeen trade. The ICU
yase Natal was approached by local inhabitants to assist in opposing
the erection of the beerhall. In the first formal protest, Champion
wrote to the Board on behalf of the 'voiceless members of our
Community' stating objections to 'attempts to obtain monies from the
low paid natives for the purposes of financing [the Board's]
advancement'.[65] Numerous meetings in Sydenham during March
indicated the level of grass-roots opposition to the beerhall. On
successive Sundays in May groups of Africans numbering between 300
and 800 marched from the ICU Hall in Durban to these meetings. A
witness of one of these marches reported that:

> They were an organised body — headed by a brass band preceded
> by a native in Highland costume — a kilt. They had a Union Jack
> and a red flag with a hammer and sickle on it... Many of them
> were dressed in uniform and carried sticks in military positions.[66]

This richly syncretic and subversive language of protest came
increasingly to signal the Union's public presence in the town. The
ICU dance hall, which survived a sustained official campaign of
proscription, played a pivotal role in forming a common sense of
identity amongst racially-oppressed workers.

The physical distance between the Union's open-air meetings and
its dance hall was short. Union demagogues made every effort to
transfer and consolidate their political message in the cultural arena
provided by the dance hall. Marching *ngoma* troupes, clad in *imitsha*
and beads, could lead hundreds of workers from Durban's 'Hyde Park',
as Champion put it, to the ICU dance hall, singing *amahubo lamabutho*
(regimental anthems) *en route*. Song was also used to provide
collective experience with a political frame of reference. One song
performed by *ngoma* dancers, most of whom were domestic workers,
was recorded as follows:

Who has taken our country from us?
Who has taken it?
Come out! Let us fight!
The land was ours. Now it is taken.[67]

Song and dance could also act as a vehicle for the creation of new identities and meanings in the town. The emergence of a new performance style known as *ingom' ebusuku* or *isicathamiya* was the result of complex processes of innovation. Although this style was rooted in the traditional idiom of wedding songs, migrant workers also appropriated elements from black mission choirs to create a remarkably syncretic song and dance style.[68]

If rural and urban identities for the majority of workers were closely intertwined, some sections of Durban's African population gave expression to a more fiercely self-conscious urbanism. Many workers, probably outside the ranks of barrack-dwellers, differentiated themselves by wearing 'Oxford bags'. No doubt they were members of a social grouping which the local composer, Reuben Caluza, celebrated in one of his songs, part of which ran:

Put on Oxford Bags like a modern man.
Men dressed in Oxford Bags are always confident
   like modern men and walk like great men.
There are young men and women who misbehave
   and who no longer return home.[69]

The Union's own brass band and choir also symbolised the emergence of more self-conscious urban identities. Ragtime music, too, might have had a particular appeal amongst members of Durban's middle classes in search of cultural idioms expressive of their particular position as an oppressed grouping. Certainly, the popular ragtime group, Dem Darkies, could expect an enthusiastic response when they performed at the dance hall. Yet non-traditionalist styles simultaneously expressed and disguised emerging class distinctions. Champion's comment that he 'captured' most of the ICU membership through the Union's cultural institutions[70] is not only revealing of his style of leadership, but is also suggestive of his skills as a cultural broker and of the way the Union's message was advanced through providing cultural expression with a political context. Financially, too, these Union-sponsored institutions were important. Their monthly income could be as much as £400.[71]

Deprived of a political voice, the Union also created its own alternative sources of authority. *Ngoma* dance and *amalaita* gangs provide the most striking examples of the way in which popular culture in Durban was infused with military symbols and rituals drawn from a pre-colonial past. The stick- and sjambok-wielding Unity League (also known as the ICU Volunteers or Mob Crowd), welded from 150 Union members, assumed the responsibility for recruiting new members and, as Champion more ominously put it, 'carrying out justice' according 'to our own law'. An equivalent vigilante body for women, the ICU Women's Auxiliary, was also formed at this time. It, too, was organised along military lines and its members led by uniformed women.[72]

'Bad Beer', Riots and *Amalaita*

In early May, in response to the proposed Sydenham beerhall, the ICU *yase* Natal formed the Anti-Kaffir Beer Manufacturing League. The league's main aim was to oppose the 'obtaining [of] monies from the poorly paid natives' through the principle of beer monopoly.[73] 'Hostile' speeches were made in Sydenham while intoxicated protesters returning to Durban left a trail of assaulted motorists in their wake. In an atmosphere increasingly charged with violence, workers in Durban symbolically smashed the windows of the Point beerhall and raided the overseer's office. In late May an incident at the overcrowded Point barracks heightened worker disaffection. At the instigation of a local Indian trader, the Compound Manager ordered the cessation of the brewing of *mahewu*. Dockworkers, who relied on *mahewu* either as a partial source of income or as a cheap and nutritious food, responded by boycotting the Indian trader's store. In addition, one worker, Mcijelwa Mngomezulu, attempted to organise a boycott of the Point beerhall. The municipal NAD acted quickly.[74] A short time after being interrogated by the Deputy Manager of the municipal NAD, Mngomezulu's *togt* badge was confiscated along with his right to work.

Workers at the Point soon called for a systematic boycott of Durban's beerhalls and took up the issue with the ICU *yase* Natal as 'a matter which affected them all'.[75] At a meeting on 12 June many dockworkers advocated strike action and were unanimous in their opposition to municipal *utshwala*. Champion, however, was less than inspiring. He was neutral on the beer issue and was actively opposed to the proposed strike action since, as he explained to the workers, it was 'not a matter between employers and themselves'.[76] On the following day, however, at a meeting in the ICU hall, the League, under the chairmanship of J.H. London, endorsed the beer boycott. In the face of unyielding *togt* worker militancy, Champion and the Union's leadership 'pledged to support' African workers in organising the boycott. As Champion later claimed: 'I did not favour the boycott... Subsequently I took advantage of (it).'[77]

In some ways the municipal beer monopoly was a singularly appropriate target for the Union's lower middle-class leadership since it was a striking example of the more general marginalisation of small black capitalist enterprise in Durban. Yet Champion's initial attempts to marshal support for the boycott by employing Christian temperance ideology, espoused at the time by a number of black nationalists, proved a dramatic failure. At one meeting he was 'extricated with some difficulty from an angered audience which resented the idea of their beer being done away with altogether'.[78] For the majority of workers the brewing of beer was both traditional and 'a national right' of which women, in particular, had been deprived. These ideas fused with notions which held that municipal beer 'burned one's insides' because it was 'doctored' and brewed by ignorant whites. Such notions, compounded of folklore, myth and daily experience, were to underpin the extensive boycott. Furthermore, the municipal monopoly was increasingly linked to low wages, deteriorating living conditions and the everyday regimentation of workers.[79]

Against a background of violence in which a crowd of beerhall pickets up to one thousand strong clashed with police, the ICU *yase* Natal held a meeting at Cartwright's Flats, attended by over 5 000 blacks.[80] The first to speak was Champion:

> They say that this trouble was started by the ICU... but from today the ICU is taking up the burden of the togt boys — and are willing to die with them... We should get money in Durban and go and build homes outside... Down with beer! (*Loud cheers*)

J.T. Gumede, the radical President of the ANC who was in Durban during May and June, also spoke at the meeting. His speech, infused with the ideas of the CPSA's Native Republic programme, served to underline rank-and-file militancy:

> The ICU has taken the place of the Congress [NNC] absolutely in
> Natal and that shows that officers of the [NNC] were wrong to
> think they could think for other people... Now let us combine and
> take our freedom... Today the Black man and the poor White man
> is oppressed... the money goes to the Capitalists... then, work
> together for the National Independence of this country.

For Gumede, the struggle was as much about passes, 'unjust laws made
by Hertzog', and exploitation, as about the beer monopoly and the
confiscation of a *togt* worker's badge. Not surprisingly, Champion
directed his invective at local forms of oppression, using the Borough
Police and municipal NAD as examples, and exhorted those present to
join the Union. Champion also claimed that *togt* workers were
'earning a very good salary' which could well have been a way of
justifying his opposition to strike action.

It is unlikely that Champion's 'lieutenants' would have uniformly
shared this opinion, least of all Sam Mabaleka and Mtshelwa Ndhlovu.
Mabaleka was a worker at the Point, and Ndhlovu, a key ICU
representative at the docks, was a railways *induna* with strong CPSA
ties. If the Union's leadership was increasingly impelled towards a
downward identification with Durban's labouring poor, this was, not
least for the Provincial Secretary, an ambiguous process.

On 17 June Durban's five beerhalls were systematically picketed by
stick-wielding workers and members of the Unity League. During
clashes with police a white motorist was killed by the workers.
Champion, in the meanwhile, secured police protection. Together with
the Chief Constable and District Commandant of the South African
Police (SAP) he went to the Point where he told workers 'there must
be a stop to this... your grievances will be considered by the proper
authorities'.[81] This call went unheeded by workers when it was learned
that over 600 white vigilantes had besieged the ICU hall in the town.
Over 6 000 workers from barracks and hostels throughout the town
converged on central Durban. Dockworkers, led by Ndhlovu wearing a
skin cap and allegedly carrying a revolver, were heard to shout the Zulu
war cry *Usuthu!* Also conspicuous were members of the Unity League
dressed in khaki shirts and riding breeches.[82] The violent clashes which
followed left 120 injured. Six workers and two white civilians were
killed.

One immediate consequence of the violence of June 1929 was the
appointment of a government commission to investigate the

disturbances. In his report Justice de Waal viewed workers' grievances as 'utterly devoid of any substance'. Moreover, Champion as a 'professional agitator', 'capable of much good, or of infinite mischief', had used supposed grievances to 'foment trouble'. The Commission vindicated Durban's system of 'native administration'. De Waal recommended the establishment of a location for married workers, the creation of an Advisory Board in terms of the Urban Areas Act, and the setting aside of adequate space for recreation.[83] For his part, Champion claimed that the ICU *yase* Natal would disband if a location for 'better class natives' and an Advisory Board were established.[84]

The Commission's agitator thesis was hardly appropriate to the realities of popular protest in Durban. The continuing ICU *yase* Natal meetings led to official fears that the position could 'become dangerous again at any moment', and the Chief Magistrate made an attempt to ban meetings under the Riotous Assemblies Act. In August, Duiker, Sitshe, Mabaleka, Tom Gwala, Nkonke Vilakazi and Macebo were sentenced to between two and three months' hard labour for violating a ban which had been placed on one Union meeting.[85] By September 1929 the ICU *yase* Natal in Durban had an estimated 700 paid-up members, although over 5 000 workers could attend regular Union meetings. Their support for the beer boycott during 1929 was unremitting.[86]

Yet patterns of organisation only partially charted by local policemen served to underpin the boycott. While opposition to municipal beer became a central motif in the speeches at Union meetings, the boycott also appears to have been secured through other, more hidden, forms of organisation. Since the turn of the century *amalaita* gangs had been a feature of Durban's social landscape.[87] Forged in the backyards of white dwellings, the gangs were one way in which migrant youth confronted the colonisation and isolation of domestic service. Yet these street gangs could also signal out symbols of local oppression as targets for their violence, as is suggested by the running battles between the police and a gang known as the *Ngqolayomlilo* (Fiery Wagons) in 1919. At a time when the municipal NAD noted with concern that a new generation of *amalaita* comprising the 'habitually idle classes' had emerged in the town, the ICU appears to have engaged in mobilising the *amalaita*. In 1929, for example, *amalaita* successfully closed down a NNC meeting.[88] Union meetings themselves could be postponed because work obligations prevented domestic workers, and therefore possibly gang members, from attending. It was at the height of the boycott, however, that the degree of gang involvement in political activities was suggested. Secret meetings between Champion and and gang leaders at C.D. Tusi's dance hall led one ex-gang leader to pronounce: 'I say that all the Lietas today are in league with the ICU.'[89] Union claims that Champion was the 'head and guide' of Durban's *amalaita*, although invoked to threaten local authority, clearly went beyond the hyperbole which could characterise Union officials' speeches.

The Women's Auxiliary was also central, and more public, in mobilising support for the boycott. This group of women, who armed themselves with sticks and dressed in the masculine women's fashions of the twenties, were responsible for extending the boycott to municipal beerhalls in Natal's rural towns during late 1929.[90] In Durban they were known for their uncompromising use of violence against boycott-breakers. For example, in November 1929 twenty-five of these women attacked workers in the newly erected Sydenham beerhall.[91] Despite the proscription of informal brewing, a largely female-controlled shebeen trade had emerged in Durban's populous peri-urban areas.[92] With the onset of depression and further legal curbs placed on brewing, there can be little doubt that women in peri-urban and rural areas found it increasingly difficult to make ends meet. The ferocity with which the Women's Auxiliary attacked workers cannot, however, be simply ascribed to an assumed involvement in the shebeen trade.[93] Men squandering wages on municipal beer became a symbolic and economic attack on the brittle integrity of the household in which women occupied a pivotal role.

Inscribed within the radicalism of these women's beer protests lay a conservative impulse: an attempt to restitute imagined female roles in an older social order. The overt 'masculinity' of these women, their denigration of 'weak men', and their oft-expressed claims that 'the men have failed and we women will show them what we can do', were an expression of this complex articulation of radicalism and conservatism.[94] One report of a speech by C. Ntombela, an ex-nurse and 'mother' of the Natal ICU, ran as follows:

> She wanted to tell those Natives who drank at the Beer Halls [that] the day of their doom was not far distant... when... they would be 'blotted out'... she warned those dogs of persons who called themselves Natives who were selling their manhood in working for the Police that their day was at hand.[95]

In the case of some Auxiliary members this usurpation extended into the sphere of their personal lives. Hilda Jackson and Bertha Mkize, two key boycott leaders, rejected female roles as mothers and wives: both were, and remained, unmarried.[96] On various occasions during 1930 a number of members were arrested for attacking men drinking in municipal beerhalls or, in the case of Jackson and Mkize, for assaulting policemen.

Against a background of soaring arrests for the possession of illicit liquor, and intelligence reports predicting a general strike and gaol mutiny, the central government intervened in dramatic fashion.[97] On 14 November 1929 Oswald Pirow, the Minister of Justice in the Pact government confirmed in office by the recent general election, arrived in Durban together with 690 members of the para-military Mobile Squadron. Over the following weeks the Squadron swooped on compounds to check workers' poll-tax receipts and embarked on an extensive operation to crush shebeens and the illicit drink traffic in the town and its peri-urban areas. Well over 2 000 workers were arrested and thousands of gallons of *isitshimiyane* destroyed. While revenue from the beerhalls remained negligible, in one week Durban's intimidated workers paid £5 000 in taxes.[98]

This undiluted repression was undoubtedly welcomed by the municipal NAD, the Borough Police and harshly paternalist Natal ideologues such as J.S. Marwick. It was criticised, however, by the recently elected liberal Mayor, A. Lamont, and a handful of Town Councillors. Their criticisms were embodied in a report of the local Joint Council which claimed that Africans were 'in that state of mind in which revolutionary propaganda easily thrives', and that 'Native opinion should be scrupulously consulted and sympathetically considered'.[99] Similarly, the Report of the Native Affairs Commission conceded that Africans had genuine grievances, particularly that of low wages. The Report stated, moreover, that the lack of a 'native village' and adequate recreation facilities had led to a situation where Africans had resorted to

> illicit drinking, listening to the ill-informed and unbalanced agitator of communistic or anti-European tendencies, the attendance of dance halls where the notaries of the national Zulu dances rub shoulders with others indulging in European dances.[100]

As a consequence, the Commission reiterated the need for a location, a Native Advisory Board and recreational facilities. The implementation of these recommendations during the early thirties represented a real victory, particularly for the leadership of the ICU *yase* Natal.

The Native Advisory Board and the Beer Boycott

The establishment of a Native Advisory Board (NAB) in January 1930 was clearly a response to a situation where Africans' shared experience of class and racial oppression had facilitated the formation of the popular alliances of 1929. As the Chief Native Commissioner noted, the NAB would 'be useful as a buffer between the mass of the people and the local authority'.[101] The Board comprised four Town Councillors and ten African representatives. In an unprecedented step of recognition the ICU *yase* Natal was allocated two seats which were subsequently occupied by Champion and James Ngcobo. The NNC was also allowed two representatives while the remaining six seats were given to residents of government and municipal barracks. The Board, however, had no legal status since it was not constituted in terms of the 1923 Urban Areas Act and was thus deemed a 'goodwill gesture'.[102]

Initially the Board members presented a united front on the issue of the boycott despite councillors' threats that rents at municipal barracks and trading quarters would have to be increased to offset the 'unfavourable position' of the Native Revenue Account.[103] Most Board members urged discussion of the 'economic question' which they regarded as integral to the beer boycott. Yet some members attempted to distance themselves from the boycott. The NNC, represented by the entrepreneurs J.R. Msimang and A.F. Matibela, passed a resolution in March 1930 stating that Congress had no 'connection whatsoever with the Beer Boycott'.[104] Indeed, the Congress movement, having lost its claims on the support of the masses, warmly embraced liberal bodies such as the Joint Councils. In Durban this took the form of endorsing the Durban Joint Council's plea for greater formal recognition of the 'difference between the umfaan' and the 'growing class of educated native clerks, teachers, artisans etc.'[105] In broader regional terms the NNC concentrated its political initiatives in attempting to gain state recognition of Solomon kaDinizulu as Zulu Paramount through Inkatha.[106] Dube suggested the recognition of Solomon as a means of dampening popular protest in Durban, and also published the contents of an anti-ICU speech by the Zulu king precisely because of the potential threat which the Union posed to Congress's political programme.[107]

Matibela clearly suggested this failure of the NNC to extend its organisational roots when he claimed that, with regard to the boycott issue, it was 'impossible' for the NNC 'to get in direct touch with the Natives whom they represented'.[108] Ironically, the continuing boycott provided Congress demands for a location for married Africans with additional ballast. The call for adequate family housing had been a central demand of Congress leaders such as Dube, as well as of a broader substratum of Durban's African middle classes for over a decade. For a *kholwa* élite there was little doubt about the eligibility of the 'raw native' for such accommodation: he was perfectly well suited to Durban's barracks.[109] This was a issue about which ICU leaders were a little more ambiguous. The frustrated artisan J.M. Ngcobo, for example, stated that the proposed location should be built by, and for, African bricklayers, carpenters and painters.[110]

If members of the Board made repeated demands for local employers and the Town Council to address the question of wages, they spent as much, if not more energy in pressing the demands of Durban's struggling petty traders. At the end of March the Native Administration Committee, having obtained evidence that Union leaders were threatening beer-drinkers with violence, resolved to increase rentals for all African traders. At this point the solidarity over the boycott, at least at the level of the NAB, collapsed. J.R. Msimang proposed a motion, which was seconded by his fellow NNC representative, that 'the promoters of the beer boycott be requested to suspend the same until such time as the proposed Native village is established'.[111]

The motion was carried by eight votes to two. Champion strategically abstained, while Ngcobo, along with the railway workers' representative, voted against the motion. Champion's abstention was hardly surprising. He was caught between a government Native Affairs Department which viewed his activities with increasing suspicion and the 'many people' who had 'grave doubts about the usefulness of the Board'. Ngcobo vehemently abused Msimang and the NNC, claiming that workers' demands for higher wages and better housing had yet to be met. Indeed, only a day before, a deputation of municipal workers, acting independently of the Union, went to the municipal NAD to protest that their wages were unable to meet the demands of taxation and the high cost of living.[112] A day after the resolution was passed, the NNC held a mass meeting in order to present their position on the boycott. The meeting, which was heavily guarded by police, was able to register only nine votes. Nearly 700 members of the assembly indicated their animosity towards the NNC by leaving prematurely. As for Msimang, he 'stood condemned in the eyes of his own people' and was forced to vacate his business premises under threat of death.[113] Msimang, who had drawn up the 1926 Constitution of Inkatha,[114] was forced to resign from the NAB when Champion laid charges of bribery and corruption against him.

Although it was reported in June that larger numbers of workers were drinking municipal beer, the boycott had been remarkably effective for over a year. Revenue from beer sales, usually comprising well over half of the income to the Native Revenue Account, fell to £6 107 during the same period. The shortfall of £47 517 'was almost entirely due to the boycott'.[115] The local press warned that even after a year the boycott was still 'influencing, and indeed intimidating, 40 000 natives in the Durban area'.[116] Undoubtedly the Union, together with its militias and *amalaita*, played an important role in sustaining the boycott. In more general terms, however, the strength of the boycott lay in broader patterns of worker disaffection. While the consumption of home-made brews in shebeens was in all likelihood cheaper than municipal beer, the beer boycott was rooted in opposition to the beerhall as a disguised form of taxation. Undoubtedly, too, it was seen as a way of expressing workers' demands for higher wages. It is likely that these notions found their way into the language of Union leaders. Hamilton Msomi, for example, reportedly claimed that the 'European could no longer exploit [workers]' and that the Town Council would have to 'make submission according to the Zulu custom and give a full explanation before any beer would be allowed to be drunk'.[117] Msomi's language also hints at those ways in which traditional views of social norms and obligations underpinned the boycott. Men and woman were motivated by the common-sense belief that they were defending a traditional right which had been violated by the authorities.

Although the ICU *yase* Natal was still able to attract a diverse cross-section of Durban's African population to its meetings, in the countryside of Natal and Zululand it had all but disappeared. Even in Durban itself Union subscriptions were not sufficient to offset its financial problems.[118] Given the Union's failure to fulfil its ambitious promises to workers, it is hardly surprising that it largely ceased to attract paid-up membership, despite implicit grass-roots support for the Union. During 1930 it is probable that the active participation of the Union on the Advisory Board did little to advance flagging rank-and-file support.[119]

Urban Militancy: The Zulu King and the Union's Imbongi

Anxiety over declining support underlay a conscious shift in the Union's strategy. At a meeting on 11 May Champion claimed that he was 'going to call a Meeting of all Native Chiefs in Natal, including Solomon kaDinizulu'.[120] While the financial problems of the Union had much to do with this shift in tactics, the mobilisation of traditionalist authority should also be understood in terms of the exigencies of local struggles in a town where many workers saw themselves as members of particular clans, bound through a network of reciprocal obligations to chiefly authority. It was on this social terrain that Union organisers responded to and manipulated particularist symbols and loyalties, while Champion continued to see himself as the last in a lineage of great organisers extending back to Shaka.[121]

At the end of May, sixty-two African chiefs and headmen from Natal and Zululand arrived in Durban. The purported reason for their presence was an invitation extended to them by Champion to discuss a ricksha strike which began on 19 May — eight days after Champion had announced his intention of meeting with Solomon and the chiefs. While crowds of workers thronged the streets, Union leaders held a closed meeting with the chiefs. The hidden agenda of the chiefs undoubtedly related to the question of wage-remittances. Rising levels of unemployment which accompanied economic depression, together with the need to ensure the continued flow of urban incomes into rural households, helped clear the way for this meeting with Union leaders. The intimate connection between agrarian and urban struggles was reflected in the resolutions of the meeting which dealt with cattle-dipping, the Land Act, taxation and restrictions on beer-brewing and black court interpreters.[122] Yet this was the first conscious attempt by leadership to link urban and rural struggles.

The following day a public meeting was held at which various chiefs addressed an audience of 6 000. Most speakers told of hunger and starvation wages, although Ngonyama kaGumbi of the Union's Pietermaritzburg branch invoked British injustice and the 'murderous acts' of whites, suggesting that Africans should 'cut the throats' of government officials 'as the Russian Communists had done'. It was also reported that:

> An elderly Native from the seats of the alleged Chiefs got up and thanked Champion publicly for what he was doing. He said that they would carry on the work undertaken by him in Durban to the country... also a younger Native from the crowd... commenc[ed] 'bongering' or singing the praises of the chiefs from the past and the warring acts. He commenced with Tshaka and ended with Champion... this is a most dangerous proceeding in a gathering of the ICU variety... the effect [is] electrical.[123]

At the close of the meeting J. Duiker shouted *Humu! Humu!* (Regiments Disperse!) while thousands of voices took up the cry of *Ematsheni!* (Beerhalls!).

There was good reason for the increasing concern of local police officials over the incorporation of traditionalist idioms and symbols into the speeches of ICU organisers at a time when the state was exploring ways in which traditionalist authority could be used as a form of domination appropriate to an industrialising society. It was not only the large number of chiefs who responded to the invitation of a 'commoner' which perturbed local authority, but also the apparent fusion of the nationalist rhetoric of ICU organisers with traditionalist folklore. If the independent appropriation from below of the language and symbols of a pre-colonial past and their reworking in the context of urban struggle was perceived as highly subversive, how much more so was the arrival of the Zulu king himself in Durban a few months later? Although Champion had opportunistically claimed that the meeting of Chiefs indicated that the 'District and Rural areas would combine with [workers] in one general movement',[124] it is unlikely that the government officials, who were watching the situation closely, expected Solomon to arrive in Durban. However, in late August, he slipped into the port town. Three days after having visited workers at the Bell Street barracks he slipped into the ICU Hall where he interrupted a concert by Dem Darkies, received a rapturous welcome, and addressed an enthusiastic meeting. After a private meeting with Champion in which Solomon apparently appealed for unity between the Union and the NNC, Champion arranged a public meeting for Solomon. The Zulu king, no doubt acutely aware of the potential repercussions which his visit to Durban would have in government circles, failed to appear and quickly retraced his steps to Eshowe.[125]

The traditionalism of the Zulu royal family constituted a potential bulwark against radical change not only for wealthier African landowners such as John Dube, but also for ideologues of segregation, the most notable of whom was the sugar baron G. Heaton Nicholls. Certainly the role which the Zulu royal family and Inkatha could play as an antidote to ICU radicalism was not missed by certain government officials.[126] Despite the occasional public antagonism between the ICU and Solomon, it is unlikely that popular support for the Zulu king and the Union were ever mutually exclusive. In 1928 Solomon had indicated a keen interest in the affairs of the ICU and claimed that he had publicly condemned the ICU the previous year because the Union did not ask his permission to hold meetings in 'his kingdom, Natal'.[127] When one of the rural organisers uttered 'we look upon Chief Solomon as a king because of hereditary blood',[128] it is likely that his words would have found a resonance amongst the urban and rural poor in both town and countryside.

It has been suggested that what might appear to be deep ethnic continuities may also be unmasked as contingent historical creations.[129] In many ways Union leaders, and for that matter the NNC, did consciously rework history to legitimate claims to cultural autonomy and political rights. Yet the creation of these continuities with the past was not entirely factitious.[130] Zulu-speakers in Natal and Zululand did share a language, a common culture, a remembrance of autonomous statehood and a tradition of resistance to white rule. Moreover, there is much evidence to suggest that by the 1920s the Zulu royal family had been invested with an almost mythological power as protectors of ordinary people's rights. Undoubtedly Solomon's visit to Durban was motivated by the self-interested desire to secure further financial and political support for his increasingly arduous quest for state recognition.[131] Yet his appearance in Durban was made increasingly feasible by local conditions of struggle.

One immediate consequence of the presence of the chiefs and Solomon in Durban was the deportation of Champion from Natal under the amended Riotous Assemblies Act. Clearly, during a period when the loyalty of traditional chiefly authority to the state was regarded as tacit, the brief public association of Solomon and a large number of chiefs with the 'radical' ICU yase Natal was, at least in the more alarmist sections of local and central government, regarded as a possible prelude to the combination of urban and rural popular protest under the symbolic leadership of the Zulu king.[132] In Durban itself the shifting tactics of the Union appear to have resulted in a brief increase in rank-and-file support. The Union, having installed a resident *imbongi* (praise-poet) at mass meetings, could claim that 'the Zulu nation was one and any future action would be as one solid action by the Zulu nation'.[133]

Conclusion: Shaka's Nemesis

When no tangible benefits accrued from the Union's purported alliance with the Zulu king and chiefly authority, mass support for the ICU *yase* Natal appears to have finally evaporated. Disillusioned workers who had paid Union subscriptions in the hope that Champion and his Union would successfully lead their struggle for better wages, demanded their money back. Certainly, economic conditions in Durban hardly favoured trade union demands for higher wages. Many workers had lost jobs through wage determinations while others were simply dismissed by employers seeking to maintain profit levels during the depression. Moreover, the municipal NAD used the Urban Areas Amendment Act of 1930 together with the Native Taxation Act systematically to eject large numbers of blacks 'with no visible means of subsistence' from the town. Durban's unskilled African workers were rendered increasingly exploitable by the presence of a large reserve army of labour in the town.

There were, however, other forces at work which served to detach Union leaders from its volatile constituency. Through the Board the grievances of a small section of Durban's African population were receiving some degree of attention. The establishment of the Board and the promise of a location at Clairwood for 'more civilised' blacks partly fulfilled their demands. The provision of this proposed housing scheme depended substantially on the decreasing revenue accruing to the Native Revenue Account, since white labour fiercely opposed the use of cheap migrant labour in the erection of houses. Not surprisingly, then, those sections of the African population which were to benefit from the proposed location also had, along with Durban's ruling classes, a stake in the termination of the beer boycott and the moulding of popular protest along more conservative lines. Although the leadership of the ICU *yase* Natal continued to support the beer boycott after Champion's departure from Durban in October 1930, their position *vis-à-vis* the labouring poor became increasingly ambiguous.

It is unlikely, too, that workers who were demanding a living wage would have enthusiastically embraced an organisation which was calling for £1 donations to the 'Champion Defence Fund', and which was partially discredited through its involvement in the affairs of the Advisory Board. Indeed, frustrated workers led by Mtshelwa Ndhlovu took the law into their own hands and severely assaulted the NAB representative for the Bell Street barracks whom they regarded as a stooge of the local Native Administration Department.[134]

It is no wonder, then, that when the CPSA began mobilising local support for its proposed pass-burning campaign at the end of 1930 it should have drawn 6 000 workers (including many ex-Union supporters and lower-level Union leadership) into its ranks and also forced the ICU to prolong its meetings in order to prevent workers from 'crossing the railway line' to listen to fiery Party speeches. Yet not all workers responded to the call to destroy passes. Older dockworkers, for example, demanded of the youthful Nkosi 'if his parents knew what he was doing?'. Others, anticipating renewed violence, simply returned to their rural homes. It was probably with more than a degree of surprise, then, that the police approached the gathering of thousands of workers on 'Dingaan's Day', witnessed the destruction of passes and heard praises of Solomon and his royal predecessors. Police intelligence had confidently claimed that the Party's campaign would attract a few hundred 'Basutos of the low type.'[135] Indeed, while the ICU leadership publicly disassociated itself from the campaign, the predominantly Basotho IICU gave what support it had to the campaign. It was not without reason that the local police stated that the 'riff-raff', 'scum' and 'habitually idle' of the town were in strong evidence on 'Dingaan's Day'. It was precisely those workers who felt most vulnerable in the face of the restructuring of the labour market, as well as unemployed urban outsiders (many of whom might have been non-Zulu and of a younger generation), which the CPSA could claim as its constituency. For these individuals the pass and the poll-tax receipt were in a very real sense 'badges of slavery' for they underpinned both low wages and restricted employment opportunities.

As men and women who retained a residual optimism that they could wrest greater recognition of their status from the ruling classes, the ICU leadership in Durban was, at the best of times, hard pressed to make the transition from tactics of litigation and the amelioration of individual worker's grievances to mass worker action. By the late 1920s the members of this middle class *manque* sacrificed their position as ideologues of the masses, in the hope of differential accommodation within local relations of domination and subordination. It was left to men such as Mbutana Vanqa, a shoemaker from the Transkei, and Cyrus Lettonyane, the local leader of the IICU who had a string of criminal convictions ranging from theft and assault to malicious damage to property, to mobilise popular support for the pass-burning campaign. Together with the most oppressed sections of Durban's labouring poor they confronted the brunt of local police repression in a last desperate attempt to challenge exploitation. With depression, state repression, unemployment and drought at their backs, their gesture of defiance marked the collapse of the popular alliances of the twenties, the retreat of political movements into factionalism and the withdrawal of workers into their own struggle for survival.

Notes

I am indebted to Charles van Onselen for his criticism of an earlier draft of this article.

1 University of South Africa (UNISA), ICU *yase* Natal Microfilm, Reel 3, General Secretary's Report of Branches, 6 March 1926.

2 *Udibi lwase Afrika,* June 1927. For early membership figures see University of the Witwatersrand (UW), Champion Papers, Champion to J. la Guma, 12 Nov. 1925; Champion to C. Kadalie, 9 Nov. 1926.

3 For an outline of these court victories, see UNISA, ICU Microfilm, 4, Manuscript by Champion (n.d.). For these formative struggles of the Union, in particular the campaign against the enforced bodily disinfecting of workers, see P. la Hausse, The Struggle for the City: Alcohol, the Ematsheni and Popular Culture in Durban, 1902-36. MA Dissertation, University of Cape Town, 1984, pp.144-52.

4 UNISA, ICU Microfilm, 4, List of Natal Delegates, 16 Dec. 1927.

5 H. Bradford, The Industrial and Commercial Workers' Union of Africa in the South African Countryside, 1924-1930. PhD Thesis, University of the Witwatersrand, 1985.

6 For attempts by the state to reformulate urban 'native policy', see *Report of the Inter-Departmental Committee on the Native Pass Laws,* 1920, U.G. 41-'42.

7 *Natal Government Gazette,* No. 3710, 10 Oct. 1908, Act to Amend the Law relating to Native Beer.

8 Native Affairs by-laws which were introduced in 1917 laid down precise procedures for work registration, passes and service contracts. The laws also introduced a harsh curfew and compulsory medical examination. See *Mayor's Minute*, 1917, p. 15.

9 Interview by P. la Hausse with Charles Khumalo and Alfred Tshabalala, Durban, 28 Aug. 1986. These are Charles Khumalo's translations.

10 See Natal Archives (NA), Police Report Book, No. 6, 4 March 1903.

11 NA, Durban Town Clerk's Files (DTCF), 63, 467, Evidence of Town Council to Native Economic Commission (NEC), March 1931; Durban Corporation, Statement re NEC.

12 Interview with Khumalo and Tshabalala.

13 NA, Durban Municipal Inquiry, August 1927, Evidence of C. Dube, p.582. See also C. Murray, *Families Divided - The Impact of Migrant Labour in Lesotho* (Johannesburg, 1981), pp. 14-16. For worsening conditions amongst rural blacks in Natal, see Bradford, The ICU, pp. 52-65.

14 Interview with Khumalo and Tshabalala; Interview by P. la Hausse and M. Marrengane with F. Zondi, Maqadini, 25 Feb. 1987. The extent of this tendency awaits further research.

15 See NA, Commission of Inquiry into Durban Native Riots, 1929, Minutes of Evidence (hereafter Commission Evidence), p. 300 (Det. Sergt R.H. Arnold).

16 For example, by 1926 the rise of white- and Indian-owned laundries had effectively marginalised African washerwomen. See *Mayor's Minute*, 1926, p. 318.

17 For women and illicit brewing, see Central Archives Depot (CAD), NEC, Minutes of Evidence, p. 6372 (Mrs Sililo).

18 NA, Durban Criminal Records (DCR), Case heard 3 Jan. 1916.

19 NA, DTCF, 103, 467B, Amendment of General By-Law No. 71.

20 See Interview with Charles Khumalo, Bruntville, Mooi River, 1 Sept. 1986; cf. A. Vilakazi, *Zulu Transformations* (Pietermaritzburg, 1965), pp. 76-77.

21 For example, see *Report of the Proceedings of the Fifth General Missionary Conference of South Africa* (Durban, 1922), pp. 73-95.

22 Interview with Khumalo and Tshabalala.

23 UNISA, ICU Microfilm, 1, Regulations for the Management and Control of Municipal Native Eating Houses; A. Mtembu and sixteen others to Manager, Municipal NAD, 13 Sept. 1929.

24 See, for example, NA, DTCF, 43, 315, Petition of Native Stall Owners' Association, 1 Dec. 1925.

25 UNISA, Champion Papers, Acc. 1, Box 1, 2.2.2., Interview by M.W. Swanson with A.W.G. Champion.

26 See UNISA, ICU Microfilm, 2, Points put forward by Deputation from Borough Market Stallholders, 18 Nov. 1929.

27 For a recent perceptive study, see S. Marks, *The Ambiguities of Dependence in South Africa* (Johannesburg, 1986), pp. 42-73.

28 See *Ilanga lase Natal*, 19 Aug. 1927 for criticism of the ICU and its constituency.

29 See UNISA, ICU Microfilm, 4, Champion to J. Astor, 7 March 1935. Bradford's discussion of the nature of the national ICU leadership is illuminating. See The ICU, Chapter 2.

30 CAD, Native Affairs Department (NTS), 7606, 49/328, Part I, Translation of *Igazi ne Zinyembezi*. Champion referred to London as a 'victim of [the] white labour policy'; see UNISA, Champion Papers, Interview with Champion. It is difficult to document the lives of the lesser-known (and less-recognised) office-holders of the ICU in Durban, of whom there were at least sixty between 1928 and 1930.

31 CAD, NTS, 7214, 49/328, Part I, Translation of *Igazi*; and UNISA, ICU Microfilm, 3, Report on a meeting called by Native Advisory Board members, 11 March 1930.

32 NA, Chief Native Commissioner (CNC), 210A, 913/1915; CAD, NTS, 7214, 56/326, Part I, Det. Sergt Arnold to Officer (CID), 6 Sept. 1929. For further information on Mkize, see UNISA, Interview by T. Couzens *et al.* with B. Mkize, 4 Aug. 1979. For the plight of teachers see, for example, *Ilanga lase Natal*, 25 March 1927.

33 Interview with Khumalo and Tshabalala.

34 Both Dunn and Maduna had been forced out of the Union by the end of 1927. See Wickins, *The ICU of Africa*, pp. 145-49; and Bradford, The ICU, p. 114.

35 NA, Commission Evidence, p.251 (Chief Constable Alexander).

36 For a discussion of the subsequent political impact of black war veterans, see B. Willan, 'The South African Native Contingent, 1916-1918', *Journal of African History*, 19, (1978).

37 These included Jim London, Bertha Mkize, Hamilton Msomi, Abel Ngcobo, James Ngcobo, George Conjwa, David Sitshe and Hilda Jackson.

38 NA, Commission Evidence, p. 305 (R.H. Arnold).

39 Ibid., p. 289 (R.H. Arnold).

40 UW, Champion Papers, Bc1, Minutes of the Governing Body of the ICU *yase* Natal, 27 June 1928; NA, Commission Evidence, p.289 (R.H. Arnold); Interview by P. la Hausse with A. Gumede, Durban, 16 April 1986. For a fascinating discussion of the upward mobility of leadership, see Bradford, The ICU, pp. 125-33.

41 UNISA, ICU Microfilm, 2, R. Tshabalala to all Provincial and Branch Secretaries, 27 Oct. 1927.

42 See UNISA, ICU Microfilm, 5, Regulations of the All-African Cooperative Society Ltd. See also CAD, Department of Justice (JUS), 920, 1/18/26, 16, R.H. Arnold to CID, 4 June 1928; Interview with Bertha Mkize.

43 CAD, JUS, 917, 1/18/26-sub, R.H. Arnold to CID, 6 Feb. 1928.

44 CAD, JUS, K22, Box 1, 6301/29, Cowley and Cowley to T.C., 5 March 1926; UNISA, Champion Papers, Acc. 1, Box 3, 5.1, Rules and Constitution of Natal Workers' Club, Durban. Membership of the Club was limited to 500, annual subscriptions were 2s.6d., while the entrance fee was also 2s.6d.

45 For the impact of black separatist thought on Champion see UW, African Studies Institute (ASI), Autobiography of Champion (MS), p. 53. Also cf. Bradford, The ICU, pp. 184-49.

46 Interview with Khumalo and Tshabalala.

47 Interview by P. la Hausse with Jacob Cele, KwaMashu, 27 Aug. 1986.

48 For the chaotic state of union finances, see CAD, JUS, K22, Box 2, Judgement of Justice Tatham in case of Champion vs Lenono, 1 Dec. 1927. Peculation and lax book-keeping, however, were not solely responsible for the financial problems of the branch. By July 1928 Cowley and Cowley, the Union's lawyers, were owed £3 000 for legal expenses.

49 CAD, JUS, 917, 1/18/26, 8, R.H. Arnold to CID, 5 May 1927. Dockworkers had taken independent strike action in 1926 and 1927. See D. Hemson, Class Consciousness and Migrant Workers: Dockworkers of Durban. PhD Thesis, University of Warwick, 1979, pp. 202-05.

50 See CAD, JUS, 920, 1/18/26, 16, R.H. Arnold to CID, 14 May 1928.

51 CAD, NTS, 7214, 56/326, 1, R.H. Arnold to CID, 24 May 1928; UNISA, ICU Microfilm, 3, Batty to Champion, 18 May 1928.

52 Cf. T. Ranger's discussion of the Beni *ngoma's* in *Dance and Society in Eastern Africa 1890-1970* (London, 1970).

53 C. Kadalie, *My Life and the ICU* (London, 1975), p.162.

54 Ibid., p. 96; Bradford, The ICU, p. 165; Interview with Cele.

55 Interview by P. la Hausse with C. Khumalo, KwaMashu, 5 April 1986.

56 See, for example, *Udibi lwase Afrika,* June 1927.

57 NA, Commission Evidence, p. 399 (A.W.G. Champion); *Ilanga lase Natal,* 9 March 1928, S.L. Plaatje to Editor.

58 For a suggestive comparative study of language and class consciousness, see Gareth Stedman Jones, *Languages of Class-Studies in English Working Class History 1832-1982,* (Cambridge, 1982), pp. 90-178.

59 CAD, JUS, K22, Box 1, 6301/29, Memorandum submitted by the Representatives of the ICU *yase* Natal to the Mayor, 19 Sept. 1928; JUS, 920, 1/18/26, 17, R.H. Arnold to Inspector (CID), 22 May 1928.

60 Arnold was a close confidant of Champion who saw it as his task to 'worm' his way into the Union in order to destroy it. He had allegedly drawn up the Constitution of the ICU *yase* Natal. See NA, Commission Evidence, p. 441 (A.F. Batty).

61 By 1928 the membership of the CPSA was predominantly black. See H.J. and R.E. Simons, *Class and Colour in South Africa 1850-1950* (London, 1983), pp. 407-09. For an examination of the programme, see M. Legassick, 'Class and Nationalism in South African Protest: The South African Communist Party and the Native Republic, 1928-34', *Eastern African Studies,* 15 (1973); B. Bunting, *Moses Kotane – South African Revolutionary* (London,1975), pp. 14-42.

62 See CAD, JUS, 922, 1/18/26, 23, Const. Hobbs to CID, 18 Feb. 1929; R.H. Arnold to CID, 22 Jan. 1929.

63 NA, Commission Evidence, p. 337-38 (A.W.G. Champion).

64 CAD, JUS, 922, 1/18/26, 23, R.H. Arnold to CID, 20 Feb. 1929. Membership of the Party at this time was probably not more than 100.

65 NA, Commission Evidence, p. 25 (C.W. Lewis).

66 Ibid., p. 24 (C.W. Lewis). Other witnesses claimed that the militia displayed the red ICU flag. That this was subject to debate is revealing in itself.

67 Margery Perham recorded a rich diversity of dance forms after a

visit to the ICU dance hall during this period. See *African Apprenticeship* (New York, 1974), pp. 196-99.

68 D. Coplan, *In Township Tonight!* (Johannesburg, 1985), pp. 65-67.

69 *U Bhungca (ama Oxford bags)*. Lovedale Sol-fa Leaflets, 7C, (translation).

70 UNISA, Champion Papers, Interview with Champion.

71 CAD, NTS, 7665, 46/332, Consultation in CNC's Office, 7 Sept. 1929.

72 NA, Commission Evidence, pp. 285-86 (Arnold); also cf. Bradford, The ICU, pp. 203-11.

73 CAD, JUS, K22, Box 1, Exhibits A-RR, Document entitled Anti-Kaffir Beer League, 5 May 1929.

74 NA, Commission Evidence, p. 46 (T.J. Chester).

75 Ibid., p. 424 (M. Mngomezulu).

76 Ibid., p. 350 (A.W.G. Champion).

77 Ibid., p. 381 (A.W.G. Champion).

78 CAD, NTS, 7665, 46/332, CNC to Secretary of Native Affairs (SNA), 31 Aug. 1929.

79 CAD, JUS, K22, Box 1, Exhibits A-RR, Memorandum of *Togt* Labourers of the Bell Street Barracks.

80 For the speeches, see CAD, K22, Box 1, Exhibits A-RR, Const. Hobbs to CID, 20 June 1929.

81 NA, Commission Evidence, p. 229 (Chief Constable Alexander).

82 See NA, Commission Evidence, *passim*.

83 Library of Parliament, Report of the Commission of Enquiry into Native Riots of Durban, 29 July 1929, Annexure 133-1929.

84 NA, Commission Evidence, p. 354 (A.W.G. Champion).

85 NA, DCR, A Court, Case heard on 28 Aug. 1929.

86 CAD, NTS, 7665, 46/33, CNC to SNA, 31 Aug. 1929; Minutes of the Native Administration Committee (NAC), 8 Oct. 1929.

87 See P. la Hausse, '"Mayihlome!": Towards an Understanding of Amalaita Gangs in Durban, *c.* 1900-1930', Unpublished Paper, African Studies Institute Seminar, University of the Witwatersrand, 1987.

88 *Ilanga lase Natal*, 5 April 1929.

89 CAD, JUS, K22, Box 2, Native Unrest in Durban, Affidavits and Statements: No. 23, G. Dhlamini, 12 Nov. 1929; No. 27, C. Nxaba, 12 Nov. 1929; No. 34, T. Myeza, 13 Nov. 1929.

90 For these struggles, see Bradford, The ICU, pp. 312-61.

91 *Natal Mercury*, 6 Nov. 1929.
92 Convictions for the possession of illicit alcohol were enormous. During a six-month period in 1928 over 2 792 Africans were convicted.
93 This was the view of some government officials and Dube. See CAD, NTS, 7665, 46/332, Meeting of Minister of Native Affairs and others in CNC's Office, 6 Sept. 1929.
94 NA, DTCF, 63, 467, W. North to Town Clerk, 19 Nov. 1930. Also see CAD, NTS, 7606, 49/328, I, Translation of *Igazi ne Zinyembezi*.
95 CAD, JUS, 823, 1/18/26, 25, R.H. Arnold to CID, 7 April 1930. (Thanks to Helen Bradford for comments on Ntombela.)
96 Interview with Khumalo.
97 CAD, JUS, K22, Box 2, Affidavits and Statements.
98 Ibid., Report on Mobile Squadron; *Natal Mercury*, 18 Nov. 1929, 20 Nov. 1929.
99 CAD, JUS, K22, Box 1, 6301/29, Statement of the Executive Committee of the Durban Joint Council of Europeans and Natives concerning SAP Raids and Demonstrations, 14-21 Nov. 1929.
100 NA, DTCF, 57, 323, Report of the Native Affairs Commission, 12 Dec. 1929.
101 CAD, NTS, 7665, 46/332, CNC to SNA, 31 August 1929.
102 NA, DTCF, 57, 323A, Memorandum for Native Administration Committee, 25 Aug. 1931.
103 NA, Minutes of the NAB, 19 Feb. 1930.
104 NA, DTCF, 21, 91, F.M. Xulu to Town Clerk (TC), 5 March 1930.
105 UNISA, ICU Microfilm, 1, Extract from Report of Joint Council of Europeans and Natives (June 1930) on the Urban Areas Act of 1930. Champion referred to the Council as 'a self-constituted body that refuses to admit the accepted leaders'.
106 These attempts to bolster traditional Zulu authority were seen as a way of securing the class interests of the propertied élite. See N. Cope, The Zulu Royal Family under the South African Government, 1910-1933: Solomon kaDinizulu, Inkatha and Zulu Nationalism. PhD Thesis, University of Natal, 1985.
107 See CAD, NTS, 7665, 46/332, Report of Meeting in CNC's office; *Ilanga lase Natal*, 12 Aug. 1927.
108 NA, Minutes of the NAB, 16 April 1930.
109 NA, Commission Evidence, p. 408 (John Dube).
110 NA, DTCF, 57, 323A, Ngcobo to TC, 6 June 1930.

111 NA, Minutes of the NAB, 16 April 1930.

112 NA, DTCF, 315E, T.J. Chester to TC, 16 April 1930.

113 *Natal Mercury*, 17 April 1930; NA, Minutes of the NAB, 16 April 1930; DTCF, 57, 323A, Msimang to TC, 12 May 1930.

114 Cope, The Zulu Royal Family, p. 224.

115 *Mayor's Minute*, 1930, p. 1ii.

116 *Natal Mercury*, 28 Aug. 1930.

117 CAD, JUS, 923 1/18/26, 25.

118 See UNISA, ICU Microfilm, 3, Champion to President and Governing Body, ICU *yase* Natal, 24 Feb. 1930.

119 CAD, JUS, 923, 1/18/26, 25, *passim*.

120 Ibid., 26, R.H. Arnold to CID, 11 May 1930.

121 UNISA, ICU Microfilm, 5, Fragment of Champion's writings (n.d.).

122 CAD, NTS, 7214, 56/326, Part I, Document entitled Resolution, 31 May 1929. For official confusion over the number of chiefs who came to Durban see NTS, 7214, 56/326, Part I.

123 CAD, JUS, K22, Box 1, 6301/29, R.H. Arnold to CID, 2 June 1930.

124 Ibid., District Commandant, SAP to Commissioner, SAP, Natal Division, 16 June 1930.

125 NA, CNC, 81, 58/7/3, N.1/1/3(32)1, R.H. Arnold to CID, 16 Sept. 1930.

126 Marks, *Ambiguities of Dependence*, pp. 40-41, 70-71; Cope, The Zulu Royal Family, Chapter 6.

127 CAD, JUS, 922, 1/18/26, 22, Report of Det. Const. M. Zondi, CID, 18 Dec. 1928. Solomon had apparently told this to Kadalie in 1928.

128 CAD, JUS, 920, 1/18/26, 17, Det. Const. Van Vuuren to Dist. Commandant, SAP, 7 May 1928.

129 G. Eley, 'Nationalism and Social History', *Social History* 6 (1981), 94.

130 See E.Hobsbawm's characterisation of 'invented tradition' in terms of the creation of a factitious continuity with the past, in E. Hobsbawm and T. Ranger (eds), *The Invention of Tradition* (Cambridge, 1983), p. 2.

131 Cope, The Zulu Royal Family, p. 380; Marks, *Ambiguities of Dependence*, pp. 15-20.

132 CAD, JUS, 582, 3136/31, I, Commissioner SAP to Minister of Justice, 19 Sept. 1930.

133 CAD, JUS, 923, 1/18/26, 28, Report of Det. J. Andrews, 2 Oct. 1930.

134 NA, DTCF, 57, 323A, A. Gumede and S. Ngcobo to NAB, 21 Nov.
       1930.
135 CAD, JUS, 924, 1/18/26, 29, R.H. Arnold to CID, 8 Dec. 1930.

Swing the Assegai Peacefully?

'New Africa', Mkhumbane, the Co-operative Movement and Attempts to Transform Durban Society in the Late Nineteen-Forties

Iain Edwards

As it becomes increasingly acknowledged that the nineteen-forties constitute a politically crucial decade, greater attention is being devoted towards various aspects of African city life during the period. Much of this work is aimed at analysing African political expression during the late 1940s, and at understanding why the African working class failed to develop stronger trade unions and political structures. Though the economy was undergoing a period of uncertainty which 'brought to a head the effects of structural changes generated at various levels of the economy during the war',[1] the significantly enlarged African proletariat was unable to take advantage of an uncharacteristically indecisive state. While many of the shantytown movements, millenarian sects and other groupings succeeded in winning piecemeal victories, by and large these newly formed communities 'were still too fluid, too diverse, too unformed to take sustained advantage of the state's fumbling indecision'.[2] By their very nature, many of these groups could be nothing other than introverted, sectional and transient.

Although such work has probably underestimated the aims and ambitions of such movements, it has nevertheless cast doubt on the acceptability of many of the recognised analyses of African political experience during the late 1940s. It is no longer adequate to assert that during this period the African working classes had, under the influence of the Communist Party of South Africa (CPSA),[3] developed a militant nationalism which radicalised the African National Congress (ANC), placing it 'at the centre of the non-racial liberation movement that has led the struggle since the early 1950s'.[4] Similarly, it is simplistic to attribute the lack of apparent political mettle in the proletariat merely to the internal weaknesses of the African trade unions, divisions within the South African Trades and Labour Council, state repression and the dissolution and subsequent banning of the CPSA. With regard to the African proletariat, it is also doubtful whether 'the two most important developments' in African politics during the 1940s were the gaining of influence by both the Congress Youth League (CYL) and the CPSA over the ANC.[5] It is also questionable that the rejuvenated ANC was able to step 'into the gap left by the absence of a mass workers party and [become] the focus for the nationwide movement of the black working people'.[6]

To study the lives of ordinary Africans in the city through analysing some of the organisations which claimed their adherence is insufficient. This can often lead to a narrow institutional history. Furthermore, the history of the Durban African proletariat's political expression during the late 1940s is mainly concerned with essentially proletarian populist movements rather than with highly structured organisations. Such movements always had an ambivalent relationship to the then established organisations.

During the late 1940s in Durban, the small local branch of the CYL and, acting indirectly through the Youth League, the CPSA, were able to begin redirecting the ANC. However, the ANC was a weak organisation with only 221 members in Durban in 1947, dwindling further to 140 members by 1949.[7] A.W.G. Champion used the organisation as his own 'feudal empire',[8] dismissive of the needs and views of Africans within the city. Some members of the provincial executive were aware both of the constraints imposed on the organisation by Champion's leadership and of the increased militancy of the African proletariat,[9] but little was to change within the organisation until the mid-1950s. While many were to attend the various mass meetings called during 1950, and while organisers then publicly stated that hundreds of new members had joined, the reality was far less optimistic than Congress members would have liked it to be.[10] Few workers stayed in the organisation long:

> Ja, of course we all went along to the meetings at Red Square. But you didn't join. No, no that came much later. I only joined with the Beerhall Riots in 1959. I had started drinking then and my wife was brewing. I had to, otherwise too much trouble.[11]

Ashmon Nene, then a Congress member and key organiser in Cato Manor, confirms the weak state of the organisation at the time:

> How could you get supporters with old Champion around? Yes, people would come to the rallies, there was a feeling about them. They were well organised — mainly by the NIC. But the real growth of Congress only started much later in the 1950s — in fact after the Defiance Campaign.[12]

Although the CYL was dominated by teachers, they had intermittent contact with and supported many issues important to the African proletariat. Communists had all but abandoned contacts with the ever-diminishing African trade unions[13] and, despite close links with the various community groupings, they were not in a position to sustain any really effective influence. During the late 1940s the political terrain of African proletarian life in Durban lay elsewhere.

The late 1940s in Durban produced, not a rejuvenating move into the various existing organisations claiming influence amongst Africans in the city, but the emergence of new movements which the proletariat saw as being able to provide them with greater control over their own lives. African life in Durban became suffused with a new moral vision: the feeling of and desire for 'New Africa'. Often incorporating millenarian images, the African proletariat saw in 'New Africa' a progressive image of themselves that would both celebrate their previous accomplishments and provide them with a vitiating image around which they could mobilise.

'New Africa' was to offer sustenance to people while never attaining the status of a well-developed and coherent ideology. The vision thrived on verbal communication within the largely illiterate proletariat. When aspects of 'New Africa's' vision appeared in writing they were always incomplete and lacked the vigour associated with the more verbal images. To many, these literate expressions appeared otiose, quaint or, more importantly, hesitant. Acting within a society undergoing rapid transitions, the proletariat saw in the verbal essence of the ideology an enduring strength. 'New Africa' thrived on change and redefinition became self-justifying.

The essential elements of 'New Africa' included the following: Firstly, there was a celebration of the dignity of the ordinary African. Africans began to gain a clearer confidence in the legitimacy of their own social relations, which became coupled with an awareness of the reasons for their living in dirty and unsatisfactory conditions. This developed into a polemic against the dominant ideology pervading the city which vilified Africans for their general uncleanliness. Secondly, the desire to gain better education and the cultivation of proletarian leadership. Thirdly, the desire for an alternative society. This arose from the confident predictions and hopes for a better way of life that had been propagated during the war by such diverse organisations such as the CPSA, the Catholic Church and the Watchtower Movement. Fourthly, certain notions of racism that had for long been evident within the local society developed into a new messianic populism. Fifthly, a belief in the legitimacy of their own struggle that the proletariat attempted to integrate into an international rather than merely local context. Sixthly, and most vitally, a militant concept of revenge.[14]

Within the proletariat there had for long existed jokes which satirically explored elements of the dominant ideology. One such joke concerned the 'white madam' who went to the local Labour Bureau looking for a 'nice clean Zulu with matric to be the garden boy' — salary: 10s. a month, but 'an extra 5 bob with mathematics!'. The poverty-stricken, uneducated young migrants, mainly from the Nongoma, Mhlabatini and Lower Tugela areas, who did accept such work became derisively known as 'Garden Boys BA': people who, although desperate for work, could still be condemned because they were prepared to accept the status quo within the city.[15] However, during the 1940s a more coherent analysis of the dominant ideology developed. Newspapers aimed at an African readership contained numerous articles which dealt with the need for Africans to develop a feeling of dignity as a step towards establishing their rightful position in Durban. One such story was an allegorical tale about an African woman called 'Miss Mouse'.[16]

Of a quiet but assured disposition, Miss Mouse enters a departmental store in the centre of Durban. Desiring to purchase an article, she approaches the white woman counter assistant, smiling in anticipation. Conscious of the implications of such an approach the assistant curtly remarked: 'Yes Annie, what do you want?' Acting innocent, Miss Mouse looks over her shoulder but sees nobody. She turns again to the assistant and 'manage[s] to look surprised'. Sensing that the situation was now becoming more complex, the assistant attempts to regain the initiative: 'You! I mean you, Annie!' This strategy backfires as a short 'hot' exchange of words takes place. The assistant backs down somewhat, explaining, no doubt in slow intonation, that she did not know the person's real name. Miss Mouse replies firmly that she wishes only to be served and not to reveal her name or engage in friendly chatter. Furthermore, she continues, she had been christened soon after birth and her name was not 'Annie'.

This story reveals important details about the spirit of the 'New Africa'. Our hero is a woman: a representative of the city's African women who, as a group, were even more marginalised than were African men. The woman is stressing her right to enter that part of the city which was then the virtual sole domain of whites. The woman is objecting to the 'white city/black city' dichotomy so entrenched in South Africa. It is important that Miss Mouse was not shopping in those areas of the city where Indian-owned shops proliferated: areas where Africans usually conducted their business and often suffered abuse of various kinds. Her strategy, which is really the central focus of this article, contains three interrelated themes. Firstly, the militancy is expressed in a polite but assertive fashion with careful reference to her Christian upbringing. Secondly, in the confrontation she requires both humour and knowledge of the attitudes of her opponent. Thirdly, in the developing situation she has to be 'hot' and determined to make her point. Significantly, however, though the concern of the article is with purchasing power rather than earning power, we are not told whether Miss Mouse ever succeeded in purchasing her sought-after article.

During the late 1940s Africans endeavoured to sustain an internationalist vision that they had developed during the war. Africans realised that their enthusiastic support for the Allied cause had not brought any real improvement in their general position. This was viewed as a bitter blow. Stanford Mtolo, a Congress Youth Leaguer, recalls:

> We were really back to the beginning. The war! We all were excited by it. All the news from outside and how we should all help. But then afterwards people still had to try to keep that thing together.'[17]

After the war, while the CPSA continued to promote an internationalist outlook, ordinary Africans' interest in the outside world was more usually stimulated by an informal communication network. Information was gleaned from two sources besides newspapers. Firstly, many demobilised African servicemen entered a local environment which was eager to listen to any recollections however brief or anecdotal. The second source of information was the harbour itself. Workers in the vicinity of the harbour constantly relayed gossip about which ships were in the harbour, where they came from, and what the sailors were talking about. This information not only helped Africans looking for work as stevedores but it also allowed others to keep abreast of international issues. One such story which is still fondly recalled probably epitomises the type of information that was available and some of the essential reasons why Africans sought such information:

> This American ship was tied up at 'A' shed. That was where the *nongoma* dance was. It was called the Liberty.[18] That ship had Negroes — black people but from America as sailors. Also others — the Europeans called them something funny but they were really Indians.[19] Now you see when they came to Durban they would not go to town but come here to Cato Manor. They said that we were brothers. This pleased us and you would entertain these people like kings.[20]

While such attempts to solicit foreign recognition were often naive and generally failed to achieve their objectives, they contributed to awareness of the power of ethnic and national mobilisation. Ashmon Nene remembers that

> Everywhere on the buses there would be groups listening to someone reading the papers. The *Guardian*. 'You see they are now free. They have their government.' This talk really did convince people that they could do it as well.[21]

The argument was made all the more compelling by manifestations of Afrikaner nationalism, as well as by transformations wrought on Durban society through the settling of post-war immigrants from Britain, Italy, Greece or Portugal. Africans were struck by the way in which Afrikaans-speakers were calling for their own trading ventures to deal solely with Afrikaners. It was striking, too, how immigrants to Durban, although declining to become integrated into white English-speaking society, yet added a vociferous new element to the general level of white racist consciousness.

Many of these newly-arrived people exploited segregatory

legislation to take over trading ventures operated by Indians, while conducting their businesses along the same extended-family lines as did the previous Indian entrepreneurs. The moral was clear. Here were people who had a concept of ethnic unity and an ambivalent relationship to the established white English-speaking community. They helped to make the dominant racist ideology more vociferous and, in so doing, prospered.

Secondly, many of these immigrants settled in the newly opened suburb of Durban North. In entrenching themselves they managed to convince the City Council to pass a by-law which restricted African access to the suburb to those who were employed in the area as domestic servants. This by-law was enforced by the South African Police and the 'cafe owner' at 'Robina Stores bus stop', the first on the bus route across the Umgeni River in Durban North. All those who did not have letters from local employers were turned back, often after a 'hiding'. At that stage family members, girlfriends and boyfriends of African employees could also obtain letters of permission. This allowed for a host of iniquitous practices and was widely disliked.

> It was no bloody good. The madam would give you a letter so you could come to visit. If you had that letter then you could stay in the khaya over the weekend. But if your girlfriend had not been good, then when you came on Friday, the madam takes the letter from you. 'OK, yes you can stay this weekend, Mary has been good!' You would get some food that night and Saturday night. On Saturday afternoon you would cut the hedge and on Sunday morning you would wash the boss's car nicely. You could only have one boyfriend and the madam chose you. It was hated.[22]

During the war the price of basic foodstuffs had risen dramatically, and these escalated even more rapidly in the years immediately following. In 1946 there were tea and rice shortages,[23] while white maize was supplanted by the inferior yellow maize.[24] The first shipment of white bread flour since 1940 arrived in Durban in 1948.[25] Topside cuts of red meat were prohibitively expensive and, with whale meat being unpopular,[26] many black workers preferred to eat less meat — usually offal — and increase their consumption of potatoes or putu (maize-meal porridge).[27] Fowls were consumed less as the prices varied around 10s. each.

Black marketeers operated often with the collusion of the manufacturers, suppliers or municipal officials.[28] Instead of bread, many workers would buy mealies from traders such as Harry Thomas and Co. which gained infamy for its high prices.[29] In 1949 shopkeepers often charged 6d. for a pound of sugar despite a regulated price of 3 1/2d. The prices of rice, soap, tea, butter and paraffin[30] were also extortionate but 'we could only buy from these bastards'.[31]

Manufacturers exploited the food shortage. Patent medicines directed at an African market included 'Feluna Pills', a 'blood cleanser' which promised to make workers fitter and thus more acceptable to wives and employers.[32] Two major bakeries engaged in a publicity war, with Pyott (Natal) advertising their bread, virtually unobtainable to Africans, by depicting a lion facing a 'Zulu' warrior armed to the teeth. Their slogan ran: 'All courageous people eat Pyott's bread — Make sure you have courage.'[33]

Tensions arose in the long queues waiting for scarce commodities. In these queues blacks gained additional first-hand knowledge of white racism and traders' duplicity. At the head of the queue Africans would be ignored until they were willing to pay the black market price:

> They would always say that they had run out of the thing. Then when the madam comes they go to the back and give it to her. So you had to go back and offer double.[34]

White women would often go to the Victoria Street Meat Market where African meat sellers would eagerly swop 'tender steaks' for the 'best white bread' leaving Africans 'only the worst'.[35]

Many Africans resorted to a form of banditry that turned the whole Warwick Avenue/Victoria Street locale into a 'no go' area.

> It was no trouble. There is the madam with her boy in the kitchen suit. Hey, they were too scared! You see that was not their area, it was ours. But if they caught you on the roads of their houses you were finished. They did not like being seen in the red and white uniforms amongst us. He would be carrying the meat and vegetables while the madam was pushing all over everybody else. And you would go up and grab from him![36]

There were other ways of procuring food. Welfare societies operated food kitchens in the African residential areas and on the roadside in the industrial area. Many Indian traders appear to have been thoroughly sympathetic, with some requesting that the CPSA assist them in distributing basic foodstuffs at regulated prices. At many stores, Africans could buy 'special food'. For around 5d. workers could get a bowl of soup and a large chunk of bread or putu.[37]

In 1946, when the basic food shortage became critical, the City Council attempted to alleviate the crisis. While rejecting calls for subsidies and rationing, the municipality did operate food canteens along Dalton Road where soup and bread cost only 3d. These proved extremely popular.[38] Municipal concern was two-fold: to provide basic provisions to the labour force, but also to compel the unemployed and dependent to leave the city. The initial idea was to serve food only at the workplace to registered African labourers.[39] After an outcry, the food supply scheme was extended to residential areas, and the controls relaxed to the extent that any African male could queue for food.[40] African males' attempts to place their whole families in the queues, in order both to procure sufficient food and to save time, failed. Similarly unsuccessful were attempts by African women to participate in the food queues.[41]

Amidst the rising anger, which saw the Durban Housewives' League becoming increasingly assertive, Africans began to raid stores and take any available products. Protest over the issue of food both revitalised community groups in the residential areas and resulted in a well-organised campaign led by the CPSA. In May 1946 the CPSA organised food raids: entering shops searching for stockpiled products and then redistributing them.[42] A meeting was held at Red Square around a large coffin inscribed with the words, 'Here lies the grave of the black marketeer'. After this meeting, which attracted thousands, both black and white, people marched to shops and assumed the task of selling goods at CPSA-regulated prices. According to Billy Nair, one of those present,

> It was a real people's revolt. From the meeting we marched to the Indian black marketeers. We took their shops over and started food committees. In the shops we would sell at our prices — Party prices. I think that we had all learnt a lesson.[43]

Encouraged by this success, the Party attempted to develop the food committees into more enduring non-racial worker organisations.

However, contact with African communities was too weak, and in any case such organisations would probably have been seen by Africans as being in competition with their own grass-roots organisations.

During the food crisis the African workers absorbed two crucial lessons. Firstly, raiding as a legitimate and justifiable activity gained widespread acceptance. In the food raids the sturdy small Coca-Cola bottle emerged as a potent weapon. With bottle clutched in one hand, people would warn hostile traders of the fragility of their shop windows. By January 1949 the real power of the bottle had been revealed, with hundreds of shop windows being broken in this manner.[44] Secondly, of the 27 000 African males who were formally employed in commerce and industry in Durban in 1946, 16 000 were employed in either the manufacture or distribution of foodstuffs.[45] Stanford Mtolo, who worked in a city dairy, recalls,

> We were there making food. We could never get it. We had to go elsewhere to find food. When people went back to the bundu they were known to receive a thrashing if they were too weak. It was a terrible position.[46]

It was in the raids that Africans began to gain confidence in their own perceptions and strategies. With the fragility of the trade union structures, people were to seek other avenues of action, mainly in forming co-operatives.

Africans also turned their attention to white condemnation of Africans as dirty and diseased. To the African proletariat the solution did not lie in Feluna Pills. The situation needed a serious analysis of the structures of local government. During this time malnutrition continued to be rife amongst African children; an average of five Africans died of tuberculosis each day, food was scarce, and accommodation in municipal and employer locations and hostels was unsanitary, ill-kept and always overcrowded. Cases of dysentery, measles and bronchitis were increasing at an alarming rate.[47]

During this period white vigilante groups formed to counter the incidence of petty theft occurring along the city beachfront.[48] This meant that any African who visited the beach area was considered a potential criminal. Africans, while not condoning thieving, maintained that the problem was one of hardship, and called for a redistribution of the city's wealth.[49] Such calls gathered force after the Council allocated additional funds to beachfront improvements while

'African women and children sleep on concrete',[50] and after its decision in 1947 to stop allowing Africans in the back rows of seats on 'white' buses.[51]

There was also growing pressure on the Council from white ratepayers for the curfew to be advanced from 10pm to 9pm.[52] The implications of such attitudes produced an angry reaction. Decrying the Native Revenue account as '"farcical" — it actually kept us from the money we helped to make', an increasing number of Africans began to seek ways in which the local power structure could be transformed.[53]

At the same time there was a popular outcry against the City Council's limited perception of the role of the Location Advisory Boards. African workers desired that the elected African leaders sit with full powers on the City Council, and condemned as 'sell-outs' those who claimed to represent them on the Location Advisory Boards. In response, many of the sitting African councillors launched a bitter attack on the City Council. At one point Champion and nine other councillors boycotted meetings.[54] The whole problem, they asserted, was the City Council's belief that it knew what was best for the 'native'. Champion argued that Africans respected the members of the Advisory Boards, and the City Council should thus confer additional power on the Boards.[55]

African workers were not mollified, and continued, with increasing vehemence, to attack the councillors. Champion and his colleagues became ever more reliant on the support of the City Council which now asserted the responsibility of educated Africans to engage in political activity.[56]

The crisis coalesced when the municipality resorted to unfair tactics during an election, and thereby managed to facilitate victory for the sitting candidates.[57] However, through the efforts of Pious Mei, trade unionist and CYL supporter, the election was declared null and void in court, and stringent rules were established to prevent future municipal interference.[58] Reportedly the success of the court case influenced hundreds of African inmates of Mzizini to view the Advisory Board less sceptically. In spite of attempts by the City Council to ban meetings in the location, Mei and fellow-trade unionists Nkwanyana and Dubazana held meetings at which their nomination for the new Advisory Board was discussed. Eventually the three agreed to stand, facing opposition from 'tame native' employees of the City Council. The election was once again rigged. A massive public protest demanded the appointment of a judicial Commission of Enquiry.[59]

While the City Council refused publicly to accede to this demand, a request from the Council for such an enquiry was made to the Union Government. In the meantime new regulations were made which outlawed any municipal interference in elections, and barred African employees of the municipality from standing for the Advisory Boards. New elections were held in all the locations and hostels in September 1947.

These elections were fought amidst much 'mud slinging and ill-feeling' with both parties printing handbills and holding mass meetings.[60] Trying to regain support, the incumbents endeavoured to co-opt a crucial element of the ideology of 'New Africa' — workers' demands for a technical school for Africans in Durban — and press for a reduction in the price of sorghum beer. Both requests were turned down by the City Council.[61]

These rejections confirmed popular disenchantment with any attempts to alter either the membership or the structure of the Advisory Boards. A worker call for a boycott was successful in Baumanville.[62] The elections at Mzizini were again rigged, with Mei being defeated by the 'educated' Africans. In Lamontville, while workers gained a court order to prevent irregularities, a second election resulted in Champion regaining his seat through municipal assistance. In Chesterville the Bantu United Zakhle led by Champion, R.R.R. Dlomo and Mwelase were victorious over the Chesterville Tenants Association nominees: Pitness Simelane, Stanford Mtolo and Oscar Ngwenya.[63]

Control of the Advisory Boards remained in the hands of Champion and his cronies. African workers had made energetic efforts to control the Advisory Boards as the first stage in gaining full representation at City Council level, and their failure had important results. Workers sought other means of organising, with the polls in later Board elections being dismally low. Champion became increasingly dictatorial in the Joint Locations Advisory Board, and was forced to collude with the Mayor of Durban in order to achieve his goals.[64] Stanford Mtolo recalls:

> There were some of us — Youth Leaguers — there. Oscar finally managed to get on. He would always fight A.W.G. about being undemocratic. But that was our fight — also against S.B. Ngcobo — a real puppet of Champion's — it was our chosen battle to isolate Champion. We in Natal had started that in 1944. We just

had to carry on because Champion was too dangerous. We were lucky because we had young Dlomo to write for us. But the workers, well we knew they would stay away — that was accepted.[65]

For workers, the shortcomings of the Boards pointed to the need to operate on a completely different political terrain. Any hope that the City Council had of deflecting the conflict through new regulations or Commissions of Enquiry were thus swept away.

During 1948 a fourth issue was raised by African workers. Africans had long opposed the municipal beer monopoly. The City Council, despite a critical housing shortage, was allocating large sums from Native Revenue to erect beerhalls. The price of the basic ingredients of beer had declined since 1945, but the Council refused to reduce the beer price and in fact raised it. The price of a large container of beer was now 1s. 6d. In 1948 a bag of sorghum cost £1.10.0 compared to the wartime price of £4.0.0. When the Joint Locations Advisory Board raised the matter with the Native Administration Committee, Councillor Nicholson said that the Board had no authority and refused to discuss the issue.[66]

Africans then proceeded to boycott the beerhalls and, it appears, during the boycott they raised other demands. Prince Pika Zulu, the *induna* and chief spy of the municipal Native Administration Department, was 'threatened'. Amongst the demands were that beerhall attendants should be Africans, and, furthermore, Africans desired to relax in 'clean pubs' and not sit in the dirty overcrowded conditions after waiting in long queues. None of the demands was met.[67]

The direct gains of these struggles were few. While the African workers were continually attempting to incorporate new issues into an increasing level of belligerency, they were never really able fundamentally to challenge the power structures of the city. The conflicts did nevertheless provide important guidelines for the future. The food crises provided evidence of the inequalities in the local economy with workers producing food they could not buy. The food campaigns also revealed the effectiveness of raiding. The quest for an internationalism deepened awareness of the force of ethnic mobilisation. The failures of involvement in the politics of the Advisory Board revealed the need to develop other strategies of transforming life in the city. To Africans it was clear that the City

Council was in no position to deal with the 'waves of discontent' that were 'sweeping through Durban'.[68] When in 1946 the City Council requested that a Commission of Enquiry be urgently appointed, they were abjectly incapable of supplying any substantial detail. Likewise, the Commissioner, Justice F.N. Broome, was also 'unable to obtain a very clear picture of the events leading up to the appointment of the Commission'.[69]

Not only was the African proletariat aware of the indecision within the City Council, but the confidence developed during the struggle contributed to the development of a popular political initiative. All the new groupings that succeeded in establishing themselves with Africans in the city achieved influence only if they maintained a localised grass-roots support base.

Throughout the late 1940s many, including Champion, were to try to reform the Industrial and Commercial Workers' Union. The aim was to supply the Natal branch of the ANC with a popular base of support that would overshadow the trade unions and the CYL and bring to Champion greater national appeal.[70] Accordingly, in 1947 the ANC called for an 'African Week'. While Champion appears to have promoted the idea in Durban with his desire to 'squash all who were against him', the event never took place.[71]

During the same period the Daughters of Africa split up after some members endeavoured to use the movement as a vehicle for starting a Natal branch of the ANC Women's League. The Daughters of Africa had started in 1939, and by 1946 was well supported by women in the Durban and Pinetown areas. The main concern of the movement was with developing African women's self-worth and dignity, with the advancement of women's particular roles in a society, and with the difficulty of maintaining a household in a city environment. Local branches started craft clubs making and selling 'boys' clothes', formed fruit and vegetable co-operatives, tried to persuade Indian shop owners to employ Africans and thereby reduce social animosity, and generally attempted to expand the woman's role and influence in broader political affairs.[72]

Though most of the members were 'congress supporters',[73] rifts appeared in the movement during and after its annual conference held in Durban in February 1946.[74] At that meeting it appears that some

members, including the wife of A.J. Luthuli and the widow of Dr J.L.
Dube, who were active on the committee,[75] attempted to direct the
movement towards incorporation with the ANC Women's League.
Whilst this latter organisation's aims were similar to those of the
Daughters of Africa, there were many Daughters of Africa who were
reluctant to allow their organisation to be so absorbed. As a result of
these disagreements and, to a lesser extent, of the interference of white
welfare bodies, the Daughters of Africa gradually declined.[76]

Simultaneously, attempts to start a provincial federation of African
trade unions also failed. In 1946 twenty-three African trade unions
with support in Durban and Pietermaritzburg formed a Council for
Non-European Trade Unions (CNETU) (Natal Branch) but unity was
shortlived.[77] In reality it appears as if the move was led by trade union
leaders with little grass-roots support. Stanford Mtolo, who later
became a trade union organiser in the dairy industry, recalls:

> That was in fact before my time in the Union. I was still at the
> dairies. I never really heard about it until just before. We all acted
> — worker unity was good but it did not come easily then. They
> were hard times for the Unions to grow. All kinds of things... The
> whole CNETU started in Johannesburg and probably it was an
> attempt to build us up through bringing it down to Durban — but
> I really don't know.[78]

By 1948 the federation, now comprising five unions and called the
Natal Federation of Trade Unions, was badly run and so poor that it
was unable to send a single delegate to the CNETU annual conference
in Bloemfontein.[79]

During the late 1940s it is clear that the African proletariat was
becoming both more politically assertive and more effective at
opposing initiatives not of its own choosing. There were few African
'leaders' who could afford to ignore the proletariat's new position in
politics.

Reacting to this new spirit of proletarian assertion, 'educated
Africans' attempted to form a literary and cultural club, based at the
Bantu Social Centre, eschewing involvement with either 'politics' or
'the ordinary native'.[80] Interestingly, the attempt failed; mainly *tsotsis*
invaded the ballroom dances,[81] and drunken *jasbaadjie* minstrels
barged into musical recitals.[82] After attempting to regroup at Ma
Phillips's nearby classy shebeen, they eventually abandoned their
efforts.[83]

Intimidated by the mood of workers, many 'educated Africans' ceased attending meetings held by the Joint Councils.[84] As Mtolo recalls:

> Those were incredible days. All you hear about now is how bad it was. Dirt, wages and the Nationalist victory and the Riots of 1949. But it was a time when normal people ruled the roost. I was a worker then and went into the union. It was like that all round. Those of us, Africans, [those] who were already exempted would ignore their brothers at their peril. Now they had to watch it. Even us in the Youth League had to be very careful.[85]

The notion of 'New Africa' was becoming more and more integral to proletarian experience in Durban. In the period from 1946 to 1950, Africans had created a new sense of residential life in the shantytowns of Mkhumbane. 'Mkhumbane our home' became the centre of attempts by Africans, in the face of their growing estrangement within the rest of the city, to establish a coherent world under their control. To many Africans, Mkhumbane was 'New Africa'.

Through the destruction of Indian-owned residential and trading property, and the virtual expulsion of Indian inhabitants from the Mkhumbane area during the January 1949 riots, Africans believed that they had 'won the battle of Cato Manor'.[86] Mkhumbane had been liberated and the area was henceforth to be controlled by the African residents 'through right of conquest'.[87] Shantytown leaders formed a civilian guard[88] and defiantly called upon both police and City Council to admit that the area was now finally out of their control and to leave the settlements alone.[89]

In the carnage, Africans were acutely conscious of their ability to create a situation where no existing power but themselves could dictate the terms. Within this social and political flux, Mkhumbane could be liberated from all forms of unwanted authority. One recollection illustrates this vividly:

> We ran up to Pelwane's place at the top. There were some other Indians living there as well. Then the cops arrived — navy in blue coats. We sat on their truck and Pelwane came out. He said we

could take everything — just leave me alone. Ja but you see we just laughed and said we just wanted his women — the police — they could take the blankets and things! He just ran away with all the others — the Indians they were cowards. They were all like Italians — always with their hands up![90]

The seizure of land and power in Mkhumbane revealed an enthusiastic unity within the shantytown. Here with the liberation of the area was a vindication of the patterns of consciousness which had developed since the mid-1940s when the nature of African settlement in the area changed markedly. Up until this time Cato Manor Farm had a semi-agricultural feel to it. Many of the Indian landowners owned market gardens, while most of the 5 000 African families cultivated their own gardens and grazed herds on the grassy hillsides.[91] While many of the African dwellings were squalid, rapidly erected and offering only basic shelter, some families owned and built more substantial shacks after concluding tenancy agreements with Indian landowners.[92] Most of the African dwellings were located in the Mkhumbane area. With the beginning of an Indian-owned bus service to newly-built Chesterville which adjoined Mkhumbane, and because of overcrowding in residential areas closer to the city centre, Cato Manor Farm came to be seen as suitable for new shantytown growth. The area was now within easy commuting distance of the main factory area, which then stretched along Sydney Road to Jacobs, and to those areas of the city which were the nexus of African city life: King Edward VIII Hospital, the municipal offices of Kwa Muhle, beerhalls, markets, bus ranks and the Grey Street/Alice Street/Warwick Avenue trading area. Cato Manor Farm was also hilly, allowing initially at least for the easy disposal of waste matter and fairly well concealed from the city centre and the surrounding white suburbs. Furthermore, Indian landowners were becoming aware of the lucrative profits which could be derived from shack settlement. By 1948 Cato Manor Farm had the appearance of a 'recently disturbed anthill'.[93] Of the 150 000 Africans then believed to be resident in the city,[94] reliable estimates placed the total African population of Cato Manor Farm at 29 000. The majority of these inhabitants settled in the Mkhumbane area.

Within this new group of shantytowns, the vast majority of people originated from areas in Natal remote from Durban. During this period agricultural production in the main reserves which surrounded Durban had not declined to the point where people were being forced to move permanently to the city. Most of the African males who came from these areas and worked in Durban commuted on a weekly or fairly frequent basis.[95] On average 60 per cent of Africans living in Cato Manor Farm came from other areas in Natal, while a further 20 per cent originated from areas outside the province, some from as far afield as Nyasaland.

During the late 1940s, shack surveys of the shantytowns revealed that about 40 per cent of the total shantytown population in the area had only recently moved to the city, mostly from rural reserves rather than white-owned farms.[96] New male arrivals in Mkhumbane were often supported by, or secured jobs at the same concern as, a relative.[97] Others with artisan skills would become shack-builders in Mkhumbane, sometimes leaving fairly secure employment.[98] Of the African women who journeyed to Durban, many came after their husbands had consistently failed to send money to the rural household. Often wives and children moved to the city after hearing tales of marital infidelity.[99] There were also numerous cases of women moving to the city in order to restart a life shattered by rural poverty and the migrant labour system. With the medical facilities in rural areas being for the most part totally inadequate, many pregnant women came to Durban seeking pre- and post-natal care. During 1947 it was reported that 500 African women were admitted to King Edward VIII Hospital after having given birth on the roadsides on their way from Durban station to the hospital.[100]

During this period Mkhumbane's demography included growing proportions of women and children: an indication of a greater degree of permanent African family settlement within the city. African women were unable easily to gain employment — young males were preferred in white domestic service, Indians were already entrenched in laundry work, and the manufacturing and industrial sectors were difficult to penetrate. This combined with the requirements of household survival to create the conditions where women's roles became continually discussed.

Amongst the African peasant families who moved permanently into Mkhumbane during the latter 1940s, were many who had been forced to remain in the city or leave the countryside through the activities of African entrepreneurs based in Durban. In addition to running fraudulent sweepstakes in the city and thus impoverishing many visitors to Durban,[101] some operators took their ventures into rural Natal. Here they encouraged peasants to sell off many of their cattle —

which were already threatened by the implementation of the Union Government's 'overstocking' policy — in order to purchase 'shares' in their operations. In so doing, these entrepreneurs 'killed each area, one by one, but never returning to the same area again'.[102] Attracted by the hope of a cash windfall and subsequently losing much of their valued capital, many families simply moved into Durban and settled at Mkhumbane.

African entrepreneurs based in Durban would also drive up to the gold mines and offer to transport Mpondo back to their rural homes. Mpondo migrants, now with brand-new decorated khaki trousers and sparkling new mine helmets purchased solely for the welcoming party back home, accepted such offers eagerly. With a fair amount of cash and possibly a few gold sovereigns, the migrants spoke enthusiastically with the driver about their home life. Stopping off at a Durban beerhall on the way, the driver would introduce the passengers to his cronies. By the time the beerhall closed 'there were the Mpondo, in their blankets and shiny hats with all their money gone'.[103] Rapidly the Draaihoek area of Mkhumbane became dominated by impoverished Mpondo, who soon built the area into one of the filthiest — and most militant — areas, even by the standards of Mkhumbane.[104]

Not everyone came to Mkhumbane through indigence. During the late 1940s a group of Basotho moved down and settled in Draaihoek.[105] Likewise, a similar group of peasant farmers from the Harrismith area settled in Newtown,[106] while other groups of sharecroppers from the Ladysmith area entered Mkhumbane intent on becoming shacklords and traders.[107] In 1947 a group of Mpondo women moved into Draaihoek and set up a lucrative *shimeyane* brewing operation.[108] In addition, a peasant family often spent valuable money educating its eldest son. When the son gained sufficient education the family would move to Durban and prosper from the son's education. J. Hlope, who lived with his family in Harding, went to school in the late 1930s and came to Durban with his family in 1946. Hlope recalls:

> My father was a farmer down the South Coast at Harding. He was good and even the Europeans respected him. He sent me to this mission school where I learnt about machines and passed Standard five or six. Then we all came to Durban... We stayed at Cabazini (in Mkhumbane) where my father had some shacks. I was a conductor and then driving the Indian buses.

The decision to move to Durban was thus made long before the drought conditions which affected the Harding area in the mid-1940s.[109]

Other people who moved into Mkhumbane during the late 1940s came from the Durban shantytown areas of the Bluff, Clairwood, Umhlatazana, Stella Hill, and the Umgeni River Sea Cow Lake. Conditions in the male barracks and hostels were constantly unsatisfactory: they were overcrowded and generally dirty, and they lacked proper amenities. Furthermore, the police persistently raided the hostels late at night in a never-ending search for 'illegals'. However these conditions did not create a massive movement into the shantytowns. Obviously male migrants did move into Mkhumbane,[110] often grouping together to purchase the required building materials and erecting their own shack cluster, but most of the barrack inhabitants preferred merely to visit Mkhumbane in their leisure time.[111] In addition, for those African male migrants intent upon sustaining more than merely flirtatious relationships whether they were married or not, the shacks of Mkhumbane were particularly favoured. Whilst there were other areas where the migrant, living in company or municipal compounds, could rent a room and start a 'townhouse' with the 'girlfriend', Mkhumbane was seen as 'new and right — it was where we were doing things properly'.[112] Mkhumbane also attracted social outcasts; the ex-convicts who were released and left impoverished and jobless outside the prison, and Africans suffering from diseases such as tuberculosis and avoiding the hospital authorities' attempts to have them deported.[113]

Two processes underlay the movement of Africans from other shantytown areas into Mkhumbane. Firstly, the municipality was attempting to formulate some policy that would enable them both to control the shack development and to restrict the entry of further people, particularly women, into the city. While they were, for various reasons, never able to gain control of the situation, their attempts to do so caused harassment to shack-dwellers, many of whom moved away to other areas. In July 1945, before the real growth of Mkhumbane, the City Medical Officer of Health admitted that:

... the stage has already been reached where the inarticulate element of the community is simply being buffetted from 'pillow to post'...[114]

However, this harassment of landowners and shack-dwellers was to continue. By 1947 the municipality grew even more alarmed, and gained increasing respect for this apparently 'inarticulate' population. Municipal officials noted that African shack-dwellers were beginning to settle with impunity on land owned either by the local authority or the South African Railways and Harbours,[115] and remarked on the manner in which shack-dwellers were uniting under 'self-elected leaders [to] build shack settlements with a greater density than previously'.[116] By 1947 the City Council had exhausted all apparent remedies for the crisis and was, along with other local authorities, calling for a new approach to the problem of African labour in the city.[117] Harassment only infuriated shantytown people who were finding it increasingly difficult to subsist within the city. The relatively sparsely populated land of Cato Manor Farm offered exciting opportunities for starting a new life. Furthermore, Cato Manor did not have a large police force present in the area.

The second reason for the move into Mkhumbane from other areas in the city concerns the unusual nature of the material base of the new shantytowns in Cato Manor Farm. In the case of Mkhumbane, the general assertion that 'squatting was a response to a situation in which the costs of family subsistence had to be met entirely from wages, yet in which wages were below the costs of subsistence' is only partially correct.[118]

For, during the late 1940s, many of the people who came to live in Mkhumbane had access to capital, which they invested in creating a range of services not available anywhere else in Durban. Some of the more wealthy investors were ex-servicemen who had returned home with a Union Government gratuity. One such ex-soldier recalls:

> Smuts said he would give us all some land. He came around and promised us this — when the war was over he would give us this. He also called us asses. But I did get an old Harley Davidson motor bike and sidecar. Some of [them] — they sold their presents and got rich in Mkhumbane. You could get some shacks... or even open a shebeen. It was all happening just then.[119]

In addition to the usual assortment of wealthy African traders and others who became involved in shack building and other commercial ventures, ordinary people living in Mkhumbane were also constantly on the look-out for alternative ways of making money. Amongst the more popular activities were the '*i-link*' sweepstakes, running crooked pavement dice and counter games, and the general practice called '*imbazo*'. Here a person with sufficient capital would buy up gallons of sorghum beer at one of the beerhalls, then sit quietly sipping from a meagre can-full. At the end of the work, shift workers would dash to the beerhall, often to find queues too long or supplies having already run out. Lucrative profits could be made: 'Ja, they were not cross, but they paid double — that's just luck.'[120]

There were other nefarious schemes that were even more lucrative. Mkhumbane became the centre of a middle-man operation whereby stolen goods were transferred from the thief to their eventual market in the city itself. In collusion with the white dockyard foremen, crane drivers, and the African winchmen on ships loading or unloading in the harbour, African dockworkers would break open a deliberately damaged crate, distributing the contents to those involved. Be they watches, clothes or other goods, much of the loot was then handed over to 'fences' from Mkhumbane, who would then sell the goods to Indian-owned shops in town.[121]

Others made their money through a fairly acute perception of racism and the ideology of work in the labour process. C. Khumalo, at the time a 'delivery boy' for a large firm manufacturing men's suits, recalls his activities at the Cato Creek railway station:

> You would stand in the queue with the boer just swearing at all the kaffir boys in the queue. Too much work. Sometimes he would just sit. Everybody would just stand there waiting. I would shout out to the clerk, 'Môre, my baas! Ek het pakkies hier.' He would shout you over, 'Waars hulle?' and you would point at some parcels on the ground. They were really in the van all the time. He would never look at you — just sing and stamp and throw it in the tray. 'Fuck away!' 'Weg jou... !' And you would thank him nicely, but you were really thanking the parcels in the car.[122]

The same informant recalls that Mkhumbane 'was a smelly place but everybody had money — everything was so cheap and there were fences selling everywhere'.

Within the shantytowns of Mkhumbane, whose population almost doubled at weekends when visitors and revellers flooded into the area, the range and assortment of activities was far more diverse than in any other area within the city. Co-operative shack shops started, often beginning on a very small scale, and shebeens appeared, much to the consternation of those endeavouring to sustain the idea of workers being morally upstanding, sober and hardworking. Indeed, Mkhumbane was an entrepreneur's paradise: money-making activities included the selling of passes and letters of exemption, often collected from the pickpockets operating on the buses to and from Mkhumbane; the making of leather goods from saddles to belts; collecting and selling empty white man's liquor nips and quarts; operating a *dagga* network originating in northern Zululand and Pondoland; the roadside selling of fruit and vegetables; and roadside open-fire cooking of offal for those tottering home from shebeens eager for 'dronk kos'. The diversity of these operations led to the oft-quoted remark about the Draaihoek area: 'There man you could get anything! It was our Chicago. Anything! If you want a poke [stab] in the back then you must go to Draaihoek!'[123]

The capital which people brought into the new shantytowns was to be invested in activities which, although often duplicating enterprises already operating elsewhere in the city, made Mkhumbane into something more impressive than any other locality: 'Mkhumbane was our home.' The capital available became known as 'our fertiliser'. T. Shabalala recalls the late 1940s in Mkhumbane as follows:

> We were all different in that place then. After the Riots things did change, but then... You see we had this fertiliser and so no one was really very poor. We could see that we were going places. Very fast.[124]

This 'fertiliser' would have meant nothing for African workers and their families trying to live in the city if it had not been used to enhance the growth of a new community in Mkhumbane. The wealthy African and Indian investor who made profits from trading and rackrenting and then 'takes our money and goes away — like Champion — he had shacks in Ridge View — but he had a big shop in Lamont. We never saw our money again',[125] were seen as contravening the morality of the new community. The success in applying the constraints on the circulation of money had much to do firstly with the complex and communal systems of shack ownership and tenancy, and secondly with the way in which the Mkhumbane residents had united in order to protect their residential space.

The African shantytowns which developed in the area after 1946 were substantially different from those which had existed in the same area previously. In the earlier period Africans who desired accommodation merely went to the Indian landowner, concluded an agreement as to rent payable and then constructed, or rented, a room suitable either for themselves or their dependants. While some of them sub-let shacks to later arrivals, most of the inhabitants lived in accommodation intended only for individual or single-family use. During the later 1940s the situation became far more complex, with both African and Indian tenants sub-letting on a larger scale. For example, in the Newtown area, which developed in 1948, there were approximately 887 Africans living in 640 rooms in 112 shacks. There was an average of 5,7 rooms per shack and an average of 1,3 Africans per room. These rooms were owned in various ways by a total of 288 people, both Indian and African.[126]

In the late 1940s the price of shack building material rose markedly.[127] The material for a three- or four-roomed dwelling could cost as much as £20 with a further £10 being charged for the erection of the structure.[128] As a result of the need to build quickly and the high outlay involved, wealthy African and Indian residents co-operated with certain coloureds trained as builders but not in possession of artisan tickets,[129] and became influential within the community through supplying the required accommodation. Often African workers would pool their savings and purchase shack material, employing young *tsotsis* to build.[130] In general the average size of the rooms was 8 ft by 6 ft (about 4,5m²), with the monthly rental being between £1 and £1.10.0.

In the late 1940s the shantytowns had developed into a densely populated ever-growing collection of shack clusters, with a vast array of footpaths and roads interlinking the various settlements. For those not resident in a particular area, the settlements were virtually impenetrable. Consciously desiring to create a degree of confusion for 'outsiders', many painted randomly selected numbers on their doors, thus obliterating the effects of municipal shack surveys: 'It was no-one's bloody business who lived there. *We* were.'[131]

During the move into Mkhumbane various shantytown movements developed. Amongst the apparently numerous groupings, the most successful was the Natal African Tenants and Peasants Association. This movement had started in the middle 1940s under the leadership of Sydney Myeza, who administered various nominal trade unions. In a dispute, Myeza would correspond with the employer demanding settlement for which he charged the worker either a straight fee or a portion of the money derived from any successful action.[132]

Myeza was a confidant of various militant Zionists and herbalists who were continually calling upon Africans to rise up and regain their 'promised land'.[133] One such person was Esau le Fleur who, while using the name Esau Makatini, was in fact descended from the Le Fleur family who had fought against white land acquisitions in the East Griqualand area in the nineteenth century.[134] With a well-established liturgy, much of it centred around the need for land, the Zionists gained widespread acceptance amongst people vigorously asserting their right to declare Mkhumbane their home. Many of these influential Zionists had moved down from the Charlestown area,[135] an important Zionist centre, as a result of the Union Government's resettlement policy in the area.[136] The Natal African Tenants and Peasants Association was able to unite various shantytown communities and to 'lead the homeless to new areas', where some maintained an impressive aura of authority, one even having its own 'police and government'.[137] At some point in the late 1940s, Myeza made contact with members of the CPSA in Durban who were at that time trying to protect shack-dwellers from municipal harassment. It was through such movements that the people of Mkhumbane became even more convinced that they had finally acquired a permanent place to stay in the city.[138]

So Mkhumbane acquired its 'first leaders'. Charismatic, undemocratic and coming from the stratum of the most wealthy African shacklords, who often charged more for accommodation than did their Indian counterparts, such people had a common conception of leadership, believing that 'had they lived outside South Africa they would have been the George Washingtons, the Thomas Jeffersons of the world'.[139] Secondly, they all felt a considerable degree of animosity towards the established African élite in the city. To them, this élite had 'forgotten the people — they had left the people behind'.[140] Thirdly, coming to the city with clear recollections of the peasant way of life, and particularly the peasants' critical focus on the economies of the market place, they enforced the idea that the wealth of Mkhumbane should 'not trickle through our hands'.[141] While often making their money through shady enterprises conducted in other parts of the city, such people never attempted to duplicate these dealings in Mkhumbane: 'They would get killed — beaten. We knew them, they were our leaders.'[142] While certainly keeping the profits individually, these people would reinvest in Mkhumbane. Nene recalls:

> The leaders, I was one, were respected because they knew what
> the people needed. A lot of people made a considerable amount of
> money there, but you would always say to someone, 'Look, so I
> hear you want to buy a sewing machine and train this girl to make
> children's clothes? Ja, well here is the money. I will help you.'[143]

Within the shantytowns, the sense of unity and community spirit was
based upon the circulation of money, commodities and services in a
way which bound the shack-dwellers together. The complexity of the
ownership of shack building materials and the various sub-tenancy
agreements were, in addition to the co-operative societies and the
stockvels, creating a social structure which was referred to by the
residents as 'robbing Peter to pay Paul'.[144] This system, which
produced wealth not solely derived from the wage labour of the
residents themselves, created a continuing cycle of acquisition and
redistribution, and resulted in people becoming aware of what
constituted a reasonable profit,[145] and highly critical of the money
economy which operated in the rest of the town.[146] Money made by
Mkhumbane residents had to be circulated within the shantytown.

The new shantytowns of Mkhumbane became pivotal to African
proletarian experience in Durban. Mkhumbane was seen as a clear
indication of the success of the vision of 'New Africa'. Here was a
community comprising both people new to the city and those who had
lived in Durban for some time, co-operating, exploring and indeed
transforming many aspects of urban life under new and respected
leaders.

Simultaneously, the co-operative movement became entrenched
within the African proletariat. The impetus for the co-operatives came
from the working class, self-employed ex-peasants, and liberal and
radically-minded whites. But the proletariat was to exercise greatest
control over the growth of the movement which became the
organisational backbone through which workers could express their
views on Durban's society. The co-operatives continually moved
between two positions: the need for improved conditions within the
existing structures and the total transformation of city life. As these

groups proliferated, Africans began to view them as the means for profound change.

To the African proletariat, there was a militant quality in the way in which the co-operatives advocated the acceptance of the industrial economy, but called for the growth of a moral community of workers.[147] Nene recalls that

> The leaders were mostly very upstanding people. One could easily call them middle-class, but they were not, and no one saw them like this. What they were really doing was calling for workers to respect themselves, then organise, and then move out. I think most people only saw it later. I did... but a lot, well some of the leaders had actually come from trade unions. Now we all knew what happened to them. Finished. You strike and you are fired. No money and someone takes your place. That's silly. Ridiculous. And I honestly do think, looking back, that they were trying to do the same things — fight, but on different lines.[148]

To see the co-operatives merely as an indication of immature working-class consciousness is insufficient. With uncertainties in the economy, rapidly decreasing real wages, changing patterns of employment among the established working class, and the influx of new people to the city, all of which occurred during the time when ordinary Africans were developing a notion of 'New Africa' that would allow them to make strategic gains, the co-operative movement was viewed as vitally important.

The co-operatives urged Africans to recall how they were 'subjected to the most horrifying discrimination during the war', and how this had worsened with exorbitant food prices, black marketeering and conditions generally deteriorating. Noting how 'the present bad situation is a much talked about issue amongst Africans in street corners and trains', the co-operatives reminded ordinary Africans that existing African political organisations were incapable 'of uniting the black nation' and were led by undemocratic and ambitious people who never really concerned themselves with the problem of the ordinary African.

The African proletariat was exhorted to unite and protect its own economic interests. Through this, politics would be transformed and the whole structure of the city would alter in ways beneficial to Africans who 'laboured on the buildings and the roads but today are treated like vermin'.[149] While accepting the need for mass action, and often evoking calls similar to Zulu Phungula's appeals for mass general trade unionism, the co-operatives maintained that it was only through workers and their families being economically united and living a new type of life that political power could be gained. Mtolo comments on the popularity of the new notion:

> It swept through people so quickly. It was so obvious. People needed to live together so that they could help each other. That's self-help. Everyone always knew that they were being cheated in the city. No-one needed to tell them that. But how to stop that... that had always been something people did not even think about. You just tried to live along. But the co-operatives changed all that.[150]

Here was the spirit of 'New Africa': through the co-operatives Africans would ensure that the future could be different. '*Mayibuye i Afrika*' became an increasingly popular slogan.[151]

In January 1946 Victor Maillie formed the African Industrial Central Society. The aim of the society was to collect funds, through the purchase of shares in the society by wealthy Africans, for the construction near Durban of a technical school and two hostels for the male and female apprentices. The school, which would train Africans as clean, Christian, law-abiding, productive workers, would then be responsible for allocating such labour to the African business sector.

The principles behind the move were three-fold. Firstly, Maillie had seen that African men were exploited in the factories and commercial sector of the city, while African women were unable to find any 'proper' employment except in degrading and badly paid work in Indian shops or in Indian or white residential areas.[152] Furthermore, there were no apprenticeship schemes for Africans in Durban,[153] and thus Africans should commence such schemes in order to compel industry and commerce to accept the legitimate rights of African workers in the city.[154] Secondly, Maillie believed that, despite the call by emerging African businessmen for Africans to trade only with Africans, these businessmen often ignored the conditions under which the majority of Africans lived. Profits derived from African business activity should be directed in ways that would allow the African working class both to strengthen and to advance. Thirdly, Maillie, who had apparently been loosely associated with many African trade unions

in early years,[155] asserted that workers should demand a clear voice in
African political movements. Throughout the period Maillie, who was
neither a member of the ANC nor the CYL, was engaged in laying the
groundwork for such a policy through his attempts to mediate between
the CYL and the ANC.[156] Mtolo, a Youth Leaguer, remembers:

> He would often tell Champion a thing or two. Champion did not
> like that kind of behaviour... but he also told us where to get off.
> You had to listen — we didn't really disagree. He was respected
> by all. He had friends in the trade unions but he would often tell
> workers not to leave their jobs, but to go to night schools.[157]

In general the plan was a combination of certain principles of craft
unionism and mission school education which had been integrated into
a broad concept of developing the economic base of a broad Africanism
in which ordinary Africans would be predominant. Embodied in the
idea were concepts of ethnicity and nationalism. However, two
essential issues should be emphasised. Firstly, it appears that many
Indian business and political leaders were receptive to such plans.
Secondly, the ideology of a militant 'New Africa' did embrace a concept
of revenge as part of its strategy of transforming the position of the
Africans in the city.

   While the African Industrial and Central Society never became
firmly established, it was to elicit a noticeably favourable reaction from
workers. It contrasted favourably with the recent proliferation of self-
help schemes aimed only at advancing the fortunes of the African
entrepreneurs who ran them. Shabalala, a resident of Mkhumbane,
explains:

> People get wise after a while. There were always ideas, often put
> forward by people who never had education but who were sharp.
> You would listen because they looked like Africans — but you
> never got bugger all. They were careful — they never showed
> their money... always in rags but you knew they had yours.[158]

Many such schemes were started in Durban in the late 1940s, such as
those offering shares in freehold land companies[159] and prospective
bus companies.[160] All such enterprises, whether initiated by the
established élite or the 'bush lawyer', were to fail in their attempts to
secure anything but meagre initial capital. Of course, the legal and

political obstacles in the way of African business activity were enormous, but it is significant that these particular schemes never really attracted lasting support. In essence such activities ran counter to the principles of 'New Africa' espoused by the African proletariat.

In Durban, the period 1946 to 1950 was the heyday of the Africans' co-operative movement. In Natal agricultural co-operatives and land banks had long been a dominant part of African rural life.[161] Many of these groups had been initiated by Father Bernard Huss and the Catholic African Union as a means to promote rural self-sufficiency and a Christian communalism to counter the growth of potentially more radical ideologies.[162] Within Durban's African population, which had always maintained close links with the rural areas, and which continually exhibited a populist consciousness, there had always been self-help and co-operative schemes.

In the late 1940s, though, the power of 'New Africa' and proletarian confidence brought to the co-operative movement a more fervent ideology. During this time African workers saw in the co-operatives not just a material and psychological bulwark against their own marginalised conditions, but the vital organisational structure through which they could begin transforming their economic and political position in the city. Gerhard Bhengu, the artist who was to illustrate *Ukubambiswano*, the Nabantukop Co-operative magazine, comments:

> We had always needed to trust one another... we had to have these ways of keeping together — even if it was small — you and your neighbours in Cato Manor... We all knew about these things from being farm boys — you know at home. But in the forties when I started drawing — Nabantukop's magazine — those people in Durban were cross — very cross. They wanted to do all kinds of things. There were these co-operatives all over the place — many even in a place like Cato Manor. It was something new that was happening and people went to the co-operatives.[163]

In April 1946 a meeting of the Durban Co-operative buying clubs was held at the Mzizini Hall despite harassment by municipal officials.[164] The meeting was chaired by W.J. Mseleku, a member of the Committee of the Natal branch of the ANC,[165] the so-called father of the co-operative movement,[166] and composer of numerous songs urging Africans to wake up, unite, and remember the dignity of their forebears.[167] In the early 1940s Mseleku had also, like Victor Maillie, been loosely associated with the African trade union movements.[168] He in fact approached Father Huss eager to discuss alternative strategies.[169] At the meeting were 109 representatives of co-operative clubs from Mzizini, Dalton Road Hostel, Chesterville, Mayville, Umlazi, Maydon Wharf, Klaarwater and Clermont. Some of the societies were wealthy, with the Chesterville Society, the Blackhurst co-operative buying club, having a capital of £300 and £190 worth of stock.[170]

These co-operative clubs were generally of three types.[171] Firstly people would often endeavour to reduce the time and costs of providing household items by contributing to a common fund and then taking turns to journey to town where bulk purchases could be made. Other clubs operated along similar lines except that the items purchased did not have to be solely food or household essentials, and all the items were intended to be re-sold by each particular member of the co-operative. The third type of society was in essence a co-operative loan bank where each prospective member would have to pay a percentage of his salary to join, and then 'around 1 or 10 shillings each month depending upon how much he could afford or wanted to'.[172] For supplying this capital the member was entitled to secure loans from the society.

> Each month you would dress up in your smartest and there would be a meeting of the club. The Treasurer would tell you about the finances and then people could stand up and ask for loans. If you wanted to build a house, children's school, hospital — not silly things — but a fine, that was OK. Then the Treasurer would tell everyone how you had contributed and we would all discuss it. After the meeting you would go and get drunk — it was because you were so happy things were coming right.[173]

Underlying the functioning of the co-operative clubs were two economic principles. While no one objected if members made a profit,[174] it is clear that the popularity of the idea of a proper and acceptable profit led to people attacking the existing industrial and commercial sectors with a new-found vehemence.

> Look if you go into an Indian store and you want to buy something you know that you are being cheated. That Indian also has a family and has to live but so does the African who works there.

> You knew that your brothers were getting peanuts so you were
> getting cheated.[175]

Here was the essence of the workers' perception of the city economy.
Africans believed that their inability to secure sufficient earnings was a
result of the bias of the market, whence the realisation through the co-
operative movements of the power of controlling at least a segment of
the city's redistributive cycle. With the evident success of Indian and
later the newly-immigrant traders, and the way in which Afrikaans-
speaking people were then boycotting non-Afrikaner shops, Africans
saw in control of the market the key to participation in the urban
economy.

From this principle came the co-operatives' attitude towards
Africans who were employed in the city. A distinction was generally
made between those who were employed as domestics or shop
assistants and those who laboured in industry. In order to exact
revenge upon shopkeepers and domestic employers and teach them
the value of African labour, all Africans so employed should withdraw
from such labour.[176] They should then receive education at the co-
operative schools held each summer and winter,[177] and either be
employed by African businessmen or operate as independent
entrepreneurs with the assistance of the co-operatives.[178] While a
strike or boycott tactic was upheld for such workers it was accepted that
these tactics were clearly inappropriate for the majority of the working
class.

> How could you do that? It's nonsense. There were no African
> industries anyway. We could teach the Indians and the madams a
> lesson but not the bosses — no, we never said that.[179]

Instead the attitude was similar to that advocated by the African
Industrial Central Society: Africans should learn the dignity of labour
and work within the factories while bettering themselves at co-
operative schools.

The second economic approach which underlay the co-operative
movement was the belief that the faster money, goods and services
could circulate the more economic wealth could be enhanced.[180]
Workers should bring into the community as much of their salaries as
possible, and there also involve themselves in selling and buying. It
was through this cycle of selling and buying that a community of

workers, families and 'unemployed' would unite. Hence the value of wages from African labour employed in industry and commerce was central to the task of transforming African city life. However, one of the implications of the approach was the dilution of working class consciousness.

As far as the co-operative societies' policies towards independent African business were concerned, the movement believed such enterprises should be destroyed, by violence if necessary, because they felt no obligations to Africans. The general attitude amongst African workers was that African business was identical to white and Indian enterprise. It was the Indian petty bourgeoisie which attracted the sharpest criticism from the co-operatives. The Indian stores, where Africans could buy on credit, were 'thriving on our hard-earned cash', and Indian property had been built on profits made from African labour. To vengefully 'kill'[181] these activities and create economic interdependence between 'ordinary Africans', people should form co-operatives. Messianic nationalism, economic transformation and racism became fused.

The number of co-operatives continued to grow. The main force behind the movement was W.J. Mseleku, leader of the Nabantukop Co-operative. This co-operative had been formed in 1945 but proved to be popular in Durban even before it officially started in the city in May 1947, when over 800 people attended the inaugural meeting. Through Mseleku's guidance, probably after consultation with Father Huss,[182] a Natal Bantu Co-operative Advisory Council was formed in April 1946 which held a series of winter and summer schools.

At the second winter school held in July 1946 prospective organisers of co-operatives were taught the following subjects: principles and practice of co-operation, hygiene, book-keeping, music and drama, and various other topics. While many of the lessons appear to have been given by Huss himself, the movement was also subject to more radical influences. An associate of Huss's comments:

> Father Huss was involved in the teaching, yes, but there were a lot of Communists around and a great many of the African co-operatives did not appreciate a tight rein. They talked to whosoever they pleased and as a result became rather radical. I do not believe there was much anyone could have done.[183]

While other schools were held for new organisers, the co-operatives also offered literacy classes, a music festival where the Municipal orchestra explained and then played various classical pieces, and other evenings of dancing, choral recitals and music played by *jasbaadjie* bands.

For the Catholic Church the co-operative societies were the basis for future social harmony. The co-operative movement would prevent the spread of trade unionism while providing Africans with a new social structure suited to the needs of the urban environment.[184] For the Catholics the conflict between 'capital and labour' produced 'not only wealth but despotic power... concentrated in the hands of a few'. Furthermore, the tendency for capital to unite and 'labour unions [to] internationalise' resulted in the creation of 'two opposing camps who consider their interests mutually antagonistic'. The solution for Africans was a co-operative society which was, according to Father Hurley,

> that form of society which is not organised according to positions in the labour market but according to the *diverse functions* which they exercise in *society*.[185]

The CPSA had developed a renewed interest in the political value of the co-operative societies during the latter part of the Second World War. In 1944 Moses Kotane, then Party Secretary, wrote a pamphlet on how to operate co-operatives. Noting that 'it is harder to break 20 matches than it is to break 1', Kotane saw in the societies the operational means whereby people 'learn *how* to do it together'.[186]

In the period after the war the CPSA in Durban became eager to promote a militant grass-roots nationalism that would prompt the ANC in Natal into becoming both more democratic and more militant. It was within this context that the strategic role of the co-operative movement appears to have been discussed. At least one CPSA member was actively engaged in assisting the movement. R.I. Arenstein explains his rationale:

> The national question usually arises in the market. It arises particularly when a group which is economically backward starts trading and goes into business and then starts trying to get its own people to buy from it in preference to buying from others. The Afrikaners did that on a big scale when they started their Reddingsdaadbond in 1938... Africans also began to use this Africanism to try and build up their business.[187]

Though both the Catholics and communists saw the importance of the co-operatives and were able to assist the movement, it is fair to say that the thrust behind the co-operatives came essentially from a grass-roots level.

The co-operative movement was to be the real site of organisational growth in Durban in the period from 1946 to 1950. While political or trade union bodies stagnated, the co-operative societies flourished, providing ordinary Africans with confidence, skills and a belief in their economic power. According to Mtolo's defence of the co-operatives,

> It was a real beginning. You tell me how many groups — African political groups — can now ignore their people. Well they could then and always did. Look at what Champion was doing. You laugh at the societies holding concerts, but the Africans are a part of the city — it was their money that bought the orchestra. We demanded our legitimate place in Durban. All that stuff about us being dirty and things. That really offended people. So we had to teach people a lesson. Showing our power by ourselves was the beginning. Up until then no other body had brought Africans to that stage.[188]

The radical nature of the co-operative movement was to be clearly seen in an article written by a Chesterville co-operative leader which appeared in *Ilanga lase Natal* on 16 August 1947:

> As an oppressed group there is a tendency, natural and understandable, to place too much accent on politics. In a sense this cannot be avoided. The vote, however useful it is, is not everything. There are other powerful forces at work besides the vote, one of them being economic power. The man who wields a financial whip is often the master, the ruler, the law. We therefore congratulate the growth of the Co-operative Movement in Durban.

The writer then went on to offer a thinly veiled criticism to the ANC: the co-operative movement 'is much more powerful, in membership and accumulated funds, than the Congress'. The article asserted that 'this movement can easily penetrate the enemy camp and strike telling blows'. The tone of the article then changed noticeably:

The authorities will only have themselves to blame if in their desperation, Africans resort to underground movements. History has shown that you cannot oppress a whole community without this happening. Already there are whisperings....[189]

But by 1950 most of the more militant and idealistic of the co-operatives had either disappeared or changed into relatively profitable groups having no interest in transforming broader society. Often those that had never sustained a militant outlook also disappeared, due to both managerial incompetence or the very fact of their success. The availability of large sums provided people with the opportunity to embezzle from the co-operatives or leave them to set up individual enterprises. A number of the African independent traders who operated in Durban from the 1950s onwards had their origins in the co-operatives. Many others arose through the 'robbing Peter to pay Paul' system which continued to expand in spite of its being often in near-total contradiction to the ideals of the co-operative movement and of 'New Africa'.

Many of the co-operatives became integrated into the expanding Nabantukop movement which had always been more middle-class in orientation. As time went by they focused more on bureaucratic issues, leaving the more visionary aspects by the wayside. As the Nabantukop foundered it also became involved in such operations as the 'selling' of letters of exemption.[190]

As the co-operatives developed, prospects for transforming the whole concept into a more communalistic socialism disappeared and they concerned themselves with marketing alone. Manufacturing co-operatives are generally accepted as more difficult to develop than marketing ones. Added to these inherent difficulties, the tight constraints of lack of capital and technical knowledge prevented any development along the lines of Victor Maillie's ideas.

Indian-owned shops and merchants effectively competed with African co-operatives through providing credit facilities and in offering certain goods, like paraffin or bars of soap, at vastly reduced prices.[191] Under the guise of assisting African co-operatives in the face of Indian competition, wealthy African traders then started 'wholesale' businesses which began to compel small co-operatives to trade with them.[192]

By 1949 the 'fertiliser ran out'. Workers' real wages were reduced, and in 1950 the City Council banned the entry of Africans from any area but those reserves which surrounded Durban and which still maintained viable agricultural production. As a result, the amount of money available for redistribution within the the city declined drastically. Shabalala, a resident of Mkhumbane, explains:

> After the Riots [of January 1949] was the time when the fertiliser ran out. That was the start of people becoming poor. No food, no jobs and lots of sickness. Then you had to look after yourself.[193]

At the same time, Mkhumbane became racked with further conflicts. Immediately after the January 1949 riots, a pro-apartheid and anti-Indian body, the Zulu Hlanganani Co-Operative and Buying Club, was formed, and gradually compelled all other co-operatives to integrate or close down.[194] In 1953 the Council started the Cato Manor Emergency Camp in the Mkhumbane area to control the population until they were removed to a then still-undecided location. The Cato Manor Welfare and Development Board was set up as an advisory body, thereby institutionalising a crucial political arena, while many of the co-operative members applied for and gained permits to trade individually in municipally-built shops in the area.[195] By the mid-1950s the Zulu Hlanganani had split into ANC and more conservative factions with some of the conservatives then attempting to restart the Inkatha movement in the late 1950s.[196] The newly rich attempted to sustain the idea of a united community through commemorating each year those Africans who had died during the January 1949 riots, noting that 'it was because of their sacrifice that we are where we are today'.[197] At these ceremonies the traders would distribute free food and drink to any passer-by in Mkhumbane.[198] Mkhumbane was to play no real part in any mass political expression until the later 1950s.

The notion of 'New Africa' was intended to stimulate mass unity between all ordinary Africans. The idea of a mass movement means a diverse leadership, but the leaders were never really able to clearly define the ideology and lacked a real notion of how the city could be restructured. Many of the ex-peasants, while providing insights into capitalist market relations, lacked real experience in the city. Many were trying to steer clear of formal wage relations. Some of the new leaders, while possessing great charisma and being able to make political capital out of the weaknesses apparent in the African élite's belief in the clear distinctions between righteousness and lawlessness, were perhaps more jealous of the position of the élite than they were prepared to admit.[199] Within the proletariat, the notion of a broad mass unity was in contradiction to the deepening class contradictions then developing amongst the city's work force. The working class had foregone struggles at the workplace, accepted the existence of the capitalist economy, and tried to sustain a notion of what it meant to be a worker through struggles outside the factory floor. Whereas the proletariat had been able to exert a clear and vociferous constraint over political expression in the city during the later 1940s, their failure to produce either radical or social democratic gains along with transformations in African society during the period, was to result in a generally reduced level of political consciousness that was to last well into the 1950s.

Notes

1 D. Hindson, 'The Pass System and Differentiated Labour-Power', Association for Sociology in South Africa Conference, 1985, p. 5.

2 P. Bonner, 'We are digging, we are seizing huge chunks of the municipality's land': Popular Struggles in Benoni, 1944-1952', African Studies Institute (ASI) Seminar, Oct. 1985, p. 1.

3 J. Simons and R. Simons, *Class and Colour in South Africa, 1850-1950*, (London, 1983), p 609.

4 K. Luckhardt and B. Wall, *Organize ... or Starve!*, (London, 1980), p. 72.

5 T. Lodge, *Black Politics In South Africa since 1945*, (Johannesburg, 1983), p. 20.

6 *Inqaba ya Basebenzi*, March-May 1984, p. 9.

7 Carter-Karis Microfilm (CKM), 2DA 19:30/2, ANC (Natal Province) Annual Report, 1947; ibid., 2:DA 19/1:44, List of Branches, 1949.

8 Interview with R.I. Arenstein, 24 July 1985.

9 Interview with A. Nene, 28 Feb. 1984; CKM 2 DA 19/1:62/1, ANC (Natal Region Annual Report), 1949.

10 *Guardian*, 10 July 1950, where M.B. Yengwa claimed that the ANC had recently recruited over 200 'volunteers'.

11 Interview with M.O.D. Kunene, 5 May 1985.

12 Interview with Nene, 28 Feb. 1984.

13 Trade Union Council of South Africa (TUCSA) Papers; South

African Trades and Labour Council (SATLC), AH646 Dc 18, Durban and District Local Committee to General Secretary, 24 Nov. 1949.

14 S. Jacoby, *Wild Justice: The Evolution of Revenge*, (London, 1983).

15 Interview with B. Nxasana, 7 May 1986.

16 *Ilanga lase Natal*, 29 Nov. 1947.

17 Interview with S.S.L. Mtolo, 10 June 1983.

18 This ship was clearly one of those cargo vessels which became known as 'Liberty' ships during the war.

19 Lascars.

20 Interview with J. Shabalala, 21 June 1985.

21 Interview with Nene, 28 Feb. 1984.

22 Interview with C. Khumalo, 14 July 1985.

23 Interview with B. Nair, 27 June 1985.

24 *Ilanga lase Natal*, 30 Nov. 1946.

25 Ibid., 30 Oct. 1948.

26 Ibid., 5 Jan. 1946.

27 Interview with A. Afrika, 25 Sept. 1980.

28 *Guardian*, 26 Dec. 1946.

29 Interview with T. Shabalala, 31 June 1985.

30 *Ilanga lase Natal*, 15 Feb. 1947; *Guardian*, 16 May 1946.

31 Interview with Nair, 27 June 1985.

32 *Ilanga lase Natal*, 29 July 1946.

33 Ibid., 29 June 1946.

34 Interview with Khumalo, 21 April 1985.

35 *Ilanga lase Natal*, 23 Aug. 1947.

36 Interview with T. Shabalala, 31 June 1985.

37 *Guardian*, 6 July 1946; Interview with T. Shabalala, 31 June 1985.

38 *Guardian*, 11 April 1946.

39 *Ilanga lase Natal*, 20 April 1946.

40 Interview with T. Shabalala, 31 June 1985.

41 Interview with T. Phewa, 21 April 1985.

42 *Guardian*, 16 May 1946. This tactic was to spread rapidly to other urban centres, particularly Cape Town. *Guardian*, 23 May 1946.

43 Interview with Nair, 27 June 1985; *Guardian* 20 June 1946.

44 Interview with M.B. Laviopierre, 31 Jan. 1981.

45 *Ilanga lase Natal*, 13 April 1946.

46 Interview with S.S.L. Mtolo, 10 June 1983.

47 *Durban Native Administration Commission* (DNAC), UG 46/47, Evidence of City Medical Officer of Health (MOH).

48 *Ilanga lase Natal*, 30 Oct. 1948.
49 Ibid., 2 Feb. 1946.
50 Ibid., 12 Oct. 1946.
51 O. Walker, *Kaffirs are Lively*, (London, 1949), p. 208.
52 *Ilanga lase Natal*, 4 Oct. 1947.
53 Interview with S.S.L. Mtolo, 10 June 1983.
54 CKM, 2:XC9:30/84, Minutes of the Native Locations (Combined) Advisory Board, 24 April 1946.
55 *Ilanga lase Natal*, 9 March 1946.
56 Ibid., 30 Aug. 1947.
57 Ibid., 4 Jan. 1947.
58 Ibid., 18 Jan., 2 April 1947.
59 Ibid., 28 June 1947.
60 Ibid., 4 Oct. 1947.
61 Ibid., 3 July 1948.
62 Ibid., 27 Sept. 1947.
63 Ibid., 10 Jan., 25 Sept. 1948.
64 CKM, 2:XC9:30/84, Minutes of the Native Locations (Combined), Advisory Board, 17 Feb. 1949; S.B. Ngcobo to Champion, 25 Feb. 1949.
65 Interview with S.S.L. Mtolo, 10 June 1983.
66 Minutes of the Native Administration Committee, 3 July 1948.
67 *Ilanga lase Natal*, 17 July 1948.
68 *Ilanga lase Natal*, 7 July 1947; CKM, 2:XC9:30/84, Minutes of meeting of the Executive Committee, ANC (Natal Branch), 1949.
69 DNAC, UG 46/47, Report of Commission.
70 *Ilanga lase Natal*, 8 Nov. 1947; Interview with S.S.L. Mtolo, 10 June 1983.
71 CKM, 2:XC30/84, Minutes of the ANC (Natal Branch), 1946; Interview with G. Bhengu, 2 Feb. 1982.
72 Killie Campbell Library, Durban (KCL), KCAV; Interview with A. Mzimela, 21 July 1982; Interview with H. Sibisi, 11 Nov. 1985; KCL, C.D.S. Mbutho Papers, A History of Clermont, 'Of Clermont I Sing of Thee'.
73 Interview with D. Nyembe, 7 July 1985.
74 *Ilanga lase Natal*, 16 Feb. 1946; Interview with Nyembe, 7 July 1985.
75 KCL, KCAV; Interview with A. Mzimela, 21 July 1982.
76 Interview with Nyembe, 7 July 1985.
77 *Ilanga lase Natal*, 16 March 1946.

78 Interview with S.S.L. Mtolo, 10 June 1983.

79 H.G. Ringrose, *Trade Unions in Natal* (Cape Town, 1951), p. 55; Natal Regional Survey, Vol. IV.

80 *Ilanga lase Natal*, 23 March 1946.

81 Ibid.

82. Interview with Kunene, 5 May 1985. Kunene, then a leading *jasbaadjie*, claims to have been involved in some of the incidents.

83 *Ilanga lase Natal*, 26 Jan. 1946.

84 Interview with Laviopierre, 31 Jan. 1982.

85 Interview with S.S.L. Mtolo, 10 June 1983.

86 Municipal Native Administration Department (MNAD), H2/CM Vol. 1, Manager, MNAD, to Town Clerk, 30 July 1949.

87 Interview with Khumalo, 21 April 1985; C.N. Shum, Personal Memorandum, 3 Nov. 1960.

88 KCL, KCAV, Interview with A. Mzimela, 21 July 1982.

89 H18/CM, Vol. 1, Sworn Affidavit of Esau Makatini, 15 March 1949.

90 Interview with T. Phewa, 21 April 1985.

91 *Ilanga lase Natal*, 12 Oct. 1946.

92 Interview with S. Shabalala, 21 June 1985.

93 DNAC, UG 46/47, Report of Commission.

94 MNAD, H2/CM, Vol. 1, Manager, MNAD, 'Native Housing Policy', Nov. 1948. This figure was 50 000 higher than estimated by the Report of the DNAC. See UG 46/47, Report of Commission. Officially the municipality refused to admit to such a high figure, citing only 110 000. City of Durban, 'Mayor's Minute', Report of the MNAD, 1947-1948.

95 MNAD, *H2/CM*, Vol.1, Chief Superintendent-Manager, MNAD, 2 March 1950.

96 MNAD, H18/CM, Vol. 1, Schedule of Shack Dwellers: Haviland Road, May 1948; Schedule of Shack Dwellers: Newtown, May 1948; Survey of Cato Manor Shack Settlement, 15 Oct. 1848. See also 19L, Vol. 1, 'Report of an investigation into the position of Natives at Cato Manor and Newlands', conducted on Tuesday 22 June, 1943, report undated.

97 Interview with M. Kunene, 21 April 1985.

98 KCL, KCAV, Interview with A. Afrika, 25 Sept. 1980.

99 Interview with Kunene, 21 April, 5 May 1985.

100 *Ilanga lase Natal*, 17 April 1948.

101 Interview with J. Mzimela, 21 April 1985.

102 Interview with Khumalo, 19 July 1985.

103 Interview with S. Shabalala, 21 July 1985.

104 Interview with Shum, 10 July 1985.

105 Interviews with S.B. Bourquin, 9 Jan. 1981 and R.F. Drew, 17 Dec. 1981.

106 Interview with S. Shabalala, 21 June 1985.

107 Interview with Shum, 18 July 1985.

108 Natalia Development Board, slide archive. Still to be numbered.

109 Interview with J. Hlope, 29 July 1985. For a valuable theoretical analysis on peasant attitudes over time see C. Meillassoux, 'The Economic Bases of Demographic Reproduction: From the Domestic Mode of Production to Wage Earning', *Journal of Peasant Studies*, 11 (Oct. 1983).

110 Interview with R.G. Willson, 21 Dec. 1980.

111 Interview with Drew, 17 Dec. 1980.

112 Interview with Khumalo, 21 April 1985.

113 *Ilanga lase Natal*, 7 June 1947, 27 April 1946, 23 Nov. 1946. While relating to a later period, Bruno Mtolo's own personal account of such a predicament is interesting. Mtolo, *Umkonto we Sizwe: The Road to the Left* (Durban, 1966), pp. 6-7.

114 Natal Archives, Town Clerk's file, 19L, Vol. 2, City MOH to Public Health Committee, 17 July 1945.

115 This had been imminent throughout the period under discussion. See 19L, Vol. 1, City Valuator and Estates Manager to Town Clerk, 9 Dec. 1941; Ibid., Vol. 5, City MOH to Town Clerk, 30 June 1949.

116 Ibid., Vol. 3, City Health Department Memorandum re Haviland Road Shanty Settlement, 22 Sept. 1947.

117 DNAC, UG 46/47; Evidence of the Durban City Council.

118 A. Stadler, 'Birds in the Cornfields: Squatter Movements in Johannesburg, 1944-1947', in B. Bozzoli (ed.), *Labour, Townships and Protest* (Johannesburg, 1979), p. 22.

119 Interview with Khumalo, 21 April 1985. The reference to 'asses' is clearly commenting upon Smuts's publicly stated belief as to the patience of Africans.

120 Interview with Kunene, 21 April 1985.

121 Ibid.

122 Interview with Khumalo, 21 April 1985. ('Good morning, boss! I've got parcels here.' 'Where are they?')

123 Interview with J. Mzimela, 28 April 1985.

124 Interview with T. Shabalala, 21 June 1985.

125 Interview with Khumalo, 21 April 1985.

126 MNAD, H18/CM, Vol. 1, Schedule of Shack Dwellers in Newtown Area, Oct. 1984.

127 MNAD, H2/CM, Vol. 4, City Valuator and Estates Manager to Town Clerk, undated; Superintendent, Cato Manor Emergency Camp to Manager, MNAD, 14 Oct. 1954.

128 *The Durban Housing Survey*, Natal Regional Survey, Additional Report No. 2 (Pietermaritzburg, 1952), p. 372.

129 Interview with Shum, 18 July 1985.

130 Interview with J. Mzimela, 21 June 1985. As a young boy in Cato Manor in the late 1940s, Mzimela had been one such 'shack *tsotsi*'.

131 Interview with Khumalo, 21 April 1985.

132 Ibid.; University of Witwatersrand Library, Historical and Literary Papers (UWL), Ballinger Papers, B.2.5.16, Natal African Tenants and Peasants Association to M. Ballinger, 30 June 1952; Interview with Arenstein, 24 July 1985.

133 Interview with Nene, 28 Feb. 1984.

134 Interview with Shum, 21 June 1985; W. Power, *The Party Annals of Kokstad and Griqualand East*, (Pietermaritzburg, repr. 1978), pp. 119-125, 164-167; R. Edgar and C. Saunders, 'A.A.S. Le Fleur and the Griqua Trek of 1917', *Journal of African Historical Studies*, 15 (1982).

135 B. Sundkler, *Zulu Zion and some Swazi Zionists* (Oxford 1976), *passim*.

136 CKM, 2:OA 19:96/1, 'Political Activities', n.d.; 2:XC9:30/84, ANC (Natal Branch) Annual Report 1946.

137 19L, Vol. 3, Natal African Tenants and Peasants Association to Mayor, 30 Aug. 1946; Natal African Tenants and Peasants Association to Town Clerk, 14 Oct. 1946; Minutes of the Native Locations Advisory Board, 19 May 1947; *Ilanga lase Natal*, 29 Nov. 1946, 8 Feb. 1947.

138 Interview with S.S.L. Mtolo, 16 July 1983. By late 1947 the Natal African Tenants and Peasants Association was clearly heavily reliant on CPSA advice and assistance. Their memorandum to the DNAC was identical to that written by G. Gokul, the then local Party Secretary, and submitted on behalf of the Natal Indian Congress.

139 C.D.S. Mbutho Papers, 'A History of Clermont'.

140 Interview with H.C. Sibisi, 11 Nov. 1985.

141 Interview with Nene, 28 Feb. 1984.

142 Interview with Kunene, 4 Feb. 1985.

143 Interview with Nene, 28 Feb. 1984.

144 KCL, KCAV, Interview with C.C. Majola, 20 June 1979.

145 UG 19/1949, Evidence of Esau le Fleur.

146 Interview with T. Shabalala, 21 June 1985.

147 *Ukubambiswano*, July 1947; Interview with Bhengu, 30 Jan. 1982.

148 Interview with Nene, 28 Feb. 1984.

149 These quotes are from *Ukubambiswano*, June 1947.

150 Interview with S.S.L. Mtolo, 10 July 1983.

151 *Ukubambiswano*, June 1947.

152 *Ilanga lase Natal*, 14 Sept. 1946.

153 Ibid., 26 Jan. 1946.

154 Interview with S.S.L. Mtolo, 10 June 1983.

155 Marianhill Mission Archives, Father B. Huss Papers; File 'Durban C.A.U.' n.d.

156 CKM, 2:XC9:30/84; V.L.D. Maillie to Champion, 15 Jan. 1950; Interview with Bhengu, 2 Feb. 1982.

157 Interview with S.S.L. Mtolo, 10 June 1980.

158 Interview with T. Shabalala, 31 July 1985.

159 *Ilanga lase Natal*, 25 May 1946; Interview with H.C. Sibisi, 11 Nov. 1985. Sibisi was one of the 'directors' of the company along with Dr Pixley Ka Izaka Seme and the Revd A. Mtimkulu, then a member of the Joint Councils, and legal advisor to the ANC.

160 *Ilanga lase Natal*, 12 April 1947.

161 Interview with Father St George, 10 Sept. 1985.

162 D. Hemson, 'Dock Workers, Labour Circulation and Class Struggles in Durban, 1940-1959', *Journal of Southern African Studies* 4 (1977), p. 108.

163 Interview with Bhengu, 2 Feb. 1982.

164 *Ilanga lase Natal*, 6 March 1946.

165 CKM, 2 DA 19/1:62/1, ANC (Natal Region) Committee Report 1949

166 T. Couzens, *The New African* (Johannesburg 1985), p. 250.

167 W.M. Mseleku, *Isingeniso*, n.d., copy in author's possession.

168 Interview with S.S.L. Mtolo, 10 June 1983.

169 Father B. Huss Papers, File 'Catholic Union Minutes Durban'; Aug. 1944.

170 *Ilanga lase Natal*, 6 March 1946.

171 For a general analysis see Ballinger Papers, 1.2.5-13, 'The Native and the Economic Question', n.d. and 'Questions on Co-

Operation'; Father B. Huss Papers, File 'Co-operatives in Durban"
passim.

172 Interview with T. Shabalala, 31 July 1985.

173 Interview with Khumalo, 7 July 1985.

174 UG 36/49; Evidence of A. Mchunu and J. Shandu.

175 Interview with Khumalo, 19 July 1985.

176 *Ilanga lase Natal,* 30 Nov. 1946.

177 Ballinger Papers, C1.2.14., File 3, 'The Co-operative Movement
among South African Natives'; *Ukubambiswano, passim; Ilanga
lase Natal,* 13 April 1946.

178 *Ukubambiswano, passim.*

179 Interview with Bhengu, 2 Feb. 1985.

180 *Ukubambiswano,* Sept.-Oct. 1947.

181 Ibid., March-April 1948.

182 Father B. Huss Papers, File 'Durban'; Huss to W.J. Mseleku, n.d.

183 Interview with St George, 10 Sept. 1985.

184 Ibid.

185 Father B. Huss Papers, File 'Issues', D. Hurley, 'The Catholic Faith
in South Africa'.

186 M. Kotane, *Let's Do It Together,* (Cape Town, 1944).

187 Interview with Arenstein, 24 July 1985.

188 Interview with S.S.L. Mtolo, 10 June 1980.

189 *Ilanga lase Natal,* 16 Aug. 1947.

190 Interview with Kunene, 5 May 1985.

191 MNAD, *Cope Trading Report,* 1953.

192 Interview with Nene, 28 Feb. 1984.

193 Interview with T. Shabalala, 21 June 1985.

194 Interview with J.J. Shabalala, 28 Oct. 1986.

195 MNAD, CM/2, 'Applications for Trading Sites'.

196 Interview with Sibisi, 15 Nov. 1985.

197 KCL, KCAV, Interview with Majola, 20 June 1979.

198 Interview with J.J. Shabalala, 28 Oct. 1986. Shabalala was one of
the key organisers of these ceremonies.

199 See, for example, Interview with Sibisi, 15 Nov. 1986.

Patriarchs, Passes and Privilege

Johannesburg's African Middle Classes and the Question of Night Passes for African Women, 1920-1931

Kathy Eales

There are few moments in history where the divisions of class, race, age and gender are collapsed into a common unity against a common grievance. African resistance to South Africa's pass laws is not one of those moments. Without close attention to the class basis of protest, one can easily be lulled into perceiving such action as a cross-class phenomenon in which participants shared identical interests and motivation. The response of Johannesburg's African middle classes to African women's inclusion in the city's curfew regulations in 1925 and 1931 suggests otherwise. Their protest was not merely against the subjection of African women to a form of pass control. To a large degree it was a plea for the defence of their status as a differentiated élite, not subject to the same legislative constraints as the majority. It was also a rejection of state interference with the right of African men to determine the affairs of their households. The purpose of this paper is to explore the context of curfews for African women, and the African middle class's responses to the measure.

Julie Wells's and Cheryl Walker's pioneering studies have done much to rectify the omission of women from most accounts of African anti-pass campaigns.[1] For example, Wells's account of the vehement Orange Free State anti-pass campaign of 1913-1917, illuminates at least one reason why African women were not included in the pass laws until the 1950s. Along with many revisionist accounts, however, her analysis tends to focus on class exploitation and national oppression, and at times even to collapse the two. Her approach often conceals the more discrete tensions at play over the politics of age and

Estimated total population	Distribution according to employment					
	Mines within Johannesburg	Municipal service	Domestic service	Employed by employers of over 25 natives	All other employers	Women and children unemployed or only casually employed
136 000	53 238 Housing, food, medical service and recreation provided by employers.	5 000 Minimum daily wage 2s. Housing, food, medical service and recreation provided by employers.	26 000 Average monthly wage about £3. Housing, food and often clothes provided by employers. About 6 000 not housed by employers	10 000 Average minimum wage about 16s per week. Mostly housed by employers.	18 949 Average minimum wage about 16s per week. A few housed by employers. Some living in municipal hostels or villages, or finding accommodation for themselves in backyards, slums, etc.	22 814 Living in backyards, slums, 'native' townships or villages.

Table compiled by G. Ballenden, 1928, See fn. 4 for source.

gender. Wells's essentially 'heroic' paradigm obscures the reasons why certain African women in Bloemfontein specifically requested women's inclusion in the city's night pass regulations in 1923 despite a 'tradition' of defiance.[2] This approach also smudges the shifting class distinctions among the African protagonists of protest action. Many middle-class African women supported restrictions on 'women of low morals' as vigorously as their spouses did.

Once South Africa's ruling classes had weathered the post-war recession of 1921-22, the 1920s was a period of economic growth. This expansion occurred across virtually all sectors of the economy. On the Rand, manufacturing industry was taking off, aided by the sheltered markets of World War I and protectionism after 1926. The non-mining industrial workforce, particularly its African component, swelled from 17 046 African men in 1916 to 35 142 in 1923. Yet, mineworkers aside, the proportion of African men in industry relative to other sectors was relatively small. Many worked in the commercial, service or municipal sectors, and domestic service outranked any other single type of employment in Johannesburg. The number of industrial workers did not exceed that of domestic workers until 1941.[3]

African wages remained relatively static throughout the 1920s at levels little changed since pre-war days. At a time when conservative estimates set the cost of supporting a four-member urban African family at £6.11.8 per month — a figure which excluded such 'luxuries' as medical care, education or clothing — the average wage for non-mining workers was £4.2.0, a figure based on the alleged cost of providing for the immediate needs of a single, migrant worker.[4] Yet statistics from the 1911 and 1921 censuses reveal a significant demographic shift, however imprecise the enumeration may have been. While the number of men working in Johannesburg rose by only 5 per cent between the 1911 and 1921 censuses, the number of women nearly trebled from 4 357 to 12 160. Clearly an increasing number of African women were moving to town to settle and establish their families there.[5]

As an urban African family simply could not subsist on the average monthly wage of £4.2.0 paid to working men, other members of the family had to contribute to the household income. Most children took some part in this — selling newspapers, hawking fuel or doing odd jobs in the neighbourhood — but the most important supplement came from adult women.[6] Many resorted to illicit, and allegedly immoral, ways of making money.

Adequately paid jobs for women were scarce in Johannesburg. The one sector of the labour market where women might expect to find work — domestic service — was dominated by men.[7] 'In town,' protested a prominent member of Johannesburg's African élite, Charlotte Maxeke, in 1919,

> the work of the women has been taken over by the men. There are houseboys, washboys and boys nursing the babies, and the women are outside unable to get anything to do. If they do get work the amount they receive is so small that they are unable to live, all on account of the competition of the men in the women's field of work.[8]

In 1925 wages paid to African women domestics ranged from 5s. to 15s. a month, with food and lodging; men, conversely, were paid between £2 and £4.[9]

Employers were apparently reluctant to hire African women for domestic work. An African woman did not carry a pass and hence could not be tied as effectively into a service contract as a pass-bearing African man. Secondly, there was little imperative to draw on female labour given the fairly plentiful supply of migrant men available for domestic service. African men could presumably also be used in a far wider range of manual household chores than women. Thirdly, and possibly most significantly, urban African women were said to be immoral and liable to pass on diseases to their young white wards. The immorality of African female domestics was perceived as being integrally related to their accommodation. Where it was provided — domestics frequently had to make their own lodging arrangements — servants' quarters were generally squalid.[10] An 'eminent physician' warned sternly:

> If the mothers saw their nurse girls' surroundings and knew of their diseases, they would abandon their pleasures and nurse their own children rather than allowing them to run the risks

they do. Your washing is done by people often rotten with venereal disease and your milk and meat may at any time be infected.[11]

Men, apparently, were not seen as harbingers of disease, and the chastity of male servants was rarely questioned; they at least did not fall pregnant and disrupt their employers' household routines.

By 1931 African women comprised a little over a quarter of Johannesburg's 26 000 domestic workers.[12] This was due not only to employers' reluctance to hire them, but also because of the lack of child-care facilities for women who went out to work. Although young children could be entrusted to the care of older siblings or friends, most women opted for home-based industries, of which washing for white families was the most common.

The returns on this back-breaking labour were small. The standard rate for doing washing at an employer's home was 2s.6d. a day, and for those who laundered from their own homes, 10s. per month. Once soap, blue, water, coal and tram fares had been paid for, women could be left with profits of less than a shilling per washing bundle each week.[13] Not altogether surprisingly, a high percentage of urban women resorted to more lucrative sources of income, such as illicit liquor-selling and prostitution.

Reliable statistics on the incidence of prostitution are hard to come by at the best of times, and particularly so for African women living in Johannesburg in this period. White authorities and several African commentators alleged that prostitution assumed alarming pro-portions, 'even when the carnal promptings of a quarter-million unattached Native males is (*sic*) taken into account'.[14] The prevalence of venereal disease was evinced as proof, although claims that 80 per cent of Johannesburg Africans suffered from VD were not borne out by medical testimony. In fact, 15 per cent of all patients coming for treatment at the city's clinics were venereally infected.[15] This figure does suggest a fair degree of promiscuity, but promiscuity is not necessarily the same as prostitution. Hence the endemic immorality described by municipal officials and missionaries presumably referred broadly to any union outside the sanction of formal marriage.

Far more common than prostitution was liquor-selling. In a survey of African family budgets in Marabastad, Pretoria, in 1933, Eileen Jensen Krige found that about 70 per cent of location dwellers derived some income from liquor sales. Ellen Hellmann's study of a Johannesburg yard, Rooiyard, in the same period, suggests that the incidence of women selling liquor in Johannesburg was comparable, if not higher.

Women who brewed beer in urban areas were not motivated purely by economic considerations. In rural African societies, the sexual division of labour allocated the task of making beer to women, and sorghum beer — or kaffir beer, as it was more commonly termed — played an integral part in many African customs and ceremonies. In urban areas it remained the duty of obedient wives to brew for their husbands. Hellmann noted that

> there are very few men who, in order to protect their wives from the constant danger of arrest to which they expose themselves by the brewing of beer, will forego the pleasure of having their beer in their own homes where they can entertain their friends.

Beer-brewing underwent certain significant changes in its relocation to an urban milieu, where it was frequently a commodity produced for sale. Furthermore, if brewed in the customary way from malted sorghum, mealie meal and water, beer took up to four days to ferment and gave off a distinctive sour smell which was immediately discernible to police on the prowl. Adulterating the brew by adding yeast, sugar and other ingredients not only accelerated fermentation, making its producers less vulnerable to police harassment, but the additives also raised its alcohol content. For customers paying for liquor that had to be downed quickly in case of a police raid, concoctions like *skokiaan*, *skomfana*, *babaton* and *Isiqataviki* provided the desired effect fast.[16]

Profits on the sale of liquor were high — a gallon of *skomfana* which fermented in two hours could be produced for 6d. and sold for 400 per cent, and a woman's weekly beer revenue could be as much as £3. African liquor sellers were not confined to the ranks of the idle and dissolute. 'Many an honest girl and woman' was tempted into the liquor trade 'because she had nothing else to make her living from', argued Charlotte Maxeke, and for most it was just a sideline. As Krige noted, 'over 90% of the evil is caused by absolute necessity on the part of the Bantu housewife to augment her husband's wages in some way or other... selling intoxicating concoctions is the most convenient way, so she follows it.'[17]

While it is impossible neatly to delineate the class composition of the liquor brewers, it seems that few women who were real or aspirant members of the élite traded in liquor. Given the formal prohibition on liquor for Africans, liquor-selling carried with it very particular connotations of illegality that were inimical to the status of the élite. Temperance was a strong strand in contemporary missionary teaching and, for those seeking assimilation and acceptance into white society, kaffir beer was a token of the world of 'heathen' rituals and tribalism.[18] Yet the temptation to brew was there. The comment of an African woman aspiring to the comforts of a middle-class life is revealing:

> It is almost impossible for us to live decently in Johannesburg. The temptation to sell this illicit liquor is almost too strong. All the women around here are making a lot of money, buying pianos and gramophones and silk dresses. Because I am a Christian and try to go straight, I have to stand here day after day and kill myself washing.[19]

In the eyes of white officials, the prevalence of liquor-brewing was the most overt indication of the growing number of African women living in town. Liquor-brewing and prostitution were usually mentioned in the same breath, or used interchangeably, and 'wherever women are found, large quantities of beer are brewed'.[20] Johannesburg was said to be 'riddled' with African 'women of bad repute, who come here not to work, but to brew'. The illicit liquor traffic was said to be 'one of the most disastrous features of native life in Johannesburg', given its allegedly close connection with crime.[21] Despite police vigilance, there was no way in which the authorities could suppress the illicit liquor trade, and fewer than 10 per cent of offenders were ever caught.[22] The solution to this and other problems of urban African administration was seen to lie in regulated housing.

Throughout the 1920s the municipality grappled with the housing issue. Though realising that adequate accommodation for Africans was an urgent priority, if only for reasons of social control, it claimed to lack the necessary funds. More specifically, as Councillor Harry Kroomer informed a Native Affairs inquiry in 1923, 'the whole point is that the Johannesburg municipality has no desire to have to provide for natives... that should be the duty of the employers'.[23] Access to housing in municipal townships was strictly regulated. Only male heads of families who could prove they had lived and worked in Johannesburg since January 1924 — when the 1923 Natives (Urban Areas) Act was promulgated — and were 'fit and proper' persons, could add their names to the waiting list for the tiny two- or three-roomed houses there. By 1925 no more than seventeen thousand people lived in township housing. The tenements, yards and slums of inner Johannesburg, conversely, housed an estimated population of between thirty and forty thousand.[24]

The Council wanted the slums cleared. It was not so much that thousands were living there illegally, or that the slums were a major health hazard, or even that they were the 'lurking places of the criminal classes'.[25] The problem was that they afforded a space where the unemployed, the underemployed, the criminal, and the respectable labourer all dwelt side by side, fairly free of official regulation. It was illegal space. As Frederick Cooper points out, the slums did little to socialise people into a world of rigid labour discipline. Instead, inner city slums simply reproduced the wrong kind of workforce. While illegal beer and sex may have contributed cheap services to low-paid male workers, they both literally and figuratively infected the working class.[26]

Providing an alternative to slum accommodation was a problem that plagued the Council for many years. At a formal level, only Africans with exemption certificates, and those who could prove they were needed by their employers after hours, were granted permits to live in town. Anyone else was obliged to live in hostels if they were single men, or municipal houses if their families lived with them. No specific provision was made for single women until 1930, and family housing was reserved for married couples only. Informal marriage was one way to escape single-sex hostels for family accommodation in the yards or municipal housing in the townships, as couples could exploit anomalies in the law. Roman Dutch law did not recognise the most common form of marriage — customary marriage — which it deemed uncivilised. This meant the state did not issue marriage certificates to those not married by the state or church, and thus could not disprove a couple's claim that they were married by customary rites.[27]

One way out of the housing crisis and the spread of slums was to introduce influx controls for women. 'The crux of the situation,' concluded Rand 'Native administrators' at a conference in 1924, 'was really the female, who was usually in industrial areas for unlawful purposes and it was they and not the males who were crowding out accommodation.'[28] The government, however, was unsympathetic to their demand that African women be included in the pass laws. The South African Party government, headed by J.C. Smuts, had accepted the conclusion of the 1920 Godley Commission into the Pass Laws. The Commission had concluded that passes exposed women to the risk of molestation, and maintained that control should instead be achieved through 'suitably controlled housing accommodation' and the removal of 'undesirables' from urban areas.[29] The report of the 1922 Stallard Commission into Transvaal Local Government took a harder line regarding the control of urban African women, and many of its recommendations were subsequently included in the 1923 Natives (Urban Areas) Act.[30] The Act enshrined the principle that 'natives — men, women and children — should only be permitted within municipal areas in so far and for so long as their presence is demanded by the wants of the white population'. It laid down that all Africans — men and women — had to report at a reception depot immediately on their arrival in town, and stay there until assigned a job.[31] African women were not included in its pass regulations, presumably because there were comparatively few women in the urban areas before the 1930s.

Municipal officials soon discovered serious deficiencies in the Act. The 'idle and undesirables' clause provided for the deportation of anyone not formally employed, but the Council found this to be of little use in deporting women it considered undesirable. As long as women did not carry passes, it was difficult to prove who was unemployed. As one administrator noted irritably, 'a woman may say, 'I am a washerwoman, and can show you that I am washing for Mrs Jones', but in the meantime she is living anyhow'. In addition, there was no reception depot for African women in Johannesburg before 1930, and thus no way of proving when a woman had arrived in town.[32]

The Johannesburg municipality considered other measures to regulate what 'type' of African women lived in town. One possibility was the medical examination of women entering the urban area, first proposed in 1912. City officials knew full well that African women would object to being examined for venereal and other diseases by white men. As Stallard had noted shrewdly in 1922,

> if the results of medically examining native women show that they become unwilling to migrate to the towns, it will not be unsatisfactory, as the presence of native women in municipal areas, except those living with their husbands in municipal villages or residing on the premises of their masters or mistresses, works for evil.[33]

The Johannesburg Public Health Committee motivated strongly for adoption of the measure in 1924. The Council, however, overruled the motivation when it was pointed out that women were more likely to contract venereal diseases after they had lived in Johannesburg for several months. By that stage it would be impossible to recall them for examination.[34]

If local officials could treat only the symptoms of the presence of 'undesirable women' in town, a curfew was one way to do it. In October 1924 the Joint Council, a liberal inter-racial forum, convened a broad-ranging Conference on Native Affairs in Johannesburg for 'Native administrators', municipal officials, representatives of church and welfare bodies and Joint Council members. The problem of young women 'escaping' parental control and coming to lead 'immoral lives' in the towns was discussed at length; no solution was arrived at, and the conference resolved to consult African opinion on measures to minimise the 'evils arising from unattached women living in town'.[35]

The intentions of this resolution were pre-empted by the central government. In late November 1924 Tielman Roos, Minister of Justice, told African delegates at a state-convened Native Conference in Pretoria that he wished 'to put a stop to natives moving about the street at night without passes'.[36] In contemporary parlance, 'Native' meant 'male African' unless otherwise specified, and the assembly did not demur. Two weeks later Reef police received orders to arrest all Africans — women included — not in a location and out of doors between 9pm and 4am without a permit signed by their employers. Arrests were to commence on 1 February 1925.[37] The official reasons given for extending the curfew to women were, firstly, 'to keep natives off the streets at night' where they might cause offence to white citizens, and secondly, to prevent 'immorality' by African women.[38]

There is little evidence that the Johannesburg Council was behind the plan, and it would be unwise to argue that the requirement for employers to sign all night passes was a strategy aimed to coerce African women into wage labour. This would suggest a degree of subtlety conspicuously absent in Council politics. Apart from a desire to minimise its obligations as much as possible, the Council had no definite Native Affairs policy in this period, and no municipal Native Affairs Department until 1927. Jurisdiction over Native Affairs in Johannesburg was divided between the government's Native Labour Bureau, responsible primarily for African labour, and the Council's Parks and Estates Committee, responsible for day to day location administration. As late as the early 1920s, the Parks and Estates Committee spent as much on African administration as it did on maintaining the city's zoo.[39]

It is unlikely that the government's Native Affairs Department supported the extension of the Night Pass Ordinance to women. It had endorsed Godley's recommendation that African women should be free of passes[40] and, by contemporary standards, was a relatively benign and paternalist body which saw its role as being a kind of 'umpire of the races'.[41] In the absence of more explicit documentation, the evidence suggests that Roos's extension of the 1902 Night Pass Ordinance aimed simply to expand the scope of police power.

On the surface, the curfew was just another petty mechanism to regulate the lives of urban Africans. African men, who had been subject to a curfew in Johannesburg for many years, had demonstrated that night passes were not a particularly effective restriction. Forgeries were readily available.[42] Its application to African women, though, was met with swift and vocal protest. Letters of protest appeared in the press, and there were terse reports of a 'mass meeting' of African women in Johannesburg on Sunday 25 January which called on the government to repeal the Ordinance which 'tended to the wholesale degradation of the Native women's honour and prestige'. Significantly, they appealed to the respectable African National Congress (ANC) to orchestrate a campaign of passive resistance.[43]

The ANC in the mid-1920s, though, was in no position to take up a mass campaign. A small body, it floundered between a refusal to associate itself with the newly formed liberal Joint Council of Europeans and Africans, and a concern to define itself in opposition to the nascent 'Bolshevism' of the Industrial and Commercial Workers' Union (ICU). It claimed for itself the role of defender of the limited rights of African people, and, at a meeting in Johannesburg in March 1925, condemned night passes for African women.[44]

In attempting an analysis of the protests, one has to tread warily. The records are sparse, and the most comprehensive surviving account appeared in the pages of *Umteteli wa Bantu*, a newspaper sponsored by the Chamber of Mines.[45] The paper articulated the views of a particular and limited sector of Johannesburg's African population, the élite, for whom the contradictions of missionary education — equality before God but not the government — were most stark.

As Philip Bonner and Tim Couzens have argued, most Africans living in Johannesburg in this period were close to poverty, which smudges sharp class distinctions within the urban African population. As the earnings of the élite and the majority hardly differed, one must turn to other than purely economic factors in delineating class distinctions. One such source is the perceptions of the élite themselves. As Bonner argues, the key distinction lay between those who thought of themselves as educated and civilised, and those they deemed were not.[46] On a national level, Couzens's analysis of the entries listed in Mweli Skota's *African Yearly Register* — a directory of the African élite in South Africa in 1931 — provides a fascinating insight into the self-definition of this stratum, and its their occupations and values.[47] One of the most striking features of the directory is the small number of those deemed worthy of inclusion amongst the élite. Education provided the entree; of the 271 persons described, 114 had gone to mission schools; 48 were teachers. These were followed, in descending scale, by clergymen and clerks. There was mention of only 8 journalists, 6 doctors and 4 lawyers. Couzens draws attention to the repetition of certain words and phrases in the pen-portraits. To be termed 'progressive' was a high accolade, and the word, as Couzens shows, becomes the ideological touchstone of the whole book. It embraced such values as diligence and perseverance (particularly in education), charity and kindliness, abstemiousness, and, of crucial importance, a rejection of tribalism and ethnocentrism.[48]

The business of being a gentleman included other codes of deportment — particularly with regard to women. A speech given by D.D.T. Jabavu to an assembly of African teachers in Natal in 1920 is particularly revealing. At the time, Jabavu was a lecturer in Bantu Studies at Fort Hare, and one of the most eminent Africans of his day; a decade later, Mweli Skota was to devote an entire page of his *Who's Who* to Jabavu's biography, alongside a full-page photograph of him. Jabavu pointed approvingly to the chivalry of men in 'civilised society':

> [They] take off their hats when greeting ladies, they remove pipes and refrain from spitting in their presence, give them the correct side in walking on pavements, and use refined language in their presence... In these countries the luggage of ladies is borne by men, with us it is the opposite.

In Jabavu's opinion, customary marriage practice was the root cause of the low status accorded African women by men. It reduced women to the level of chattels — 'a commodity that is purchased by the highest bidder' — and obliged them to populate the home with as many children as possible 'as a return for the cattle'. Such matrimony was neither holy nor monogamous. This 'primitive state' would begin to disappear when African women were liberated from 'unreasonably heavy' agricultural work. Once freed, women would be able to

> practise better cooking, to beautify their homes, to bring up their children under their personal attention, to improve their own health and that of the race in general.

The crucial point was this: 'If we mean to rise in this world and to command the respect of other nations we must begin by raising up our women.'[49]

The notion that 'no nation can rise higher than its womanhood' was expressed repeatedly throughout this period in the speeches and writings of the élite. Jabavu's wife ('Mrs D.D.T. Jabavu') was not merely echoing her husband when she wrote in 1928 that, 'no nation can advance without race pride, and such pride depends on the motherhood of the nation and the self-confidence that can be engendered only by the mother in the home.'[50]

In part, this veneration of women and motherhood was a reflection of ruling-class Edwardian thought. As Davin has argued, English mothers in the early twentieth century were urged to do their bit for the cause of Empire by raising strong and healthy sons, and to seek fulfilment in the realm of the ever more private and child-centred home. Married women were not to clog the labour market.[51] These ideas were introduced into South Africa largely by English missionaries, and, with little regard for the practicalities of urban subsistence, Christian African women were urged to strive for the same ideals.[52] In a leading article in 1922 in *South African Outlook*, a female English missionary argued that women were to be given new importance as the 'queen of the home':

> The man has his kingdom in his home. That gives him the impetus to work... His wife is the queen of that dwelling, and all that is best and sweetest in life reigns there. [Her] work is symbolised by the letter H — Humanity, Homes, Husbands, Housewives, Hygiene, Happiness, and lastly, Heaven.[53]

The pages of *Umteteli wa Bantu* repeatedly stressed similar notions.[54]

The African élite's emphasis on morality, motherhood and the 'proper' sphere of female endeavour was not only a reflection of prevailing English values, nor was their rhetoric aimed only at members of their own stratum. It was aimed at Africans generally. The élite strove for acceptance into white society, and they recognised that this would not necessarily be achieved on individual merit alone. Much as they wished to distance themselves from the mass of 'tribal' Africans, they perceived that their fortunes, and those of the majority, were not necessarily distinct. Recognition by whites of the humanity of Africans, they believed, would come only with the 'upliftment' of the race as a whole, and, as 'no race could rise above' the level of its womenhood' the status and behaviour of African women had to be brought into line with the alleged norm elsewhere.

The majority of African women living in Johannesburg in this period, however, were stereotyped by whites as immoral. The white press, in particular, ran frequent stories on the allegedly prevalent vice and crime among Africans, to which African women contributed as prostitutes and liquor-sellers. As hard evidence made many of these claims difficult to disprove, the élite viewed this characterisation with alarm. The life-styles of many African women living in Johannesburg simply did not accord with the conception of grace, beauty and domestic fulfilment outlined for them. This threatened to jeopardise the status not only of African women as a whole, but of the African élite as well. An essay competition run by *Umteteli* in 1923 on 'The Dangers of Town Life' neatly illustrates the élite's concern. The winner of the £1 first prize addressed his comments to women newly arrived in town, and exhorted them to 'keep your hands so full of work that the Devil will have to display his 'situations vacant' column to someone else'.[55]

When it came to the issue of night passes for women, the élite distinguished themselves by their ambivalence. Night passes for African women, they said, were perhaps not wholly bad, particularly in view of declining parental authority in the towns. At an ANC meeting in March 1925 a number of African women in the audience qualified the meeting's condemnation of night passes with an appeal for more parental control,[56] a refrain that echoed through virtually all strata of Africans at the time. Discriminatory though the regulation may have been, it could potentially constrain the waywardness of young African women by keeping them at home at night.

Those among the élite who opposed the curfew premised their

protest on four basic objections. Firstly, the curfew cast a slur on the morality of all African women. And, in the opinion of S.M. Magkatho, ANC president in 1925, 'European women were the worst prostitutes' — yet few curbs were placed on their mobility.[57] Secondly, if women were to carry passes, they would be subject to checks by police empowered to arrest transgressors. If convicted, offenders faced either a 10s. fine or a week in prison. Pass offences thus carried with them the very real threat of criminalising large numbers of African women.[58] A more immediate problem was the potential for verbal or sexual abuse by police, and indeed there was no lack of evidence of police 'acts of indecency and molestation' against women.[59] Thirdly, both the Moffat and Godley reports had come out strongly against any form of curfew regulation for women. The 1920 Native Affairs Act had enshrined the principle that no change would be made to this or any other matter 'affecting natives' without proper consultation with African representatives. That the government had overridden the commissions' recommendations, and furthermore had made no attempt to consult with Africans about the issue, was seen as a serious breach of faith.[60]

Finally, passes for women shifted the fulcrum in the unequal balance of power between men and women, and undermined the right of men to be sole masters of the affairs of their households. As an editorial in *Umteteli* said:

> The Native man is himself the arbiter of his women's conduct and is resentful of any interference in his matters marital. The Native woman has not progressed so far in public affairs as her British prototype, nor has she ventured so unwisely on the road to masculinity. Her husband is still her lord, and it is because of this old fashioned and very desirable relationship that any incursion damaging to the domestic state of the Native people becomes an extremely hazardous proceeding.[61]

Arguably, this was as much an appeal to the values of the white male élite as it was to fellow-Africans. It was an appeal for men to close ranks in defence of their right to determine the affairs of their households.

There was another, more sensitive issue at stake. The curfew cut across class. Most female members of the élite were not exempted, and were thus subject to the curfew. There were fewer than six hundred

exempted Africans in Johannesburg in 1925, and most were male.[62]
Women who met the educational and property criteria —
independently or through their spouses — could qualify for
exemption, yet few applied; in the absence of pass laws for women,
they brought few privileges women could not enjoy through their
spouses' exempt status.[63]

The night pass issue was hotly debated in the pages of *Umteteli*. On
the one hand, womanhood was said to be sacred — 'the natural
modesty of women makes it unnecessary for them to carry a pass'. On
the other, 'we know it is no longer the case with a large number of
women in our towns':

> It has been said that passes are unnecessary since they are under
> the control of their husbands and fathers. We know that is the
> case in Native life, but we cannot for a moment believe that the
> swarms of over-dressed Native girls who parade the streets at
> night are in the control of anybody.

Quite simply, 'the Transvaal town [was] no place for Native women.'[64]

The Joint Council, meanwhile, had taken matters into its own hands.
It condemned the arbitrary manner in which the curfew had been
imposed, and demanded a meeting with the Prime Minister.[65]
Hertzog, head of the newly elected Pact government, subsequently
agreed to a four-month moratorium on the understanding that the
Joint Council would put forward a viable alternative to passes for
women by 1 May.[66] The Johannesburg Joint Council then began work
on a counter-proposal, based on consultation with 'representative'
Africans, something the committee itself certainly could not claim.
The members of the Joint Council committee were drawn from the
ranks of the eminently respectable — the Native Mine Clerks'
Association, the Transvaal Native Teachers' Association, the
Transvaal Native Ministers' Association, and the Bantu Women's
League.[67] The Ministers' Association's 'fierce objection' to the curfew
was particularly interesting — 'it will give license to evil doers to
accomplish their evil desires with the connivance of the
Government'.[68] The ANC and ICU refused to work either with the
Joint Council or each other in putting forward an alternative.[69]

By mid-March the Joint Council's proposals were ready. More far-
ranging and restrictive than anything ever proposed by the
government, they hinged on bolstered parental control — 'the only

way we can see of stemming the flowing tide'.[70] If the influx of young women into the cities led to their downfall, they should be stopped before they left home. The Joint Council proposed that any woman who left home for the towns unaccompanied by her husband or natural guardian had to have a permit signed by the local magistrate which certified her parents' permission, and proof that she had both work and accommodation waiting for her. Without this permit, she could be returned to her parents at any time. On arrival in town, she was to report to a Native Rest House and wait there until claimed by an employer. The proposal's sub-clauses were worse. Cohabitation without marriage was to be made a criminal offence, and wives who deserted their husbands in urban areas were to be treated as idle and undesirable, and repatriated.[71]

Premising the proposals on parental control was an astute move. It resonated deeply with the complaints of many African parents who bemoaned their declining control over their children and diminishing filial respect, issues which were themselves symptomatic of broader dislocations in traditional authority systems.[72] The loss of rural women to the towns had particular significance for rural families. Women played a crucial role in rural subsistence, particularly as men were drawn into the migrant labour nexus in increasing numbers.[73] In addition, it was necessary for married women to be kept at home by their husband's kin to serve, effectively, as hostages for the return of their migrant spouses and the repatriation of their earnings.[74] And for families living as labour tenants on white-owned farms, the desertion of adolescent children — from whom the farmer could claim terms of unpaid labour — could lead to eviction. Judging from the correspondence solicited from 'representative' Africans at the time by the Joint Council, there was virtually unanimous support for the stern reinforcement of parental control.[75]

This bolstering of traditional authority structures was not without its drawbacks. Parents might indeed be provided with greater sanction over their daughters, but this permission needed the seal of white officials. Arch Mbelle, a prominent member of the élite, spelled out the consequences. If implemented, the plan would

> instil in the minds of our women folk the idea that Government officials have more paternal and marital power of control over them than their own fathers and legal and lawful husbands.[76]

Once again, the message was clear: domestic politics were not to be tampered with by officials of the state.

The Joint Council, of course, had proposed a pass system more stringent than the Night Pass Ordinance itself. This was particularly ironic given the participation of the Bantu Women's League in the drafting committee and its stance as defender of the rights of African women. The League had been formed in 1913 specifically to oppose proposed health checks for women and the Free State women's pass laws. However, A.G.W. Champion, a member of the Mine Clerks' Association and an ICU leader, later claimed he was 'reliably informed' that 'no meeting of the Bantu Women's League was ever held to determine the opinion of native women' on the pass issue.[77]

The government was not prepared to enforce or administer such a far-reaching control measure, and rejected it as impractical. The Joint Council's endeavours were not entirely wasted, however, as Hertzog did agree to one modification. The curfew for women would be enforced not from 9pm but 10.30pm, as of 1 June 1925.[78]

The ANC responded to the severity of the Joint Council's proposals with anger and derision. More significantly, at its annual conference in Bloemfontein in April 1925, it used the issue to berate the ICU by accusing it — erroneously — of endorsing the Joint Council's proposals. 'Here the ICU were playing the part of Judas Iscariot right through,' declared S.M. Makgatho.[79] Lengthy discussion ensued as to the best course of protest against the curfew. Makgatho appealed to all African women in the employ of whites 'to give notice at the end of April 1925, so that at the end of May 1925 there would be no native females working'. This proposal was flatly rejected on the grounds that many women were working to support their parents, and it would be their parents who would suffer. Delegates eventually resolved to appeal to the Minister of Justice to repeal the regulation, and, if necessary, to take the matter before the Privy Council.[80]

By early May protest rhetoric was flowing thick and fast. The ICU was said to be threatening passive resistance (which it later changed to a strike call and subsequently abandoned) 'as a protest against the unwarranted interference with Native women', and a number of African congregations on the Rand observed Sunday 3 May as a day of mourning. The only hint of concrete action came from a meeting of women in Doornfontein who resolved to elect ten women to 'give themselves for test case purposes'.[81]

It was such test action that led to the lifting of the curfew for women.

In August two African women appeared in the Pretoria Supreme Court to appeal against their conviction under the Ordinance — Helena Detody from Pretoria, and Sinah Ngema, possibly one of the Johannesburg volunteers.[82] Ngema's counsel unsuccessfully argued abrogation of the Ordinance's applicability to women through disuse. Detody was defended by the eminent barrister, A.B. Davis KC, whose services were hired by the ANC at a cost of £300.[83] Her defence was initially dismissed, but subsequently upheld in February 1926 when a bench of three judges reconsidered and agreed that the original Ordinance had not been intended to include African women.[84] African women in Johannesburg were now legally exempt from the curfew.

While the Detody case was being debated in court, a struggle of a different order was being waged in the streets of Johannesburg. Slum clearance had begun. Six thousand Africans were ordered out of inner Johannesburg between January 1924 and December 1925.[85] All pretence of being able to regulate the number of people living in town by controlling the number of permits issued was now abandoned. Instead, officials planned to proclaim 'white areas', suburb by suburb, and systematically clear them of their African residents. Only exempted Africans would be spared. For workless women unable to prove they had a husband who had been living in Johannesburg since January 1924 when the Urban Areas Act was promulgated, slum clearance posed problems of subsistence that the formality of night passes could never rival. Removal could spell repatriation, and hundreds were repatriated.[86]

The Urban Areas Act had laid down that 'no extension of the permanent [urban African] population should be encouraged or even permitted'. By the mid-1920s, factors beyond the control of municipal officials were at play that overrode legislative fiat and extruded thousands of newcomers into the city. Nineteen twenty-four marked the beginning of a decade of drought which exhausted the resources of many rural families — white and black — who had managed to weather earlier crises, and many abandoned their land for the towns. In addition, the government was channelling massive funding into white farming, while tightening the noose of farm labour and anti-squatting legislation.[87]

The number of immigrants from the reserves was increasing too. Many migrants did not return from the mines or towns. The fact that hundreds of women from all parts of the country and beyond were said to be coming to Johannesburg in search of their husbands in this period cannot be ascribed to sentimental reasons alone.[88] Many arrived only to find their husbands living with other women, and were obliged to make independent subsistence arrangements. Municipal officials noted with alarm the number of women who turned to other men, or liquor-brewing, or both, to survive:

> Particularly is the large influx of women a danger and a menace to society and the fair name of Johannesburg. They are either liquor sellers or prostitutes, or are living an illegal life with a man. The Johannesburg City Council has spent over a million and a half in housing natives, but, unless we can control the influx, to what purpose?[89]

Women living in town were 'an embarrassment' to the municipality. Worse still, 'they are the people who produce the detribalised family'.[90] More serious than the horrors of urban women brewing liquor, prostituting their bodies, tempting respectable men and contributing to vice and crime, was the spectre of their 'detribalised' children who, through improper socialisation and early exposure to vice and crime, would make poor workers. Native administrators were acutely aware of this: 'it is the infantile population that is going to create trouble. They will only make very cheap labour, and you can never send them back to their tribal conditions.'[91]

Regulated housing as a form of influx control was a farce. The number of municipal houses fell far short of the demand, and slum clearance was halted in 1926 by a court ruling because of insufficient alternative accommodation.[92] Nor were the pass laws particularly effective in controlling the influx of Africans into Johannesburg. Control over issuing passes was in the hands of the Government Native Labour Bureau, which, to add insult to injury, consistently refused to hand over pass revenue to supplement housing costs.[93]

The obvious solution to the crisis, in the eyes of the municipality, was influx control for women. If the number of women in town could be controlled, there would be fewer men demanding family housing, and fewer 'detribalised' families for whose accommodation the Council was responsible. Housing could be restricted to bona fide workers, and it would be easier to deport 'idle and undesirable' women whose passes would show they were not employed. Furthermore, men's wages could not support an urban family, and it was frequently the financial contribution of women — often by illegal means — that made urban subsistence viable.[94]

In October 1927 three City Councillors were despatched to Cape Town to plead their case before the government. Hertzog, then Minister of Native Affairs, was reported to be 'sympathetic' to their pleas for greater control measures for African women;[95] yet, when the bill amending the 1923 Act was presented in Parliament, there was no reference to passes for women. There was, however, provision for a curfew for both men and women included at the specific request of the Johannesburg municipality. Despite the protests of the Joint Council and the condemnation of the liberal National European-Bantu Conference which met in Cape Town in October 1929, the night pass regulation remained.[96]

The Nationalist Party romped to victory in the 1929 general election. It maintained its coalition pact with the conservative white Labour Party, as Hertzog needed this added support to push through Native Affairs legislation. The 1930 amendment to the 1923 Natives (Urban Areas) Act was but a small part of Hertzog's grander plan, yet for the Johannesburg City Council it was adequate. No African woman would be admitted to an urban area without proof that she was going to join her husband or father. Accommodation had to be available, and her relative had to have been resident and continuously employed in the area for at least two years. Any woman unable to produce a certificate issued by the local authority to this effect could be prosecuted and repatriated. The 'idle and undesirable' clause was amended to allow for repatriation of anyone convicted more than once for selling or possessing liquor, and the 1902 Night Pass Ordinance, declared *ultra vires* for women in 1926, was given new legislative effect.[97]

For reasons that remain unclear, the municipality did not enforce the provisions requiring women to report to the local authority on arrival until the late 1930s. But, on 22 May 1931, a small notice appeared in the Government Gazette proclaiming Johannesburg under Section 19 of the amended Act. From 1 June all unexempted Africans in Johannesburg would be subject to a 10pm curfew. Ten days after this notice appeared the first arrests were made.[98]

The new curfew was symptomatic of the state's unease over control of the burgeoning urban African population. By 1931, the depression in Western economies was taking its toll in South Africa. African wages, which had barely risen in over a decade, were cut.[99] Unemployment soared, the problem compounded by the fact that Johannesburg's African population had swelled from an estimated 83 457 people in 1928 to 96 000 by 1931.[100] For the first time since the recession and drought of 1906-07, the mines had more labour than they could use, and unemployed urban workers who volunteered in desperation for mine work were turned away.[101] Hundreds of African workers in the municipal and state sectors were replaced by whites as a result of 'civilised labour' policies, introduced in 1926.[102] Even paltry washing profits were no longer secure; a petition signed by more than a thousand women from Western Native Township in May 1929 claimed that the increasing number of commercial laundries in town was depriving them of their living. By mid-1931, over half the residents of that township were consistently behind in their rent.[103] More alarming to the state was the fact that a small number of white and black workers were taking to the streets in displays of inter-racial protest against unemployment.[104] It was in this context of growing unemployment, accelerating urbanisation, and rising militancy that night passes for women were re-introduced.

The protests precipitated by the new curfew were more bitter and vociferous than anything seen in 1925, and for a while the Council was forced on to the defensive. It feigned ignorance of the fact that the new curfew would include women, and hastily made interventions to ensure that the police suspended arrests until further notice. It was 'unfair', stated the mayor, G.W. Nelson, that African women should be 'pestered by the police for passes'. 'Instead of advancing, we would simply be going back to the old days when the natives were oppressed.'[105] Contemporary accounts described the whole affair as a most unfortunate administrative error, and G. Ballenden, manager of Municipal Native Affairs, was said to have made 'a bloomer'.[106] Although he had been the architect of the scheme — 'wanting a grip on these questionable women' — Ballenden piously denied any premeditation.[107]

In late June a Council deputation went to interview the Ministers of Native Affairs and Justice to appeal for a suspension of the measure. Their request was turned down. Four years earlier, the Council itself had specifically requested the curfew and — the Ministers pointed out — 'in black and white it says male and female'.[108] The curfew would remain, unaltered. On 26 June the arrest of transgressors was resumed.[109]

Johannesburg's African middle classes were outraged by the new regulation. At both a political and economic level, their status was under attack. 'It is an unhappy coincidence,' wrote I. Bud Mbelle in a letter to *Umteteli* in August 1931, 'that just when the European women are given the franchise the Bantu women are subjected to such humiliation.'[110] In 1930 Hertzog, as head of state, had virtually doubled the size of the electorate by enfranchising white women in a conscious bid to dilute the voting strength of enfranchised Africans in the Cape. As R.V. Selope Thema, a prominent African politician and frequent contributor to *Umteteli*, commented, 'all hope of getting full citizenship rights was now closed'.[111]

Economically, the depression compounded new legislative measures affecting the middle and aspirant middle classes. The 1924 Apprenticeship Act specifically excluded Africans from training and certification in artisan trades. Their frustrations emerged clearly in this statement, in 1931, by a representative of the Sophiatown and Martindale Ratepayers' Association:

> Our teachers are the worst paid public servants, education for our children not only neglected but starved, and the rest of the revenue derived from us goes to provide jobs for European lads now employed in all Pass offices and Native Commissioners offices, mutilating our language and keeping imperfect records.[112]

The curfew was a further example of the government's betrayal of the élite. 'It does not pay to be loyal,' wrote Mweli Skota.[113] Once again, the curfew cut across status as so few middle-class women were exempted. An African minister complained:

> The night pass regulations do not affect only the wives of ordinary men, but the wives of chiefs and ministers of religion too. We are all put and boiled in one pot. It does not matter whether one is a respectable native or not.[114]

'I can't express myself politely on this subject,' A.B. Xuma, a doctor trained in Edinburgh and Budapest, told members of the Johannesburg Rotary Club. 'This is the grossest insult.'[115]

Night passes also assumed that all women had an employer to sign their night passes. It was a point of pride for many 'respectable' African women that they were not employed and did not need to work outside their homes.[116] Furthermore, night passes carried with them the more insidious presumption that any woman who went out at night did so for immoral purposes unless she could prove otherwise by means of a pass. Having 'failed to weed out undesirables' the authorities were now 'burdening even respectable natives with this degrading badge of inferiority.'[117]

The ANC assumed leadership in the campaign of protest, and called for urgent, militant and mass action. The organisation's General Secretary, Mweli Skota, urged women to defy the law, and called for 'a day of demonstration' when neither men nor women would go to work. Elaborate preparations were said to be under way throughout the Reef to inform the authorities that 'the time has come for all passes to go'.[118] At a mass meeting in central Johannesburg on Sunday 21 June the ANC executive was mandated to organise a national campaign.[119] Other protest meetings were held in Western Native Township, Eastern Native Township, Evaton and Klipspruit, and evidence of a petition from as far afield as the 'Native Community of Zeerust Town and Marico District' in August suggests widespread opposition to the Johannesburg curfew.[120]

Once again, the regulation was seen as an attack on the 'manhood' of African men:

> Rightly or wrongly, we consider this action of the Government as a challenge to our manhood... We have all along trusted in the goodwill of the white race and its sense of justice, but today we have found that our trust has been betrayed. As men we can submit to injustice as long as we must; but we cannot tolerate the subjection of our womenfolk to the indignities and barbarities of the pass laws.[121]

Again, this was an appeal to cross-cultural assumptions of male supremacy, and the need for the strong to defend the weak. This paternalism and sense of betrayal was echoed in a statement issued by the Independent Industrial and Commercial Workers' Union (IICU). Pointing out that neither the 'wildest savage' nor 'wild animal' would 'allow its female to be tampered with', it warned that 'this regulation will convert sober-minded and moderate native leaders into extremists and enemies of constituted law and order'.[122]

It was an inaccurate prediction. By September 1931 even letters of protest to the press had stopped. The ANC lacked the mass base necessary to sustain large-scale action in this period, and the proposed anti-pass campaign was quietly shelved. The ICU, by 1931, was a spent force, racked by leadership disputes and its failure to deliver the goods it had promised its members. The recent demise of the ICU possibly had had broader repercussions: those who could potentially be mobilised were disillusioned with formal political activity and were wary of further rhetoric.

One crucial question remains unanswered: why was there virtually no evidence of resistance to the measure outside institutional politics, particularly from African women? Such a question assumes that there was unanimous and unqualified rejection of the measure by the majority, but this was not necessarily the case. While it would be facile and presumptuous to suggest that the majority of Africans supported the curfew, one should bear in mind that it could benefit sectional interests. In Bloemfontein in 1923, 'the better class' of African women specifically requested that local curfew regulations include all African women in the city 'with a view to assist[ing] the young girls to become respectable and useful'. They argued that 'being free to go where and when they will, Native women and girls have abused their privileges and have developed undesirable night practices'.[123] From this perspective, curfews could clearly be exploited by parents in the interests of morality and discipline.

Night passes could also be used to buttress male authority. Certainly, the curfew allowed the state a foot in the door of household politics. Equally, however, it had the net effect of keeping women at home and indoors at night. The available evidence suggests that while women's contributions to the majority of urban household incomes were recognised as important, they could also potentially undermine the pre-eminence of the male household head.[124] Furthermore, women in traditional African societies were denied the means to accumulate wealth through their exclusion from control over cattle.[125] It would be naive to imagine that many Africans who lived in Johannesburg did not retain at least some of the assumptions that informed rural customs, even in an urban context far removed from a cattle-based economy. None the less, through domestic work, liquor-selling, and a range of other activities, the towns afforded women an opportunity to accumulate wealth — one many seized with fierce pride.[126]

This surely must have had some impact on African men's perceptions of the changing status of women. The comments by ICU leader A.W.G. Champion that 'the working woman has more money than the working man' and 'the wives do support the men rather than the men support their wives in town here' suggest some unease, as do pejorative references to 'kept husbands' and 'gentlemen of leisure' supported by their wives.[127] Marriage arrangements, too, were changing. In a complete inversion of customary norms, some urban African women were said to have earned the money with which their spouses paid their *lobola*.[128] Many insisted on church weddings in addition to customary marriage, suggesting not merely a desire for a public formalisation of marriage, but a marriage that barred their husbands from taking a second wife, and made them legally accountable for household maintenance.[129]

In the face of this growing assertiveness by African women, there seems to have been a backlash — argued most explicitly in the black press — which posited a return to traditional values of wifely submission and obedience. African women were said to be

> using every opportunity to break asunder the chains of tradition and custom... This claim of equality with men by Bantu women is at the root of the destruction of Bantu family life. It is not the right kind of equality... No community in which the men are without control over their women can hope to build up a healthy social system.[130]

One may speculate that these sentiments were inspired by men wanting to preserve a niche of power within the family in the face of eroded power beyond. Significantly, these notions were articulated not only by men, but by women too, concerned to check the declining morals of their daughters, distance themselves from 'fallen' women, and establish a respectable sphere of authority for themselves. This was the context of the implementation of the night pass regulations. Those women who succeeded in circumventing its aims were already beyond the power of the existing laws.

The inclusion of African women in Johannesburg's curfew regulations in 1925 and 1931 occurred in the context of a colonial and racist state grappling with the management of industrialisation and social change. The state's responses to issues of social control among Africans were crude and blatantly racist. It wilfully ignored the distinctions of class and status asserted by the African élite itself. The protest of the African élite was framed in terms of 'natural guardianship' over their wives and daughters, in which the state had no right to intervene.[131] Yet, more important to the male members of the African middle classes than the fact that 'their' women were now obliged to carry passes, was the erosion of their status as a distinct and privileged élite. It was an appeal for the retention of privilege, both in the politics of gender — as men over women — and the politics of class — as the élite over the majority. It was an appeal dismissed by the white state on the basis of race.

Notes

1 J. Wells, The History of Black Women's Struggle against the Pass Laws in South Africa, Unpublished PhD Thesis, Columbia University, New York, 1982; C. Walker, *Women and Resistance in South Africa*, (London, 1982).

2 *Umteteli wa Bantu*, 19 May 1923.

3 Figures drawn from A. Proctor, 'Class Struggle, Segregation and the City: A History of Sophiatown 1905-40', in B. Bozzoli (ed.), *Labour, Townships and Protest: Studies in the Social History of the Witwatersrand*, (Johannesburg, 1979), p. 53; Union of South Africa, Office of Census and Statistics, Special Report 26 of 1925: Industries on the Witwatersrand 1915-1923, p. 12; B. Freund, The Social Character of Secondary Industrialisation in South Africa, 1915-1945, Unpublished African Studies Institute Seminar Paper, University of the Witwatersrand, April 1985, p. 8.

4 Figures drawn from G. Ballenden, Memorandum submitted to the Native Economic Affairs Commission (NEC), 1930-31, Annexure B, in Evidence before the Native Economic Affairs Commission (ENEC), University of the Witwatersrand Library, Department of Historical Papers (UWL), AD 1473, Box 7 (Memoranda submitted to the NEC are cited by reference to the box, and verbatim evidence by page number); Archdeacon Hill, Memorandum, p. 3, ENEC, Box 10.

5 D. Gaitskell, Female Mission Initiatives: Black and White Women in three Witwatersrand Churches, 1903-1939, Unpublished PhD Thesis, University of London, 1981, p. 106.

6 See, for example, D. Maud, ENEC, pp. 7611-12.

7 See Johannesburg Non-European and Native Affairs Department, Survey of the African in Industry in the Municipal Area of Johannesburg, 1939, p. 12; see also Charles van Onselen, 'The Witches of Suburbia: Domestic Service on the Witwatersrand, 1890-1914', in his *Studies in the Social and Economic History of*

the Witwatersrand, 1886-1914, Vol. 2 (Johannesburg, 1982), pp. 1-73.

8 Quoted in the *Rand Daily Mail*, 19 May 1919.

9 Letter from the ICU, Johannesburg, to the Special Committee, House of Assembly, May 1925, in Karis and Carter Microfilm Collection, UWL, Reel 13B, 2:LI 1:41/2.

10 Ballenden, ENEC, p. 7712; Dorothy Maud, ENEC, p. 7619; H.G. Falwasser to the Medical Officer of Health, Johannesburg, 12 May 1925, in Joint Council Papers, UWL, AD 1433, File Cj2.1.5; and see Van Onselen, 'The Witches of Suburbia', *passim*.

11 Lieut.-Col. F.A. Saunders, quoted in the *Star*, 13 May 1920.

12 Ballenden, ENEC, p. 7712.

13 Hill, Memorandum, ENEC, Box 10.

14 *Umteteli wa Bantu*, 22 Sept. 1928.

15 *Rand Daily Mail*, 14 May 1928; Witwatersrand Committee for Health Work among Non-Europeans, 'Venereal Disease', in *Report of the National European-Bantu Conference*, 1929, (Cape Town, 1929), p. 187.

16 This section is drawn from E. Krige, 'Some social and economic facts revealed in Native family budgets', *Race Relations*, 1:6 (1934), p. 96, and 'The social significance of beer among the baLobedu', *Bantu Studies*, 6:4 (1926/27); E. Hellmann, *Rooiyard: A Sociological Study of an Urban Native Slum Yard*, (Cape Town, 1948), pp. 39-47.

17 This paragraph is based on Hellmann, *Rooiyard*, p. 41; Superintendent of Location's Report 1922-25, in Records of the Johannesburg Municipality, Central Archives Depot, Pretoria (CAD), Minute Books of the Special Native Affairs Committee; Evidence before the 1918 Moffat Commission of Inquiry into the Witwatersrand Disturbances, p. 151, quoted in Gaitskell, Female Mission Initiatives, p.129; M. Janisch, 'Some administrative problems of Native marriages in urban areas', *Bantu Studies* 15 (1941), p. 4; E. Krige, 'Some social and economic facts revealed in Native family budgets'.

18 Editorial in *Imvo Zabantsundu*, 12 May 1922; A.J. Cooke, *Why Not the Durban System?* (Cape Town, 1922), pp. 13-14.

19 Quoted in R.E. Phillips, *The Bantu are Coming*, (New York, 1930), p. 126.

20 Report of the Director of Native Labour, 1925, Government Native Labour Bureau, CAD, Government Native Labour Bureau

(GNLB) 137, File 2756/13/54.

21 *Star*, 22 Feb. 1919; Johannesburg Native Affairs Department Report, 1922-25, p. 7, in GNLB 380, File 11/11.

22 Union of South Africa, *Report of the Select Committee on the Working of the Transvaal Liquor Laws* (SC 2-'18), 1918, p.40.

23 Councillor H. Kroomer, Evidence before the Special Committee on Native Affairs (SC 3a-'23), 1922, p. 201.

24 These figures are estimates as there was no official census between 1921 and 1936. In 1923 there were 6 548 people living in the municipal townships of Western and Eastern Native Townships and Klipspruit and, allowing for new housing and population growth, the 1925 figure was probably around 8 000 (Col. S.A.M. Pritchard, Evidence before Select Committee on Native Affairs, SC 3-'23, p. 200); Sophiatown, Martindale and Newclare housed an estimated population of 4 000 people, a figure based on a generous increase on the 1921 figure of 2 643 (see A. Proctor, 'Sophiatown', p. 58); Alexandra had a population of roughly 5 000 in 1925 (Aston Key, Memorandum on Alexandra Township, 10 Nov. 1925, in GNLB 419, File 8514; see also *Rand Daily Mail*, 6 May 1919; *Star*, 12 Jan. 1927).

25 The phrase was a headline in the *Star*, 16 Aug. 1937.

26 F. Cooper, 'Urban Space, Industrial Time and Wage Labour in Africa', in F. Cooper (ed.), *The Struggle for the City: Migrant Labour, Capital and the State in Urban Africa*, (Beverley Hills, California, 1983), pp. 32-33.

27 Report of the Medical Officer of Health to the Public Health and Parks and Estates Committees, 26 Jan. 1923, in Pim Papers, UWL, A 881, File Fa 9; M. Janisch, 'Some administrative problems of Native marriages in urban areas', p. 2; and see J. Lewin, 'Some legal aspects of marriage by Natives in South Africa', *Bantu Studies*, 15 (1941); D.W.T. Shropshire, *Primitive Marriage and African Law: A South African Investigation*, (London, 1946, 1970 edn), pp. 18-19, and *passim*.

28 Report of the Conference of Native Affairs Officials, Municipal Representatives and Location Superintendents, Johannesburg, 11 Sept. 1924, in Joint Council Papers, File Cj2.1.4.

29 Union of South Africa, Report of the Interdepartmental Committee on the Native Pass Laws 1920 (UG 41-'22), p. 15, para. 63.

30 See D. Hindson, The Pass System and the Formation of an Urban

Proletariat in South Africa: A Critique of the Cheap Labour Power Thesis, Unpublished D Phil Thesis, University of Sussex, 1983, pp. 27-72; Wells, The History of Black Women's Struggle against the Pass Laws, pp. 193-201.

31 Union of South Africa, Report of the Transvaal Local Government [Stallard] Commission (TP 1-'22), 1922, p. 47, para. 267, and see pp. 49, paras 275, 276.

32 Ballenden, Evidence before the Select Committee on Native Affairs (SC6a-'29), 1929, p. 7.

33 Report of the Transvaal Local Government Commission, TP 1-'22, para. 279.

34 *Rand Daily Mail*, 1 Sept. 1924; *Star*, 1 Sept. 1924; *Johannesburg City Council Minutes*, 2 Sept. 1924.

35 Resolution 12 in Resolutions of the Conference on Native Affairs, 30 Oct. 1924 — 1 Nov. 1924, Johannesburg City Health Archives, Transvaal Intermediate Archives Depot, Johannesburg (TIAD), SGJ 24, File A 3554.

36 *Star*, 19 Jan. 1925.

37 *Umteteli wa Bantu*, 27 Dec. 1924.

38 *Star*, 19 Jan. 1925; J.B.M. Hertzog to the Secretary, Johannesburg Joint Council, 22 Jan. 1925, in Pim Papers, File Bl 4.

39 J.P.R. Maud, *City Government: The Johannesburg Experiment*, (Oxford, 1938), p. 101.

40 J.F. Herbst, Secretary for Native Affairs, to W. Webber, 17 June 1925, in Joint Council Papers, File Cj2.1.5.

41 Saul Dubow, 'Holding "a just balance between white and black": The Native Affairs Department in South Africa *c*.1920-33', *Journal of Southern African Studies* 12 (1986), p. 225, and *passim*.

42 *Umteteli wa Bantu*, 3 Sept. 1927; ICU Memorandum, printed in ibid., 25 Aug. 1928.

43 Ibid., 31 Jan. 1925.

44 *Rand Daily Mail*, 14 March 1925.

45 Tim Couzens, *The New African: A Study of the Life and Work of H.I.E. Dhlomo*, (Johannesburg, 1985), p. 43; Philip Bonner, 'The Transvaal Native Congress, 1917-1929: The Radicalisation of the Black Petty Bourgeoisie on the Rand', in S. Marks and R. Rathbone (eds), *Industrialisation and Social Change in South Africa: African Class Formation, Culture and Consciousness, 1870 – 1930*, (London, 1983), pp. 276-77.

46 Bonner, 'The Transvaal Native Congress', pp. 276-77.

47 Couzens, *The New African*, pp. 3-14; and see T.D. Mweli Skota, *The African Yearly Register: Being an Illustrated National Biographical Dictionary (Who's Who) of Black Folks in Africa*, (Johannesburg, 1930).

48 Couzens, *The New African*, pp. 5-7.

49 D.D.T. Jabavu, 'Native Womanhood', in *The Black Problem*, (Lovedale, n.d.), pp. 145-53

50 Mrs D.D.T. Jabavu, 'Bantu Home Life', in J. Dexter Taylor, (ed.), *Christianity and the Natives of South Africa*, (Lovedale, 1929), p. 173.

51 A. Davin, 'Imperialism and Motherhood', in *History Workshop*, 5 (Spring, 1978), pp. 9-57.

52 D. Gaitskell, 'Housewives, maids or mothers: Some contradictions of domesticity for Christian women in Johannesburg, 1903-39', *Journal of African History* 24 (1983), *passim*.

53 M.M. Waters, 'The need today of Native women and girls', *South African Outlook*, 59, May 1922, p. 7.

54 See, for example, H. Selby Msimang in *Umteteli wa Bantu*, 27 Aug. 1927, and R.V. Selope Thema, ibid., 20 June 1931; see also Mrs C.M. Maxeke, 'The Progress of Native Womanhood in South Africa', in Dexter Taylor (ed.), *Christianity and the Natives of South Africa*, pp. 177-82.

55 *Umteteli wa Bantu*, 3 Nov. 1923.

56 J.D. Rheinallt Jones to W.A. Russel, 28 April 1925, in Joint Council Papers, File Cj2.1.5.

57 Quoted by the Divisional Criminal Investigation Officer, Witwatersrand, 25 April 1925, in Department of Justice (JUS) Archives, CAD, JUS 3/1064/18, 'Report on Bolshevism on the Rand'.

58 *Umteteli wa Bantu*, 10 Jan., 25 Jan. 1925.

59 Ibid., 3 Jan. 1925; Report of the Interdepartmental Committee on the Native Pass Laws, 1920 (UG 41-'22), p. 15, para. 63.

60 See, for example, Editorial in *Umteteli wa Bantu*, 25 Jan. 1925.

61 Editorial in *Umteteli wa Bantu*, 3 Jan. 1925.

62 UWL, Joint Council Records, Cj2.1.6a, Secretary for Native Affairs to Thema, 13 July 1926.

63 UWL, SAIRR Archives, AD 1715, Box 5, Rheinallt Jones, Misc. correspondence, 1933-36, 'Exemption Certificates'.

64 *Umteteli wa Bantu*, 10 Jan. 1925.

65 *Star*, 19 Jan. 1925.

66 Prime Minister's Office to the Secretary, Johannesburg Joint Council, 22 Jan. 1925, in Pim Papers, File Bl 4.

67 *Rand Daily Mail*, 14 March 1925.

68 *Umteteli wa Bantu*, 6 June 1925.

69 Prime Minister's Office to the Secretary, Johannesburg Joint Council, 22 Jan. 1925, in Pim Papers, File Bl 4; Clements Kadalie to Skota, 14 Feb. 1925, in Karis and Carter Microfilm Collection, UWL, Reel 13B, 2:LI:41/1.

70 UWL, Joint Council Records, Cj2.1.5, Rheinallt Jones to Russel, 28 April 1925.

71 Ibid., 'Passes for Native Women'; *Rand Daily Mail*, 14 March 1925.

72 See W. Beinart and P. Delius, ' "The Family" and Early Migrancy in Southern Africa', Unpublished Seminar Paper presented to the African History Seminar, University of London, School of Oriental and African Studies, 9 May 1979; D. Gaitskell, 'Wailing for Purity: Prayer Unions, African Mothers and Adolescent Daughters, 1912-1940', in Marks and Rathbone (eds), *Industrialisation and Social Change*, pp. 338-43; J. Guy, 'The destruction and reconstruction of Zulu Society', in ibid., pp. 175-80.

73 See B. Bozzoli, 'Marxism, feminism and South African studies', *Journal of Southern African Studies* 9 (April 1983); M. Kinsman, 'The Uses and Abuses of Anthropology', Unpublished Paper presented at the Pre-colonial History Conference, University of Cape Town, 1986, pp. 6-9; M. Hunter, 'Results of culture contact on the Pondo and Xhosa family', *South African Journal of Science*, 1932.

74 A point made by Kenneth Little in *African Women in Towns*, (London, 1973), p. 18.

75 UWL, Joint Council Records, Cj2.1.5, Correspondence File, 1925.

76 Ibid., Arch S. Mbelle to Rheinallt Jones, 6 April 1925.

77 Ibid., A.G.W. Champion to Rheinallt Jones, 24 March 1925.

78 Ibid., Herbst to W. Webber, 9 May 1925; Herbst to the Secretary of the Johannesburg Joint Council, 17 June 1925.

79 Quoted by the Divisional Criminal Investigation Officer, Witwatersrand, 25 April 1925, in JUS 3/1064/18, 'Report on Bolshevism on the Rand'.

80 Ibid.

81 *Umteteli wa Bantu*, 9 May 1925.

82 Ibid., 8 Aug. 1925; *Rand Daily Mail*, 5 Aug. 1925.

83 *Umteteli wa Bantu*, 27 June 1931, repr. in T. Karis and G. Carter (eds), *From Protest to Challenge: A Documentary History of African Politics in South Africa, 1882-1964*, Vol. 1, *Protest and Hope, 1882-1934*, (Stanford, 1972), p. 310.

84 *Umteteli wa Bantu*, 27 June 1931; Pretoria Appeal Court Register, CAD, 1925-6, Rex vs Detody, *SA Law Reports*, Appellate Division, 1926, p. 202; *South African Outlook*, March 1926.

85 *Star*, 11 Dec. 1925.

86 See correspondence, 1925, in GNLB 284 File 52/18/72; *Umteteli wa Bantu*, 16 March 1929.

87 See especially Msimang, 'Addendum to Paragraph 2 of the Report on the Natives (Urban Areas) Act', n.d., in Pim Papers, File Fa 9.

88 See, for example, A.B. Xuma, Memorandum, pp. 5-6, ENEC, Box 10.

89 E.O. Leake (Chairman of the Johannesburg Native Affairs Committee), before the Select Committee on Native Affairs, quoted in the *Star*, 25 March 1928.

90 H.S. Cooke, evidence before the *Select Committee on Native Affairs*, SC 6a-'29, pp.1-11.

91 Leake, quoted in the *Star*, 25 March 1928.

92 For a review of the legislation, see *Rand Daily Mail*, 13 Jan. 1926 and 7 Feb. 1927; for a discussion of later court action, see Laura Menachemson, Resistance Through the Courts: African Urban Communities and Litigation under the Urban Areas Act 1923-59, Unpublished BA Hons Dissertation, University of the Witwatersrand, 1985.

93 See correspondence between the Magistrate, Johannesburg, and the Director of Native Labour, 1920-23, in JUS 289 3/127/20; see also evidence of Kroomer before the Select Committee on Native Affairs, SC 3a-'23.

94 See evidence of Leake and Ballenden before the Select Committee on Native Affairs, SC 6a-'29, pp. 1-11.

95 *Johannesburg Mayor's Minute*, 1928.

96 *Umteteli wa Bantu*, 20 June 1931.

97 Act No. 25 of 1930, Sections 7 and Section 19.

98 'Night Passes', *South African Outlook*, July 1931.

99 Union of South Africa, Bureau for Census and Statistics, *Union Statistics for Fifty Years*, (Pretoria, 1960), G20-1, 27,31.

100 Both figures exclude mineworkers; Ballenden, Memorandum, ENEC, Box 10.

101 H.M. Taberer, ENEC, p. 7396.
102 Hill, ENEC, p. 9704.
103 *Rand Daily Mail*, 17 May 1929; Ballenden, ENEC, p. 7739.
104 E. Koch, 'Doornfontein and its African Working Class, 1914-1936', Unpublished MA Dissertation, University of the Witwatersrand, 1983, p. 173.
105 *Star*, 10, 11, 16, 26 June 1931; *Rand Daily Mail*, 13 July 1931.
106 'Night Passes', *South African Outlook*, July 1931, p. 3; Gaitskell echoes this view, erroneously, in 'Christian Compounds for Girls: Church Hostels for African Women in Johannesburg, 1907—1970', Unpublished Paper presented at the History Workshop, University of the Witwatersrand, February 1978, p. 9; J.E. Holloway, ENEC, p. 9051.
107 Rheinallt Jones, ENEC, p. 9051.
108 *Johannesburg City Council Minutes*, 3 July 1931; Rheinallt Jones, ENEC, p. 9051.
109 *Rand Daily Mail*, 29 June 1931.
110 *Umteteli wa Bantu*, 1 Aug. 1931.
111 Quoted in T.R.H. Davenport, *South Africa: A Modern History*, (Johannesburg, 1977, 1978 edn), p. 208.
112 Sophiatown and Martindale Ratepayers' Association, Memorandum, ENEC, Box 7.
113 *Star*, 10 June 1931.
114 Revd L.S. Matsepe (General Secretary of the African Native Ministers' Association) to the *Star*, 26 June 1931.
115 *Rand Daily Mail*, 12 June 1931.
116 Revd A.B.L. Karney to the *Star*, 13 June 1931.
117 Skota (General Secretary of the African National Congress) quoted in the *Star*, 10 June 1931.
118 *Star*, 10 June 1921.
119 Ibid., 19 June 1931; *Rand Daily Mail*, 22 June 1931.
120 Ibid., 15 June 1931; *Rand Daily Mail*, 16, 22 June 1931; *Umteteli wa Bantu*, 27 June 1931; 'Petition presented to His Excellency the Earl of Clarendon by the Native Community of Zeerust Town and Marico District', 21 Aug. 1931, in Governor General's Records, CAD, GG 1185 File 50/1414 (thanks to Graeme Simpson for this reference).
121 *Umteteli wa Bantu*, 27 June 1931, repr. in Karis and Carter, *From Protest to Challenge*, Vol. 1, pp. 310-11.
122 Independent ICU Memorandum to the Minister of Native Affairs,

E.J. Jansen, quoted in the *Star*, 16 June 1931.

123 *Umteteli wa Bantu*, 19 May 1923.

124 For a discussion of the benefits to men of the family wage, see Heidi Hartman, 'The Unhappy Marriage of Marxism and Feminism: Towards a More Progressive Union', in L. Sargent (ed.), *The Unhappy Marriage of Marxism and Feminism: A Debate in Class and Patriarchy*, (London, 1981), pp. 21-23.

125 For a discussion of the subordination of women in pre-colonial Tswana polities, see M. Kinsman, 'The Uses and Abuses of Anthropology'.

126 See, for example, E. Mphalele, *Down Second Avenue*, (London, 1973), p. 41.

127 Champion, ENEC, p. 8233; H.I.E. Dhlomo, *An African Tragedy*, (Lovedale, 1931), p. 8.

128 Champion, ENEC, p. 8237.

129 A point made by Helen Bradford in '"We are now men": Women's Beer Protests in the Natal Countryside, 1929', in B. Bozzoli (ed.), *Class, Community and Conflict: South African Perspectives* (Johannesburg, 1987), p. 30; and see E.J. Krige, 'Changing conditions in native marital relationships and parental duties among urbanised natives', *Africa*, 9 (1936).

130 Thema, in *Umteteli wa Bantu*, 20 June 1931.

131 *Umteteli wa Bantu*, 27 Dec. 1924.

African Settlement and Segregation in Brakpan, 1900-1927

Hilary Sapire

Until recently, the literature dealing with the creation of an urban African working class and the evolution of urban segregation has tended to ignore the presence of a permanently urbanised African population in the main industrial centres of South Africa in the early twentieth century. While vast mining compounds housing migrant African workers dominate the landscape of turn of the century social history, the contemporaneous patterns of permanent African settlement and urban culture prior to the emergence of segregatory institutions such as locations or 'native villages' have remained virtually hidden in most accounts. By contrast, popular African urban life in the later period, from the 1920s onwards, has received considerably more scholarly attention, and in recent years there has been an efflorescence of studies of permanently settled African communities and social movements in slumyards, freehold townships and locations.

Most of these studies focus on Johannesburg, the Rand's hub and pacemaker. Yet Johannesburg's very nature as the country's principal city means that the experiences of urban life and the evolution of urban segregation there were far from typical, even on the Witwatersrand. Few towns for example could boast of the substantial areas of freehold African township such as Sophiatown and Alexandra in Johannesburg. Just a modicum of research conducted in the last few years tells us that the pace, timing and nature of African urbanisation and settlement varied regionally according to local patterns of economic development and exploitation, both in the towns and in their immediate hinterlands. Similarly the various attempts by local authorities to administer and control the burgeoning African populations were regionally diverse, determined by highly specific local conditions. This was perhaps no more evident than in their attempts to implement the government policy of urban segregation. For, notwithstanding the 1923 Natives (Urban Areas) Act, which made provision for the establishment of 'native locations' by municipalities, the unfolding of urban segregation in the 1920s was determined more by local labour needs, the patterns of African settlement and resistance, the politics of local authorities and by the geography of land ownership than by overall government policy.[1]

This essay does not aim to provide a comprehensive corrective. It intends, through the narrow prism of the Brakpan case study, to demonstrate how one town's economic, social and political characteristics determined the nature and contours of African settlement. It examines the way in which the specific circumstances of the local authority shaped its responses to government 'native policy' and to local demands for urban segregation.

Brakpan represents an unusual hybrid case study. On the one hand, it shared many characteristics with small platteland towns such as Heidelberg, Kroonstad and Potchefstroom with their large black populations and an almost total absence of manufacturing industries. Like these towns, which were situated on the fringes of agricultural districts, Brakpan also operated as a staging post for migrants, labour tenants and women on their way to the larger employment centres on the Rand. On the other hand, it differed dramatically from these towns because of the large gold mines with their massive migrant African populations living in compounds on the verge of the town. In this, Brakpan was typical of the mining centres of the East and West Rand. The interaction between permanently urbanised Africans and migrants presented particular problems of social control which were not experienced in other small towns. The Brakpan case thus reveals aspects of both small town urbanisation as well as the problems of managing and controlling vast African populations — migrants and urbanites — which were faced by the larger Reef municipalities.

The Emergence of a Permanently Urbanised African Population in Brakpan, 1900-1927

Although the Heidelberg district, in which the Brakpan settlement lay, had long been settled by the African agriculturalists, the first trickle of Africans to the area began in the early 1890s with the opening of the Apex and Brakpan collieries and with the establishment of a transport riders' camp on the Weltevreden Farm. Apart from the coal mines, before the Anglo-Boer War the 1 100 Africans living at the rough settlement could be found working in the transport riders' camp, the 'native stores', Maskell's Hotel, the Rand Central Electrical Company, in boarding-houses and on the farms and homesteads on the outskirts of the village. Just how permanent this settlement was is unclear and it appears that together with the colliery workers some of these early Brakpan residents departed from the Rand with the outbreak of the war.[2]

With the opening of deep-level gold mining on the Far East Rand in the post-war years, the complexion of this small African population changed dramatically. In 1905 Brakpan Mines began sinking operations to produce its first gold in 1908, and the Rand Collieries opened in 1905 to supply cheap coal to fuel this new mine. From this date, a constant stream of migrant African workers arrived at Vitoli, Skilpot, Zweegoed and M'shlambomwa, as Africans designated the gold and coal mines in the region.[3]

The establishment of the gold mining industry also stimulated permanent African urbanisation, for, with the growth of the white mining population and the appearance of a small industrial and commercial sector, new employment opportunities opened for Africans who had made their way to the Reef independently of the mine recruiting agencies. This urbanisation occurred at a comparatively leisurely pace. It was only during the First World War and afterwards that any significant industrial and commercial expansion took place and that the number of permanently settled Africans in the area demonstrably increased. Unlike the neighbouring towns which were transformed during the war by the spurt of industrial growth catalysed by wartime protectionism, Brakpan's development was tied to the expansion of the gold mining industry. In 1914 'State Mines', which was to become the world's most productive gold mine in the 1930s, produced its first ore.[4] In the wake of this development, the white working- class population in the engineering and commercial sectors increased, but unlike that of most towns in the region Brakpan's engineering industry, made up of seven factories, was diminutive. Its productive methods were antiquated and its activities remained entirely subservient to the needs of the local gold mining industry. Even when it came to producing ammunition for the war effort, it was in the workshops of State Mines rather than in the engineering shops that the lead was taken.[5] Unlike the engineering sector of Brakpan's neighbours, that of Brakpan was only able to employ a small number of Africans. Victoria Engineering, for example, employed only two African labourers, while it was only in the 1930s that Davies Engineering began to engage African labour.[6]

More significant as employers of African labour were the municipality (which employed 300 men in the 1920s), a mineral water factory, the town's four brickyards, the crushing works and the timber yards. In addition, intermittent employment could be found by African work-seekers in the rash of building activities which followed the establishment of the municipality of Brakpan in 1920. The commercial sector offered jobs to African men in the three bakeries, the dairies, hotels, general dealers, butcheries, 'kaffir eating houses' and the abbattoir.[7] Finally, servants, gardeners and agricultural labourers worked on the vast agricultural smallholdings which surrounded the town. It is difficult to obtain definitive population figures for the 1920s. One report in 1921 reckoned that there were 14 790 mining men and 462 of their womenfolk living in the mining compounds, and 2 316 non-mining men and women scattered throughout the municipal area. The number of permanently settled Africans living in the town (excluding those squatting on mine properties and smallholdings) was estimated at 2 540 in 1924.[8]

In the 1920s Brakpan's industrial identity and social character was firmly stamped upon it by the huge gold mining industry which had given it birth. Accordingly, the bulk of the African population were migrant miners on the mines or contract workers in the Victoria Falls Power Station (VFP). Yet, alongside these temporary migrations, a constant stream of rural immigrants sought permanent employment and homes in the town. Dislodged by the advance of rural capitalism, which was particularly evident in Natal, the Heidelberg area and the neighbouring Reef farms, rural immigrants were drawn into the smallholdings, kitchens and factories of Brakpan.[9] This phase of urbanisation often entailed the movement of whole labour tenant families from white farms to the town. So marked was this phenomenon that the Native Commissioner of Benoni remarked in 1925 that many 'whole families have established themselves in the area'. He accordingly pressed the local authority to provide accommodation for the local African population on 'a family basis'.[10]

African Occupational Patterns, 1900-1927

Amongst men, employment patterns were characterised by considerable movement between jobs in Brakpan, whether on the mines, the smallholdings or in the town, and between other industrial centres. In the mid-1920s, oscillation between the East Rand and the diamond diggings of the Western Transvaal was not uncommon.[11] Such mobility, though, was usually dependent upon some level of skill or education, and often it was those originally from the more mission-influenced regions who enjoyed this leverage. One early Brakpan resident, E. Maleko, recalled how after leaving the 'family farm' in the Transkei in 1923, because of 'starvation and the "lack of crops"', he had begun his working days on the Rand as a messenger in Boksburg. Shortly after that he took a similar job on the mines in Springs, then he found a post as a policeman in the Springs Native Affairs Department in 1925, before finally winding up as a teacher in a mission school on the West Springs Mine.[12] In general, however, few male work-seekers in Brakpan were literate and thus able to follow such an upward occupational path. Although they did tend to move from job to job, most working men found their scope confined to manual work with the municipality, the engineering factories, in the domestic service sector, the brickyards, quarries, and the few commercial establishments. Thus T. Mosuku, who started off as a labour tenant or 'squatter' on the property of Van Dyk Mines, was successively a labourer at the VPF station, a messenger at Hunt Leuchars and Hepburn Timber warehouse, and again a labourer at E.W. Summersons Engineering. Yet, because of the 'old fashioned' machinery and the proprietors' failure to 'stress safety', Mosuku did not 'last long'.[13] Wages paid to working men in Brakpan were pitiful. While the average wage was estimated at £3 per month, municipal labourers, 'boss boys', and drivers employed by the Council were paid between 2s.3d. and 2s.6d. per day, and manual labourers, 15s. per week.[14]

Female experiences of work were strikingly different. African women in Brakpan (a conservatively estimated 530 in 1926) ranged from the wives and dependents of miners to single women who had escaped from patriarchal controls and poverty of the Reserves, and those who had arrived in the town with their labour tenant families. Because the male wage patterns were determined by the mining industry which paid 'bachelor' wages, the establishment of family life depended upon access to an income beyond the males' principal wage. If some form of urban employment was crucial to family subsistence, it was equally necessary for single women to secure work in the town. Yet the domestic service sector which provided jobs for women in other Rand towns was extremely limited. White householders who did engage domestic labour preferred to employ male 'houseboys', many of whom had previously been miners. According to one informant, few white working-class householders employed full-time female domestic servants and, more often than not, the servant's room in the backyards housed poor white relatives from the rural areas of the Orange Free State and the Transvaal rather than African 'maids'.[15] Where women were employed, this was usually as weekly chars. There is no precise breakdown of the sexual composition of the domestic labour force of the town. However, the gender profile of the juvenile domestic labour force suggests a preponderance of males in this sector. In the 1920s, out of the town's 980 domestic servants, 184 were juveniles (under the age of 15). Of these, 162 were male, while the 22 girls were classified as 'nursemaids'.[16] Given the considerable agitation amongst white residents in the mid-1920s against domestic servants roaming the streets, the fear of 'black peril' incidents, and the oft-expressed preference for men (or women of 'staid' years) as domestic servants,[17] it seems probable that the majority of the remaining 806 servants were male.

Few women obtained formal employment outside the domestic service sector. Where they did, it was often through the operation of kinship networks. When Mrs Motlakeng accompanied her husband from Mount Fletcher in the Transkei to the compound of State Mines in 1925, her brother who worked in a bakery in Brakpan secured work for her there. She was one of three women employed by this concern, and, as she expressed it, 'Many peoples in the kitchen, two ladies and there was me... that's all... boys, boys, all boys, making bread'.[18] As 'kitchen' or domestic work was so hard to come by, and as the material rewards were paltry (Mosuku recalled how his domestic servant mother earned between £1 and £1.5 per month), the only other avenues of economic activity open to women were hawking, selling food, prostitution, and the brewing and selling of beer to workers. It was to the production and sale of beer that most women turned.

One last component of this African population was an extremely small petty bourgeoisie made up of teachers, clerks, interpreters and informal traders and craftsmen. This group was small because opportunities to exercise its talents, skills and training were few. The absence of a location, municipal offices and a local magistrates' court until the latter part of the decade meant that there were few clerical posts in the town. Some educated Africans found work as interpreters and clerks in neighbouring towns and on the mines. Simon Ziswana, an official of the local Transvaal Native Congress (TNC) branch, for example, worked as an interpreter in the magistrates' court of Benoni. The four 'native schools' on the mines in the area provided some scope to trained teachers.[19] If circumstances did not favour the growth of a professional and clerical stratum, neither did they encourage the growth of African entrepreneurship. Capital accumulation by individual Africans received little support from a local government which viewed Africans as temporary sojourners in the town and which was thus anxious to pare the African population to a figure commensurate with its limited labour needs. Likewise, elements of local capital, particularly those engaged in the lucrative 'native trade' with miners, did not look kindly upon the competition that African businessmen, traders and craftsmen were likely to afford. White 'native traders' in the town and concession store owners on the mining properties jealously guarded their business with local miners and had successfully eliminated trading competition from Indian and 'Assyrian' hawkers by pressuring the Council to refuse them trading licences.

Aspirant entrepreneurs were constrained further by the ruling that no Africans could own 'kaffir eating houses' in the town. Craftsmen and traders faced other restrictions. The self-employed required a daily labourer's pass, the granting of which was contingent upon an almost non-existent municipal accommodation.[20]

It was from this small lower middle-class stratum that political leadership in Brakpan was drawn. The branch secretary of the TNC for example, C.H.K. Morotolo, was an interpreter and messenger in the municipal offices. The small rank and file of this organisation also sprang from municipal employees in office work, shop assistants and higher-paid workers hovering on the verges of the African petty bourgeoisie. The signatures appended to a TNC petition to the Council in 1923 probably represented a fair reflection of both the size and social composition of the local TNC and, indeed, of the petty bourgeoisie. Of the twenty-four signatories, twelve signed themselves as municipal employees, six as employees in commercial concerns, two as interpreters, two as mine clerks and one as an 'office boy'. The local African petty bourgeoisie was thus even more 'stunted and repressed' than their counterparts in the larger Reef centres, and they represented a minuscule fraction of the local African population. Both these factors and the scattered nature of African residence until 1927 were seriously to limit the ability of the TNC to appeal to a wider constituency.[21]

However fluid and scattered it may have been, by the 1920s a permanently urbanised African population had emerged in Brakpan. Whereas their white working-class counterparts were settled in modest, neatly laid-out suburbs, the local authority made no provision for the accommodation of permanently settled African workers and their families. This resulted in the profusion of hovels, slumyards, shacks in vacant stands, and squatter settlements on the surrounding smallholdings and mining land. Even as late as 1927, four years after the promulgation of the Natives (Urban Areas) Act, there was no location in the Brakpan municipal area. Until the latter half of this year, many African workers and their families lived in an ensemble of informal living arrangements deemed by a perturbed Government Health Inspector to be 'most unsatisfactory'.[22]

African residential patterns in Brakpan, 1900-1927

In the 1910s and 1920s some 9 100 African gold and coal miners lived in the compounds of State Mines, Brakpan Mines and Apex Colliery. The compounds, designed with the aim of keeping the costs of feeding and housing temporary workers to the barest minimum, were notorious. Workers lived in poorly ventilated rooms with tiered concrete bunks and muddy floors. The food was inadequate and was often used as an instrument of social control. Managers, izinduna and the compound police meted out harsh disciplinary measures, while little supervision was exercised over health and sanitary conditions. When the Government Health Inspector visited the Brakpan Municipality in 1927, for example, after inspecting only one mine compound he judged all the others in the municipal area to be 'satisfactory'.[23] Yet despite the compound's pre-eminent labour-repressive function, workers enjoyed some freedom through their contact with the population which lived outside the compounds on the remote farms and plots surrounding the town and in the backroom shebeens in the town.

Compounds were not the exclusive form of accommodation for miners. In the post-South African War period of labour shortages, as an inducement to attract African workers, compound managers allowed for the development of 'mine locations' where miners and their families were permitted to reside. As a result, by the 1910s, informal locations had mushroomed on vacant mining land throughout the Witwatersrand. As more and more families flocked to the Rand, and as the fledgeling industrial and commercial sector began to develop, the mine locations soon accommodated a far more varied African population. The families of Africans who worked in the towns, as well as single women, soon made these 'mine locations' their homes. Because mining companies did not provide services and because municipalities had no authority over these locations, the living conditions rapidly deteriorated, and these areas of African occupation became notorious for their insanitary nature and for the evolution of a robust drinking culture.[24] The 1906 Report of the East Rand Local Government Commission described the 'dwellings' in these 'irregular mine locations in the immediate vicinity of the mines' of the Far East Rand as 'insanitary shanties', and observed that 'very little control appears to be exercised' over them.[25] One such location had appeared at Rietfontein Colliery close to Brakpan itself, while another had mushroomed on Brakpan Mines. The informal location at Rietfontein had been established on private stands sub-leased to 'Jewish shop keepers of a low type'. Here African families crammed into huts fashioned of old corrugated iron and tin boxes. In 1907 the Director of Native Labour was alarmed to hear allegations that most of the huts were occupied by women 'of a very low class who live by brewing and selling kaffir beer and prostitution'. In the huts and narrow lanes separating them, the police had found barrels and cans of 'kaffir beer in all stages of fermentation', and had reported how during the weekend's 'excessive drinking and debauchery' brawls frequently ended in fatalities.[26]

In most Rand municipalities in the second decade of the century, the 'mine locations' had disappeared as a result of Milnerite policies of reducing the disorganisation in the pattern of settlement of black workers and their families. Some mine locations were constructed at this time. The Boksburg, Germiston and Springs municipalities took over the administration of the 'mine locations' within their municipal boundaries. Although married quarters were constructed on the property of State Mines, a large informal 'location' remained on the Brakpan Mines property. One informant recalled how in the 1920s clusters of 'squatters' camps' peppered the mining land between Brakpan Mine and State Mine, in the plantation which separated the town from State Mine, as well as on the open land in the vicinity of Apex Mines.[27]

Although the compound system did not serve as the exclusive form of worker accommodation even on the mines, it set the standard for the accommodation provided by the major employers of African labour in the town, such as the municipality, Hunt Leuchars and Hepburn, Rowe and Jewell Engineering and Parrack Brickyard. In 1920, soon after attaining municipal status, the Brakpan Town Council constructed its own brick and iron compound adjacent to the municipal stables. Here, three hundred single men lived under conditions similar to those of their miner counterparts. They were issued with staple mine fare and the bunks, floors and sinks were all constructed out of concrete and cement. Like the mining companies, the Council was determined to maintain the costs of housing and feeding their workforce at the lowest possible figure. This meant that not only were the facilities themselves inadequate from the start, but that the Council was not prepared to take any steps to ameliorate the rapidly deteriorating living and health conditions. Thus little was done to prevent the disease caused by the constant plague of flies which bred in the nearby stables. By 1928 the municipal compound was so overcrowded that forty men had to be accommodated temporarily in the produce storeroom. The Council was unable to build an extension to the compound because it could not house the labourers required to do the work.[28]

Conditions and the degrees of controls imposed by managements varied greatly from compound to compound. While controls in the VFP compound were extremely stringent, in the compound attached to Hunt Leuchars and Hepburn timber company the regimen was more relaxed. This company provided communal kitchens in which workers could prepare their own food.[29] Nevertheless, even in these smaller, considerably less tightly regulated compounds, irksome restrictions and regulations inhibited the recreational, family and social lives of their inmates. One of the most irritating rulings was the requirement that workers obtain passes from their employers before leaving the business premises for, unlike the miners and the VFP labourers, most compound workers in the town had families living in Brakpan and in its surrounds.

Some concerns such as the VFP allowed a section of their workforce to construct huts on their premises or provided huts where workers could live with their womenfolk and families. On the whole, however, family accommodation had to be sought elsewhere. Many Brakpan workers lived in the neighbouring locations of Springs and Benoni.[30] This was not ideal, particularly in the absence of municipal transport. In any case, this option closed for many Brakpan employees in 1923 when the Springs Municipality expelled all Africans not working in its magisterial district from the overcrowded location. This exacerbated the growing accommodation shortage in Brakpan as hundreds of expelled workers appeared in the town in search of shelter.[31]

In the absence of municipal accommodation for African families, a variety of informal residential patterns emerged both within and outside the township. Many Africans lived on the vast, sparsely settled agricultural smallholdings on the edges of the town. In 1921 both the South African Land Exploration Company (SALLIES) and the Rand Collieries applied for the subdivision of their lands, Witpoort No. 1 and Rand Collieries respectively, into smallholdings. While these rural plots were originally envisaged as 'healthy residential areas for phthisis victims and sufferers and other pensioners',[32] smallholders other than phthisis victims and pensioners settled here. Artisans, transport riders, dairy farmers and Italian and Portuguese market gardeners supplemented their incomes through keeping chickens, cows and small vegetable gardens.[33] Just as the plots and the nature of activities carried out upon them varied, so too did the 'squatting', employment and tenancy arrangements with African men and women. Despite the fact that the title deeds for both the Rand Collieries and Witpoort Smallholdings legalised the residence of domestic and other servants only, a whole range of 'irregular' tenancy relationships grew up. Usually permission to build shacks and to keep stock and chickens was granted to African labourers and their families in lieu of a cash wage. Some plot-holders allowed miners, workers, petty criminals and beer brewers to squat on their properties in return for rents. Their more law-abiding neighbours frequently charged that the 'shacklords' were raising their monthly incomes by extracting extortionate rentals from their tenants.[34] Even industrial concerns occasionally came under fire from several white smallholders for allowing and encouraging Africans to live on the plots. For example, many white smallholders were outraged when Rowe and Jewell Engineering allowed fourteen African employees to live in two wood and iron sheds on their property on Rand Collieries. They were also angered by a township company which had permitted the construction of 121 huts by Africans on its property at the Rand Collieries. But it was the absentee landlords, mining companies and 'European owners who live in the town' who were most reviled by white plot-holders for sanctioning African settlement, cultivation and stock keeping. Absentee landlords on the Withok Estates, for example, incurred white plot-holder ire by

allowing African 'farming on their own account'. Similarly, because
SALLIES refused to hand over the jurisdiction of open land on
Witpoort Estates to the Council, 'native grazing' in these areas
continued well into the decade. As one smallholder expressed it, the
sparseness of the white population on the plots was 'an invitation to
such acts by Natives'.[35]

The overwhelming impression from the evidence is that this
settlement both on mining land and on individual plots occurred on a
family basis. For many of the families who had arrived here from the
'white farms' of Natal and the Transvaal, the plots served as a
temporary halt and breathing space in the inexorable process of
proletarianisation. One informant recalled how his parents, having
lived and worked 'under feudal conditions' as labour tenants in Natal,
migrated to the plots belonging to Van Dyk Mine, next to the Brakpan
township. As tenants, they continued in agricultural work, 'tilling the
soil, looking after cattle and helping sell vegetables'. They were
allowed to keep their own cattle and goats and, according to their son,
Mosuku, this represented a marked improvement upon their existence
in Natal. When the municipal location was finally built in 1927, they
were removed from the plots, into the location and into wage labour in
the town.[36]

The plots also acted as a staging post for miners, many of whom
established their women and/or families there.[37] The smallholdings
thus accommodated a diverse and heterodox population of Africans in
different stages of proletarianisation. Alongside 'labour tenants' and
independent agriculturalists, lived gardeners, servants, miners, town
workers and their families, beer-brewers and prostitutes.

The density of African settlement on the plots soon became a source
of concern to the local authority and to many white residents. By the
mid-1920s the smallholdings were pockmarked with 'insanitary huts'.
The shacks were uniformly squalid and overcrowded. Made up of
pieces of iron, sacking and other debris, they were dark, damp and
condemned as so 'dilapidated, defectively constructed and overcrowded
that they are injurious and dangerous to health'.[38] The shacks were
generally congested. On one plot owned by a transport rider, for
example, six male drivers, their wives and dependants were all
crowded into two poky huts. Another plot was reputed to
accommodate eighty African people.[39]

Apart from the squalor and the threat of 'contagion' which it posed
to the white residents, the fact that so many squatters were employed

neither by smallholders nor in the town was viewed with alarm. Labour tenants and Africans squatting on vacant mine-owned land were accused of disrupting farming activities on the plots. As one irate plot holder complained,

> Native squatters make free use of grazing in our area. They collect all the cattle from outside areas, dump them on plots and, in consequence, the small amount of grazing available to plot-holders is reduced.[40]

Smallholders also suspected African squatters of agricultural sabotage. One smallholder asserted in the early 1920s that 'these boys [who were] responsible for grass fires here two years past now, destroyed our grazing'.[41] Beer-brewers and prostitutes attracted scores of mineworkers to the plots, seeking some escape from the alienation and exigencies of work in the shebeens.[42] Paul Jensen and '76 others' complained of a case where liquor was 'freely distilled' in the huts on a neighbouring plot, while neighbours of a transport rider, a Van Rensburg, were disturbed by the 'crowds of natives who visit these native girls' on his property, and sight of 'drunken boys' roaming the plots at weekends.[43] Yet despite the plot-holders' fears for the safety of 'white women lonely during the day', surrounded by 'superfluous natives' creating a 'nuisance... through drinking and riotousness', the Council did little to prevent African settlement on the smallholdings. As the smallholdings met the housing needs of many of the town's employees they were loath to take action. The Council's reluctance to prevent African settlement on the plots was also dictated by the inadequacy of the local police force. Municipal parsimony and the remoteness of the plots from the town meant that the smallholdings were never properly policed.[44] Moreover, as a South African Police (SAP) official of the Brakpan-Springs area told the Town Clerk in 1929, criminal proceedings against plot-holders harbouring non-workers on the plots could not be instituted until the area was proclaimed under the Natives (Urban Areas) Act. Free from official harassment, shacks on the smallholdings became the most sought-after form of accommodation. The freedom from prosecution and police interference made the plots particularly attractive to women, the unemployed, the marginalised, and all those who had entered the urban area passless. The plots also provided homes for African workers with their families who, in the absence of municipal accommodation in the town, had little choice but to become 'squatters'.

Formally, the regulations of 1912 of the Brakpan township required that the township

> or any portion of it shall not be transferred, loaned or in any manner assigned or disposed to any coloured person and no coloured person other than the domestic servants of a registered owner or his tenant shall be permitted to reside thereon or in any manner occupy the same.[45]

In practice this regulation was rarely observed, and hundreds of Africans lived, often with the approval and permission of their employers, in backrooms in the town. The mineral factory, P. Sullivan and Sons, for example, was 'in the habit of allowing [our] boys to rent rooms in the township'.[46] Quarters could be found by African families in back rooms, garages, above shops and business premises, in crude shelters on the vacant stands in the town, and in the surrounds of the VFP pan. By the mid-1920s slum yards began to develop where the families crammed into 'grossly overcrowded backrooms' which abutted on to concrete courtyards. After surveying such establishments in 1925, the Government Health Inspector urged that:

> The building of a municipal location is a pressing matter as the conditions under which native employees in the town are at present housed is most unsatisfactory and unhygienic. They are crowded together in backrooms of private persons and sometimes into rooms opening on to yards as is the case behind the butcher shops.[47]

Yet, despite this and similar other exhortations to rid the town of families residing in such conditions, from the mid-1920s the Council failed to evict permitless Africans from the town. This was due partly to the fear of political militancy that such action might provoke, and partly to the Council's inability to construct a location. Both these issues are dealt with later in this article. The following section turns to the range of white fears centring on unregulated African residence which fed into the demands for urban segregation.

As was the case in most urban areas in which fear of epidemics supplied the rationale for the establishment of early African locations,[48] the 'sanitation syndrome' loomed large in the segregationist discourse in Brakpan. The rapid growth of an African population squeezed into virtually every nook and cranny in the township gave rise to intense concern amongst the townsfolk about the health dangers it posed to the white population. In 1924 J. Bezuidenhout and 536 others attempted to take legal action against the Council to persuade it to build a location. 'The natives squatting in the back rooms and shops', their legal representative wrote, 'is nothing short of a danger to the health of the community.'[49] In addition to the widespread concern about the dangers to public health posed by uncontrolled African residence in the town, white citizens became alarmed by a vigorous drinking culture which had emerged, and by the prevalence of 'Sunday quarrelling and fighting' amongst African workers. The brawling and 'noise', they asserted, invariably occurred in the 'aftermath of the previous night's drink parties'.[50] The drunken brawls prompted a deputation of the town's clergymen to the Council in 1921. These gentlemen impressed upon the Council the necessity of providing municipal services and amenities for the local African population. 'This', they urged, would 'direct natives from the deteriorating influences' - beer-brewers and prostitutes who plied their trades in the town's backrooms. Especially vociferous was the invective against the back rooms of Power Street, a street notorious on the East Rand as a 'native trading zone' where all the evils of drink and sex were allegedly concentrated. These stores were owned by 'a low class of European', Jews of Russian descent who catered to an almost exclusively African miner clientele. The shopkeepers rented out the rooms at the back of their premises to African women. To the Council's concern, for the sake of inflated rentals and the custom which the women drew to their stores, the store owners

> tolerate and in the majority of instances... countenance the brewing of intoxicating liquor by innumerable native women who reside in their backyards, ostensibly as their servants.[51]

The back-room brothels and shebeens of Power Street acted as a magnet for miners, drawing them into the heart of the town. Power Street traders ignored official censure of the activities in the backrooms, and indeed effectively encouraged them. In order to ensure miner-patronage of their stores, the traders sent lorries to the compounds to transport customers to their stores and to the brothels.[52] The traders' refusal to co-operate with the police in their efforts to root out prostitution and beer-brewing gave rise to an indignant campaign which, because of the ethnic exclusivity of the 'native trade', acquired a bitter anti-Semitic edge. The traders were accused of having 'no sense of responsibility', and of being 'out for their own ends only'.[53] White residents and churches were constantly outraged by the 'carousing and immoral conduct' which spilled out of these 'dens' and into the streets of the town. The Apostoliese Geloof Sending,[54] for example, was shocked by displays of public indecency:

> Native girls can frequently be seen entering these premises. Under the pretext of doing minor work, they emerge with goods under their dresses and these are distributed to the natives in the immediate vicinity. Subsequent acts of indecency take place and natives expose their persons to the women and children.[55]

But public pressure, the warnings of compound managers, the strictures of clerics, and regular police investigations had no effect on the gathering of large numbers of African men and women in Power Street. To the Council's chagrin, there was no law under which they could successfully prosecute the traders.[56] Power Street thus came to constitute one of the most vivid symbols of the dangers of an ungoverned African population living in the midst of the town. Pervasive drunkenness, sex across the colour line, and crime all provoked a wave of segregationist demands in the 1920s.

These phenomena were also in part a consequence of the large numbers of African men in domestic service. A particularly gory 'black peril' case in 1927, in which a 'houseboy' assaulted his mistress, galvanised a group of white residents into renewing pressure on the Council to construct a location.[57] A further outgrowth of the male dominated domestic service sector was the *amalaita* gangs of black servants.[58] While these gangs provided male domestic servants with a measure of collective security in a world of low wages, 'black peril' witch hunts, and unemployment, the white townsfolk regarded them as a threat to public peace. One of the early white residents recalled how *amalaita* gangs, in their distinctive white garb and *takkies*, 'gathered in the area of the pan for weekly fights' in the early 1920s.[59] Alarmed by large numbers of domestic servants abroad at night, the residents called for a curfew bell. It was to be placed in the Market Square to ring at night at 8.45pm and again at 9.00pm, 'so that all kaffir servants should know to be in at that time'.[60] Ideally, however, it was felt that local segregation and the establishment of a municipal location would be the best means of reducing the ubiquitous crime, noise and brawling.

One of the themes in the segregationist discourse of white residents was the prevalence of crime in the region. Historically, the Far East Rand had earned for itself a certain notoriety for criminality, and from the turn of the century the isolated small town had become a target for a growing band of black criminals. The problem of crime in the region, explained the Deputy Commissioner of Police in 1912, was 'probably due to the Cinderella Prison [being] situated in that district' and the 'large numbers of seasoned native criminals imprisoned there, (whose release constantly adds to the ranks of native habitual criminals on the East Rand where they are to be found in large numbers)'.[61] Charles Van Onselen's work has shown how both the Cinderella Prison in Boksburg and the mining compounds of the East Rand disgorged squads of 'Ninevites', the secret organisation of robbers and criminals which preyed on the Brakpan-Benoni-Heidelberg district.[62] In 1911 and 1912 the Heidelberg area was in the grip of a housebreaking epidemic, and in 1912 it was estimated that four to five hundred robberies and housebreaking incidents had occurred in the area between Germiston and Springs.[63]

Although the Ninevites had been dealt a severe blow by a series of state measures by 1914, the turbulent post-war years witnessed a brief resurgence of criminal activity as the value of real wages declined and the cost of living soared. This in turn led to the growth in numbers of African criminals and the swelling of prison populations.[64] The increase in crime in the early 1920s may also have resulted from the decline of the metalworking industry.[65] White officialdom ascribed much of the crime in Brakpan in the 1920s to the establishment of a new location in Springs which had resulted in the exodus of 'bad characters' from that municipality into Brakpan. Many of these criminals secreted themselves into 'odd corners' in Brakpan and on the vast, unregulated smallholdings.[66] Police resources were stretched to their limit, and as a result of the shortage of manpower valuable policing time was drained in routine tasks such as the preparation of cases, framing charge sheets and summonses, appearing in court, and the typing of preparatory records. As the African population was so widely distributed, it was impossible to carry out effective searches and to restrain black criminal activity. It was widely believed, particularly by the police, that the high levels of criminal activity, which had created 'a feeling of insecurity with residents',[67] were due to the absence of a location and of the controls over the influx and efflux of 'undesirables' that segregation was believed to ensure.[68]

The wave of crime in the early 1920s was one of the responses to the changing conditions which stimulated a crescendo of political radicalism on the Rand from 1918 to 1920. This in turn caused a systematic rethinking of 'native policy' in the Union and, in particular, in the urban areas of the Witwatersrand.[69] With the start of inflation in 1917, popular ferment began in the compounds and locations of the East Rand. Prices of commodities rocketed while African wages remained stationary. In the underground caverns of the mines around Brakpan, white officials were disturbed by rumours of a proposed 'native uprising' in Natal to which Zulu miners, summoned by their chiefs, were supposedly to return. In the following year a boycott of mine stores commenced, with occasional acts of violence and retribution against concession-store owners. Two years later a mineworkers' strike of 71 000 black miners paralysed the mines in and around Brakpan.[70] The shock waves were rapidly transmitted to other concerns. The VFP management, for example, complained that 'the presence of agitators' had caused the 'unsettled state of natives at this compound'.[71] In Brakpan Mines 300 white miners struck over dismissals, leaving 3 500 of a 4 500-strong black workforce standing idle. At State Mines, African workers were found to be 'restless', and reports of 'agitators' who had 'been going round telling people to strike' fed the growing fears of mine-owners of the subversive effects of the interaction between town dwellers and compound workers.[72]

Apart from the outbursts of resistance by miners, the period between 1918 and 1920 also witnessed the most intense radicalisation of urban black political leadership in South Africa before the Second World War. Under the impact of working-class militancy, the largely petty bourgeois TNC joined hands with the industrial working class in a brief display of mass class action.[73] The widespread disaffection resulted in a Reef-wide TNC-organised 'shilling a day' and anti-pass campaign. Discontent over living conditions significantly infused the ferment. Throughout the Rand, material conditions were squalid and depressed. The conditions in Johannesburg, the centre of TNC activity, are well known. On the East Rand, these were perhaps worse, and it is therefore small wonder that the campaign of 1918 evoked such an intense response in this region. Most East Rand locations had been constructed adjacent to municipal sewage depositing sites. Under austere location regimes, residents were subjected to arbitrary measures such as continual liquor and pass raids.[74] It was in Benoni, Brakpan's parent municipality, that the most regular demonstrations and outbursts occurred. This 'storm centre of the Reef' witnessed bitter struggles with crowds stoning the police. In response, all white constables in the area were summoned to round up twenty African males suspected of travelling through the district spreading disaffection among the 'mine natives'. In Springs similar episodes of crowd clashes with the police were reported, and in Boksburg meetings in the location similarly culminated in a fracas with sixty arrests.

Although there is one reference in the documentation to a Brakpan resident, a Mr Batho, who was sentenced to five months in prison for his part in the 'strike against pass laws' in 1919,[75] the municipal and central government records reveal little about the effects of this wave of protest on the Brakpan township. It is difficult from the available material to confirm whether local Africans and the TNC branch participated in the campaign. That Brakpan and Benoni were officially regarded as one and the same might explain the lacunae in the documentation. It is more likely, though, that the documentary silence reflects a situation of political quiescence in Brakpan township. A TNC branch had indeed been established, with its offices in Northdene Avenue in the centre of the township. However, because of its relatively conservative and cautious leadership, the small size of its membership, the scattered nature of African settlement, the absence of working-class pressure from below, and the fact that Brakpan Africans were free from some of the most irksome controls which characterised urban life elsewhere, it was hardly militant. Although the documents record TNC requests for public meetings in the public park in the 1920s and although, according to an informant, regular TNC meetings over the need for housing were held near the 'Jew Stores' at State Mine,[76] dealings with the local authority were characterised by mutual courtesy. There is no evidence of militant grass-roots pressure on this organisation for a more radical and combative political stance.

Nevertheless, the lessons of the recent upheavals in most Reef towns were not lost upon Brakpan's white citizenry, and from 1920, the year in which independent municipal status was bestowed upon the town, attempts to provide a location began to assume an urgency amongst the newly appointed municipal officialdom. The central government's Native Affairs Department also became perturbed that Brakpan was the only Rand town without a 'native location'. In 1920

Major H.S. Bell, the Native Sub-Commissioner of the Witwatersrand, warned the Brakpan Town Council of the dangers attendant upon further dilatoriness in the provision of a location.[77] The upsurge of militancy on the Rand had made Bell particularly aware of the social consequences of 'native slums' and of the possibilities of African middle-class disaffection resulting from government neglect of their needs.[78] He impressed upon the Council the urgency of implementing government policy of segregation which he contended was aimed to 'create an environment calculated to raise the moral tone of the native and make him a useful member of society instead of a potential criminal'.[79] In addition, from this date local TNC pressure on the Council began to mount steadily. From 1920 to 1923 the congestion, crime and drunkenness of Africans in the township had assumed such alarming proportions that the police and magistrates initiated a fresh wave of harassment in their efforts to ferret out criminals and beer-brewers.[80] It was in this situation that the construction of a location became an increasingly attractive solution to many of the TNC adherents, and this in turn prompted the first TNC deputation to the Town Council in 1922. Because of the generalised chaos in the town caused by the 1922 white miners' strike, however, the Director of Native Labour, Colonel S.M. Pritchard, refused to allow this meeting to take place. One year later, however, the Council agreed to meet a TNC deputation. At the meeting, the delegates informed the Council of the hardships endured by Africans in the town and of the urgency of building a location. As the Council reported, the deputation told them that:

> At present natives are being arrested in a wholesale manner and are being fined by the magistrate for living in the township without permits from the standholders. He (Ziswana, the TNC branch chairman) further stated that the Springs location would be closed in approximately three months' time and that hundreds of natives would as a consequence be rendered homeless.[81]

Following this deputation, Ziswana requested permission for the delegation to sit in on the meetings of the Finance Committee in order to reach some agreement on the solution to the housing problem in Brakpan.[82] While the Council did not grant this request, it conceded that until a location had been constructed no further prosecutions of permitless Africans in the township should be carried out, 'unless in the opinion of the Chief Sanitary Inspector, a distinct nuisance is being created and that they be requested to exercise discretion in the matter'.[83]

By the mid-1920s then, for a variety of motives, the call for segregation was being voiced in several quarters in Brakpan, black and white. Some of the calls originated in the extreme exclusivism of the white working-class inhabitants who complained that 'natives' walking along footpaths and gathering in front of Maskell's Hotel were making it 'impossible for Europeans to pass on sidewalks'. Beneath the racism, however, lurked a very real dread of permanent African settlement and acquisition of skills in the town. The plea for segregation was also motivated by philanthropic concern over the squalor, poverty and disease which bred in the town's slumyards and smallholdings. Others simply believed that the ubiquitous crime, prostitution, and illicit drinking, and the potential for working-class militancy could best be contained in a municipally controlled location. For many African workers, too, who lived in the single-sex compounds or back-room hovels, a location with family accommodation seemed infinitely preferable to the prevailing situation and was actively called for by the TNC. Yet even after 1923, when the state made provision for the construction of municipal locations, the haphazard, informal patterns of African residence persisted as the municipality struggled to overcome local obstacles in order to implement government policy.

Brakpan and Municipal Segregation

The story of the location goes back to the turn of the century, and it is to this topic that this article now turns. Although the development of the Brakpan settlement began to occur in a more purposeful and planned direction in the post-Anglo-Boer War years, the Milnerite social planning for 'orderly settlement' passed this crude colliery settlement over. It was in this period that 'poor whites' were winnowed out from the popular districts of most Reef towns and that Africans were settled in locations administered by local authorities. In the towns of Springs, Germiston and Boksburg on the East Rand, the 'mine locations' were taken over and run by the newly established municipalities.[84] By contrast, no action was taken by Benoni, Brakpan's parental municipality, to settle Brakpan's African inhabitants in an 'orderly' manner. This was largely because the numbers of Africans living in the Brakpan settlement did not warrant such consideration, and because the growth and extension of Brakpan beyond a residential area for white miners had never been envisaged. With more foresight, the Transvaal Coal and Trust Company, the owners of Brakpan Mine and the company responsible for the laying out of the township in 1912, had secured surface rights under the provision of Section 71 of the 1908 Transvaal Act for a site for a future 'native location' in 1911.[85] Yet, when the Brakpan township was laid out and established in 1912, no action was taken to establish a 'native location'. The proposed location site was considered unsuitable. Situated a mere 300m from the town it was felt to be uncomfortably close to a white residential area. At this stage, prior to the war-time growth of the town and of the African population, Benoni officialdom felt little urgency in looking for a better site.

In the war and post-war years, however, the failure of the Benoni Town Council to segregate the town led to extensive local white dissatisfaction with the Benoni Municipality. Indeed, in its secession campaign of 1916 to 1920 one of the charges of neglect which Brakpan ratepayers flung at the Benoni Municipality was the latter's failure adequately to control and regulate the local African population. In 1915 little heed had been paid to local agitation for the establishment of a separate pass office for Brakpan, and in 1920 the Brakpan Ratepayers' Association instituted an enquiry into the absence of a location.[86]

Although a separate new municipality considerably more receptive to white ratepayer interests was established in Brakpan in 1920, it too failed to take steps to segregate the town. Many factors contributed to this recalcitrance. Most important were municipal penury, the attitudes of the chief employers of African labour towards African settlement, white ratepayer opposition to subsidising African housing, the confusing and overlapping jurisdictions and responsibilities of municipal, provincial and central authorities, and the reluctance of the chief landowners in the region to part with surface rights for the purposes of establishing a location.

One of the chief problems faced by the municipality was its narrow fiscal base and the antipathy of the dominant economic groups in the town towards subsidising the housing of a permanently urbanised African workforce. Although mining capital owned vast tracts of land within the municipal boundaries, it was exempted from municipal rates on the land it owned, paying tax only on buildings and improvements to the land. All revenue from taxes and mineral values was channelled towards the central state rather than in the direction of the local authority. Nor did the mining industry, operating under severe cost constraints, favour permanent African residence in the urban area and the expenses this would entail. Thus not only was the local authority deprived of the wealth generated by the mining industry but also, as the largest landowner, mining capital was able to dictate to it the use of urban space. Throughout the 1920s mining companies were successfully able to block the Council's attempts to find land for an alternative site for an African location. It was only in 1926 that the government agreed to persuade the mining companies to part with their surface rights for the purposes of a location.

Manufacturing capital would have had a considerably greater interest in promoting a stabilised, adequately housed workforce, but it was unwilling to supply the necessary financial resources. As discussed earlier, the manufacturing sector was extremely undeveloped. The actual labour forces of factories were small and most employers, with the exception of larger concerns such as Rowe and Jewell and Hunt Leuchars and Hepburn which provided compounds for their workers, were content to see their employees living either on their business premises, in rooms in the town or on smallholdings.

From 1920, when Brakpan became an independent municipality, the onerous financial burden of the administration of the town fell exclusively upon the shoulders of the white ratepayers, an almost entirely working-class constituency. Part of the agreement upon seceding from Benoni was that Brakpan would raise £14 000 to pay the Star Life Assurance in respect of a loan obtained by Benoni (in return for taking over the assets within the Brakpan municipal area valued at £33 988).[87] In addition, the new local authority had to construct municipal buildings and a water and electricity scheme, provide safety measures at the Springs railway crossing, pay officials' salaries, and buy equipment, livestock and vehicles. Because the loans which the provincial Administrator was prepared to sanction for these purposes were regarded as inadequate,[88] rates were high, particularly so for a white working-class population subject to the vagaries of unemployment and poverty. In 1922, the year of the white miners' strike and of widespread unemployment, the collection of rates was well-nigh impossible and was one of the reasons given by the Administrator when he refused to authorise further loans to the new Town Council.[89] In 1926 the burden of rates weighed even more heavily upon the population when site values were increased by 1d., only to be reduced in 1937.[90] Thus while the white population desired

tighter controls on the African workforce and the establishment of a
location, the extra financial responsibility of housing the African
labour force was unwelcome, particularly as the chief employers of
black labour appeared to be abrogating all such responsibility.

Most importantly, the political complexion of this constituency
governed their attitudes to subsidising black housing and to permanent
black settlement in the town. This was a mining and artisan
community to whose interests black urbanisation and the consequent
acquisition of industrial skills were inimical. The militancy of this class
against the encroachment of black labour was violently and
dramatically expressed in the 'Rand Rebellion' of 1922. The violence
perpetrated against scabs, the attacks on African miners, and the
armed conflict on Brakpan Mine in which twenty-three people were
wounded and eight killed, marked Brakpan as one of the storm centres
of the revolt. So severe were the attacks on black miners that on
Brakpan Mine 10 000 black men armed with sharpened jumpers
threatened to settle accounts with the strikers.[91] In the 1924
parliamentary elections the successful Labour Party candidate,
'General Waterston', leader of the Brakpan 'hooligan commando', was
swept into power with his promises of protection from the
competition of black labour.[92] Three years later in the municipal
election, Dai Davis, the Labour Party candidate, won on a platform
opposing the influx of Africans into the town. If elected, Davis
promised, he would see to it that the municipality obtained 'further
powers to prohibit Natives coming into the municipal areas unless
they have work to come to'.[93] In a poor municipality where the
interests of a white working class predominated it was unlikely that the
local authority would be willing to undertake the financial
responsibilities for subsidising the reproduction of a permanently
urbanised African working class. The financial deadlock was only
resolved in 1925, when the Central Housing Board extended a loan for
location purposes. But conflicts over the siting of the location would
yet delay the establishment of a location for a further two years.

In 1920 it was hoped that a joint location could be established with
the Springs Municipality. It was a much favoured idea, particularly for
property owners who had no desire to see the emergence of an African
location as close to the town as the original plan had envisaged.[94]
However, when overtures were made to the Springs Town Council, it
was learned that this local authority had already chosen a site for their
own location, one which the Brakpan Council deemed 'unsuitable'.[95]

The town engineer was now instructed to design a location for the original site on Weltevreden farm. By April 1921 these plans were completed and the Public Health Committee met with Major Bell, the Assistant Director of Native Labour to discuss the establishment of the proposed location. At the meeting, Bell stressed both the importance of situating the location at least one and a half miles from the town, and the necessity of providing space for expansion so that the problems of teeming slums which characterised areas of African residence in Springs and Johannesburg could be obviated.[96] The Brakpan No. 5 or Weltevreden site, however, met neither of these requirements. After war-time population growth, its 32 morgen was considered too small to house an estimated population of 4 000. It was also situated too close to the township boundary. No expansion could take place without the permission of Brakpan Mine which owned the farm Weltevreden. According to the mine management, the site was 'too close to the township and would therefore be a great source of trouble to both the Mine and Township Administration'.[97] The management of this mine was fearful that a nearby location with the attractions of liquor and women 'would lead to serious disorganisation of mining operations and further losses'.[98] Other obstacles to the siting of the location rapidly arose. Any expansion of the location would block further growth of white residential areas as well as the development of the proposed provincial hospital, while property owners stressed the likelihood of a location depressing the value of their properties.

Because of the overwhelming opposition to the site, the Council endeavoured to find an alternative. They attempted to secure a site on the Schapensrust of Koolbult No. 13 farm, an area of 100 morgen situated 2 miles (about 3,5 kilometres) from the town. This site was favoured by the Council, the Department of Native Affairs and Pritchard, the Director of Native Labour. It had numerous advantages above that of the original site of Weltevreden. It was considerably larger, and from a white viewpoint a more convenient distance from the town. The old NZASM railway station at Schapensrust would be available for immediate use to transport workers to town, thereby relieving the Council of the responsibility of providing bus transport. Finally, the Rand Water Board pipeline in the immediate vicinity could supply water to the location. So enamoured was the Council of this site that a further plan for a location to accommodate Africans, coloureds and Indians was drawn up and approved, and applications were made for the surface rights of 61 morgen on this property.[99] Yet the

Schapensrust option was foreclosed in 1921 when the Mining Commissioner of Boksburg announced that he could not support a request for a permit for the surface rights as Brakpan Mine held the coal rights on Koolbult on behalf of the Consolidated Mines Selection Company and was not prepared to cede the necessary permit for building a location to the Council.[100]

Another lobby, the shopkeepers of Power Street, also voiced opposition to the Koolbult site. In the expectation that a location would be built at Weltevreden, they had established a string of shops on the road leading to that site. In a petition signed by the Power Street traders, it was asserted that if a location was to be built at Koolbult bankruptcy would stare them in the face.[101]

By this date, however, the Council was determined to continue negotiating for the Koolbult site and to establish a location there as soon as possible. Yet, at this stage in 1922, the Director of Native Labour advised them to delay further action until the draft Natives (Urban Areas) Bill had been passed by Parliament. Pritchard hoped that this would open the way for government pressure to be exerted upon the owners of Koolbult.[102]

But by the time the much awaited legislation made its appearance it was too late. By 1923 the Witpoort farm on the borders of the Koolbult property had been carved up into smallholdings and a location on the fringes of the plots was now considered inappropriate. As Councillor Price expressed it, 'it would encroach on the residential privileges of the plot-holders at Witpoort by reason of its abutting on the estate'.[103] Given the absence of other alternatives and the congestion in the town, attention shifted back to the original site, Weltevreden. In the following year the Council applied to the Mining Commissioner for the release of a further 30 morgen adjacent to the proposed location site at Weltevreden.[104] By this date, the Minister of Native Affairs was persuaded that 'the establishment of a Native location is an urgent necessity', and agreed to lend his support in negotiating for more land at Weltevreden.[105]

Although ministerial intervention in the matter resulted in the purchase of an additional 30 morgen for the proposed location from Parrack Quarry, the Council and the Department still had to overcome the implacable opposition of the mines which now closed ranks. New State Areas Mine which lay on the border between Brakpan and Springs and which was next to the Weltevreden site insisted that with the establishment of a location at Weltevreden, mine natives would be able to obtain liquor in the location, with the result that drunkenness amongst natives would cause serious disorganisation of work on the mine with consequent financial loss to the Company and this government.[106]

Its management raised the spectre of 'tribal fights' being staged by 'natives under the influence of liquor' and of rampant sexual activity which they asserted could only result in venereal epidemics. They recalled how the patronage of miners of the entertainment in the old Springs location had undermined the efficiency of mine labour. Indeed, so determined was New State Areas to prevent African miners from visiting the shebeens that it contributed £2 000 towards that location's removal. Brakpan Mine chimed in, opposing not only the granting of additional land for the location site but also the siting of the location there at all.[107] The SAP, who had long advocated the establishment of a location, were also critical of the site. Engaged in an interminable battle against the liquor trade in the Springs location, the police objected to the verdant plantation near the Weltevreden site which they believed was 'ideal for liquor smuggling'. They predicted that control of the illicit liquor sales would be impossible if a location with a population of 4 000 was to be placed alongside compounds housing 13 499 single black men.[108]

By this time, though, despite mining capital's intransigence and the police's objections to the site, the Council was determined to establish a location as soon as possible at Weltevreden. Plans for the location were already far advanced, and the Central Housing Board had agreed to grant £15 000 for the construction of the first houses.[109] A deputation of councillors had a meeting with the Minister of Native Affairs in November 1925 to secure his support in siting the location at Weltevreden. The Minister, however, felt that the obstacles in the way of the Weltevreden site were too great, and urged the Council to explore the viability of the farm Rietfontein No. 4, land owned by Apex Mine.[110] Although the Council duly entered negotiations for the release of this land, at a Council meeting in December 1925 it was resolved that, notwithstanding the objections of New State Areas and the police, the provincial and central government authorities were to be convinced of the urgent necessity of the immediate erection of a location at Weltevreden.[111] Early in the following year, at a meeting with the Secretary of Native Affairs, J.F. Herbst, the Councillors told him of the pressing urgency of bringing the question of the location site to a settlement as the overcrowding of Natives in the town was a serious menace to the public of Brakpan.[112]

More correspondence and wrangling ensued until finally, on 26 October, the Council was informed that the Department of Native Affairs would now assist them in executing the Weltevreden scheme and in obtaining additional land from Brakpan Mine.[113] A further 32 morgen was thus acquired from Brakpan Mine and, although only 62 morgen in area, the Brakpan Native Location was finally established in the final months of 1927.

With the building of the location at Weltevreden in 1927, the way was clear for the resettlement of African residents. Families and single men and women on the smallholdings, shacks, backyards and backrooms were dislodged and herded into municipal houses. A distinct new identity was belatedly bestowed upon a hitherto scattered and fragmented African community and the conditions laid for the growth of a new urban culture and new forms of association. A satisfied white population and Town Council believed the new location to be the panacea of the town's social problems. It brought about the final regimentation and control óf the town's labouring classes and the mechanisms required for the expulsion of the 'dangerous classes', the unemployed and 'idle and dissolute'. The local authority could also now bask in the moral comfort that, in segregating the town, the loftiest human ideals had been realised. As the *Brakpan Herald* reflected,

It stands as an axiom that, when natives are housed well, they will respond to civilising influences and not only be healthier and happier but render better service. But looked at from the higher point of view, it is but a measure not only of selfish policy, but of justice and humanity to see to it that these people whose wages are small and outlook so limited should have a chance to live decently and to make the best of themselves.[114]

Notes

1 See J. Cohen, A Pledge for Better Times: The Local State and the Ghetto, Benoni, 1930-1938, BA Hons Dissertation, University of the Witwatersrand, 1982; D. Gilfoyle, An Urban Crisis: The Town Council, Industry and the Black Working Class in Springs, 1948-

1958, BA Hons Dissertation, University of the Witwatersrand, 1983; P. Bonner, 'Family, Crime and Political Consciousness on the East Rand, 1939-1955', Paper presented to the History Workshop, University of the Witwatersrand, Feb. 1987.

2 F.J. Nothling, Die Ontstaansgeskiedenis van Brakpan, 1904-1922, MA Dissertation, University of Pretoria, 1969, Ch.1, and 'The Story of Brakpan', Unpublished manuscript; S. Webster, 'The Brakpan Story', Unpublished manuscript, pp. 1-5; *Star*, 15 July 1895.

3 For the history of the gold mining industry in this region, see Nothling, Die Ontstaansgeskiedenis van Brakpan, Chs 1 and 4; Transvaal Archives Depot (TAB), Secretary for Native Affairs (SNA), 8 852/1902; F.J. Nothling, 'Die Vestiging van Nie-blankes in Brakpan 1888-1930', *Kleio* 2 (May 1973), pp. 15-27, and 'The Story of Brakpan', Ch. 14.

4 Nothling, 'The Story of Brakpan', p. 23.

5 J.X. Smith, *Brakpan-Transvaal*, (Johannesburg, 1970), p. 23.

6 F. Stark (ed.), *Achievement Brakpan 1919-1952*, pamphlet issued by the Town Council of Brakpan and the Chamber of Commerce, 1952; Interview with S. Webster, Dec. 1986.

7 J.X. Smith, Brakpan-Transvaal, pp.36-41; Central Archives Depot (CAD), Brakpan Municipal Records (BMR), P4/142,. Report on Systematic Health Inspections of Brakpan Municipality by Dr E. Cluver, 24, 30 June 1927 (Cluver's inspection).

8 CAD, BMR C2/2, Town Clerk to Director of Census, 18 Jan. 1921; ibid., Brakpan Census, 1921, Provisional figures forwarded by the Assistant Resident Magistrate, Benoni, per telephone; CAD, BMR, H2/117 Engineer to Town Clerk, 3 Dec. 1926.

9 Archives of the Church of the Province of South Africa, University of the Witwatersrand Library, Historical and Literary Papers, AD 1438, Box 2, Evidence of Archdeacon Hill to the Native Economic Commission, 1931; Report of the Native Economic Commission, 1930-1932, U.G. 22, 1932; H. Bradford, 'A Taste of Freedom: Capitalist Development and Response to the ICU in the Transvaal Countryside', in B. Bozzoli (ed.), *Town and Country in the Transvaal*, (Johannesburg, 1983), pp. 128-50.

10 CAD, Native Affairs Department (NTS) 179/313, Native Sub-Commissioner, Benoni to Brakpan Municipality, *c* 1925.

11 See the case of Elliot Tsheleza in CAD, Court Appeal Records, Brakpan Municipality v. Elliot Tsheleza, TPD 184/29.

12 Interview with E. Maleko, Tsakane, Jan. 1985.

13 Interview with T. Mosuku, Tsakane, Jan. 1985.

14 CAD, Benoni Municipal Records 2/2/1, East Rand Municipal Conference, 15 Feb. 1921, Native Wages.

15 Interview with S. Webster, Brakpan, Dec. 1986.

16 CAD, Government Native Labour Bureau (GNLB) 323 84/20/243, Return Showing Numbers of Daily Labourers and Native Juveniles Employed in Labour Districts on the Reef, 30 Nov. 1922.

17 CAD, BMR N3/1, Mrs Lewis to Superintendent, Brakpan Native Location, 19 July 1923. (As no location existed in 1923, this and similar letters regarding the employment of African labour were transmitted to the Town Clerk.)

18 Interview with Mrs Motlakeng, Tsakane, Jan. 1985.

19 CAD, BMR P4/142, Cluver's inspection.

20 CAD, Department of Mines (MNW) 364 9/12, Mine Traders' Association Interview with Minister in regard to: (1) Trading by hawkers to the detriment of concession stores, (2) Mines trading in compounds, (3) Trades carried on in recreation halls, (4) Application for the appointment of a special Inspector under the Mining Commissioner who shall inspect compounds and generally look after the trading question, 1912; CAD, GNLB 323 84/20/243, Native Sub-Commissioner, Benoni, to Director of Native Labour, Johannesburg, 12 Oct. 1926.

21 CAD, BMR N3/1, Petition from Simon Peter Ziswana and twenty-six others. For a discussion on the Rand's African petty bourgeoisie, see P. Bonner, 'The Transvaal Native Congress: The Radicalisation of the Black Petty Bourgeoisie on the Rand', in S. Marks and R. Rathbone (eds), *Industrialisation and Social Change in South Africa*, (London, 1982), pp. 270-313.

22 CAD, BMR P4/142, Cluver's inspection.

23 Ibid.

24 S. Moroney, 'Mine Married Quarters: The Differential Stabilisation of the Witwatersrand Workforce 1900-1920', in Marks and Rathbone (eds), *Industrialisation and Social Change in South Africa*, pp. 259-69; A. Potgieter, Die Swartes aan die Witwatersrand, 1900-1933, PhD Thesis, Rand Afrikaans University, pp. 126-53.

25 Report of the East Rand Local Government Commission, 1906.

26 CAD, GNLB 1 2192/07, Government Native Labour Bureaux

Director to Secretary for Native Affairs, 17 Dec. 1907.

27 CAD, BMR A3/2, Assessment Rate: Remission of Mine Property; Interview with Webster.

28 CAD, BMR C/26, Town Clerk to Chairman of the Finances and General Purposes Committee, 5 April 1928; CAD, BMR P4/15, Minute of Meeting of the Finances and General Purposes Committee, 14 Sept. 1920; CAD, BMR P4/142, Cluver's inspection.

29 Interview with Webster.

30 CAD, BMR P4/15, Minutes of the Meeting of the Finances and General Purposes Committee of SAR Native Employees, Brakpan (undated); CAD, GNLB 1 2192/07 Government Native Labour Bureaux Director to Secretary of Native Affairs, 17 Dec. 1907; CAD, BMR C2/2, Town Clerk to Director of Census, 18 Jan. 1921; CAD, BMR P4/15, Minutes of the Meeting of the Finances and General Purposes Committee, 17 Aug. 1920.

31 CAD, BMR N3/1, Ziswana to Town Clerk, 22 March 1923.

32 Nothling, 'The Story of Brakpan', p. 81; CAD, BMR A4/6, Secretary, Townships Board, to Town Clerk, 26 Nov. 1921

33 CAD, BMR A4/6, Minutes of a Special Council Meeting, 26 Feb. 1926.

34 CAD, BMR A4/6, Evidence of D.H. Bester to the Commission of Enquiry into the Excision of the Witpoort and Rand Collieries Smallholdings, 21 July 1921. The rents charged to African tenants helped smallholders pay rates and licence fees which were seen as particularly onerous for artisans earning an estimated 20s. a day. Also see CAD, BMR A4/6, Minutes of a Special Meeting of the Town Council, 23 Feb. 1926.

35 The account of 'irregular' African settlement on the plot is based on the correspondence and evidence in file CAD, BMR A4/6, Excision of Witpoort and Rand Collieries Smallholdings, 2 July, 1926, and especially the evidence of H. Maskell. See also CAD, BMR C2/2, Town Clerk to Director of Census, 18 Jan. 1921; CAD, BMR P4/47, Minutes of the Meeting of the Finance and General Purposes Committee, 19 Nov. 1927; CAD, BMR A4/7, Minutes of the Meeting of the Finances and General Purposes Committee, 24 Feb. 1927.

36 Interview with Mr Mosuku.

37 Interview with Mr E. Pakade, Tsakane, Jan. 1985.

38 CAD, BMR P4/15, Public Health Report, 31 Jan. 1929; CAD,

BMR P4/15, Letter circulated to 32 people on Witpoort plots, 25 Aug. 1930.

39 CAD, BMR P4/47, Minutes of the Meeting of the Town Council, 26 March 1926; CAD, BMR A4/6, Minutes of the Meeting of the Town Council, 25 Aug. 1930.

40 CAD, BMR A4/6, Evidence: Commission of Enquiry into the Excision of Witpoort and Rand Collieries Smallholdings, 21 July 1926; CAD, BMR A4/6, Minutes of the Special Meeting of the Finance Committee, 1 Dec. 1926.

41 Ibid., Evidence of J.P. Fouche.

42 Ibid., Evidence.

43 See complaints in CAD, BMR P4/6, Witpoort and Rand Colliery Smallholders' Association to Town Clerk.

44 CAD, BMR P4/47, SAP Officer Commanding Brakpan-Springs area to Town Clerk, 18 June 1929.

45 Webster, 'The Brakpan Story', p. 21.

46 CAD, BMR N3/1, P. Sullivan to Town Clerk, 23 Feb. 1923; CAD, BMR N3/1, Minutes of the Meeting of the Finances and General Purposes Committee, 17 April 1923.

47 CAD, BMR P4/142, Cluver's inspection; CAD, BMR P4/15, Memorandum: Squatting at VFP Pan, 14 Sept. 1920.

48 M. Swanson, 'The Sanitation Syndrome: Bubonic Plague and Urban Native Policy in the Cape Colony 1900-1909', Journal of African History, 18 (1977), pp. 387-410.

49 CAD, NTS 179/313, Mr Legate to Town Clerk, 1 April 1924; CAD, BMR P4/17, Public Health Report for Year ending 30 June 1928.

50 CAD, BMR N3/1, Minutes of the Meeting of the Town Council, 8 Aug. 1924.

51 CAD, GNLB 2756/13/34, Sub-Inspector Officer Commanding SAP, Brakpan-Springs Area, to District Commander, SAP, Boksburg, 17 Dec. 1927; CAD, BMR N3/1, Report of the SAP at the meeting of the Town Council, 28 Aug. 1924.

52 See correspondence in CAD, GNLB 2756/13/54, Illicit Liquor Traffic in Brakpan; CAD, Evidence to the Commissioner of Enquiry into Trading on Mining Ground, 1935.

53 Ibid.

54 Apostolic Faith Mission.

55 CAD, GNLB 2756/13/24, V. Acton to Resident Magistrate, 8 Dec. 1927.

56 *Star*, 14 Dec. 1927.

57 CAD, NTS 179/313, Mr Legate to Town Clerk, 1 April 1924.

58 C. van Onselen, *Studies in the Social and Economic History of the Witwatersrand*, Vol. 2, *New Nineveh*, (Johannesburg, 1982), pp. 1-73.

59 Interview with Webster, Brakpan, Dec. 1986; S. Webster, 'A Glimpse of Brakpan's Past', Unpublished manuscript, Brakpan Municipal Library.

60 CAD, BMR N3/1, Brakpan Ratepayers' Association to Town Clerk, 3 Sept. 1920.

61 CAD, Department of Justice (JUS) 3/778/12, Deputy Commissioner, SAP, Pretoria, to Secretary, Transvaal Police, Pretoria, 13 June 1912.

62 Van Onselen, *Studies in the Social and Economic History of the Witwatersrand*, Vol. 2, pp. 171-201; CAD, JUS 144 3/778/12. Sub-Inspector Officer Commanding, Benoni Police, to District Commissioner, Transvaal Police, Boksburg, 20 June 1912.

63 CAD, JUS 144 3/778/12, Sub-Inspector Officer Commanding, Benoni Police, to District Commissioner, Transvaal Police, Boksburg, 20 June 1912.

64 Van Onselen, *Studies in the Social and Economic History of the Witwatersrand*, Vol. 2, pp. 192-93.

65 A. Sitas, African Worker Responses on the East Rand and Changes in the Metal Industry 1960-1980, PhD Thesis, University of the Witwatersrand, 1984, p. 67.

66 CAD, BMR Pll/l, Minutes of the Meeting of the Town Council with Colonel Godley, Deputy Commissioner of Police, Witwatersrand District, 2 Sept. 1923.

67 See correspondence in file CAD, BMR /011/1, Police Headquarters.

68 CAD, JUS 3/911/21, District Commander East Rand District, Boksburg, to Deputy Commissioner, Commanding Witwatersrand, SAP, Johannesburg, 23 July 1927.

69 P. Bonner, 'The 1920 Black Mineworkers' Strike: A Preliminary Account', in B. Bozzoli (ed.), *Labour, Townships and Protest*, (Johannesburg, 1979), pp. 273-97, and 'The Transvaal Native Congress, 1917-1920', pp. 270-313.

70 Bonner, 'The 1920 Black Mineworkers' Strike', p. 273.

71 CAD, JUS 3/127/20, Sub-Inspector, SAP, Benoni, to District Commander, SAP, Boksburg, 26 Feb. 1920; CAD, JUS

29/3/337/20, Sub-Inspector, SAP, to District Commander, Boksburg, 7 April 1920.

72 Bonner, 'The Transvaal Native Congress', pp. 270-313.

73 CAD, JUS 29/3/337/20, Sub-Inspector, SAP, to District Commander, Boksburg, 7 April 1920.

74 CAD, GNLB 84/20/243, Statement of H.S. Bell, Sub-Native Commissioner, Witwatersrand, before the Local Government Commission, 12 July 1920; J. Cohen, 'Twatwa: The Working Class of Benoni in the 1930s', *Africa Perspective*, No. 20, (1982), p. 77; Gilfoyle, An Urban Crisis: The Town Council, Industry and the Black Working Class in Springs, 1948-1958, Chapter 2.

75 CAD, Nigel Municipal Records, 1/3/3, Report of the Location Superintendent, 31 March 1936.

76 Interview with Mrs Motlakeng; CAD, BMR P1/6, C.H.L. Morotolo, Secretary, Transvaal African Congress, Brakpan Branch, to Town Clerk, 19 July 1926.

77 CAD, BMR N3/1, Town Clerk's Memorandum, 8 Oct. 1927.

78 CAD, GNLB 313 84/20/243, Statement of Evidence of H.S. Bell, Sub-Native Commissioner, Witwatersrand, before the Local Government Commission, 12 July 1920.

79 CAD, BMR N3/1, Town Clerk's Memorandum, 17 April 1923.

80 CAD, BMR N3/1, Minutes of the Meeting of the Town Council, 17 April 1927.

81 CAD, BMR 149 N3/1, Minutes of the Meeting of the Town Council, 17 April 1927.

82 CAD, BMR N3/1, Ziswana to Town Clerk, 22 March 1923; CAD, BMR N3/1 Minutes of the Meeting of the Finances and General Purposes Committee, 10 April 1923.

83 CAD, BMR N3/1, Minutes of the Meeting of the Finances and General Purposes Committee, 10 April 1923.

84 A. Potgieter, 'Die Swartes aan die Witwatersrand, 1900-1933', PhD Thesis, Rand Afrikaans University, 1978, pp. 126-53.

85 CAD, NTS 129/313, Town Clerk to Secretary of Native Affairs, 15 April 1924.

86 *East Rand Express*, 30 Oct. 1915; CAD, BMR N3/1, Minutes of the Meeting of the Town Council, 3 Sept. 1920.

87 Nothling, 'The Story of Brakpan', pp. 37-39.

88 CAD, BMR L5/3, Report of the Finance Committee, 30 Jan. 1923.

89 Nothling, 'The Story of Brakpan', p. 41.

90 Ibid., p. 61.

Members of the Durban Borough Police unearthing illegally-brewed *isitshimiyane* during the beer boycott in the town, 1929.

Migrant workers being guarded in a compound by a member of the South African Police during the raids of the Mobile Squadron in Durban, November 1929.

The aftermath of a raid on African compounds, Durban, 1929. Members of the CID display hundreds of sticks confiscated from migrant workers. Note the dummy gun being held by the policeman on the right.

Women hawkers, Johannesburg, 1927.

Durban's ICU *yase* Natal Governing Body, c. 1928. A.W.G. Champion holds a walking-stick.

The speaker is saying, 'All nations buy from shops of their own nation. So where are our shops?'

The caption reads: Watch! Nabantukop is reviving the idea of the co-operatives — Nabantukop will be touring Natal and KwaZulu. Further information will be given in October 1948. (*Ubambiswano* Vol. 1, No. 12, Sept./Oct. 1948)

A home in Rooiyard, Doornfontein, 1933.

The Queen of the Home on her wedding day. An ideal many women aspired to.

Without kin networks, public child-care facilities or trusted friends to look after young children, many women were obliged to work from home, often as laundrywomen.

Chief Nyabela

An **Ndebele** woman in a bridal cloak standing in front of a wall decorated in the less ornate style prevalent until the 1940s.
(©Constance Stuart Larrabee 1989)

Informal music-making: the small public pleasures of working-class life.

The Americanised cinema — post-war District Six.

91 Nothling, 'Die Ontstandsgeskiedenis van Brakpan', Ch.4.
92 *East Rand Express*, 10 May 1924.
93 *Brakpan Herald*, Oct. 1929.
94 *Star*, 11 Aug. 1925.
95 CAD, BMR N3/1, Minutes of the Meeting of the Town Council, 12 Nov. 1921.
96 CAD, BMR N3/1, Minutes of the Meeting of the Town Council, 15 April 1921.
97 CAD, BMR N3/1, General Manager, Brakpan Mine, to Town Clerk, 6 June 1921; CAD, BMR N3/1, Memorandum: Visit of Colonel S.M. Pritchard and Major H.S. Bell to Brakpan, 20 May 1921.
98 *Star*, 11 Aug. 1925.
99 CAD, BMR N3/1, Town Clerk to Director of Native Labour, 6 June 1921; CAD, BMR N3/1, Town Clerk to Mining Commissioner Boksburg, 16 Sept. 1921.
100 CAD, BMR N3/1, Town Clerk to Director of Native Labour, 6 June 1921; CAD, BMR N3/1, Minutes of the Meeting of the Finances and General Purposes Committee, 19 June 1923; CAD, BMR H2/117, Office to the Registrar of Mining Titles to Town Clerk, 30 April 1921.
101 CAD, BMR N3/1, Minutes of the Meeting of the Town Council, 25 March 1924.
102 CAD, BMR N3/1, Minutes of the Special Meeting of the Finances and General Purposes Committee, 11 May 1922.
103 Ibid.
104 CAD, BMR N3/1, Minutes of the Meeting of the Town Council, 22 April 1924.
105 CAD, NTS 179/313, Secretary of Native Affairs to Secretary of Mines and Industries, 3 June 1924.
106 CAD, NTS 179/313, General Manager, New State Areas Ltd, to Administrator of the Transvaal, 20 Oct. 1925.
107 CAD, NTS 179/313, General Manager, Brakpan Mine, to Provincial Secretary of the Administrator, 23 Dec. 1925.
108 CAD, BMR N3/1, Minutes of the Meeting of the Town Council, 27 Nov. 1925.
109 Ibid.
110 Ibid.
111 *Rand Daily Mail*, 23 Dec. 1925.
112 CAD, BMR N3/1, Minutes of the Meeting of the Town Council, 23

March 1926.
113 CAD, BMR N3/1, Minutes of the Meeting of the Town Council, 23 Nov. 1926.
114 *Brakpan Herald*, 30 Sept. 1927.

Managing Black Leadership

The Joint Councils, Urban Trading and Political Conflict in the Orange Free State, 1925-1942

Paul Rich

The Joint Council movement is an important dimension in inter-war black politics in South Africa for it acted as one of the crucial links between local community organisation and 'high' politics at the level of the state and government legislation. In addition, the various Joint Councils that were formed in the 1920s and 1930s on the basis of the parent body in Johannesburg were key sources for the spread of a liberal political ideology of 'inter-racial cooperation' which white 'friends of the native' believed was vital both as a means of trying to humanise government policy by rational persuasion, and as offsetting more radical and potentially disruptive creeds such as Garveyism and the Marxism propagated by the Communist Party of South Africa (CPSA) through its night school movement. The Joint Councils, indeed, had been established by liberal white missionaries, teachers and academics in 1921 partly in order to defuse the tense post-war situation in South Africa characterised by a strike wave on the Witwatersrand and other towns, an ANC pass burning campaign in 1919, and an African mine strike in 1920.[1] The councils had been modelled on inter-racial bodies in the United States and represented a more 'modern' approach to the question of 'race relations' compared to the older Victorian paternalism of the various welfare societies and missionary bodies. They were still marked, though, by a strong faith in the idea of a generally quiet campaign of proselytisation on essentially Fabian lines. As one of the secular intellectuals involved in the movement, the Natal educationalist, Charles T. Loram, remarked on being appointed to the Native Affairs Commission in November 1920, 'Today with our democratic and even anarchistic conditions we cannot revert to the paternalism of a Grey or a Shepstone... If General Smuts

approves I hope to stump the country in an attempt to awaken the
conscience regarding Native matters among Europeans. I have a
profound belief in the sense of justice of the white South Africans.'[2]

The liberalising goals of the Joint Councils have sometimes been
accepted by historians when writing on inter-war South African
politics. Peter Walshe, especially, has argued that for African political
leaders in both the ANC and the All-African Convention (AAC) the
Councils 'became not only beacons of hope but a welcome distraction
from the ruthlessness, drudgery and discipline of mass action and
political aggression — the fond hope of an easy way out in an
increasingly alarming situation of racial aggression'.[3] Other historians
of the period, though, have sought to emphasise the degree to which
the Councils intervened in African politics and manipulated black
political leadership in the interests of maintaining social control.
Martin Legassick has seen the Councils as part of a wider body of liberal
opinion in inter-war South Africa that was moulded by an
intelligentsia based on the English universities. In essence the Councils
were instruments for the spread of a conservative liberal ideology that
accommodated to the doctrine of racial segregationism and mediated,
as 'agents of social control', an evolving class struggle that
accompanied industrialisation in the 1920s, 1930s and 1940s.[4] Baruch
Hirson, too, has emphasised the de-politicising function of the
mainstream Joint Councils, though conceding that they also contained
more radical whites who did not share the lukewarm liberalism of
Loram, J.D. Rheinallt Jones and the group of Witwatersrand liberals
who eventually formed the South African Institute of Race Relations
(SAIRR) in 1929.[5] The present writer has carried this discussion
further by also emphasising that the Councils only partially co-opted a
compliant African political leadership in the 1920s and that the
SAIRR did not define all white liberal opinion, since rival minority
groups like the Friends of Africa, organised by William and Margaret
Ballinger, remained distrustful of the political course mapped out by
Rheinallt Jones and Alfred Hoernlé in the late 1930s and 1940s.[6]
More recently, Richard Elphick has questioned the degree to which
the university intelligentsia were able to shape the general body of
inter-war liberal thought in South Africa, arguing that a far more
important influence stemmed from what he termed 'the benevolent
empire' of international missionary organisations. This perhaps at least
partially explains the weak understanding of the course of South
African politics under the dominant creed of racial segregationism and

the rather naive faith that modes of rational persuasion derived from European — and especially British — parliamentary lobbying could be applied in the same manner in the South African context.[7]

The disparate nature of local conditions in South Africa during the inter-war years in fact tends to belie Legassick's thesis that it was the university intelligentsia who were able completely to organise the liberal movement in accordance with a 'grand design' that came to be spelt out by Alfred Hoernlé in his Phelps-Stokes lectures, *South African Native Policy and the Liberal Spirit*.[8] In the Cape the African franchise continued to prevail until 1936, and the Witwatersrand liberals had still to work in alliance with a liberal movement that had roots in the Eastern Cape missions, the remnants of the African peasantry, and opposition white newspapers. Indeed, James Henderson, Principal of Lovedale, had helped to get the Joint Council movement off the ground in 1921, and the Councils remained indebted to the Lovedale Press for the publication of their material and the announcement of their activities in the *Christian Express*.[9] Similarly, in Natal a local liberal movement began to develop in the inter-war years under the guiding hand of such individuals as Mabel Palmer, Maurice Webb and, after 1934, Edgar Brookes, which the Institute liberals could only indirectly control.[10] Thus while it is probably true to say that there was an emergent South African 'liberal establishment' growing up in the inter-war years centred on the Witwatersrand, it had many of the facets of an alliance of local groups that tended to interact with their local environments in different ways, especially through bodies like the Joint Councils.

One interesting but rather neglected area in which the Joint Councils and liberal activists tried to involve themselves was the unpromising terrain of the Orange Free State (OFS). Here there was no African franchise or strong tradition of liberal missionary education in the manner of Lovedale or Healdtown. A 'traditional' pattern of race relations stretching back to the Boer Republic before 1899 had become remodelled in the interests of a burgeoning white capitalist agriculture in the twentieth century. It had been pressure from OFS farming interests which had partly led to the passing of the 1913 Natives Land Act, driving extensive numbers of African *bywoners* off white farms to roam at random, losing their livestock and drifting into the urban locations as a newly proletarianised work force for both agriculture and the mines, a process Tim Keegan has seen as one of the most dramatic in South Africa.[11] In the early 1920s, though, the population of many of these locations began to be organised by the Industrial and Commercial Workers' Union (ICU), and in January 1925 Clements Kadalie, addressing a meeting in the Waaihoek location of Bloemfontein, boasted that the Union had asked the government for a Minimum Wages Bill, and linked economic demands with nationalist ones as he claimed that Africans now had no time for British ideals and traditions.[12] The following April the location experienced a riot in which one African was shot dead as the police tried to enforce the prohibition of *momela* (sprouted corn) and the brewing of beer in the location.[13] The incident undoubtedly reflected a crisis in the management of the rapidly growing locations, and the OFS in the late 1920s began to acquire a reputation for being one of the harshest and most backward areas of the Union. The importation of cheap labour from Lesotho drove down farm wages for the migrants to anything as low as 15s. or £1 compared to local wages of £3 to £4.[14] However, for some of the Witwatersrand liberals, the OFS was by no means seen as an entirely unpropitious area in the late 1920s and 1930s, and the question turned towards establishing newer modes of contact with the African locations as well as building up an educated African class which was schooled in the ideals of Christian 'brotherhood'.

The OFS, indeed, served in many ways as a litmus test of the willingness of the English-speaking liberals to collaborate with the Dutch Reformed Churches in a local variant of the wider international 'benevolent empire' of inter-war missionary organisations. The original idea, for example, of the 1923 conference organised by the Federal Council of the Dutch Reformed Churches on 'European and Bantu' in Johannesburg had come from the Revd A.F. Louw, Minister of the Dutch Reformed Church (DRC) in Bloemfontein North.[15] The conference had made a powerful impression on some of the English liberals, and Loram especially continually warned his colleagues throughout the 1920s that the Joint Councils needed to steer clear of political issues such as the Cape African franchise through fear of shaking the alliance with the DRCs.[16] Thus the situation seemed ripe as the impetus of the ICU in the OFS began to wane in the late 1920s. The Union in 1927-28 sought co-operation with the Johannesburg Joint Council on the campaign for higher African wages and against the pass laws,[17] though some Council activists also looked for an alliance with other African interests centred around urban trading and the location advisory boards, established under the 1920 Native Affairs Act.

By 1928 the ICU began to fragment into a number of rival local groups, and in the OFS two main factions emerged. The 'ICU of Africa' owed allegiance to William Ballinger, the Scottish trade unionist imported to try and reorganise the Union, and had as its local organiser Robert Sello in the Kroonstad location in the northern OFS. In addition, there was the rival 'ICU of the OFS' which was run by the former radical union organiser Keable Mote, who had fallen out with the Communists over the direction of the Union's programme. The decline of the ICU led to accusations by an anonymous correspondent 'Enquirer' in the black newspaper *Umteteli wa Bantu* at the end of 1928 on alleged Joint Council interference with African politics. The writer pleaded for African leadership to free itself from the 'interference and control' of the Councils along with the annual European-Bantu conferences which were seen as halting African political initiative.[18] The charges were strongly repudiated by Rheinallt Jones, one of the main organisers of the Joint Councils, who argued that the Councils could never take the place of a 'strong and healthy Congress'.[19] He privately admitted though that there was 'just enough truth' in Enquirer's charges to 'make it a dangerous statement', so ensuring that it was necessary to 'build up the Congress again'.[20]

In 1930 the radical faction in the ANC, led by its President Josiah Gumede, lost out to a conservative element under Pixley Seme, one of the original founders of the Congress in 1912. In contrast to Gumede's radical ideas of using the ANC to build links with organised black labour through a separate Congress labour department,[21] Seme returned to older notions of building up a prosperous black peasantry which would market its produce in the white dominated towns and cities. In 1929, with a capital of £25 000, he had had a Native Development and Trust Company registered with William Ballinger, and in the early 1930s the ANC rapidly abandoned any notions of building bridges with the urban black working class and concentrated instead on promoting co-operative trading by buying goods in bulk from white manufacturers and distributing them through Congress-owned stores.[22] Some vocal support was given, too, to the interests of African leaders in the urban townships like Bloemfontein who were denied trading licences by the local municipality, though the continuation of disaffection with Seme's leadership by groups like the Transvaal African Congress made the ANC's task of actual organisation all the more difficult.[23] The decline of Congress membership and the shortage of funds meant that the Congress ceased to act as a serious political force, and there thus remained widespread scope for continuing white liberal intervention in African politics. It was in this context that Rheinallt Jones began to mobilise a section of 'moderate' African political opinion in the OFS behind the issue of urban trading licenses after pressure from Loram to strengthen the activities of the rural Join Councils.[24] This led to the establishment of political links which were to prove of considerable importance when he came to fight the election in 1937 as a 'native representative' for the Transvaal and OFS under the 1936 Representation of Natives Act. This emerges from the example of the northern OFS town of Kroonstad.

Black Trading and the Kroonstad Joint Council

The trading licences issue in the OFS developed in the 1920s in the wake of the 1923 Natives (Urban Areas) Act which established a nationwide pattern of urban racial segregation. Under Section 22 of the Act local authorities were empowered, if they so wished, to license African traders in municipal locations. In the case of Bloemfontein, however, the issue of licences in 1927 by the local Licensing Board to African general dealers and vegetable sellers led to the Bloemfontein Municipality taking the matter to court and establishing that the wording of Section 22 of the 1923 Act that municipalities 'may' grant licences only denoted discretionary powers. As a result of this case all the municipalities in the OFS, under pressure from white commercial interests, refused to grant licences. In Kroonstad some 35 stores were classified as 'catering for the native trade' with stocks valued at £27 945, and the local Chamber of Commerce opposed the issue of black trading licences, warning of increases in rates for white ratepayers and that urban trading would encourage the drift of 'farm natives' into the location, so increasing the illicit liquor traffic.[25] The intransigence of the municipalities led to a campaign by the African petty bourgeoisie in the OFS for the right of Africans to hold trading licences. Links began to be established with black liberals on the Johannesburg Joint Council, such as Victor Selope-Thema, who in 1927 attacked the 'impossible demands' of the ICU in their campaign of that year to avoid paying rates.[26]

Similarly, the issue was taken up by the Location Advisory Boards Congress which was run by R.H. Godlo of East London. In 1930 the Congress, while supporting the trading rights issue, also accepted the principle of urban segregation contained in the 1923 Urban Areas Act and its amendment of 1930.[27] The trading rights issue was also debated at the first conference in 1930 of the Non-European Traders' Association as it began to establish an OFS branch.[28] The question of allocation of trading rights thus became one of growing importance in the early 1930s as the ICU of Africa circulated a letter from its secretary Robert Sello to all ANC members in the hope that there could be re-established in the OFS a 'Federal Free State Industrial and Commercial Workers Union of Africa'. Sello expressed concern at the way the trading rights issue could possibly cut off African trading interests from trade union organisation. 'Agitation for such things as exemptions and trading rights,' he wrote to William Ballinger, 'will benefit only a few natives, who are advanced educationally and in civilization and... the granting of these and other rights will lead to the formation of and generation of a small middle class among the Natives which will exploit the uneducated mass and [not] benefit it one jot. We also see this danger and feel that co-operative enterprises would be the only means of evading it and that this would be preferable to individual enterprises.'[29]

This dilemma of seeking to reconcile individual trading aspirations to organised labour reflected the increasing difficulty the ICU had in trying to prevent the fragmentation of political leadership. Sello and Mote tried to organise a 'unity conference' in April 1931 in order to revive the ICU, but none of the ICU leaders — Kadalie, A.W.G. Champion or Ballinger — made an appearance, and only Selby Msimang turned up. In the event 57 delegates from various parts of the OFS attended and Msimang was elected President and Mote General Secretary. Msimang sought to link the OFS organisation with a remodelled national ICU shaped on federal lines so that the differing interests of particular provinces could be organised on a local basis. The advantage of this for the OFS organisation would be that it could concentrate on farm workers.[30] But the ICU of Africa remained weak as its leader William Ballinger shifted his interests in the early 1930s to a study of the Protectorate territories of Lesotho, Swaziland and Botswana. The idea of a radical organisation of farm workers was thus only promoted by a branch of the CPSA in Kroonstad which was established in October 1932 as a 'Young Citizens Association' under the chairmanship of Sidney MacKay. The branch campaigned for the re-establishment of a single ICU under the leadership of Harry Maleke and Jason Jingoes, assisted locally by Jason Binda and John Mancoe.[31]

The local population seemed very suitable for some political mobilisation as migrants from Lesotho crowded the location, leading to a growth in the location from 3500 in 1921 to 7228 in 1928, concentrated at 7,2 per stand.

Little came of these attempts at re-establishing the ICU, and a far more significant organisation to develop in the early 1930s was the Kroonstad Joint Council, which was initially established in September 1928 with a membership of 18 whites and 18 Africans. Mancoe, Binda, Sello and Mote were all members, while the white members included J.R. Brent, the location superintendent of the Kroonstad location. As local farm wages reportedly declined from 2s.1d. per day in August 1929 to 1s.5d. in December 1930, the Council began to take up the trading rights issue and sent representatives to the Advisory Boards Congress in 1931.[32] A 'Unity Movement' was established in October of 1931 between the Joint Council and a group in the local location led by Robert Sello with the objective of developing a separate African local economy, working in 'co-operation' with the 'European' one.[33] This development led to the Council's chief figure, Martin Knight, securing a local inquiry into the trading rights issue. The resistance from the local Kroonstad Council led to a progressive accommodation by the Joint Council towards segregation in the OFS. An initial Joint Council memorandum on the trading rights issue drafted in July of 1931 ended up being watered down when it came to the question of rights for Africans. The initial draft, written by Knight who was Secretary of the Joint Council and 'Manager' of the Kroonstad United (Bantu) School, emphasised that it was 'in every way desirable that natives should regard themselves as permanent residents in the locations where they have chosen to live' and urged the need for general trading rights beyond those of mere 'hawking' which had been granted by some OFS municipalities'.[34] The published memorandum, however, removed this sentence in favour of the goal that 'reliable Natives should be encouraged to regard themselves as "citizens" of the locations in which they live' and included a further consideration that since the 1923 Urban Areas Act 'aims at partial segregation, the right to trade is an integral part of the measure'.[35]

The pro-segregationist memorandum of the Joint Council failed, though, to have any effect on the OFS Municipal Congress which in December reaffirmed unanimously its opposition to African trading. From Johannesburg, Rheinallt Jones began to express interest in the issue which he saw as linked to a more general missionary concern with economic distress amongst the rural African population in South Africa in the early 1930s.[36] Rheinallt Jones especially hoped that the Joint Councils could take up the issue on a national scale as part of a strategy of building closer ties with the Advisory Boards Congress for, as he wrote to the Secretary of the Germiston Joint Council, 'with handling these Boards can become very useful bodies, but I am certain that any developed form of 'self-government' in town locations is going to be a slow process'.[37] A similar idea was expressed by J.R. Cooper the following year (1932) at a European-Bantu Conference in Bloemfontein in which 'efficient and sympathetic administration' over the urban African population was envisaged as occurring in collaboration with both the Advisory Boards and the Joint Councils. Cooper thought the Boards could serve as 'training schools for native thought'.[38]

It thus appeared that as Rheinallt Jones began building up the SAIRR in Johannesburg in the early 1930s, the Joint Councils locally could acquire new functions of bridge building with the government. An initial approach in August 1931 to the Secretary of Native Affairs, Major J. Herbst, for a deputation of the Advisory Boards Congress, Native Traders' Association and the Kroonstad Joint Council on trading rights was rejected on the grounds that the 'delicate' nature of the matter led the government to hope it could persuade the OFS municipalities through covert pressure rather than organised lobbying.[39] The following year, 1932, Rheinallt Jones discovered that the Native Administration Department (NAD) had instituted its own inquiry into the issue, and delayed taking a lead on the matter while there still appeared to be a chance of a change in government policy. The Johannesburg Joint Council warned the Minister of Native Affairs in October of a mood of 'dangerous apathy' amongst the African population and a 'state of discontent... bordering on despair',[40] though Rheinallt Jones turned down a request by the Kroonstad Joint Council in January 1933 for further action on trading rights 'while the political situation is so uncertain'.[41] The situation continued for another two years, and in February 1935 Rheinallt Jones still continued to caution delay on the Kroonstad Joint Council as the matter had now been referred to the Native Affairs Commission for consideration.[42]

The general ineffectiveness of the political lobbying by the Advisory Boards, the Joint Councils and Location Superintendents led some of the Advisory Board activists increasingly to widen their own area of political involvement. The Advisory Boards were generally seen as timid and pro-segregationist organisations, though by the end of 1933 the General Secretary of the Advisory Boards Congress, N.M. Motshumi, began calling for the Congress to assist in the regeneration of the ANC.[43] In 1934 the Kroonstad Advisory Board began to press for a minimum wage for local African workers of 3s.6d. a day compared to an average one of 2s.1d. a day by December 1933. 'The final evil effect of native wages being below subsistence level,' it warned in a memorandum to the Industrial Legislation Commission, 'is the fact that owing to the mother and elder children having to go out to work or char in order to supplement the family budget, the young children are neglected and run wild. Junior 'Amaleita' gangs, 'Marabi' gangs and juvenile pilfering especially from cars at the municipal market result'.[44]

This was still a general conservative political position and supportive of the idea of promoting social order through the organisation of the family in the townships. It was buttressed by Keynesian arguments pointing to a multiplier effect in the local economy through a boost to African spending power. The arguments of the Kroonstad Joint Council, in contrast, were geared to the operation of the 'civilised labour policy' inaugurated by the Pact government in the mid-1920s. While not disputing the decline in African wages in the 1930s from an average 2s.3d. a day in 1931 to 1s.6d. in early 1934, the Joint Council campaigned for a minimum wage of 5s. a day for a small group of workers irrespective of colour, a second group of 'casual' workers on 2s.6d. a day and a third group of permanent location inhabitants on 2s.11d. to 4s.11d. a day who would 'need to be trained to a higher standard of efficiency'.[45] The general emphasis of policy, the Joint Council pointed out, should be that 'town dwellers, both white and black, who are none of them content to be classified with the barbarous and undeveloped people' of the Prime Minister's definition should be protected from the unfair competition of reserve and farm natives, who have other resources with which they can supplement their inadequate earnings in the towns, while at the same time so long as it is necessary these unwilling immigrants will have certain facilities for earning the ready money they need'.[46]

The difference of emphasis reflected to a considerable degree the dominance of white rate-paying interests in the Kroonstad Joint Council, which increasingly failed to maintain its African supporters as the issue loomed of segregating the Cape African voters under the Representation of Natives Bill and of establishing a separate system of 'natives' representation' in the Senate and House of Assembly. Throughout the OFS, in fact, various local groups and committees emerged in opposition to the measure, though they generally remained ill-coordinated and without a strong popular following. The general weakness of the ANC under Seme meant that the AAC tended to have a greater presence, though in cases like that of Thaba Nchu, the local organisation tended to be dominated by farming interests led by Dr James Moroka who became the AAC's treasurer.[47] In Kroonstad, however, a large gathering in the location turned out on 20 April 1936 to hear John Maraba, the chairman of the local AAC, and further support came from the African Interdenominational minister the Revd S. Mangehane. A campaign to raise five million shillings was inaugurated, and from this time onwards the Joint Council lost most of its influence in the location, despite a plea made on its behalf by Brent.[48]

The Election Campaign for the Senate

By the time Rheinallt Jones began the campaign to be elected as senator for the Transvaal and OFS in 1937, little remained of the old Joint Council support. The Kroonstad Joint Council even lacked funds to send a representative to an SAIRR meeting in Johannesburg in June,[49] and later changed its title to 'native welfare society' to try and attract further white support.[50] Rheinallt Jones found the change of name disconcerting, given that the Joint Council movement had been developed, 'not on the basis of condescension on the part of Europeans, but with a view to developing self-regard and independence of thought on the part of the natives. In the case of Kroonstad, I gather that it was the European who failed by the natives.'[51] The failure of the Councils left the question of establishing an organisational base for the election campaign, and Rheinallt Jones tried to find support from the remnants of the alliance that had been forged with the Advisory Boards and former ICU leadership in the early 1930s.

The key figures for Rheinallt Jones to turn to were clearly Sello, Mote and R. Cingo who had been active in Kroonstad organising the AAC's five million shillings campaign. Further support came, too, from the local AAC treasurer, the Revd J.S. Litheko, who had been secretary of the convening committee that had established the Joint Council in 1928, as well as Secretary of the local United Bantu School in the location and secretary of the OFS circuit of the Methodist Wesleyan

Church. These individuals, together with the indefatigable Brent, proved crucial when it came to mobilising popular support against Rheinallt Jones's rivals, the former ICU organiser William Ballinger, and the ex-CPSA member, Hyman Basner. The municipal offices in Kroonstad served effectively as the centre of operations for Rheinallt Jones's election campaign as Sello worked as a clerk there. Furthermore Sello, Binda and Mote, with the permission of the Kroonstad Native Commissioner, followed the meetings of magistrates around the OFS in a taxi (that cost Rheinallt Jones about £2 per meeting), haranguing African voters.[52] Rheinallt Jones's African agents hoped to persuade him to provide a car, though limited funds prevented this, and Brent urged Rheinallt Jones to attend many of the OFS centres in person in order to neutralise the propaganda of Basner's 'communist' agents organised by the builder Thomas Mapikela of Bloemfontein. Brent felt that a number of the OFS locations were 'safe' by mid-February with strong local figures like the Revd Z.R. Mahabane in Winburg, Jacob Nhlapo at Reitz and the teacher, Sol Crutse, at Ladybrand coming out for Rheinallt Jones.[53] In other cases the Advisory Boards came out for Basner. The Vice-President of the Advisory Boards Congress, J.B. Sesing, issued a circular letter to African voters urging them to support either Basner or Ballinger as future 'Bantu liberators', though this appeared to be more in opposition to Rheinallt Jones's tepid position on trading rights than due to any positive support for his electoral rivals.[54]

In fact, the decision of Mote to support Rheinallt Jones proved especially damaging to Basner's and Ballinger's campaign, despite an attempt by Ballinger to counteract this by suggesting that Mote's only reason for supporting Rheinallt Jones was that more money was involved.[55] As one of the key organisers of the ICU in the OFS, Mote had quite a strong local following which, after winning over the AAC in Kroonstad, he was able to use in a number of locations in order to gain support from local advisory boards. After being prevented from participating in political activities by an education department circular, he got leave from his teaching post and was paid a salary by Rheinallt Jones of £6 a month.[56] Mote then toured the OFS locations such as Kopjies, where the Chairman of the Advisory Board, George Majoe, chaired a meeting he addressed. Further support came from the Advisory Boards of Brandfort, Bultfontein, Wesselsbron and Bothaville where, on 11 April, some 1 000 'taxpayers' reportedly attended a local meeting to back Rheinallt Jones.[57] Only in

Bloemfontein, with its 12 000 votes, was there significant opposition to Rheinallt Jones organised by Thomas Mapikela, though here Mote addressed in April a meeting in the local AME church and gained the unanimous endorsement of the Advisory Board.[58]

Rheinallt Jones's campaign was overwhelmingly assisted by the restricted nature of the franchise which excluded rural farm workers and so buttressed the support of chiefs and wealthier farmers. The election in fact confirmed an earlier set of links that Rheinallt Jones had been forging in Thaba Nchu with a small group of landowners led by Moroka, while he refused to take up pleas for assistance from the Barolong Progressive Association (BPA). This had been formed in 1928 with the objective of trying to build Barolong tribal solidarity and of opposing the regulation of the Barolong Reserve Board depriving anyone absent from the reserve for more than seven years of land rights. Rheinallt Jones, indeed, wrote to the BPA secretary, Jeremiah Soldaat, in 1933, stating that the Association's objective of restoring the land held at the time of incorporation into the OFS in 1884 was a hopeless one, and urged it to go through the Reserve Board and 'official channels'.[59] The Secretary of the Advisory Boards Congress, N.M. Motshumi, on the other hand, was more successful in securing Rheinallt Jones's support in putting the case for Barolong land-holding before the Native Land Commission, with payment for these services coming from Moroka.[60] As a consequence Rheinallt Jones secured strong support in 1937, though in the following year the BPA held a series of meetings without the approval of the chiefs, and agitation mounted over access to land acquired by the South African Native Trust.[61]

Rheinallt Jones's overwhelming election victory in the OFS — where he secured 90 per cent of the vote — as well as in the Transvaal, acted as a considerable ideological confirmation of the government policy of territorial segregation. There were reservations by some African political leaders such as Msimang that Rheinallt Jones's election might 'compromise us in the effort of gaining influence with the Government'.[62] But the generally ill-coordinated nature of the AAC and its dependence on a series of local committees prevented the same kind of campaign as that mounted by Rheinallt Jones, where there was at least enough money to pay Mote to tour the region either by taxi or train, while Rheinallt Jones himself travelled some 20 000 miles visiting 500 places.[63] Often, too, the AAC's campaign was confused, as in the case of Kroonstad where it simply kept its options open behind all three candidates, a tactic the Communist Edwin Mofutsanyana condemned as an 'indirect vote' for Rheinallt Jones.[64] It was thus not altogether surprising that on the first ballot Rheinallt Jones gained 305 333 votes in the OFS to Basner's 77 349, with Ballinger coming only fifth with 4 757. On the second ballot, Rheinallt Jones's vote rose to 404 047 and Basner's actually fell to 66 334.[65]

Some African leaders saw confirmed in the election the kind of white liberal interference in African politics that had been raised by the anonymous 'Enquirer' in the late 1920s: '... some of the friends of the Native,' Alfred Xuma complained to James Moroka, 'are better friends to themselves than to the Native people.'[66] A number of African nationalists began to despair of the AAC developing into a nationwide movement, though in places like Kroonstad the body had worked alongside the ANC. Mote, who was provincial secretary of the AAC in the OFS, began to establish an ANC branch in April 1938 following pressure from Mahabane, the new President General.[67] The objective of a strong and independent African political organisation seemed ever more urgent as Rheinallt Jones, in response to further pressure from the Advisory Boards, led another ineffective deputation to the Minister of Native Affairs in October 1938 on the issue of trading rights. Rheinallt Jones was now accompanied by such figures as the Alexandra businessman, R.G. Baloyi, and Mapikela, who now represented the Advisory Boards on the Natives' Representative Council in Pretoria. The Minister, H.A. Fagan, took the same position of refusing to compel municipalities to accept African trading under the 1923 Urban Areas Act, as the fear of the United Party government of losing white political support to the National Party under D.F. Malan on the issue was especially pressing in the late 1930s in the wake of the centenary of the Great Trek.[68]

Growing Polarisation

Even though unsuccessful in reversing government policy on the issue, Rheinallt Jones became aware, during the course of his travels throughout the OFS in 1937, of the growing political polarisation in the region. In January 1938 at a Council meeting of the SAIRR he urged a study of farm wages in the province after expressing surprise and shock at the 'bitter feeling which existed between farmers and Natives'.[69] The resulting report by Leo Marquard published in 1939, *Farm Labour in the OFS*, represented an important early study of the effects of proletarianisation of African farm labour, pointing out that the conventional assumption long upheld both by Joint Council and Advisory Board activists that farm labourers were able to return to the reserves to supplement their meagre incomes was largely false, for 'today we have to deal with a permanent labouring class of people who have lost access to the land and have only their labour power to sell'.[70] The study pointed to the absence of trade union organisation to raise wages on the farms, though it also considered that attempts artificially to restrict African entry into urban areas would be defeated by the forces of supply and demand, indicating an early statement of the economic liberal school's reliance on market forces to erode racial segregation.[71] Curiously, though, the document also considered the future of agriculture to lie either in collective organisation or through peasantisation, with the latter alternative the more likely. The study recommended that the Department of Agriculture undertake a study into the minimum number of morgen for ploughing and stock for economic grazing in the furtherance of a conservationist ideology which by the Second World War became generally known as economic 'betterment' of the reserves.[72]

The Marquard study pinpointed the development of liberal thinking in SAIRR circles towards more state-directed social engineering in the late 1930s and 1940s, reflective of a South African variant of a wider climate of thinking on colonial development and welfare.[73] There was little room within this Fabian centralism for much attention to local details, and Rheinallt Jones began to be seen by some African leaders as ignoring the people in the OFS who had helped him in the senatorial election of 1937. Mote, now based in Pretoria, accused Rheinallt Jones, in August 1939, of only bothering to go to select places and failing to visit the OFS constituency since he was elected, although with the threat of a boycott of white stores by the OFS African Traders' Association Rheinallt Jones visited the area in 1939 to outline his senate motion on trading rights. African political opinion began to be mobilised by the late 1930s against the more conventional lobbying methods that had failed to produce any significant changes in government policy. The OFS African Teachers' Association, too, complained that they were not allowed to participate in location advisory boards and political affairs, thus reducing their position merely to that of 'good boys'.[74] In Kroonstad an African Commercial and Distributive Workers' Union was formed in 1941 by Sello, Cingo and A.P. Modibedi to cover workers in the commercial, distributive and catering trades.[75] The Union donated 10s. to the ANC in the same year.[76] These more general questions of wages and the cost of living began to eclipse the trading rights demand, which was finally accepted by the OFS Municipal Association in the context of the war-time economic boom.[77]

The revival of African political organisation after the start of the Second World War tended to undermine what remained of the patron-client relationships established by Rheinallt Jones on the basis of the system of African representation established in 1936. Most of the local Joint Councils in the OFS by this time were effectively defunct, and by 1941 there seemed to be no bodies to which Rheinallt Jones could appeal to take up the 'important matters that the interested people should know'.[78] As a result he began to come under pressure from a newer set of alliances forged at the local level between the emerging African unions and the African traders on the one hand, and the Advisory Boards on the other. These bodies were now less interested in seeking out Rheinallt Jones's help on single issues like trading rights, and indeed viewed his political role in this regard with suspicion, since it was apparently 'useless' to follow his advice and appeal to local municipal councils.[79] Sello, as secretary of the Kroonstad Advisory Board, tried to pressure Rheinallt Jones to take up the question of the cost of living for Africans, given the war-time inflation.[80] The Board complained in a joint memorandum with local unemployed African shop assistants of the dismissal of older African shop assistants once the determinations of the Wage Board had raised local wages, in some cases replacing the older men with cheaper female labour.[81] Sello also wrote to Ballinger stating that Rheinallt Jones intended to act against the Advisory Board recommendations, a charge Rheinallt Jones vehemently denied, but one which still eroded his political standing.[82]

The progressive radicalisation of a number of OFS Advisory Boards undoubtedly contributed to Rheinallt Jones's defeat by Hyman Basner in the election as Natives' Representative in the Senate in 1942. Basner stood with the opposition of the CPSA, though he had by this time forged close links with the ANC despite the unwillingness of the President, Alfred Xuma, formally to endorse him. Rheinallt Jones, on the other hand, was far less committed to standing again, and his main boast was that he had been able to persuade the Prime Minister, J.C. Smuts, to appoint the Smit Committee to investigate African living conditions in urban areas.[83] However, splits within the Johannesburg SAIRR to some degree undermined his position and caused his attention to be directed to attacks from local groups led by the Registrar of the University of Witwatersrand, I. Glyn Thomas.[84] Rheinallt Jones himself was unwilling to let the election campaign force the SAIRR to come out with a formal political position, despite the fact that it was coming under criticism from Xuma and the ANC for its attempted neutrality. 'The Institute is not the instrument of a party,' Rheinallt Jones wrote angrily to Robert Shepherd, 'but if it becomes politicised (in the sense that it has adopted a political platform) it will become the victim of a struggle between the various groups of the left.'[85]

With a strange twist of the ironic, this professed objective of Rheinallt Jones's coincided with the ideas of another important figure to emerge from OFS politics in the early 1940s. The African teacher Anton Lembede was teaching in the small OFS town of Heilbron while Rheinallt Jones fought and lost the 1942 senatorial election. The local Advisory Board had traditionally been a conservative one, and in 1938 it had eulogised Rheinallt Jones's work in that 'you and we play in a film where you beat the yoke of Moses and we that of Israel'.[86] By the early 1940s the changing political climate led Lembede to berate the OFS African Traders' Association (OFSATA) for failing to develop a strong organisation such that 'branches are left to their own lot, their own fate. Centralisation is not strong enough. The Association's propaganda section - if there is any such — is a failure.'[87] Lembede eventually left the OFS in 1943 to move to Johannesburg where he worked in Pixley Seme's law firm. But undoubtedly the experience of both the poor organisational strength of African political movements and their continual patronage by groups of white liberals through the Joint Councils or SAIRR left their mark in his later thinking. As one of the moving influences in the formation of the Congress Youth League, Lembede urged the development of autonomous African political action, though he warned the ANC leadership at the end of 1944 to be 'cautious and under no circumstance allow the national movement to be commuted into a battleground of European ideologies, nor allow the national movement to be dragged into the clash or conflict of these national ideologies'.[88] The experience, indeed, of OFS politics was undoubtedly one that encouraged Lembede to seek a purist return to Africanist fundamentals free of modern ideological forces which he saw disintegrating the peasant African society in which he had been brought up.[89]

The Longer-term Consequences

Lembede, however, was no more able to seek a return to such an agrarian African tradition than the SAIRR ideologists such as Marquard and Rheinallt Jones. The post-war industrial boom and the opening up of the OFS gold mines hastened the rate of African proletarianisation, while in many instances land promised from the South African Native Trust under the 1936 Native Trust and Land Act was not forthcoming. In the late 1940s peasant unrest in areas such as Thaba Nchu and Witzieshoek against the government's 'betterment' programme reflected an upsurge in rural class conflict in the OFS, though it remained ill-coordinated with the activities of the ANC under Xuma until 1949 and Moroka from 1949 to 1952.[90] The organisation of the ANC remained weak in the OFS in the late 1940s, though the Provincial Secretary, S.M. Elias, offered Xuma his assistance to organise the local Congress branches provided he could be paid a 'living wage', a suggestion the ANC President summarily rejected.[91] The situation continued to prevail in many areas of the OFS where Africans were not even aware what the ANC was, and the organisation report for the Province at the end of 1947 complained that the ANC leadership 'fail, or cannot, or are unwilling to make the average African understand where he is being led'. In all, it was estimated that only eight branches existed in the OFS consisting of 351 men and 256 women, of which 235 were in Bloemfontein alone.[92]

In this situation, the small groups of Advisory Boards and the pockets of educated African intellectuals organised through OFSATA had not been completely unsuccessful in helping to defeat Rheinallt Jones in the election of 1942. If the role of the Joint Council movement and the SAIRR had been a mediating one in the 1930s, preserving the essential structures of social control, they had still not been able completely to dominate and manipulate African political leadership as 'Enquirer' had suggested. The patronage of the white liberals had to a considerable extent depended upon the willingness of African political groups to cooperate, and this clearly broke down once it appeared that such an alliance was proving ineffective in changing the law on the issue of location trading rights, or even in taking up the issue of dismissal of African workers once the Wage Board had increased black wages after the start of the Second World War. Nevertheless, the experience of African political leaders in the OFS during the 1930s was a crucial one, not least in the area of urban segregation which, as a process, was being entrenched in the area. While analysts have often looked to Durban or Cape Town for the origins of urban segregation in the early years of the century, the neglected example of the OFS indicates that other urban struggles between white and black trading interests continued to have a local dynamic of their own, even in predominantly rural areas of the platteland. Finally, the relative weakness of the liberal paternalism of the Joint Councils in the OFS contributed to a political climate in which the ideal of African political self-reliance could take root. The writings of Anton Lembede, especially, were to prove of crucial significance in the formation of an Africanist political consciousness within the African National Congress in the late 1940s through the organisation of the Congress Youth League.

Notes

1 For the development of the Joint Council movement see Paul B. Rich, *White Power and the Liberal Conscience: Racial Segregation and South African Liberalism, 1921-1960*, (Manchester and Johannesburg, 1984), pp. 10-32.

2 Bodleian Library, Oxford, Bryce Papers, MSS UB 48, C.T. Loram to Earl Buxton, 18 Nov. 1920.

3 Peter Walshe, *The Rise of African Nationalism in South Africa* (London, 1970), p. 188.

4 Martin Legassick, 'Liberalism, Social Control and Liberation in South Africa', Unpublished Seminar Paper, University of Warwick, 1974.

5 Baruch Hirson, 'Tuskegee, The Joint Councils and the I.C.U.', in *The Societies of Southern Africa in the 19th and 20th Centuries*, Collected Seminar Papers, Vol. 10 (London, 1981), pp. 65-76.

6 Rich, *White Power and the Liberal Conscience*, pp. 22-27, 34-35.

7 Richard Elphick, 'Mission Christianity and Interwar Liberalism', in R. Elphick, J. Butler and D. Welsh (eds), *Democratic Liberalism in South Africa: Its History and Impact* (Cape Town, 1987), pp. 64-80.

8 Legassick, 'Liberalism, Social Contract and Liberation'.

9 Paul B. Rich, 'The Appeals of Tuskegee: James Henderson, Lovedale and the Fortunes of South African Liberalism, 1906-1930', *International Journal of African Historial Studies*, 20 (1987), 271-92.

10 Sylvia Vietzen, 'Mabel Palmer and Black Higher Education in

Natal, *c.* 1936-1942', *Journal of Natal and Zulu History* VI, (1983), pp. 98-114.

11 Tim Keegan, 'The Restructuring of Agrarian Class Relations in a Colonial Economy: The Orange River Colony 1902-1910' *Journal of Southern African Studies* 5 (April 1979), pp. 234-54.

12 *Imvo*, 20 Jan. 1925.

13 Baruch Hirson, 'The Bloemfontein Riots, 1925: A Study in Community Culture and Class Consciousness', in *The Societies of Southern Africa in the 19th and 20th Centuries*, Collected Seminar Papers, Vol. 13 (London, 1984), pp. 82-96.

14 Jagger Library, University of Cape Town (JL), Margaret Ballinger Papers, Diary BL 345.

15 University of the Witwatersrand Library (UWL), AD 1433, Records of the Joint Council of Europeans and Africans (Joint Council Records) read at the Conference on Native Affairs, 27-29 Sept. 1923, for the Federal Council of the Dutch Reformed Churches, n.p., n.d. (1923?), p.9.

16 Ibid., Cj 2.1.6c, Loram to J.D. Rheinallt Jones, 22 Sept. 1926; C.T. Loram, 'The Dutch Reformed Churches and the Native Problem', *South African Outlook* 2 Feb. 1925; Rich, *White Power and the Liberal Conscience*, p. 28.

17 Ibid., Minutes of Meetings of the Johannesburg Joint Council, 6 Oct. 1927 and 22 Aug. 1928; *Imvo*, 27 April 1928.

18 *Umteteli wa Bantu*, 9 Oct. 1928 and 25 May 1929.

19 Ibid., 13 Oct. 1928.

20 UWL, A 881, J. Howard Pim Papers, Notes of Rheinallt Jones, 13 Sept.1930.

21 *Umteteli wa Bantu*, 9 July and 20 Aug. 1927; Walshe, *The Rise of African Nationalism*, pp. 176-78.

22 *Umteteli wa Bantu*, 18 Feb. 1933.

23 Ibid., 30 March and 25 May 1919, 16 Dec. 1933; *Bantu World* 24 June 1933.

24 UWL, Joint Council Records, Cj 2.1.7, Loram to Rheinallt Jones 6 May 1927.

25 Ibid., CK 5, Economics — Native Trading, Memorandum by Kroonstad Chamber of Commerce (1932); see also Joint Council MSS, Statement by Councillor C.J. Felland, Mayor of Kroonstad, and Councillor H. Heubane, Chairman of Native African Committee, to Enquiry, held at Kroonstad, 5 Sept. 1932; *Kroonstad Times*, 9 Aug. 1932.

26 *Natal Witness*, 13 Sept. 1927.

27 *Imvo*, 25 March and 23 Sept. 1930.

28 *Mochochonono*, 23 July 1930.

29 JL, *W.G. Ballinger Papers*, BC 347 A5, V.20, R.A. Sello to W.B. Ballinger, 28 July 1931; *Native Economic Commission*, Minutes, Evidence of R. Sello, 18/17 Feb. 1931.

30 *Kroonstad Times*, 10 April 1931; *Umteteli wa Bantu*, 18 April and 16 May 1931. A meeting was also held in Bloemfontein in June, *Ikwezi le Afrika*, 18 July 1931. Mote especially hoped the Unity Movement would form a political base for African intellectuals to 'harness themselves for the economic emancipation of the race and the incubus of ignorance', *Umteteli wa Bantu*, 7 Nov. 1931.

31 *Ikwezi le Afrika*, 2 May 1931.

32 Ibid., 10 Oct. 1931.

33 UWL, Joint Council Records, CK 5, Joint Council MSS, M. Knight to Rheinallt Jones, 10 Sept. 1931.

34 Ibid., Economics — Native Trading, Martin Knight, Draft of Memorandum on the Granting of Trading Rights in Locations', to be presented to the Kroonstad Joint Council on 29 July 1931, dated 8 July 1931, enclosed in Knight to Rheinallt Jones, 8 July 1931.

35 Ibid., Joint Council of Europeans and Natives, Kroonstad, *Memorandum on the Granting of Trading Sites in Locations in the Orange Free State*, Lovedale Press, n.d. (1931?).

36 UWL, AD 843/B, Records of the SAIRR, Part I, 71.1, Distress and Unemployment Among Natives, Report of an Interview with the Minister of Native Affairs, 26 Oct. 1932.

37 Ibid., Rheinallt Jones to A.A. Henderson, 17 Nov. 1931.

38 Ibid., AC 6, J.R. Cooper, 'Urban Conditions with Special Reference to the Urban Areas Act and Municipal Administration', in *Some Aspects of the Native Question: Some Addresses delivered at the Fifth National-European-Bantu Conference*, Bloemfontein, 5-7 July 1933 (Johannesburg, 1935), p. 97. See also Paul B. Rich, 'Administrative Ideology, Urban Social Control and the Origins of Apartheid Theory, 1930-1939', *Journal of African Studies* 7, (Summer 1980), pp. 70-82.

39 Ibid., CK 5.1, Secretary of Native Affairs to Rheinallt Jones, 29 Aug. 1931.

40 Ibid., CJ 2.1.13, Johannesburg Joint Council to Municipal Native Administration Department, 30 Oct. 1932.

41 Ibid., CK 5.1, Rheinallt Jones to R. Shepherd, 27 Feb. 1935;

Rheinallt Jones to C. Martin, 23 Feb. 1935.

42 Ibid, Rheinallt Jones to Shepherd, 27 Feb. 1935; Rheinallt Jones to Martin, 23 Feb. 1935.

43 *Bantu World*, 30 Dec. 1933.

44 UWL, Joint Council Records, CK 5, Memorandum submitted to the Industrial Legislation Commission by the Native Advisory Board, Kroonstad, 21 Nov. 1934, pp. 3-4.

45 Ibid., p. 5.

46 Ibid, Kroonstad Joint Council, Memorandum submitted to Industrial Legislation Commission, at Kroonstad, 13 Nov. 1934.

47 *Umteteli wa Bantu*, 11 July, 5 and 12 Dec. 1936.

48 Ibid., 2 and 9 May and 27 June 1936.

49 UWL, Joint Council Records, CK 5.1, Martin to Lynn Saffery, 21 June 1937.

50 Ibid., Martin to Rheinallt Jones, 24 Aug. 1937.

51 Ibid., Rheinallt Jones to Martin, 21 Aug. 1937.

52 Ibid., J.R. Brent to Rheinallt Jones, 4 Feb. 1937; Sello to Rheinallt Jones, 4 Feb. 1937.

53 Ibid., Sello to Rheinallt Jones, 15 Feb. 1937; Brent to Rheinallt Jones, 15 Feb. 1937.

54 Ibid., Brent to Rheinallt Jones, 15 Feb. 1937. The Executive Committee of the Advisory Board Congress left it up to local boards to choose between Rheinallt Jones and Ballinger, *Umteteli wa Bantu*, 9 January 1937.

55 Ibid., Rheinallt Jones to Brent, 16 Feb. 1937. However, Mote, Binda and Sello denied writing to Ballinger, ibid., Brent to Rheinallt Jones, 18 Feb. 1937. Mote had earlier bought a car from ICU funds for some £395.

56 Ibid., Mote to Rheinallt Jones, 12 March 1937. Mote was able to secure the support too of Jason Jingoes in the Transvaal for Rheinallt Jones's campaign.

57 *Umteteli wa Bantu*, 17 April 1937.

58 Ibid., 24 April 1937.

59 UWL, SAIRR AD843/B, 62.11, Native Land, 1933, Rheinallt Jones to J. Soldaat, 7 June 1933, and to Resident Magistrate, Thaba Nchu, 23 Feb. 1933. For the BPA, see Colin Murray, 'Land Power and Class in the Thaba Nchu District, Orange Free State, 1884-1983', *Review of African Political Economy* 29 (July 1984), pp. 42-43.

60 Ibid., 3.2.1., N.M. Motshumi to Rheinallt Jones, 9 Jan. 1937;

Umteteli wa Bantu 20 March 1937.

61 UWL, Joint Council Records, CK 5.1, Brent to Rheinallt Jones, 15 Feb. 1937; Murray, 'Land Power and Class', p. 43; *Umteteli wa Bantu*, 20 March 1937.

62 W.B. Ballinger Papers, BG 347 C5.1.3.1. Selby Msimang to S.H. Thema, 9 Feb. 1937, p. 43; *Umteteli wa Bantu*, 10 April 1937.

63 Killie Campbell Library, Durban, Maurice Webb Papers, KCM 21929, Rheinallt Jones to M. Webb, 22 June 1937.

64 *South African Worker*, 20 Feb. 1937.

65 *Umteteli wa Bantu*, 3 April and 3 July 1937.

66 UWL, A.B. Xuma Papers, ABX 370203, A.B. Xuma to J. Moroka, 3 Feb. 1937.

67 *Umteteli wa Bantu*, 23 April 1938.

68 Ibid., 29 Oct. 1938; *Umlingi we Nyanga*, 15 Nov. 1938.

69 Archives of the SAIRR at the South African Institute of Race Relations, Johannesburg, Proceedings of the Sixth Annual General and Twelfth Ordinary Meeting of the Council of the South African Institute of Race Relations, Hiddell Hall, University of Cape Town, 7 and 8 Jan. 1938.

70 Leo Marquard, *Farm Labour in the Orange Free State*, (Johannesburg, 1939), p. 15.

71 Ibid., p. 36.

72 Ibid., p. 44. See also William Beinart, 'Soil Erosion, Conservationism and Ideas about Development: A Southern African Exploration, 1900-1960', *Journal of Southern African Studies* II (Oct. 1984), pp. 32-83.

73 Paul B. Rich, *Race and Empire in British Politics*, (Cambridge, 1986), pp. 145-49.

74 UWL, AD 843/RJ/H, Economics — Native Trading, Resolution taken at Meeting of OFS African Trading Association, 3 July 1939; UWL, Rheinallt Jones Papers, Mote to Rheinallt Jones, 12 Aug. 1939; *Umteteli wa Bantu*, 22 July, 11 and 18 Nov. 1939. Mote's view was not unanimously held by African political leaders at this time for I. Bud Mbelle advised Rheinallt Jones to attend meetings of the Advisory Board Congress in order to neutralise the 'irresponsible opinions that might alienate white political support', ibid., Mbelle to Rheinallt Jones, 16 March 1938.

75 *African Teacher*, Dec. 1937.

76 *Umteteli wa Bantu*, 20 Sept. 1941; Joint Council Records, J.E.F. van Zyl to Rheinallt Jones, 10 Oct. 1941.

77 UWL, A.B. Xuma Papers, ABX 410528, R. Cingo (?) to Xuma, 28 May 1941.

78 UWL, Joint Council Records, CK 5, Rheinallt Jones to Father A. Amor, 9 Aug. 1941.

79 UWL, SAIRR, AD 843/RJ/M, Economics — Native Trading, Abner Manoto, President, OFS Bantu Traders' Association, to Rheinallt Jones, 5 May 1939.

80 Ibid., CK 5, Sello to Rheinallt Jones, 28 March 1940.

81 Ibid., Van Zyl, Native Administration Department, Kroonstad, to Rheinallt Jones, 1 Nov. 1941, enclosing Memorandum from Sello to Van Zyl, 1 Nov. 1941.

82 Ibid., Rheinallt Jones to Sello, 22 Oct. 1941.

83 Ibid.

84 W.M. MacMillan Papers, in the private possession of Mrs Mona MacMillan, J. Lewin to W.M. MacMillan, 3 Dec. 1942. Lewin described Basner as 'a rough type, full of sound and fury against the government and I fear that even educated Africans have not yet learned to distinguish the noisy from the industrious candidates'.

85 Cory Library, Rhodes University, Grahamstown, R. Shepherd Papers 14, 713(n), Rheinallt Jones to Shepherd, 25 Dec. 1942.

86 UWL, Rheinallt Jones Papers, Native Advisory Board, Heilbron, to Rheinallt Jones, 14 Oct. 1938.

87 *Umteteli wa Bantu* 8 Nov. 1941.

88 *Ilanga lase Natal*, 9 Dec. 1944.

89 See in particular Gail M. Gerhart, *Black Power in South Africa: The Evolution of an Ideology*, (Berkeley, Los Angeles and London, 1978), esp. pp. 51-67 for Lembede's Africanism, which initially bore some admiration for European fascist ideologies until Lembede was persuaded to the contrary by A.P. Mda. Lembede's parents had been sharecroppers in the Georgedale district of Natal before moving to Isabelo in the late 1920s.

90 Baruch Hirson, 'Rural Revolt in South Africa, 1937-1951', in *The Societies of Southern Africa in the 19th and 20th Centuries*, Vol. 8 (London, 1978), pp. 115-32.

91 UWL, AB Xuma Papers, 460602, S.M. Elias to Xuma, 2 June 1946; A.B.X. 460606, Xuma to Elias, 6 June 1946.

92 School of Oriental and African Studies (SOAS) Library, London, S.M. Molema Papers, microfilm, SOAS, London, Organiser's Report for the Year ending Dec. 1947, OFS Province.

School Boards, School Committees and Educational Politics

Aspects of the Failure of Bantu Education as a Hegemonic Strategy, 1955-1976

Jonathan Hyslop

In 1955 the Nationalist government moved to implement the Bantu Education Act of 1953. Among the measures provided for in the Act was the establishment of bodies at a local level which would participate in the administration of schooling in black areas — the school boards and school committees. These were designed to play an important role in the new Bantu Education system. That system was aimed at the rapid expansion of black schooling on the cheapest basis possible. At the same time it had to underpin, politically and ideologically, the state's intention to incorporate blacks within separate political structures. The school boards and committees were clearly part of this programme. Through them the state could transfer much of the burden of financing education, and some of the burden of administering it, on to local communities. The Nationalists intended that these structures would also provide a community leadership role for officially acceptable representatives of black interests, enabling more conservative figures in the community to strengthen their position by exercising a degree of real local power. The intention was to incorporate sections of the community ideologically into the apartheid project by providing an illusion of self-government.

That at any rate was the intention. What this paper aims to show is that the school board and committee system failed to play the hegemonic role which it was designed to fulfil. Established in the midst of the great political mobilisations of the 1950s, it was subject to immediate political attacks which undermined its legitimacy from the outset. The members of the committees and boards tended to be marginal and unpopular figures. At the same time, the authorities maintained an authoritarian and arrogant stance towards the boards and committees themselves, refusing to listen to their suggestions, and unseating members who would not toe the official line. By the late 1960s and early 1970s practices such as these, and the Department of Bantu Education's imposition of ethnic segregation in the urban areas, had begun to turn some of the boards and committees against the Department. While in the Bantustans the boards and committees did help the state to incorporate traditional chiefs and Bantustan petty-bourgeoisie, the corruption and brutality of this stratum's use of the system did nothing to strengthen its legitimacy. Finally, the usefulness of the whole mechanism to the state was called into question with the controversy over the Afrikaans medium of instruction in 1974-76. In this period it was the school boards in the urban areas that initially led opposition to the state's new policy before being overtaken by the students in 1976. The instrument had turned against its creator. But this final rebellion came too late to restore any real popular legitimacy to those elements involved in the board and committee system. For all practical purposes, the 1976 uprising dealt a fatal blow to any hope on the part of the state that the boards and committees would play the hegemonic role intended for them.

A particularly important aspect of this failure was the inability of the board and committee system to integrate teachers. Teachers were a key group for the state to draw into its new order. They represented, at least in the 1950s and 1960s, the most important section of the educated black workforce, and enjoyed as a group a measure of respect in many communities, and sometimes a position of community leadership (although to a lesser extent than in the pre-Bantu Education period). Moreover, they were at first glance a group disposed towards a certain conservatism: they enjoyed a relatively privileged position within the racially discriminatory and segmented labour market; they followed solidly conservative teachers' organisations from the early 1960s until after the 1976 uprisings; from the late 1960s many of them were upwardly socially mobile — as opportunities developed for black clerical and junior managerial employees in industry many tended to see their future in terms of career advancement rather than social change; and professionalist and gradualist ideologies were pervasive in teaching circles. Indeed teachers did not, as an organised force, really turn to militant opposition to the regime even in the 1970s. But throughout the period, the best the state was able to obtain from them was their acquiescence, rather than their real incorporation and support. Obviously this has to be understood primarily in terms of teachers' membership of an oppressed majority. But it was also in part an outcome of the fact that the board and committee system affected teachers in ways which militated against their incorporation. The boards and committees exerted considerable powers over teachers at a local level. Often their members, drawn from more traditionalist and less educated strata, handled teachers in a manner tinged with an underlying class hostility. This conflict was intensified with the elaboration of the Bantustan system, as the boards and committees often became the tools of local petty despots. Pretoria displayed a total insensitivity to the plight of the teachers and to their responses to these circumstances. School boards were made the conduit of many of the Native Affairs Department's (and later the Bantu Education Department's) unpopular decisions about the teaching profession, and, at the same time, the government subjected teachers to a grossly racist ideology and practice which could not in any way offset their negative reactions to the boards and committees.

Thus the role which the school boards and committees were supposed to play in underpinning the hegemonic project of Bantu Education was undermined by the assertive bigotry of officialdom, by the state's abandonment of teachers to the mercy of local tyrants, by the government's refusal to listen to criticisms of policy voiced by the representative structures which it had itself established, and ultimately by the long simmering traditions of popular resistance.

Establishment of the School Board Structure

Christie and Collins[1] have rightly drawn attention to the hegemonic character of the Verwoerdian design for Bantu Education. Verwoerd and his cohorts did aim to provide mechanisms for the incorporation of blacks within the new political order which they were propounding. The 'homelands' would provide the arena within which black political advancement and educational development would take place. The Nationalist government therefore sought to provide means by which the allegiance of sectors of the black population to a conception of their future as in the homelands could be secured. In order to do this, structures would have to be created within which such ideologically incorporated sectors would come to see themselves as having a role in determining their future. This illusion of self-determination would

enable the dominant social groups to exercise control without being
perceived as doing so.

Verwoerd quite explicitly outlined his aims in education in these
terms in his notorious speeches to Parliament on Bantu Education in
1953. In these he called for a form of black participation in black
educational administration

> which will make him ['the Bantu'] feel that he is co-responsible
> for his education but that he is also assisted by the guardian ['the
> European'] in so far as he is incapable of assuming co-
> responsibility for it...[2]

The school boards and committees were the means chosen for this
purpose. Not only would they play the essential ideological role of
winning parents' allegiance to Bantu Education, but they would also
provide a means of squeezing black communities financially in order to
subsidise the kind of cheap mass education which the National Party
was aiming at. Thus Verwoerd argued that black parents should be
made co-responsible for their children's education and

> that co-responsibility is two-fold — it is co-responsibility for
> control, but associated with that is co-responsibility in respect of
> finances.[3]

Accordingly the Bantu Education Act (No. 47 of 1953) gave the
responsible Minister sweeping powers to provide for black
participation in educational administration by establishing 'such
regional, local, and domestic councils, boards, or other bodies as he may
deem expedient' or to place any government school under bodies such
as the 'Bantu Authorities'.[4] As we shall see, the sweeping powers over
such bodies granted by the Act to the Minister were not always used in
a way which was consistent with their hegemonic design.

Regulations laid down that the school committees, which were
immediately responsible for a particular school, would be partly elected
by the parents. In both rural and urban areas, four to six of the
committee members could be elected by parents.[5] Clearly this was
aimed at drawing local communities into the new system. In order to
strengthen the strata participating in homeland structures in the rural
areas, the local authority was given the right to nominate six of the
members of the committee. However, these nominations were subject

to approval by Pretoria, and the Secretary of Native Affairs could appoint a further two members.[6] In the urban areas the remainder of school committee members, comprising a majority, were direct appointees of the Secretary for Native Affairs or the local Native Commissioner.[7]

The committees were to be the key link to the community, controlling school funds, erecting new buildings, and advising the school boards.[8] What real power was embodied in the system subsisted, however, in the school boards. These were wholly appointed bodies, with one school board controlling a group of school committees. In the urban areas all the members were appointed by the Native Affairs Department (NAD). In the rural areas the members were nominated by the Department and by the 'Bantu Authority'. It seems that as the homeland system developed the proportion of homeland authority appointees was allowed to increase.[9] The boards had considerable powers over local schools and teachers. From 1955 all African teachers' salaries were paid as subsidies to the school boards, which meant that the boards effectively controlled hiring and firing (although central government could force the board to sack a teacher by withdrawing the subsidy in respect of a particular person).[10]

From this brief description some of the inherent weaknesses of the system ought to be apparent. The hegemonic aims of the school committee structure were undermined by the Native Affairs Department's reluctance to concede real control to parents by insisting on a majority of appointees. The Native Affairs Department wanted parental participation without giving up real control. The boards did do something towards strengthening the power of homeland authorities. But appointees dominated the boards, and the fact that they were not responsible to the parents of local students also undermined their legitimacy. This structure tended to encourage the emergence of tyrannical school boards, subservient to Pretoria and resented by local parents and teachers.

Resistance to School Boards

The school board system was immediately challenged by the mass political movements of the time, which saw it an intrinsic part of Bantu Education's imposition of a totally separate and inferior education system. At a meeting of the national executive committee of the African National Congress (ANC) in Durban on 6 March 1955, a call was made for a boycott of the boards and committees.[11] The Unity Movement also opposed the board system, and indeed, unlike the ANC, saw such a boycott as the main strategy against Bantu Education.[12] Although nationally insignificant compared with the ANC, the Unity Movement was in a position to affect the struggle over this issue in the Cape because of its control of the Cape African Teachers' Association.

During the two years following the introduction of the boards and committees, there were numerous instances of resistance to their establishment. J. Dugard, then Regional Director of Bantu Education in the Cape, writes that

> where the ANC was active only very brave men would agree to be government nominees on the boards and it was quite impossible to organise meetings to choose representatives of parents.[13]

In May 1955 parents at Langbuya Location, Paarl, voted not to elect a school committee after a speaker suggested that 'it would be better if Dr Eiselen came to explain things himself'.[14] Langa, in Cape Town, proved a particularly hard nut for the NAD to crack. When meetings of parents were arranged for five schools there in August 1955, all but one of the schools voted against establishing a committee.[15] (There was suspicion that the sub-inspector had rigged the ballot on this issue at the fifth school.[16]) A further attempt the next year to establish committees in Cape Town was also unsuccessful. At Langa High School the chairman of the meeting arranged for this purpose was chased out of the meeting. Parents at Langa Methodist School disrupted the meeting there, and the school board member presiding fled via the window. St Cyprians parents also refused to elect a committee, while at an Athlone school the secretary of the Peninsular School Board was reduced to accepting nominations of committee members from the CID members attending the meeting.[17] There was also significant resistance to the new structures in the Eastern Cape and Transkei. A Grahamstown meeting to elect a committee was broken up by ANC members from East London.[18] It was reported in March 1955 that in the Tsomo and Mount Ayliff districts the overwhelming majority of school boards were being boycotted.[19]

The school boards and committees thus met a great deal of opposition at their inception, which to some extent stamped them in the popular imagination as organs of an oppressive system. This was clearly a major threat to their intended aims. But just as there were sectors of the dominated groups who resolutely rejected them, there were also those who sought to enter the system for whatever advantages might be gained. Those who were participating in the 'Bantu Authority' system in the homelands, members of urban elites who hoped for advancement through the advisory board system, and less educated rural people who resented the relative social prestige of teachers, were prime candidates for such incorporation. Furthermore, there were those opposed to the existing order who did not see the boards and committees as worth opposing. All this is reflected in the fact that despite strong opposition the state did manage to put the system in place. By 1956 there were 300 school boards and 4000 committees in existence.[20] Education officials found that in the rural areas it was not difficult in most places to find 'men and women of some standing in the community' to serve on the boards.[21]

In urban areas establishing credible school boards was more difficult: those willing to stand were often clergy and ex-teachers who lacked much popular support.[22] But some prominent figures, such as Dr W. Nkomo and Paul Mosaka, could be found advocating the idea of joining school boards in order to fight Bantu Education from within.[23] It also seems that not all ANC members adhered to their organisation's line of total boycott of the committees. At an ANC public meeting in Dube in June 1955 a speaker advocating a school boycott counterposed this strategy to a boycott of the committees:

> ...they forget that in School Boards there are elements [who are present] only because they are getting their bread.[24]

It seems that in New Brighton in Port Elizabeth some ANC members participated in the election of a school committee.[25] These events should be seen in the context that it was only in the 1950s that the ANC moved away from judging participation in state structures on tactical grounds. The reality of the growth of the school boards and committees should warn us against a simple conception of the rise of Bantu Education in which 'the people' rejected the system, while only a handful of 'traitors' participated in it. There was broad-based opposition to the system, but there were also significant constituencies, who, for varying motives, were willing to enter it.

The School Boards in Action

The operation of the school boards rapidly justified the forewarnings of their opponents. The boards were placed in a position where they were responsible for carrying out the parsimonious state educational spending policies of Dr Verwoerd. In many matters the apparent discretion given to the boards was quickly shown to be illusory. For example, the boards were 'allowed' to discontinue school feeding schemes if they wished. The money thus saved could then be spent on 'amenities'. But 'amenities' were taken to include the hiring of more teachers.[26] The demise of feeding schemes was thus assured. The boards also set about the supervision of the raising of money by the committees for the construction of new schools.[27] Considerable resentment was caused by the plight of areas which had been levied heavily by school committees and did not benefit proportionately from new school buildings.[28]

The boards also became the instrument of the state's purge of politically dissident teachers from the profession during the late 1950s.[29] In a series of cases it seems that school boards made spurious charges against teachers as a way of simultaneously discrediting and getting rid of them. A teacher at Langa Methodist School, for example, was dismissed in 1956 for alleged sexual misconduct with a pupil. The student's father wrote to the school board saying that there was no truth in the charge. The teacher was then summoned to a meeting with the secretary of the school board, who demanded that he sign a statement admitting his guilt. A scuffle broke out, and the teacher was charged with assaulting the school board chairman. But when the case was heard the Magistrate threw it out, and advised the teacher to appeal against his dismissal.[30] Similarly, the Unity Movement activist, V.K. Ntshona, was sacked by the Moroka-Jabavu School Board for supposed neglect of duties. When he applied to another school he obtained a temporary appointment, but was then turned down by the school board on grounds of his political activity after the board had been visited by the Special Branch. A subsequent attempt to obtain a post for Ntshona was frustrated when the NAD informed the school board that it would not provide a subsidy for any post held by Ntshona, and the board duly excluded him from consideration.[31]

Some board members positively revelled in the power that they now enjoyed. The Revd Lediga, Chairman of the Langa School Board, informed a meeting in 1958 that 'from now on he would see to it that the Board put its foot down and dealt more severely with the teachers'. He went on to inform the gathering that 'there has never been such a learned government as we have in the present'.[32]Much of the animosity between teachers and school boards was fuelled by the way in which teachers, formerly a prestigious social group, were placed under the control of bodies often consisting of persons less educated than themselves.[33] There was an anti-democratic as well as a democratic component in the objections raised by teachers to the new structures. At the 1957 conference of the conservative Cape African Teachers' Union (CATU) a resolution was passed that members of school committees ought to have completed primary education, and members of school boards some post-primary education.[34]

Teachers and Bantu Education Ideology

The board system worked in a way which undermined the position of teachers as professionals. Hence it served as an obstacle, and not as an aid to their ideological incorporation into the Verwoerdian social order. The possibilities of such incorporation were similarly undermined by the staggering crudity of the administrative and ideological practices of the central educational authorities. The change from provincial to central control of the educational apparatus meant that the liberal paternalism which had characterised much of the administration of education was replaced by brute authoritarianism.

Inspectors with a knowledge of local conditions and African languages were often replaced by people who lacked both.[35] Administrators with educational experience were sometimes replaced by NAD officials who knew nothing of education and were notoriously rude to their subordinates.[36] These developments in part reflected official determination to root out what were seen as liberal influences in African education, especially in the Cape where the government was particularly suspicious of the ideological proclivities of educational administrators.[37] Dr Verwoerd himself is said to have commented to the Director of Bantu Education, 'A lot of your inspectors are just plain liberals'.[38] Official racism in black education really came into its own, however, when W.A. Maree became the first Minister of an independent Department of Bantu Education in 1958.[39] Maree was responsible for the issuing of a circular to white inspectors forbidding them to shake hands with blacks.[40] Maree also occupied himself with such weighty matters as personally reprimanding Inspector Martin

Potgieter for drinking tea with the black teachers at Lovedale.[41] The Ministerial approach rapidly permeated to local level. At Adams College the dishwasher was upbraided for washing the cups of black and white staff in the same sink.[42] For black teachers used to the paternalism of the missions and the relative paternalism of the pre-inspectorate such experiences were shocking. The aggressive gut racism of those charged with implementing Bantu Education overrode the hegemonic imperatives of the system. Squeezed between the bullying of school boards on the one hand and the abuse of racist administrators on the other, teachers fell into a grumbling acceptance of the status quo. But that did not amount to an allegiance to it.

The 1960s and Early 1970s: A Period of Acquiescence

The defeat of the mass African nationalist movement in the early 1960s created a wholly different political context for the school boards. From then until the early 1970s they were no longer under overt political attack. The new conditions did much to strengthen the boards. One senior departmental official found that in this period holding a seat on a school board became far more acceptable in black communities.[43] By 1969 there were 509 school boards and 4 108 school committees, involving over 50 000 people.[44] But while the numbers of those serving on the school boards may have increased, their structure and policies continued to be ones which generated friction between them and community members and teachers. The lack of accountability of the boards to parents allowed them to trample over grass-roots opinion. A memorandum by Transvaal teachers in 1966 complained that school boards were ignoring or overturning recommendations made by school committees.[45] Furthermore, the board and committee system continued to be used by the state to extract financial contributions to education from parents. By 1971 these contributions had risen to the level of R1,7 million — of which only R350 000 was spent on repairs and new buildings, while the remainder was spent on teachers' salaries.[46] Urban parents in particular bore a heavy burden because of the state's determination during this period to restrict funds spent on urban black schooling. In 1964 in Moroka 100 out of 600 teachers were being paid by the board.[47] This practice also further alienated teachers from the boards as board salaries could be 45 to 55 per cent lower than regular departmental salaries.[48] The authorities thus generated a relatively limited amount of extra finance for education services, while at the same time creating a powerful source of parent and teacher resentment of the boards.

The Bantu Education Department's treatment of urban school boards themselves also served to undermine their credibility and their loyalty. Members of boards and committees who were politically suspect were arbitrarily removed from their positions.[49] In at least one case where the Department disapproved of the actions of members of a school board, the board was dissolved (Moroka, 1968).[50] The Department also stifled the initiative of the boards by refusing them permission to raise funds from outside donors.[51] The Vanderbijlpark school board was 'warned' by the Department in 1971 for accepting R3 000 toward the building of a school library.[52]

The contradictions of the boards were further intensified through their being loaded with responsibility for the state's policy, introduced in the late 1960s, of separating out urban schools on an ethnic basis.[53] This policy resulted in utter chaos. When it was implemented in Meadowlands in 1968, artificial overcrowding was created in the Tswana schools.[54] In other cases disastrous mismanagement of the ethnic reorganisation brought about such consequences as the allocation of junior primary students to a secondary school.[55] The Department acted with its customary lack of finesse in the matter, engaging in the wholesale expulsion of Zulu-speaking students from a Soweto school where they constituted the majority in 1973,[56] and bringing about a situation where in 1975 there were no junior secondaries for Tsonga and North Sotho speakers in Diepkloof.[57] All this scarcely brought much lustre to the boards.

School Boards in the Bantustans

During the 1960s and 1970s school boards in the Bantustans increasingly became a means by which the chiefs and homeland politicians exercised their sway over rural society. The boards provided these groups both with ways of disciplining parents and teachers and with profitable sources of misappropriated funds. These tendencies were accelerated from 1967 when the state moved to transfer administrative control over education in the Bantustans to their 'territorial authorities'.[58] The rural school boards exercised their authority ferociously over the teachers. At one school in the Tswana Territorial Authority area the Vice-Chairman of the school board told the school committee that 'Teachers are but dogs. We can dismiss them at any moment.'[59] Once again, the way in which such school boards and committees operated undermined their hegemonic purpose. While they were able to underpin the incorporation of chiefs and some homeland élites into the Bantustan scheme, the arbitrary way in which they exercised their authority alienated numbers of potential supporters amongst teachers and parents. The dominant groups in the homelands tended to loot the institutions which were placed in their trust for wealth and power, rather than using them as instruments of a hegemonic strategy.

Illustrative of these processes is the story of Philip M. Malebye, the Principal of Itotleng-Baralong secondary school in the Lichtenburg area during the late 1960s. Malebye came into conflict with the local authorities over the various forms of corruption to which they subjected the school. The local chief imposed on those pupils who came from outside the Ratlou Baralong Tribal Area a R6 tax which was paid into tribal funds. The school committee raised a levy of R3 a head from students for the building of latrines but then did not carry out this work. In November 1968 they bought 100 bags of cement for the flooring of four new classrooms. The cement was then mysteriously used up without the planned work being done - presumably appropriated by members of the committee. Malebye's resentment of such corruption apparently engendered tensions between him and the school board and school committee. The conflict was finally precipitated when a pupil approached Malebye in 1968 with evidence that she had been sexually harassed or abused by the principal of the primary school. Malebye passed this evidence on to the school board for their action. However, the primary school principal was an ally of the chief, and so instead of attempting to investigate the issue, the chief and school board began to try to get rid of Malebye. An allegation of embezzlement was then brought against Malebye, but an investigation by the responsible administrative official found that no money was missing. A charge was then brought against Malebye in the Delareyville Magistrate's Court that he had stolen a R15 cheque from the local storekeeper.[60] However, during the trial in February 1969 the storekeeper admitted that he had conspired with the chief to frame Malebye for the offence.[61] After a brief respite the board and committee moved simply to dismiss Malebye. An advertisement for his post was placed in the *World* and he was given notice to quit his post by 1 April 1969.[62] To add insult to injury, the chief's henchmen also stole some of Malebye's property. Although Malebye had plans for legal action, it seems that little came of this.[63] Malebye's tale illustrates well the manner in which those who exercised power in Bantustan structures enhanced their power through their control of the school boards, but also shows how this control was not exercised in such a way as to bring these bodies greater popular support.

Some of the most intense conflicts involving teachers in rural areas took place in the central and northern Transvaal during the early 1970s. Two dimensions of Bantustan politics need to be understood here. Firstly, in Lebowa the period was dominated by a conflict between those forces linked to the chiefs, who wanted to bolster chiefly power, and a grouping, apparently led by sections of the petty bourgeoisie and educated employees, who stood for a reduction in chiefly power. Up to 1972 the Lebowa Territorial Authority had been led by Chief Masermule Matlala, a stern traditionalist and an extreme conservative.[64] However, in 1972, with the transition of Lebowa to 'self-governing' status, Matlala was replaced by Cedric Phathudi, who became Chief Minister as the leader of an anti-traditionalist faction. In 1975, after Phathudi had failed, because of South African government opposition, to force the chiefs into a separate upper house in the Lebowa legislature, he brought about a compromise with Matlala, joining together to fend off attacks from a group around the former Interior Minister, Collins Ramusi, who wanted a more determined attack on chiefly power.[65] Secondly, there was considerable political turmoil within Lebowa, Bophuthatswana and surrounding 'white' areas over the creation of KwaNdebele. The state had originally not intended to establish a separate Ndebele 'homeland' but rather to allow the existence of Ndebele territorial authorities within Lebowa and Bophuthatswana. However, a combination of the particularism of the existing Bantustan leaders who wanted to force out 'foreign' elements, particularist forces amongst the Ndebele chiefs, the labour needs of the Pretoria-Witwatersrand-Vereeniging area, and the ideological dynamics of the state's commitment to a distinct ethnic basis for Bantustans, brought about during the 1970s an attempt to construct a single ethnic unit for the Ndebele.[66] The result was the formation of the least viable of all homelands — KwaNdebele. This process involved considerable friction between Ndebele communities and the Lebowa and Bophuthatswana governments.

The seventies thus saw severe friction in the region between traditionalist and 'modernising' leaderships and between various ethnically defined leadership groupings, and this had a severe impact on teachers in particular. One of the most spectacular results of this was a spate of incidents in which teachers were forcibly circumcised by traditionalist elements. These actions were, I would suggest, a way in which traditionalists warded off the threat to their power by more urbanised and educated groupings by subjecting them to a supposedly traditional ritual. These actions underscored the conflict in rural society between rural élites. Teachers, the bearers of a heavily Westernised identity, defined themselves against the forms of tradition invoked by the more conservative élites. A teacher who had been subject to such a forced circumcision replied in this fashion to his cross-examination during the trial of the culprits in the Potgietersrust Regional Court:

> — Was the circumcision done according to Bantu custom?
> — I don't know.
> — Do you have no knowledge of the customs of the tribe involved here?
> — The heathens, yes, they use that custom.[67]

Here the distance between 'the heathens' — a term of abuse drawn straight from a missionary vocabulary — and the teacher is clearly demarcated. This demarcation reflects a real depth of hostility.

In another such case, Amos Motsepe, principal of Metsangwana primary school and Chairman of the Transvaal United African Teachers Association (TUATA), Elands River Branch, was the victim. On 31 May 1970 Motsepe was dragged out of his motor car, beaten and taken to a circumcision school run by Headman Lesolo Maloka and under the control of Chief Motodi Matlala. The next day he was forcibly circumcised. Motsepe was later moved to another camp and held until the end of July, when he was released. Eventually in 1974, with the financial assistance of TUATA, Motsepe was able to bring a legal case against Chief Matlala, Headman Maloka and their henchmen.[68] Motsepe duly won the case, and considerable damages against Chief Matlala were awarded. However, when he tried to collect these damages he found it virtually impossible to do so. Motsepe's attempts to recover what had been awarded to him were an object lesson in the difficulties faced by anyone trying to challenge chiefly power in the Bantustans. An investigator sent to the Chief's area by Motsepe's attorneys found that the Chief and his brother Chief Mokogome Matlala had a considerable income: they imposed not only their own poll tax in the area but also an annual levy on patients at the local mission hospital, they received salaries as officials of the Lebowa government, split the proceeds of tribal funds between them, and pocketed half of any fines imposed in their Lekgotla. In addition, the Chiefs received a portion of the produce of of all land farmed. But it was to be very difficult for Motsepe to lay his hands on any of these assets. Matlala dispersed his cattle amongst the herds of the local people, thus making it impossible for them to be identified and seized.[69] It became clear that further investigations would place the attorney's agent in danger.[70] When the attorneys tried to serve a writ on the Chief, they could not find a Deputy Sheriff who was willing to enter the area for this purpose.[71] In 1980 the attorneys were still struggling to have the judgement enforced, even though Matlala had now suffered a decline in his fortunes and was in jail on a charge of stock theft.[72]

In other cases the results of forced circumcision were more tragic for those involved. In 1971 a group including school teachers were forcibly taken to a circumcision school in the Zebediela area and subjected to circumcision. One teacher, Gideon Mokoena, suffered a sepsis and died as a result. When those charged with the crime appeared in the Potgietersrust Regional Court they were let off with a fine.[73] Interestingly, forced circumcision has continued to be a weapon of traditionalist political forces in the rural Transvaal seeking to control those representing any form of challenge. During 1986 Venda's local Trujillo, Chief Mphephu, ordered all uncircumcised males to attend circumcision schools.[74]

Another aspect of the conflicts within the Bantustans was the way in which the Bophuthatswana authorities tried to force non-Tswana minorities out of their 'state'. In particular there was a determined attempt in the mid-1970s to force the amaNdebele-a-Moletlane chiefdom under Chieftainess Ester Kekana to leave for KwaNdebele.[75] The Bophuthatswana government tried to force the tribes' schools to teach in Tswana, but met with resistance from the tribal authority.[76] Eventually Chieftainess Kekana was deposed from her position.[77]

In summary, there was extensive conflict between and within Bantustan élites. In this conflict the school boards often became instruments of those who were strongly placed within the Bantustan social order — especially the chiefs. Because the most conservative of these elements often saw teachers as bearers of ideas contrary to their interests, and because of the avenues of corruption which school boards opened up, they were often operated by chiefs in a way which adversely affected teachers and parents. Thus, although the boards brought some benefits to dominant Bantustan élites, they did not really serve to build constituencies supporting the apartheid order.

Teacher Resentment

It should by now be clear that teachers were placed in a structurally powerless position by the school board system, and that this explains in large part their lack of incorporation in the new education order. Through the 1960s and 1970s there were complaints from teachers and parents about intimidation by the boards;[78] about manipulation of boards by the inspectors;[79] about what one teacher called the 'incompetent and unscrupulous management of our schools';[80] and about extortion of bribes by board members in matters of teachers' employment, transfer or promotion.[81] An editorial in the *World* in 1966 reflected the attitudes of black salaried employees and the urban petty bourgeoisie towards the system when it denounced the situation where teachers 'are more and more being exploited by small men who are in power over them in some school boards'.[82]

However, the state's failure to obtain real support from teachers for the board and committee system was also underpinned by its inability to articulate an ideology which could effectively draw in teachers to a new perception of their role, in line with the aims of apartheid. It is true that the Bantu Education Department and its publications did make much of the concept of professionalism, and this certainly had a resonance with some sections of teachers.[83] But for the most part the Department's ideologists put forward themes that were crudely racist and loaded with menace against any form of dissent. Such approaches could scarcely gain the allegiance of many black teachers. The crudity of the Department's pronouncements was quite staggering. The Department's mouthpiece, the *Bantu Education Journal*, is notable here. On one occasion it informed its teacher-readers that to them South African whites were the most important whites in the world: 'honest and sincere in their actions to all, people whose word is their bond and who will not be frightened by violence'.[84] Even more bizarre was this 1965 editorial in the *Bantu Education Journal*:

It is about time that we take a look at our South African Bantu population to see in what respects they have exceptional qualities... choral singing is one of our strong points... Another talent which is manifested in our children is their neat handwriting... *subversive activities* and *sabotage* are not our strong points. There are some of our fellow men who, following the instigation of strangers, attempted this but they were bound to fail. They failed because these things have never had a share in our traditional way of life and because they are not intrinsic abilities of the Bantu.[85]

Here the gut racism of the Bantu Education Department's officials was clearly subverting their attempts to create a coherent ideology which could hegemonise teachers.

The 1970s: Rebellion of the Urban School Boards

In the early 1970s the consequences of the failure of the school board system for the state became apparent when school boards and committees in urban areas became foci of protest against aspects of state educational policy. In the urban areas it was harder for the state to find appointees for the boards who would be tractable than it was in rural areas where conservative groupings around chiefs could easily be yoked in. Moreover, there was more space for parents to elect competent people to school committees than in the rural areas because the way they were chosen did not involve so great an element of official nomination. With the rise of new oppositional politics, there was an increasing confidence on the part of urban black élites of their ability to assert themselves. Thus in some urban areas from around 1971 there was growing protest from school boards and committees about various state policies, culminating in their taking a significant role in challenging the policy which precipitated the 1976 student uprising — the use of Afrikaans as a teaching medium. This is not to suggest that the boards and committees were simply transformed from being collaborationist bodies into some form of popular leadership. But it is to say that in certain areas they began to articulate themes contrary to those of state policy, even if they were in fact too enmeshed in a supplicant relationship with the state to be bodies which could organise militant opposition.

The first such issue around which conflict arose was the state's attempt in the early 1970s to separate urban schools along ethnic/'tribal' lines, and to establish similarly distinct school boards for different ethnic groups. In late 1971, at a meeting with Departmental officials, members of Soweto school boards expressed their opposition to the state's plans to reorganise the boards, saying that this move would create administrative problems and generate conflict between different groups.[86] In March the following year a meeting of Soweto school committee members and parents objected to the scheme to establish 'tribal' schools and threatened to withdraw their children from the schools if it were imposed.[87] In Alexandra township in 1973 school committees and parents met and protested about the ethnic separation of the schools. The Alexandra school board then withdrew its instructions to principals to pursue this policy.[88]

There were also some incidents in which school boards came to the defence of politically victimised teachers. In two such incidents in 1972, Abraham Tiro, the Turfloop student leader (later to be assassinated in Botswana) and Edward Kubayi, who, like Tiro, had been expelled from Turfloop, were ordered by the Department to be removed from the teaching posts they had taken in Soweto. However, the responsible school boards both refused to implement the Department's decision.[89]

Thus by 1974 urban school boards, at any rate on the Rand, had developed a degree of autonomy from the Department, and were in some way voicing educational and other grievances within the community.

Writings on the student uprising of 1976 have generally ignored the role of the school boards from 1974 in opposing the imposition of Afrikaans as a teaching medium. This conflict exemplified the factors making for the ultimate failure of the boards. An issue confronted township communities on which there was near unanimity of feeling: there was virtually no support for the Bantu Education Department's decision to insist on half of school subjects being taught in Afrikaans. The school boards and committees voiced protests in this connection. But throughout the period from 1974 to 1976 the Department showed no inclination to listen to these views. It responded to the boards' opinions with threats or disciplinary action. Here was the central contradiction of the board system, namely that the state wanted it to incorporate blacks into participation in the education system, but it was not prepared to give the boards the decision-making powers that would have been essential if they were to establish a real social base. The Department wanted community participation in education, but only as long as the community's views coincided with its own. This approach guaranteed in advance the failure of boards as a hegemonic structure.

Discontent about the Afrikaans policy resulted in a meeting of ninety-one delegates from school boards of the Southern and Western Transvaal areas held in Atteridgeville on 21 December 1974. The tone of the meeting was relatively mild but nevertheless strongly opposed to the use of Afrikaans as a medium of instruction. A memorandum was drawn up demanding an end to the policy, and a deputation was chosen to meet the Department of Bantu Education on the matter.[90] The views of the meeting were couched in terms of support for the homeland leaders' views that secondary education should be conducted in English.[91] The meeting also supported the idea of seeking a Supreme Court injunction if the Department proved intractable.[92] Some, however, did express more combative views: Mr M. Peta, a member of the Atteridgeville school board, called for a school boycott if the policy were not reversed.[93] The very limited demand of the school boards was met with implacable opposition from the Department. A further meeting of school boards was held in January at which 'great dissatisfaction' was expressed by the boards at the Department's refusal to compromise with them. However, the Department was determined to repress any opposition to its policies. A joint meeting of school boards planned to be held later at Sebokeng was banned by the circuit inspector of Vereeniging.[94] In Atteridgeville the chairman of the school board, J. Mahlangu, was sacked for his opposition to the Afrikaans policy, provoking a school boycott.[95] Circulars Nos 6 and 7 of 1975 were issued by the Department to firm up its position: they reaffirmed the 50-50 English-Afrikaans rule, and forbade school boards to decide on the medium of instruction in their schools.[96] W.C. Ackermann, the Regional Director of Bantu Education for the Southern Transvaal, told one school board which had instructed its teachers to use English that their grants for teachers salaries would be cut off if they did not co-operate.[97]

These strong-arm policies did not, however, crack the school boards' opposition to the Afrikaans medium of instruction policy. Several school boards in Soweto persisted in instructing their teachers to use English as the sole medium.[98] Boards in the Port Elizabeth area also took up the issue. In February 1975 the school boards in the Port Elizabeth townships presented a joint memorandum to the local Inspector calling for abandonment of the 50-50 policy.[99]

With the beginning of the 1976 school year, the conflict in Soweto deepened. On 20 January the Meadowlands Tswana school board met the local circuit inspector to discuss the issue. The inspector took an approach characteristic of his Department's chauvinism: he argued that as all direct tax paid by blacks went to homeland education, black education was being paid for by whites. The Department thus had a duty to 'satisfy' white taxpayers.[100] Not surprisingly, the board members were unimpressed by this analysis, and voted unanimously that English should be the medium of instruction in schools under their control.[101] Following this, two members of the school board were dismissed by the Department and the other seven members resigned in protest.[102] Thereupon a students' school boycott broke out in the area, demanding the reinstatement of the board members.[103]

The story of the period leading up to June 1976 is in part one of the refusal of the Bantu Education Department to listen to its own school boards. On 13 March 1976 at a public meeting of the Diepkloof school board it was announced that the board was making it compulsory for teachers to teach in English.[104]

Yet the role of the boards in opposing the Department had brought them little credibility in the community. Creatures of the Bantu Education system, they were never given the power to establish a real base for themselves in their communities. A few days before 16 June parents in Soweto began to establish their own representative committees, precisely because they felt that the boards were not representing them properly.[105] The student movements were already by-passing the school boards. With the coming of the 16th of June the school boards and the education order they represented were swept aside, as an entirely new era of political and educational struggle opened up.

Conclusions

What then are the implications of the tale sketched out above? Bantu Education was not simply a coercive strategy. It did embrace an attempt to win the consent of sections of black South Africans. However, the state's drive toward such a hegemonic strategy was undercut by the personal racism and the authoritarianism of its agents. Through their individual abuse of key figures in local communities, and through their reluctance to accord any decision-making powers on policy to the school boards and committees, the officials of the Native Administration Department and the Bantu Education Department destroyed the possibility of these bodies being able to sway popular views of the education system. Once the initial attempts to prevent the construction of the boards and committees had failed, they did, despite their limitations, become important arenas of conflict over education. Bantu Education was able to draw significant constituencies into these administrative structures, and though they mainly functioned to prop up the system, they did also, in certain circumstances, provide vents for oppositional activities. This story illustrates very well the bankruptcy of the homeland governments' and state-identified urban élites' attempts to entrench themselves in this period. They proved incapable of providing ideological direction which would really draw mass support to the systems in which they were implicated. The failure of the state to provide for the ideological and structural integration of teachers in the new education system produced amongst this vital grouping merely a sullen and resentful acquiescence in the new order, stopping short of any real identification with it. The limitations of the educational politics of this period were precisely that it remained an intra-élite politics. The prerequisite for this politics to flourish was a willingness on the part of large sections of workers and the rural poor to recognise the power of the élites. With the rise of mass student and labour movements in the 1970s, this willingness was swept away.

Notes

1 P. Christie and C. Collins, 'Bantu Education: Apartheid Ideology and Labour Reproduction', in P. Kallaway (ed.), *Apartheid and Education: The Education of Black South Africans* (Johannesburg, 1984), pp. 172-75.

2 *Hansard*, Vol. 82-3 (1953), col. 3581.

3 Ibid.

4 Act No.47 of 1953, para 12(1), Statutes of the Union of South Africa 1953.

5 *Torch*, 12 April 1955; M. Horrell, *A Decade of Bantu Education* (Johannesburg, 1964), p. 45.

6 Horrell, *A Decade of Bantu Education*, p. 45.

7 *Torch*, 12 April 1955; Horrell, *A Decade of Bantu Education*, p. 45.

8 Horrell, *A Decade of Bantu Education*, p. 44.

9 Ibid., p. 43.

10 *Torch*, 25 Jan. 1955.

11 University of the Witwatersrand Library, Historical and Literary Papers (UW), Treason Trial Collection, AD 1812, Ea 1.2, ANC Press Release, March 1955.

12 See J. Hyslop, 'Teacher Resistance in African Education from the

1940s to the 1980s', in a forthcoming volume on South African education to be edited by M. Nkomo and published by Africa World Press.

13 J. Dugard, *Fragments of My Fleece* (Pietermaritzburg, 1985), p. 101.

14 *Torch*, 24 May 1955.

15 *Torch*, 16 Sept. 1955.

16 Ibid.

17 *Torch*, 20 March 1956.

18 Dugard, *Fragments of My Fleece*, p. 101.

19 *Teacher's Vision* XII (Jan.-March 1955).

20 South African Institute of Race Relations (SAIRR), *A Survey of Race Relations in South Africa 1955-56* (Johannesburg, 1956).

21 Dugard, *Fragments of My Fleece*, p. 101.

22 M. Wilson and A. Mafeje, *Langa: A Study of Social Groups in an African Township* (Cape Town, 1973), p. 103.

23 *Torch*, 14 June, 1955.

24 UW, Treason Trial Collection, AD 1812, Ea 1.8.3, Untitled transcript of a meeting in Dube on 19 June 1955.

25 *Torch*, 10 May 1955.

26 *Torch*, 24 Jan. 1955.

27 *Torch*, 21 Aug. 1956.

28 *Torch*, 11 Nov. 1958.

29 See for example *Torch*, 17 April 1958.

30 *Torch*, 12 June 1956.

31 *Torch*, 30 July 1957.

32 *Torch*, 1 April 1958.

33 Dugard, *Fragments of My Fleece*, p. 31.

34 University of South Africa Archives, (UNISA), AAS 212, File: CATU Conferences I, Resolution of the 1957 CATU Conference.

35 E. Brookes, *A South African Pilgrimage* (Johannesburg, 1977), pp. 69-70.

36 Dugard, *Fragments of My Fleece*, pp. 89-90.

37 Ibid., p. 90.

38 Ibid., p. 106.

39 Ibid., p. 125.

40 Ibid., p. 92.

41 Idem.

42 Brookes, *A South African Pilgrimage*, p. 69.

43 Dugard, *Fragments of My Fleece*, p. 132

44 *Race Relations News*, Feb. 1969.
45 *TUATA*, May 1966. (TUATA is the name of the journal of the Transvaal United African Teachers Association)
46 *Eastern Province Herald*, 1 May 1971; Se also *Evening Post*, 11 Feb. 1969.
47 *Star*, 6 May 1964.
48 *Evening Post*, 1 May 1964.
49 *Rand Daily Mail* (*RDM*), 19 July 1968: the case discussed in this article is that of Henry Tshabalala, a former treason trialist, who was removed from two committees and a school board.
50 *RDM*, 27 March 1968.
51 *RDM*, 21 Dec. 1971.
52 *RDM*, 2 May 1971.
53 SAIRR, *A Survey of Race Relations in South Africa 1972* (Johannesburg, 1973), p. 354; *Sunday Times* (Township Edition), 18 Feb. 1973; *Star*, 9 June 1975.
54 *RDM*, 17 Jan. 1968.
55 *Star*, 1 Feb. 1974.
56 *Sunday Times* (Township Edition), 18 Feb. 1973.
57 *Star*, 9 June 1975.
58 *RDM*, 16 Sept. 1967, 13 Dec. 1967.
59 UNISA, AAS 121 (File: TUATA correspondence, unsorted), J.M. Ditlhage, Phokeng Higher Primary School, Rustenburg, to the General Secretary, TUATA, 30 Jan. 1968.
60 Ibid., P.M. Malebye, Itotleng-Baralong Secondary School, Lichtenburg, to Regional Director, Batswana Education and Culture, Mafikeng, 17 March 1969.
61 UNISA, AAS 121, Malebye to Regional Director, Letter cited; UNISA AAS 121 (File: TUATA correspondence, unsorted), P.M. Malebye, Itotleng-Baralong Secondary School, Lichtenburg, to General Secretary, TUATA, 7 March 1969.
62 UNISA, AAS 120 (File: L.M. Taunyane, legal cases), P.M. Malebye, Itotleng-Baralong Secondary School, to Regional Director, Batswana Education and Culture, 17 March 1969.
63 UNISA, AAS 121 (File: TUATA correspondence, unsorted), P. Malebye, Swartruggens, to General Secretary, TUATA, 7 August 1969.
64 SAIRR, *A Survey of Race Relations in South Africa 1969* (Johannesburg, 1970), pp. 128, 131; SAIRR, *A Survey of Race Relations in South Africa 1976* (Johannesburg, 1977) pp. 251-53,

citing *RDM Extra*, 30 Dec. 1975, 13 Jan., 25 March, 5 April 1976; Speech by Chief M. Matlala, Verbatim Report of the 1974 Session 4 March-15 March: Second Lebowa Legislative Assembly, pp. 221-23; Surplus People Project, *Forced Removals in the Transvaal: The SPP Reports: Vol.5 The Transvaal* (Cape Town, 1983), pp. 40-41.

65 Surplus People Project, *Forced Removals in the Transvaal*, pp. 40-41; SAIRR, *Survey 1976*, pp. 251-53; SAIRR, *A Survey of Race Relations in South Africa 1975* (Johannesburg, 1976), p. 138, citing *Star*, 30 Dec. 1974, 4 March, 16 May, 28 July 1975 and *RDM*, 5 March, 28 April 1975.

66 Surplus People Project (1983), *Forced Removals in the Transvaal*, pp. 38-58, 89-109.

67 UNISA, AAS 120 (File: L.M. Taunyane, legal cases), In Die Streekhof Van Die Streekafdeling Van Transvaal Gehou Te Potgietersrust: Die Staat Teen Patrick Kekana... The original reads:
-Is die besnydenis gedoen ooreenkomstig bantoegebruik?
-Ek weet nie.
-Dra jy geen kennis van die gebruike van hierdie betrokke stam nie?
-Die heidene ja hulle gebruik daardie gebruik.

68 Ibid., McMullin, Bowens, Attorneys to the Vice-President of TUATA, 11 March 1974.

69 Ibid., Report by M.J. Molelo to McMullin, 21 Dec. 1976.

70 Ibid., McMullin, Bowens to Taunyane, TUATA, 7 Feb. 1977.

71 Idem.

72 Ibid., McMullin to Taunyane, 2 May 1980.

73 UNISA, ASA 121, 'In Die Streekhof...', document cited.

74 *Star*, 11 Aug. 1986.

75 Surplus People Project, *Forced Removals in the Transvaal*, p. 50.

76 UNISA, AAS 120 (File: L.M. Taunyane, legal cases), Statement by AmaNdebele-a-Moletlane Tribal Authority, 21 April 1976; Secretary of Education, Bophuthatswana, to M. Sono, Hans Kekana High School, 6 Sept. 1976; Secretary of Education, Bophuthatswana, to M.J. Langa, Kekana Higher Primary School, 7 June 1976; Inspector, Mabopane Circuit, to M. Sono, 25 May 1976.

77 Surplus People Project, *Forced Removals in the Transvaal*, p. 50.

78 *RDM*, 4 Feb. 1966.

79 *Natal Witness*, 17 Feb. 1964.

80 *RDM*, 4 Feb. 1966.
81 *TUATA*, September 1966, quoting Editorial from the *World*, 26 Sept. 1966.
82 Idem.
83 *Bantu Education Journal (BEJ)*, April 1965.
84 *BEJ*, June 1964.
85 *BEJ*, March 1965.
86 *Star*, 2 Nov. 1971.
87 *RDM*, 30 May 1972.
88 *RDM* (Township edition), 10 April 1973.
89 *RDM*, 20, 31 Oct. 1972; *Star*, 11 Oct. 1972; *Natal Witness*, 30 Oct. 1972.
90 *Report of the Commission of Inquiry into the Riots at Soweto and Elsewhere from the 16th of June 1976 to the 28th February 1977*, Chairman: Cillie J., Vol. I (Pretoria, 1980), p. 56, (Cillie Commission); SAIRR, *Survey 1975*, pp. 222-23, citing *RDM*, 23 Dec. 1974, 13 Jan., 15 May 1975.
91 *Star*, 23 Dec. 1974; SAIRR, *Survey 1975*, pp. 222-23.
92 *RDM*, 23 Dec. 1974.
93 *RDM Extra*, 23 Dec. 1974; Cillie Commission, p. 57.
94 Cillie Commission, p. 57.
95 Ibid., pp. 61-63.
96 Ibid., pp. 58-59; *Friend*, 14 Feb. 1975.
97 *Friend*, 14 Feb. 1975.
98 Cillie Commission, pp. 57-58.
99 *Eastern Province Herald*, 19 Feb. 1975; *Weekend Post*, 22 Feb. 1975.
100 Cillie Commission, p. 73.
101 SAIRR, *South Africa in Travail: The Disturbances of 1976-77: Evidence Presented to the Cillie Commission by the Institute of Race Relations* (Johannesburg, 1978), p. 1.
102 Cillie Commission, pp. 60-61; SAIRR, *South Africa in Travail*, p. 2.
103 Cillie Commission, pp. 60-61.
104 Ibid., p. 76.
105 SAIRR, *South African in Travail*, p. 6.

The Ndzundza Ndebele

Indenture and the Making of Ethnic Identity, 1883-1914

Peter Delius

Until the dramatic struggles of 1986 against 'independence' for KwaNdebele the southern Transvaal Ndebele were best known for their material culture. From the 1940s their intricate beadwork and their vivid wall decorations have attracted growing numbers of photographers, purchasers and researchers.[1] However, another aspect of these communities which has often been commented on is their perceived conservatism. In 1914 a well-informed commentator remarked, 'the tribe... holds to its tribal conditions closer than any other natives'.[2] In 1920 an official wrote that they were 'the most conservative natives... to be found in the Transvaal. They still cling tenaciously to their old customs, dress and life style'.[3] In 1949 the anthropologist Isaac Schapera commented on the fact that, while other Transvaal Ndebele groups had virtually lost a separate identity, the Southern Ndebele had 'preserved to a remarkable degree their language and much of their traditional culture'.[4] Recent research has also yielded up an image of 'strong traditionalism' amongst certain communities.[5]

The Ndebele have been seen as an example of a community with a vibrant ethnic or traditional culture. This predictably commended them to some of apartheid's ideologues. But even serious scholars have gone so far as to suggest that 'Nguni pride and cultural aggressiveness' have shaped their history and society, and concluded that as a result they have 'embraced the idea of an independent homeland with enthusiasm' - a view which has been rather overtaken by recent events.[6]

Popular resistance has made a mockery of the crude cultural determinism which has disfigured some analyses. But the problem remains of how to explain the cultural distinctiveness, tenacity and creativity of the Southern Ndebele. It cannot be accounted for in terms of a relatively undisturbed continuity with pre-colonial society. The main chiefdom, the Ndzundza, suffered a particularly brutal and disruptive process of colonial conquest. At first sight the surprising thing is that they survived as a distinctive community at all.

Ndebele identity cannot simply be put down to the endorsement and manipulation of ethnic divisions by the state. In recent decades the state has sought vigorously to foster a distinct Ndebele identity. But until the 1940s little attempt was made from that quarter either to prop up Ndebele chiefly power or to maintain the Ndebele as a separate group. Their requests for land were repeatedly refused, and it was not until 1970 that provision was made for a separate Ndebele 'homeland'. Neither were anthropologists and missionaries central in the shaping of Ndebele identity and culture, for these professions paid relatively little attention to the Ndzundza until well into this century. Partly as a result, an educated élite emerged relatively late from these communities, and there is little evidence in the years before 1950 of such a grouping rediscovering and elaborating 'tradition' for the wider society.

It seems plausible to suggest that the explanation for both the 'traditionalism' and the artistry of the Ndzundza lies in part in their responses to the particular processes of conquest and dispossession which they experienced. This may seem self-evident to some, but while scholars have gestured in this direction little attempt has been made to research the modern history of the Ndebele with this (or any other) proposition in mind.[7] This paper attempts to start to fill this gap by examining a central episode in their history - the defeat of the Ndzundza chiefdom in 1883 and the response of its subjects to division and indenture.

———————————

It is often assumed that the Transvaal Ndebele were stragglers left behind by Mzilikazi, and this has led to speculation that a martial heritage accounts for their distinctive culture.[8] In fact their origins can be traced to the movement of Nguni-speaking communities into the interior in or before the seventeenth century. The Ndebele have been classified into Northern and Southern sections broadly divided by the Springbok Flats. While the former have been heavily influenced by

'Northern Sotho' language and social forms, the latter show clearer evidence of their Nguni origins.[9]

The Southern Ndebele divided in turn into two main groups - the Manala chiefdom in the Pretoria area and the Ndzundza chiefdom which was located near the Steelpoort River.[10] Both chiefdoms suffered heavily in the years of the *difaqane* — not least at the hands of Mzilikazi's regiments. The Manala chiefdom barely recovered, and by the early 1870s its remnants were living on the Wallmansthal mission station and the surrounding Boer farms.[11] The Ndzundza weathered these storms rather better, and in the 1830s and 1840s re-emerged as a significant chiefdom under the leadership of Mabhogo Mahlangu and under the political umbrella of the Pedi paramount Sekwati.

The Ndzundza, like other societies in the region, developed fortified mountain strongholds. By the 1860s their capital, Erholweni, was probably the most impregnable single fastness in the eastern Transvaal. The security and the resources which the chiefdom offered attracted a steady stream of refugee communities to settle within its boundaries.

In the 1840s the arrival of parties of Trekkers presented a new challenge to the society. After an initial uneasy coexistence, conflicts flared, with the Ndzundza refusing Boer demands for labour and denying their claims to ownership of the land. Boer exactions ensured that the flow of refugees to the chiefdom maintained its momentum, and the Ndzundza also secured large numbers of guns through migrant labour, trade and raiding. A number of Boer attempts to subdue the chiefdom failed, and by the late 1860s many farmers who had settled in the environs of the Ndzundza trekked away in despair. Those who remained recognised the authority of the Ndzundza rulers and paid tribute to them. A breach also developed between Mabhogo and the new Pedi paramount Sekhukhune who succeeded in 1861.

The external relations of the Ndzundza chiefdom during these years are reasonably well known but its internal social organisation is little understood. This is largely because no missionaries settled within it and there is thus a paucity of documentation. It is, however, possible to piece together some relevant impressions. The first and probably the most important of these relates to the composition of the chiefdom's population. Informed contemporary observers stressed the heterogeneity of its subjects and commented that they were mainly a mixture of Sotho- and Nguni-speaking peoples.[12]

This heterogeneity is hardly surprising when one considers the role

that in-migration played in the chiefdom's development after the
difaqane. Communities sought security and resources rather more
vigorously than they strove for cultural similarity in the areas to which
they moved. And ruling groups intent on building up their power
welcomed followers of diverse origins. There were processes of
assimilation at work, but the continuing arrival of new groups
presumably kept cultural homogeneity at bay. The society also lacked
the social institutions - like standing regiments - and the mobile way of
life which made for very rapid social and cultural incorporation
amongst some of the societies spawned by the *difaqane*. The probable
result was a chiefdom in which the aristocracy was most clearly 'Nguni'
but in which the commoner stratum was composed of an amalgam of
Sotho- and Ndebele-speaking groupings. There were also a number of
subordinate chiefdoms ranging from mainly Sotho to mainly Ndebele
in composition.[13]

This kind of interaction between Sotho and Ndebele groupings also
probably had a considerably longer if less dramatic history. The
Ndebele had at various times been subject to broader - mainly Pedi -
political systems and there is some indication of intermarriage with
neighbouring Sotho chiefdoms. This interaction appears to have
influenced Southern Ndebele norms and institutions. Crucial examples
are the practice of male initiation and the formation of regiments. It
seems, too, that the Ndzundza capital was very similar to the various
chiefly strongholds in the heartland of the Pedi paramountcy, and that
both groups shared a pattern of dispersed fields. And twentieth
century evidence suggests that Ndebele homestead design and
marriage preferences show some similarities to those of their Pedi
neighbours. Even the wall murals which are the most celebrated form
of Ndebele art are a development of 'North Sotho' practices.[14]

This is not, of course, to deny that significant differences in political
structures, the definition of local groups and other areas of social life
existed. It is, however, to insist that these communities must be
understood in the context of a lengthy process of interaction between a
wide variety of groups and cultures which so clearly shaped the nature
of societies throughout the central and eastern Transvaal. It is also to
suggest that it is more than a little misplaced to see the Southern
Ndebele as 'pure Nguni stock', and to posit that the key to their
traditionalism, distinctiveness and creativity lies in the extraordinary
vitality of 'Nguni culture'.[15]

The late 1860s and the 1870s were the apogee of Ndzundza power and prosperity. The chiefdom had a population of about 10 000 and held sway over a considerable area. But by the late 1870s changes were taking place which had ominous implications for the future of the society. The British annexation of the Transvaal in 1877 resulted in a restructuring and strengthening of the state, and in 1879 a British-led army (with Swazi and Ndzundza assistance) finally defeated the Pedi paramountcy. As the balance of power swung away from the African states in the region, landowners and speculators started to press claims to formerly unoccupied farms and to those which had been worked only on sufferance of the Ndzundza rulers. Shortly after retrocession, the Ndzundza and the restored Republican administration found themselves at loggerheads over competing land claims and over whether the chiefdom fell under the authority of the Zuid-Afrikaansche Republiek (ZAR). In 1882 the Pedi pretender Mampuru sought refuge amongst the Ndzundza after having murdered his brother Sekhukhune. Nyabela's refusal to hand him over to the ZAR brought the wider conflicts to a head.[16]

The war that followed was one of attrition. The Boer force and their African - mainly Pedi - auxiliaries baulked at direct attacks on the Ndzundza strongholds and adopted a policy of siege. Ndzundza crops were destroyed, their cattle were seized, and a number of their smaller refuges were dynamited. By the middle of 1883 widespread starvation made it impossible for them to continue the struggle, and in July Nyabela surrendered. His subjects streamed out in desperate condition while behind them their abandoned capital - torched by the victorious burghers - provided 'glorious illumination' of their plight.[17]

The ZAR now confronted the question of what to do with their defeated opponents. Mampuru, Nyabela and twenty-two Ndzundza royals and subordinate chiefs were taken as captives to Pretoria. Mampuru and Nyabela were tried, convicted and sentenced to death. The British resident protested against these sentences and Nyabela's sentence was commuted to 'levens-lange gevangenis-straf met harde arbeid in ijzers' (lit., life-long imprisonment with hard labour in irons). But Mampuru went to the gallows. The twenty-two remaining prisoners were sentenced to seven years' imprisonment with hard labour.[18]

The larger and more pressing problem facing the ZAR was how to handle the remainder of the chiefdom. Emergency supplies of grain were brought from the Botshabelo mission station but the continued supply of relief was not a course of action which recommended itself to the burghers and their leaders. They also wished to prevent the Ndzundza finding refuge amongst the other chiefdoms in the region and thus slipping beyond their control.[19]

A number of considerations shaped the policies which were finally adopted. Landlessness and labour shortages were perennial problems amongst the burghers of the ZAR. Many of those who had participated in the campaign probably suffered from one or both of these disabilities and anticipated that its successful completion would bring them some respite. These issues were also constantly brought before the Volksraad and the Uitvoerende Raad. In addition, the war had been long and costly, and the state was determined to recoup some of its costs and to provide a salutary lesson to other African communities of the dangers involved in resisting its authority.[20]

The Volksraad decided on drastic measures. There remained 15 000 morgen of the heartland of the chiefdom to which farmers and speculators had not yet secured title. These were opened on a first-come first-served basis to all burghers who had done service on the commando. They could claim smallholdings on condition that they occupied and improved the land. The area was 'rushed' in October of 1883, and although some speculation took place it remained relatively densely settled by mainly poor farmers. But it was decreed that 'kaffer kraals or tribes large or small [would] not be permitted... on this land'.[21]

The Volksraad further decreed that the population of the chiefdom 'in the interests of order, safety and humanity' would be dispersed amongst the burghers and indentured for a period of five years, with preference being given to those who had fought in the war and those without labour. In order to distance this device from the infamous *inboekseling* ('apprentice') system, to still criticism, and to make the strategy effective, it was stipulated that families were not to be separated.[22] But what exactly constituted a family was not defined.

The state also attempted to cater to its own financial needs. The regulations laid down that each family's service was to be paid for in food, clothing and wages to an amount not exceeding £3 per annum. But each employer was also responsible for paying a £5 fine as well as the tax arrears dating back to 1879 which the state demanded from each family head. It was proposed, however, that these sums could be deducted from the wages due to each family, and so, in theory, a finely-meshed method of tax collection had been devised. By the 1880s the state was aware of the chaos that uncontrolled transfer and speculation could make of the best-laid plans, and individuals were barred from making over contracts of indenture. It also had more than an inkling of the problems of control involved, and attempted to bolster the strategy by threatening severe consequences for any chief who gave shelter to refugee Ndzundza.[23]

The terms of indenture were drawn up with an eye to potential British objections. The Pretoria Convention prohibited any changes in 'native' legislation without Imperial sanction,and the ZAR authorities feared renewed charges of slavery against the Republic.[24] In the event the British reaction was mild. Since the Imperial authorities had no desire to become embroiled in a diplomatic confrontation so shortly after retrocession, no real attempt was made to condemn the practice of involuntary indenture. The British had permitted similar practices during the annexation period and the ZAR had wasted no time in exposing this fact. The British Resident did convey concern at the length of the indenture, suggesting that the period should not exceed twelve months, but when his representations were rebuffed he urged his superiors to drop the matter.[25]

The pattern in the ZAR was that legislation in relation to 'native affairs' was honoured more often in the breach than in the observance. Certainly the view of the British resident was that the indenture would have little effect. He argued that 'enforced service is a thing of the past... Her Majesty's Government need not feel any apprehension that any indentureship for a longer period than twelve months will practically be imposed on these people.'[26] Some historians have taken their cue from this remark and suggested that these measures were ineffective.[27] But other researchers have come to very different conclusions. One recent account suggests that the Ndzundza were

> utterly defeated, without a leader, scattered from friends and relatives, alienated from their own land and having to work on Boer farms for a mere pittance. It would be many years before they would have the energy and will to gradually find one another again.[28]

At first these views appear entirely contradictory. They do however have a common element, which is that neither provides any real understanding of the impact of indenture on the Ndzundza. The years from 1883 to 1914 constitute a yawning gap in our understanding of the history of the society. This is largely because after the defeat of the chiefdom the Ndzundza faded from both the official and the missionary view. Although the often fragmentary information that does exist has been insufficient to attract historians, it is none the less adequate to provide a rather fuller account than has previously been available.

There is no surviving description of the way in which the surrendered Ndzundza were parcelled out, but it is possible to give an impression of how this took place. The Boer commando which had laid siege to the chiefdom consisted of burgher contingents from the districts of Lydenburg, Middelburg, Standerton, Wakkerstroom, Potchefstroom and Pretoria which had served on a rotational basis. [29] By September 1883 the Ndzundza had been taken to these districts, the bulk of them going to Pretoria, Middelburg, Lydenburg and Standerton, whose burghers had made up the majority of the commando. They were then allocated to those who had done a stint of commando service. Others who laid claim to families were those without labour; those who enjoyed the favour of the local officials were also well placed to secure a share.[30]

Central to the process of division was the model of the family which was employed by the Boers. It is clear that this was of a nuclear family consisting of a man and his wife or wives and their unmarried children. A proportion of the families were polygamous, but the overwhelming majority included only one wife. There is some evidence that husbands were divided from their wives and that parents were separated from their children, but this does not appear to have been the dominant pattern. The records also show that significant numbers of 'orphans' and 'widows' were indentured. And, although the evidence is inconclusive, there is some indication that the aged and infirm were not often included in the definition of the 'family'.[31]

Division into nuclear families did not of course accord with the realities of Ndzundza society. In most instances nuclear families were embedded in wider units - homesteads (*umuzi*). These groups would have undergone changes in their scale and composition throughout their developmental cycle, but would often have centred on an extended family consisting of two generations of married adults. The rupture of homesteads may, however, have been partly lessened by the existence of extended families and localised clusters of kin within Boer society. The surviving registers of indenture show that in a significant number of cases three, four or more 'nuclear' families were contracted to an equivalent number of Boer families with the same surname living on a single farm. It is possible that in these circumstances homesteads could regroup.[32]

The concept of an 'orphan' was one which had long been used within the Transvaal as a specious justification for the seizure and indenture of children. Even where children had lost both parents there were a number of mechanisms within Ndzundza society which would have ensured that they were readily reincorporated. And 'widows' were clearly not always women who had lost their spouses. But where they were the Ndzundza also had a variety of means of absorbing them.[33]

These rather dry observations can convey little of the impact of these events on the Ndzundza. At the end of a bitter and prolonged war, individuals who had belonged to a powerful and independent chiefdom with rich resources found themselves scattered across the breadth of the Transvaal. Their villages had been destroyed and their land had been alienated. They had lost their stock and their weapons. The full effect on their consciousness of defeat and indenture cannot now be recreated and indeed defies imagination.

Some sense of the transition that they experienced, and the values which dominated the world they entered, is conveyed by the names that the heads of families were given by their masters when they were contracted. These were often derived from months of the year with 'September', the date of indenture of many, the most common. 'Stuurman' was also a popular name, and presumably referred to the anticipated role of the labourer as wagon driver and plough leader. Perceived physical characteristics prompted names like 'Swartbooi', 'Geelbooi' and 'Kleinbooi'. The continuity between land and labour in the thinking of some farmers was expressed in names like 'Swartland' and 'Rooiland'. The Bible also provided a source of inspiration and the character that came most readily to the minds of many was 'Jonas' (Jonah). This was presumably because he was the first Hebrew prophet or missionary sent to a heathen nation, and some Boers rationalised indenture as a step towards christianising the Ndzundza. The fact that Jonah had a very torrid time of it before he accepted his calling may also have suggested parallels. Units of currency, for example 'Rijksdalder' and 'Halfpond', provided a point of reference. Other names suggest language skills. Those named 'Jack' were probably able to speak some English, while those dubbed 'Oorlam' presumably had some command of Dutch. Many defeated by the exercise, or uninterested in it, settled for 'Booi', but a handful attempted to render a version of the Ndebele names of their new workers. Finally, the recurrence of 'Adonis' in these records reveals a sardonic humour which probably boded ill for the future of the indentured family.[34]

The Ndzundza clearly suffered considerable dislocation as a result of this experience. But the suggestion that it put an end to Ndzundza resistance for decades flies in the face of the evidence. No sooner was the process of division complete than reports and complaints started to pour in from the districts that labourers and families were fleeing from the farms. The ZAR had no standing army or police force, and this movement proved extremely difficult to control. Local commandos had to be mobilised to track down the fugitives, and burghers were often reluctant to spend time and energy on uncertain pursuits. Repeated requests from district officials that rewards should be offered and that local police forces should be created to deal with the problem were, however, refused by the central government on the grounds of the costs involved. The pattern that emerged was that in districts where considerable numbers of Ndzundza had been indentured it was possible to mobilise the burghers to pursue fugitive families. But those areas with few indentured labourers witnessed a corresponding apathy on the part of most of the burghers to the problems of control. However, even in those districts which were relatively tightly policed, the problem remained acute as the Ndzundza developed increasingly sophisticated and co-ordinated strategies for escape. A number of families would flee from different farms in diverse directions on the same night, or they bided their time until the burghers were engaged in activities — like ploughing — which they were loath to abandon.[35]

For a time it appeared that the British Resident would prove correct in his belief 'that within months scarcely any of the people now indentured will be found to be still in their masters' service'.[36] But despite considerable movement the predicted wholesale abandonment of Boer farms for African chiefdoms did not occur. There were a number of reasons for this. One already touched on was that commandos were mobilised and some fugitive Ndzundza from the central and eastern districts were hunted down. But the hazards involved in escape went beyond the dangers of immediate recapture. It was by no means as easy for fugitives to find refuge in African chiefdoms in the 1880s as it had been for *inboekselings* to do in the 1860s. The sharpest difference was, of course, that most of these had been conquered, collaborators had been entrenched, and networks of informers had been created. Beyond this, the major chiefdom adjacent to the heartland of indenture was ruled over by the Pedi paramount, Kgoloko, who had actively assisted in the destruction of the Ndzundza, and who was closely linked to J. Abel Erasmus, the Lydenburg Native Commissioner. Chiefs locked in local conflicts were also prepared to denounce their rivals for harbouring refugees.[37]

A case which demonstrates some of these dimensions involved the Zebediela chiefdom. In January 1883 Cornelis Erasmus appeared before the Public Prosecutor in Pretoria and said that while passing through Zebediela's area his wagon driver had told him that he had seen two Ndzundza women. Then a neighbouring chief Klaas Makapan had repeated the allegation. Zebediela was issued with a stern warning, and Abel Erasmus approached Kgoloko who agreed to send spies to check on the validity of the allegation.[38]

African societies in the 1880s had not only been defeated militarily but their members were also either cooped up in inadequate locations or were tenants on private land. The Ndzundza, stripped of their cattle and firearms, and without cash, were not necessarily attractive additional subjects. In 1884 the costs of affording them sanctuary were made clearer still when a number of chiefs were heavily fined for harbouring refugees. Clearly some Ndzundza were absorbed into neighbouring societies, but without resources to ease their entrance they would have had low and even onerous status. It also seems that women and children were more readily incorporated than were families or individual men.[39]

The domains of chiefdoms thus hardly provided areas in which the dispersed Ndzundza could easily shelter or regroup, and to seek refuge there was also to accept fragmentation. The evidence suggests that many Ndzundza who had evaded capture in 1883 or who had fled the farms initially adopted an alternative strategy. This was to settle in rugged zones in the eastern Transvaal on the periphery of both Boer and chiefly domains. But these areas afforded a very precarious freedom, and a number of communities were located, broken up and re-indentured. Probably only those groups that remained relatively small and mobile survived for any length of time.[40]

Possibly the most important form of resistance was revealed by the complaints about the movement of Ndzundza between farms. This was shaped by a number of factors. Much of the impetus came from individuals, who struggled to locate and reclaim their spouses and children. Their efforts were sometimes facilitated by their masters who hoped to secure additional labour. Some used formal channels. For example, in 1885 'September', indentured in the Middelburg district, petitioned the Uitvoerende Raad for assistance in securing the return of his five children who were in the possesion of J. Kock, the Landdrost of Potchefstroom. This official surrendered one child but was determined to hold on to the rest. Others adopted more direct methods. In 1884 'Kameel' arrived at the farm of Jacobus Uys in the Ermelo district in the owner's absence and fled with two Ndebele women and three children. Uys tracked down Kameel and one of the women and brought them back to the farm. But then Kameel — who was clearly a resourceful man — persuaded the farmer to let him go and fetch the missing woman and children. That night Kameel returned to the farm, rescued the woman who had been captured with him, and fled once more.[41] Through these kinds of efforts it also seems probable that the regrouping of households was facilitated.

The overall effect of this mobility conformed to a long-standing pattern within the ZAR. This was the tendency for Africans to move from the farms of poor Boers, who had limited labour and made relatively heavy demands on them, to the lands of wealthier farmers whose exactions were less onerous. In some cases this involved settling on the second — sometimes bushveld winter-grazing — farms of more prosperous burghers in exchange for seasonal labour or service on the main estate. One of the advantages of this tactic was that powerful burghers could offer some protection against capture and re-indenture. But for this to be possible the refugees needed to move away from the original areas of indenture. The result appears to have been a two-way process. Ndzundza indentured in the middleveld found refuge on highveld farms and *vice versa*. As this process continued, poorer Boers, especially, despaired of maintaining control over the indentured families. In consequence another old Transvaal strategy came to the fore. This was that while farmers were prepared to abandon the struggle to keep adults on their farms, they attempted to keep their grip on children. It was hoped that children socialised on the farms would become relatively skilled and malleable labourers and in time form part of the *Oorlams* stratum within rural society.[42]

Thus, while many Ndzundza fled from their contracted masters, large numbers none the less remained on the farms. Some moved back to the farms in the Middelburg and Pretoria districts. There were regular alarms amongst the burghers that Ndzundza were congregating in the Mapochsgronden but these proved to be without substance. These lands, relatively densely settled by poorer Boers, offered scant shelter. But Ndzundza did settle on farms adjacent to the old heartland of the chiefdom. This movement presumably reflected not only a return to familiar territory, but also the extent to which the concentration of Ndzundza in these districts afforded the possibility of drawing on, and reviving, wider social networks, and of partly overcoming the atomisation which they had suffered.[43]

There is evidence not only that Ndzundza stayed on the farms but also that significant numbers in the Pretoria and Middelburg districts stayed with their original employers. One source of confusion is the kind of replies given to a circular sent out by the Superintendent of Natives in 1886 enquiring about rates of desertion in the districts. These responses painted a picture of mass desertion. But this evidence has to be treated with caution. Although many burghers had paid taxes due on their labourers at the time of indenture, there were still numbers of them who owed outstanding taxes or fines. During six months of 1885 there were petitions to the Volksraad from 263 burghers asking to be spared from having to make these payments. These were refused, and it was probably the failure of these requests that shaped the responses to the subsequent circular of 1886. If burghers who were still being pressed to meet their financial obligations by the central government could demonstrate that their labourers had absconded, they were relieved of these payments. Thus both burghers and local officials — who wished to avoid bitter disputes with their constituents — had reason to deny that indentured families had remained in their districts.[44]

It seems safe to conclude that the British Resident's predictions proved to be inaccurate. Equally, the image of the Ndzundza as utterly demoralised is belied by the evidence that they both resisted and shaped the reality of indenture.

Initiatives came not only from below but also from Ndzundza royals. Before his arrest Nyabela had made attempts to ensure chiefly continuity. In late 1883 a group of burghers searching for Ndzundza who had evaded capture found an old man, 'Moentoe', and a child of twelve hiding in the Steenkampsberg with eleven head of cattle. Their interrogation of the captives revealed that the child was a son of Nyabela who, along with the cattle, had been placed by the chief in the care of the old man. The cattle were divided among the burghers, and the boy was indentured to a Lydenburg Veldcornet, D.J. Schoeman.[45] But this official had no place for the old man and so the youth and his mentor were separated. The designated heir, Fene Mahlangu, the son of Nyabela's elder brother, was a child at this time but later recalled that he and his mother 'wandered all over the country like wild animals'.[46] Ultimately they settled on a highveld farm in the Pretoria district. Messages were also conveyed from Nyabela to his subjects.[47] However, a juvenile heir and messages from prison were tenuous supports for a society whose foundations were in peril.

A more secure focus of royal power started to emerge in the Middelburg district in the 1880s. The precise manner in which this took place remains unclear but there are some tantalising though conflicting pieces of evidence. Fene Mahlangu, speaking in 1917 (and with reason to play down the legitimacy and significance of this process), told how a man called Japhta (Matsitsi) was 'elected' as headman.[48] But Matsitsi's descendants tell a more dramatic tale, and one that asserts Nyabela's sanction for this development. A tradition collected in 1983 recalls that in the early years of indenture

> these tribespeople had no chief or leader... so the Chief and council who were in prison decided that one of them must try to escape, so that he could return to look after his people. They chose Matsitsi [Nyabela's brother] to be this man. This was the plan of escape: every Wednesday they were given some snuff, of which they would only take a little and store the rest. One morning they went off to work, with all the snuff they had collected in Matsitsi's pocket. Matsitsi was the coffee boy; he made coffee and gave it to the warder, who then told Matsitsi to clean his shoes. Matsitsi threw the snuff in the warder's eyes, then ran away.
>
> [He hid for a period in a number of different places.]
>
> After this, he went to the white farmers at Kafferskraal where his family was living, and told them that he had been sent by Nyabela to rule his people in Nyabela's place. The whites agreed. Matsitsi called a big meeting of all the Ndzundza, who came from all the far away farms to hear what message Nyabela had sent them from prison. Matsitsi told them that Nyabela had sent him to be their ruler. They were all satisfied with this arrangement.[49]

There is evidence which lends credence to aspects of this account. At least two imprisoned Ndzundza leaders escaped in 1885. In one incident four prisoners in a group were taken to work in a quarry. For a period they were left with a single guard, and one of them, 'Maschiela', took the opportunity to flee. But the escapes had severe consequences for those that remained in custody: thenceforth they were kept in irons.[50]

The establishment of this political focus to some extent allowed chiefly ritual and judicial functions to be resumed. But probably the most important step taken to maintain a degree of social and cultural continuity and cohesion was the holding of male initiation (*wela*) and the formation of regiments. Initiation played a number of key roles within the society. It marked the transition from boyhood to manhood. During its course youths were schooled in the traditions and dominant values of the society. They even learned a special language which would allow them to converse without being understood by the uninitiated — especially women. Each school was led by a senior royal, and the virtues of loyalty to their leader and the society's rulers were drummed into the young men. These schools were normally held every four years and the most intensive section lasted about two months. A short period after they were completed youths were usually given leave to marry.[51]

A *wela* had been due in 1883 but had to be postponed because of the war. Remarkably, however, in 1886 an outraged Abel Erasmus reported that youths were asking for, and getting, passes from farmers to go to initiation. It is unclear where the impulse for this came from or where the initiation schools were held. But it may be more than mere coincidence that male initiation was restarted in early 1886, the year after the escapes of the Ndzundza royals. The tradition quoted above recalls that one of the first things that Matsitsi did was to call Ndzundza youths to an initiation school at the farm Kafferskraal, fifteen miles (about twenty-five kilometres) from the old capital. And as important for communities which had lost all their stock was the sanction — presented as coming from Nyabela and passed from family to family on the farms — for youths to marry without having to pay bridewealth. It is also probable that female initiation was continued, but as this was conducted within individual homesteads it was less likely to attract attention and excite comment.[52]

Part of what is surprising about this development is that the farmers permitted it to take place at all. Abel Erasmus argued that these events constituted a threat to peace and order, while the Superintendent of Natives, P.J. Joubert, was incredulous that a chiefdom which in his view no longer existed could hold initiation. Throughout the 1880s and 1890s sections of settler society reacted with very considerable alarm and vehemence to any sign of the revival of the Ndzundza chiefdom. The initiation that was held in 1886, and those that took place in the years thereafter, were testimony of the extent to which Ndzundza resistance had changed the balance of power on the farms. By 1886 many farmers must have recognised that to deny youths permission to attend would almost certainly result in their desertion. A number of them may also have been prepared to accept some manifestations of chiefly organisation as long as this did not result in the permanent movement of their labourers off their land.[53]

In September 1888 the period of formal indenture came to an end. Some Ndebele clearly waited for this day with keen anticipation. Reports quickly arrived in Pretoria that families were well aware that their contracts had expired and were asking for trek passes. It seems unlikely, however, that the expiry of their five-year contracts had a major effect on the conditions under which they lived. There was no area of land set aside for them to settle on, and it is unlikely that they had accumulated sufficient resources during the period of indenture to be able to buy or hire land. Farmers and local officials took a very frosty view of requests to leave farms, and they had a formidable weapon which they could deploy against groups which attempted to gather on absentee landlord land. This was the Squatters Law of 1887 which stipulated that no more than five families could live on a farm occupied by whites, and that only two families could live on 'unoccupied' land. In the main this law proved ineffective because powerful Boers with large concentrations of labour under their control or on their land were able to thwart its implementation. Indeed, they were often precisely the officials charged with the responsibility for its enforcement. There was also the threat of widespread and violent resistance by the many African chiefdoms settled outside the locations to any real attempt to execute the policy. But the Ndzundza, dispersed and disarmed, were the one group who were vulnerable to the application of this legislation.[54]

An incident in 1891 provides an illustration both of this reality and of the actions taken to prevent any major regrouping of Ndzundza under royal leadership. In early 1891 the last imprisoned leaders — aside from Nyabela — were released. One of these was a subordinate chief known in contemporary documentation as 'Tappies' who had commanded one of the major strongholds during the 1882-1883 war. Lurid stories about his activities soon started to circulate amongst some farmers. In November Abel Erasmus reported that Tappies had settled near the Steelpoort River and was gathering his former subjects about him. The Native Commissioner argued that this was in contravention of the Squatters Law and posed a danger to the surrounding white population. With the approval of the central government, Erasmus despatched his assistant, D.J. Schoeman, with twelve burghers. On their arrival they discovered that the reports were considerably exaggerated as there were only nine families to be found. None the less, six families, including that of Tappies, were seized and divided amongst the burghers.[55]

It seems probable that the main impact of the end of the period of formal indenture was to facilitate the degree of movement of Ndzundza between farms. Some took the opportunity to start — or renew — the search for their wives and children.[56] Others moved to farms which provided less uncongenial terms of service, but always at the risk that they would incur the wrath of the farmer whose land they left. A process of regrouping probably took place, but this would have been possible on any scale only with the compliance of local officials and wealthy and powerful landlords who could withstand demands for the redistribution of labour emanating from poorer farmers.

Ndebele informants recall their grandparents' accounts of the last decades of the nineteenth century as being a time of suffering, when men who were thought to be 'lazy' or 'cheeky' were beaten within an inch of their lives, and when men, women and children toiled long hours in Boer fields and kitchens. Farmers provided their tenants with land to work but gave no other payment. Thus one of the central struggles of these families was to restock, and their main means of achieving this was trading. This may have involved some exchange of grain, but the trade which informants describe was in feathers. The Ndzundza trapped finches and 'after catching them pulled out the tail feathers, skilfully binding them together into a beautiful object... these feathers were in demand in Zululand, for two works of art you received one cow.'[57]

After 1891 Nyabela was the last Ndzundza royal in prison. He had petitioned in 1888 for his release, promising never again to disturb the peace, but this and subsequent pleas were rejected.[58] Finally in 1898 the ZAR, partly prompted by the Government Surgeon's evidence that he was in failing health, released him. His freedom was conditional on his remaining under close supervision, not leaving the Pretoria district, and refraining from assembling his followers. Before he left the prison he had an interview with the Kommandant-Generaal who told him:

The State President has decided to release you. You have had ample time to think about, and to learn to understand, what constitutes the difference between the Godless and idolatrous life lived by you and your councillors in the caves and murderers' shelters of the Mapochsgronden, and the life of a town like Pretoria.[59]

But even after the fifteen years Nyabela had spent incarcerated and in irons, some burghers in the Middelburg and Pretoria districts were outraged at his release. They feared that it would encourage rebelliousness amongst the labourers on their farms and they demanded that he should be re-arrested and kept in prison until he died.[60]

Thus neither the end of formal indenture nor the release of the royals breached the barriers erected against the Ndzundza moving off the farms. It was to take the massive rural upheaval caused by the Anglo-Boer War to undermine the farmers' control of their captive labour force. As the fabric of rural society started to unravel, the Ndzundza left the farms in large numbers. The majority gathered around Matsitsi at Kafferskraal, but there was also a concentration of Ndebele round Fene and Nyabela in the Pretoria district. Initially, despite this exodus from the farms, the Ndzundza retained a peaceful relationship with the Boer forces and were even entrusted with Boer cattle. After all, the Ndzundza with relatively few arms were in no position to challenge Boer authority directly. But there was widespread, although by no means universal, support for the British amongst the Ndebele tenants. And as the war ground on, Matsitsi and his followers moved towards more active forms of resistance. This shift was partly prompted by the arrival in the area of contingents of national scouts led by British officers who made contact with Matsitsi and supplied him with guns. Thereafter a number of bitter and bloody clashes occurred between Ndzundza and Boer forces, and Matsitsi's regiments also participated with Pedi and British soldiers in a major battle against the local commando in the closing stages of the war. The Ndebele also lost considerable quantities of the stock they had so painstakingly acquired through both Boer and British exactions. None the less, by the time the Treaty of Vereeniging was signed many Ndzundza appeared to have made a decisive break with their circumscribed past. They had re-assembled and they had guns. But this recovery was to be short-lived.[61]

The Ndzundza, along with many other Africans in the Transvaal, were to find that British rule had objectives which were not compatible with a significant improvement or transformation of their pre-war situation. The Milner administration was intent on reviving the economy and securing the conditions for continued capitalist development. It also set out to create a political climate and context which would ensure long-term British interests and influence. The consequence of this strategy was a marked disinclination to allow any challenge to the racial patterns of power and property which had existed before the war. In the countryside the point was hammered home that the Boers had not been dispossessed.[62]

Nevertheless, at first the Boers appeared to have been broken by the war. An Ndebele tenant recalled that

> we received the report that the war was over. The rumour-mongers started saying that the Boers were returning home, those that had survived were coming back to their houses. Oh yes truly we saw our poor Boers arriving in a little wagon. Hawu, what a sorry sight, they were lean and emaciated. In they came and there they sat... seeing that the cattle were captured by the English they were asking for donations of donkeys... as well as one small plough for each family — no matter in what poor condition the plough was. Starvation! They planted potatoes. The soil proved good for these potatoes. They were living on potatoes.[63]

But soon it was the Ndzundza who found themselves in a tightening vice. Hopes, and possibly promises, that the new administration would permit chiefly authority to be reunified were dashed. In 1902 Nyabela visited the Middelburg district. On his arrival he was arrested, lectured before his councillors, fined £5 and removed to Pretoria. The Native Commissioner also 'told him clearly that he would never go back to his old location'. Nyabela died later the same year and was succeeded by Fene, and in the ensuing years a rift between Fene and Matsitsi opened and widened.[64]

The Ndebele were also pressed by local officials to return the cattle that they had been given by, and had raided from, the Boers. Some three hundred head of cattle from the diminished Ndebele herds were handed over, but the Boers refused to return stock they had seized, and Africans had to have recourse to the courts. The Ndzundza were once again forced to surrender their arms and this time the process was particularly thorough.[65]

By 1903 they found that even their regrouping was under threat. The Sub-Native Commissioner for Middelburg reported that

> it is quite true that natives have congregated on certain farms in this district... Efforts are now being made to prevail upon them to scatter [and] everything is being done to induce the natives to go back to the farms upon which they resided before the war but without much success as far as the Mapoch tribe under Jafita [Matsitsi] are concerned.[66]

None the less, steady pressure, facilitated by the provisions of the Squatters Law and the limited carrying capacity of the farms on which groups had congregated, did result in dispersal. By the end of 1903 the local official could report that 'the natives who had gathered in large numbers on private farms... have now in great measure returned to their former masters', although a considerably diminished concentration of Ndzundza did remain at Kafferskraal.[67]

The groups who remained on the farms and those who returned there found themselves facing mounting labour demands. Before the war farmers in the district had been mainly stock farmers concentrating on rearing cattle and sheep. After 1902 those who remained on the land turned increasingly to the far more labour intensive production of cereals. Many of them were struggling to recover from the war and were strapped for both capital and cash. It was reported in 1903:

> Farmers cannot afford to pay the high prices given for labour on the mines and must have native tenants who in return for ploughing ground, grass, wood, water and a place to reside on, give a part of a year's labour.[68]

In 1904 most farmers were said to 'pay native tenants no wages. They practically work gratuitously.' But tenants were also prevented from becoming labour migrants, and the only way they could secure cash to pay taxes was to send their children out to do seasonal work. In 'many cases', however, children were kept fully occupied on the farms, and farm labourers were the main tax defaulters in the district.[69] Not all the Ndzundza on the farms were subjected to terms as harsh as these. A handful in the Middelburg district were rent tenants but this was more common in the Pretoria district. Some of the more prosperous may even have been amongst the small number of sharecroppers in these areas.

The main prospect for the Ndebele of improving their situation seemed to lie in securing a location or in purchasing land. But neither of these paths proved to be open to them in the first decades of the century. Despite repeated requests by their chiefs and spokesmen, pressure from farmers ensured that their claims were routinely rejected by both location and land commissions. The Ndzundza were also poorly placed to muster the resources to buy land — a strategy adopted by a number of communities in the Transvaal at this time. In the years before 1913 Fene 'bought land several times on the instalment principle and failed to carry out his agreement in full and thus frittered away a lot of money'. Contemporary commentators put this down to the fact that Fene 'lacked in brains' and was a 'poor hand at finance', but it seems clear that rather wider considerations than these have to be taken into account.[70] The Ndebele, politically divided, dispersed and short of cash, could not sustain the heavy payments which more cohesive communities with access to market and migrant income could carry.

The evidence suggests that the end result of these processes was that by 1914, while there was doubtless differentiation within it, Ndebele society consisted mainly of farm labourers who were in a relatively disadvantaged position. Matsitsi testified before the Beaumont Commission:

> My people are in trouble. We are being driven from the lands, and even from where we reside. We are working on the farms without pay — for nothing; every member of the family has to work, we receive no remuneration.[71]

And the Sub-Native Commissioner of the Middelburg district gave a still more graphic account:

> Compared with other natives, farm labourers in the Transvaal are very poor... Take a definite tribe — the Ndebele for instance; compared to other tribes, they are as poor as mice. They were broken up after they were subdued by the South African Republic; they work for no wages: and going out to the mines is, to say the least, openly discouraged.[72]

Conclusion

It is the argument of this paper that the distinctiveness and cultural creativity and tenacity of the Southern Ndebele which has so often been remarked on cannot be explained by notions of Nguni pride and cultural aggressiveness. These characteristics are better understood in the context of the particular processes of conquest and dispossession which these communities experienced. The ZAR set out to destroy the chiefdom and to disperse its subjects. One of the crucial ways in which the Ndzundza fought back was through their attempts to regroup and to revive key social institutions like the homestead and male initiation. The material basis of chiefly power had been destroyed, but the chiefdom and the cultural forms associated with it continued to offer a model of an alternative and preferred social order to life on the farms. Ndzundza royals played a part in this process but they were in no position to enforce it. The 'traditionalism' which developed was made possible and defended by the resistance and initiative of ordinary men and women. It is also probable that in this process a rather more homogeneous culture was created than had existed within the independent chiefdom.

The removal of many of the central supports of chiefly power ensured that emphasis was placed on its ritual and judicial dimensions. But increasingly, after the turn of the century, maintaining elements of the chiefdom was also bound up with gaining access to land. Groups of farm labourers stood little chance of being allocated land by the state, but a constituency defined as the Ndebele chiefdom had some prospect of securing a location.

Also crucial to sustaining a distinctive Ndebele identity was the particular place which these communities occupied within the rural class structure. The fact that they had been stripped of land, cattle and weapons resulted in their ending up in a relatively disadvantaged position within rural society. Thus both a history of struggle and a particular economic position served to underwrite a distinctive identity.

The experience of the Ndzundza serves as a reminder that while ethnic identities and traditions may be moulded or even invented by élites, they can also be crafted from below by men and women working with available elements of culture to fashion ideologies and identities which help to sustain them in a harsh and changing world. The analysis of ethnicity needs to take into account both these realities.

Postscript

Although the history of these communities after 1914 remains to be fully researched, a number of key perspectives can none the less be identified. In some respects their responses are similar to those of the 'red' communities in the Transkei who developed an ideology of traditionalism as a means of coping both with colonial conquest and with the increasing centrality of migrant labour to their lives.[73] The crucial difference is that the Ndebele were largely excluded from labour migrancy, and although this meant less exposure to the socially corrosive effects of migrancy, the intensifying exploitation on the farms created deep tensions within homesteads in the twentieth century.

In order to meet farmers' demands for labour and to create some space for their own production, homestead heads had to have a secure grip over their wives and children. Traditional definitions of gender and generational roles provided them with powerful ideological ammunition in struggles within the homestead. These norms were also part of a system of beliefs which underpinned royal status. As the twentieth century progressed there may well have been a tacit alliance between homestead heads battling to maintain their positions and royals seeking recognition. It is striking that by the 1920s initiation schools were drumming the virtues of generational as well as royal authority into youths. Although the struggle for control of their children was one that homestead heads lost with increasing frequency as the balance of power on the farms swung still harder against them, the youths who fled intensifying exploitation on the land seldom returned to challenge the dominant values which they had left behind.[74]

In the twentieth century farmers also increasingly enforced their own version of traditionalism. This was shaped by their hostility to the politics of the African élite, and by their desire to insulate their labourers from outside influences and to extract the maximum labour from them. It consisted partly of a deep antagonism to any signs of 'Westernisation'. In the decades after 1900 the Ndzundza wore

> skins... You were not even able to wear a pair of trousers. You dare not come on to the farm wearing... clothes — You would be shot dead! A kaffir wearing clothes — No![75]

Tenants were also discouraged from other forms of Western consumption.

> For our meals we ate porridge mixed with fat. The whites just couldn't give us sugar, not even coffee, who were we to be given that? Even those who worked in the kitchen were not given sugar or coffee. Only whites ate those things.[76]

But the main struggle took place over education.

> There was no education for either the parents or their children. One person took his children to school unaware that the Boer farmer had been keeping a record of his children's births. One day he called this man and asked him about his children, who were by then of working age. He wanted them to start working on the farm. The man replied that his children were staying with his sister in the town. After two days the Boer again enquired about these children and claimed that they were attending school, he said that if he was correct, then this man would have to leave the farm.[77]

This conflict simmered for decades and finally came to a head in the 1950s when large number of families were evicted from the farms.

> [This] resulted from the children demanding to leave the farms because they were sick and tired of farm life and ill-treatment by the Boers. They said they wanted education... Then the Boers said we should go along with them. So we left.[78]

There were thus a number of strands which made up the traditionalism of the Ndzundza, and these were combined differently by different constituencies. It was a form of resistance to defeat and life on the farms, a buttress to the position of chiefs and homestead heads, and the only means allowed by farmers to their tenants to express a degree of independence. There is also evidence that by the 1920s educated groupings were starting to elaborate a distinct Ndebele identity. But their efforts and organisations remained remote from the lives of farm labourers.[79]

Finally, it would be wrong to imagine that because an image of traditional chieftainship was retained, and even celebrated as one element of their ideology, Ndebele communities would readily accept the co-optation of the chiefly strata by the state. Quite the reverse: as with the 'red' communities in the Transkei, a popular model of the traditional role and duties of chiefs could provide a devastating critique of the modern degradation of chiefly office.[80]

Notes

The genesis of this paper lies in comments I made some years ago when asked to explain the 'traditionalism' of some contemporary Southern Ndebele communities. See D. James, 'From Co-operation to "Co-operative": Changing Patterns of Agricultural Work in a Rural Village', Unpublished Paper, History Masters Seminar, University of the Witwatersrand, Sept. 1984, personal communication cited on p.15. The refining and reworking of those ideas which this paper represents owes a good deal to conversations with Deborah James and to the generous access she has given me to her research material. Patrick Pearson and Maureen Swan also made helpful comments.

1 See, for example, the scholarly work by E.A. Schneider, Paint, Pride and Politics: Aesthetic and Meaning in Transvaal Ndebele Wall Art, Unpublished PhD Thesis, University of the Witwatersrand, 1986; and the rather more popular work by M. Courtney-Clarke, *Ndebele: The Art of An African Tribe* (New York,1986), for two works which give a sense of the range of the recent literature.

2 Report of the Native Land Comission (UG 22-14), Evidence of T. Edwards, Sub-Native Commissioner, Middelburg District, p. 413. For earlier expressions of a similar view see Transvaal Native Affairs Department Annual Report (TNADAR), 1903, p.23.

3 The original reads, 'die mees konservatiewe naturelle... wat in die Transvaal aangetref word. Hul hou nog met hand en tand vas aan hul ou gewoontes, drag en lewenswijze.' H.C.M. Fourie, *Amandebele van Fene Mahlangu en hun Religieus-Sociaal Leven*, (Zwolle, 1921), p.206.

4 I.Schapera, 'The Ndebele of South Africa', *Natural History*, (Nov. 1949), p.206. Schapera is heavily dependent on the work of N.J. van Warmelo which is cited below.

5 Anthropological fieldwork conducted within a mixed Southern Ndebele and North Sotho village in 1983 produced evidence of a

relatively 'strong traditionalism' amongst the Ndebele, 'not only in the respectfulness of their attitudes towards traditional authority, but also in things like the large size of extended families, the persistence of polygyny, the strictness of customs such as *hlonipha* which requires a woman to show extreme respect to her in-laws, and so on'. See James, 'From Co-operation to "Co-operative"', pp. 15-16.

6 E.A. Schneider, *African Arts* 18 (1985), 66. The source for the comment on Nguni pride is given as a personal communication from W.D. Hammond-Tooke. See also Schneider, Paint, Pride and Politics, pp. 214, 218-219. The concept of Nguni culture is, even in less determinist usage, a slippery one. Nguni is, after all, a broad linguistic category which encompasses a wide variety of societies and cultures. Other exponents of ethnic determinism, although of a somewhat narrower variety, are C.J. Coetzee, Die Strewe tot Etniese Konsolidasie en Nasionale Selverwesenliking by die Ndebele van die Transvaal, Unpublished PhD Thesis, Potchefstroom University, 1980, and C.J. van Vuuren, 'Ndzundza-Ndebele en die Mapochsgrotte', *South African Journal of Ethnology*, 8 (1985), 39-47. Schneider does not rest her entire argument on Nguni culture, see below: note 7.

7 Schneider makes an attempt to situate the Ndebele in historical context — in particular that of defeat and dispersal, see Paint, Pride and Politics, Ch. 7, but her work is marred by an unresolved tension between 'Nguni' determinism and an awareness of historical process. It is also based on a narrow range of mainly published sources and thus can only provide a superficial account of Ndzundza history which is particularly weak on the late nineteenth century, and which presents an overly monolithic view of the society in the twentieth century.

8 See, for example, N. Haysom, *Mabangalala: The Rise of Right-Wing Vigilantes in South Africa*, (Johannesburg, 1986), p. 62.

9 N.J. van Warmelo, *A Preliminary Survey of the Bantu Tribes of South Africa* (Pretoria, 1935), pp. 88-89. North Sotho is also a highly artificial category which encompasses a range of societies and dialects.

10 This overview of Ndebele history is based on F.A. van Jaarsveld, Die Ndzundza-Ndebele en die Blankes in Transvaal 1845-1883, Unpublished MA Thesis, Rhodes University, 1985, and P. Delius, *The Land Belongs to Us* (Johannesburg, 1983).

11 *Berliner Missions-berichte (BMB)*, 1875, pp. 132-133. See also N.J. van Warmelo, *Transvaal Ndebele Texts* (Pretoria, 1930), for discussion of Manala history and society. The Manala, despite living on mission land, remained mainly resistant to christianity.

12 A. Merensky, *Erinnerungen aus dem Missionsleben in Transvaal* (Berlin, 1899), p.133; Transvaal Archives (TA), SN1/105/75, Landdrost, Lydenburg, to Superintendent of Natives (SN), 31 May 1879; *BMB*, 1875, pp. 132-33.

13 TA, SS487/R4978/80, G. Roth to Colonial Secretary, 13 Nov. 1880; SS1097/R4128/89/R3287/80, H. Shepstone to Colonial Secretary, 8 July 1880; SN8/299/82, S.P. Grove to SN, 14 June 1882; Delius, *The Land Belongs to Us*, pp. 88-90; T. Wangemann, *Maleo und Sekukuni* (Berlin, 1868), p. 61.; Van Jaarsveld, Ndzundza-Ndebele, p. 212; J.D. Omer-Cooper, *The Zulu Aftermath* (London, 1966).

14 TA, SS1907/R4128/89/R4474/80, A.Kuhnissen to G.Roth, 18 Oct. 1880; Delius, *The Land Belongs to Us*, pp. 10-19, 91-92; A. Kuper, 'Fourie and the Southern Transvaal Ndebele', *African Studies*, 37 (1978), 114-15, 120; Schneider, Paint, Pride and Politics, pp. 16-30; Schapera, 'Ndebele', pp. 408-11. The vividly coloured wall murals also only developed from the 1940s.

15 The first quotation reflects Fourie's view, see Kuper, 'Fourie', p. 10. The second is drawn from Schneider, Paint, Pride and Politics, p. 218. See also N.J. van Warmelo, 'The Classification of Cultural Groups', in W.D. Hammond-Tooke (ed.), *The Bantu-Speaking Peoples of Southern Africa* (London, 1974), pp. 67, 73-74.

16 Delius, *The Land Belongs to Us*, Ch. 8; Van Jaarsveld, Ndzundza-Ndebele, Ch. 5.

17 Van Jaarsveld, Ndzundza-Ndebele, Ch. 6; Schneider, Paint, Pride and Politics', pp. 200-204.

18 C.3841, No.17, Derby to L. Smyth, 18 Aug.1883; No. 22, Derby to L. Smyth, 29 Aug. 1883; No. 23, L. Smyth to Derby, 13 Aug. 1883 and enclosures; No. 49, L. Smyth to Derby, 24 Sept. 1883; No. 50, L. Smyth to Derby, 25 Sept. 1883; No. 53, British Resident to High Commissioner, 27 Sept. 1883; No. 62, L. Smyth to Derby, 9 Oct. 1883 and enclosures; No. 63, L. Smyth to Derby, 30 Oct. 1883; TA, SS7389/R10817/98, Speech by Kommandant-Generaal, 28 July 1898 (this is the source of the quotation in the text).

19 Van Jaarsveld, Ndzundza-Ndebele, pp. 235-37.

20 P. Naude, Boerdery in die Suid-Afrikaanse Republiek 1855-1899',

Unpublished D Litt Thesis, University of South Africa, 1954, pp. 60-105, 185-228; TA, SS828/R3073/83 Krygsraad resolution, 18 June 1883, minutes and enclosures.

21 TA, SS833/R3455/83, Secretary of the Volksraad to State Secretary, 21 July 1883, minutes and enclosures; Naude, Boerdery, pp. 74-75.

22 TA, SS828/R3073/83, Krygsraad resolution, 18 June 1883, minutes and enclosures; SS833/R3455/83, Secretary of the Volksraad to State Secretary, 21 July 1883, minutes and enclosures.

23 Ibid.

24 Ibid.

25 Staats-Courant (ZAR), I Dec. 1881; C.3841, No. 48, British Resident to High Commissioner, 7 Sept. 1883 and enclosures.

26 Ibid.

27 S.Trapido, 'Aspects of the Transition from Slavery to Serfdom: The South African Republic, 1842-1902', Institute of Commonwealth Studies Collected Seminar Papers, 20 (1974-1975), 29.

28 Schneider, Paint, Pride and Politics, p. 205.

29 Van Jaarsveld, Ndzundza-Ndebele, p. 213.

30 TA, SN10/22/84, Answers to circular re run-away Mapoch kaffers, n.d., 1884; SN10/305/84, Census of the natives of the tribe of Mapoch in the district of Pretoria, n.d., 1884. These files contain the surviving lists of indenture of the Ndzundza and are fullest for the Pretoria, Middelburg and Standerton districts.

31 Ibid.; SN11/396/85, Statement of September, 21 July 1885; KG, CR/653/89, L.C. Janse van Rensburg to Kommandant-Generaal, 14 March 1889.

32 Ibid.

33 Ibid.; Delius, The Land Belongs to Us, pp. 30-40, 136-47; Fourie, Amandebele, pp. 101-03, 157.

34 Names like 'Swartland' and 'Rooiland' were also common names for oxen and thus may have reflected still wider continuities, while a name like 'Halfpond' has connotations of size as well as currency; TA, SN10/22/84, Answers to circular re run-away Mapoch kaffers n.d., 1884; SN10/305/84, Census of the natives of the tribe of Mapoch in the Pretoria district, n.d., 1884; See note 30.

35 C 3841, No. 86, British Resident to High Commissioner, 12 Oct. 1884; TA, SN9/369/83, J.A. Erasmus to SN, 19 Nov. 1883; KG, 148/84, Landdrost, Standerton, to Kommandant-Generaal, 30 March 1884; SN10/198/84, J.A. Erasmus to SN, 5 April 1884;

SS948/R2665/84, J.A. Erasmus to SN, 17 May 1884; SS987/R4631/84, Landdrost, Lydenburg, to SN, 27 Sept. 1884; SN12/259/86, Responses to circular BB 12/6/86.

36 C 3841 No. 48, British Resident to High Commissioner, 12 Sept. 1883.

37 P. Delius, 'Abel Erasmus; Power and Profit in the Eastern Transvaal', in W. Beinart, P. Delius and S. Trapido (eds), *Putting a Plough to the Ground* (Johannesburg, 1986).

38 TA, SN10/54/84, Declaration of C. Erasmus before the Public Prosecutor, 24 Jan. 1884, minutes and enclosures.

39 TA, SN9/369/83, J.A. Erasmus to SN, 19 Nov. 1983; SS955/R2953/84, Minutes of a meeting between J.C. Winterbach, J.A. Erasmus and S.W. Burghers, n.d., 1884; SS960/R3297/84, S. Grove to SN, 17/7/84; SS987/R4631/84 D.J. Schoeman to J.A. Erasmus, 17 Nov. 1884.

40 TA, SN10/252/84, Native Commissioner, Middelburg, to SN, 2 May 1884; KG, 628/85, J.N. Boshoff to P.J. Joubert, 5 Sept. 1885; Landdrost, Lydenburg, to SN, 27 Sept. 1884.

41 TA, SN11/396/85, Statement of September, 21 July 1885; SN10/279/84, J. Uys to P.J. Joubert, 19 May 1884.

42 Ibid.; Delius, *The Land Belongs to Us*, Ch. 6; Naude, Boerdery, pp. 185-207; TA, SN13/31/87, J.W. Luck to SN, 10 Dec. 1887; SN12/390/86, J. Boshoff to SN, 6 Oct. 1886; SN12/259/86, J.A. Erasmus to SN, 29 May 1886; SN12/336/86, P. Minnaar to J.A. Erasmus, 24 May 1886; SS1166/R519/86, J.N. Herman to State Secretary (SS), 1 Feb. 1886;

43 TA, SN13/31/8 7, J.W. Luck to SN, 10 Dec. 1887; SN12/259/86, Answers to circular BB12/6/86; SS1166/R519/86, J.N. Herman to SS, 1 Feb. 1886; David Mahlangu interviewed by Deborah James, Nebo, May 1983. I am grateful to Deborah James for drawing my attention to this source, and for giving me permission to use it.

44 TA, SN/12/259/86, Answers to circular BB12/6/86. Despite the gloss placed on the returns, they still indicate that the bulk of the Ndzundza who remained on the farms were concentrated in the areas adjacent to the old heartland of the chiefdom. *Staats-Courant* (ZAR), Supplement, 15 July 1885: these petitioners were mainly from the Pretoria and Middelburg districts. There are few population statistics of any reliability for this period or for the 1890s. Census data from 1904/5, however, suggests that there

were approximately 11 000 Ndzundza living on farms in the
Middelburg district, and approximately 9 000 Ndzundza living on
farms in the Pretoria district. See TNADAR, 1904, pp. 69-71, and
1905, p. 72. These districts were the only ones which contained any
significant noted concentration of Southern Ndebele by the first
decade of the twentieth century. Given that approximately 10 000
Ndzundza were indentured in 1883, these figures suggest that a
considerable proportion of the society ended up living on farms in
these districts.

45 TA, KG, 144/84, D. Schoeman to CG, 20 Feb. 1884.

46 Eastern Transvaal Natives Land Committee 1918 (UG32-18),
Evidence of Chief Mfene Mahlangu, pp. 110-11

47 TA, SS1195/R1468/86, J.A. Erasmus to SN, 8 March 1886.

48 UG32-18, Evidence of Chief Mfene Mahlangu, p. 110

49 Interview with D. Mahlangu.

50 TA, SS1132/85, investigation into the escape of the prisoner
Maschiela; *Staats-Courant* (ZAR), 2 Dec. 1885.

51 Fourie, *Amandebele*, pp. 124-38.

52 Ibid., p. 203. Fourie gives the date as 1887 and the leader as
Magaduzula; Interview with D. Mahlangu. This account runs
together three separate initiation schools which probably took
place in 1886, 1890/1? and 1894/5?. It is also possible that there
was a mainly localised pattern of initiation which may have led to
local variation in the timing of initiation. The revival of female
initiation was probably equally important, if not more so, but this
took place within individual households, and therefore was not as
visible a social phenomenon; the documentary record contains no
relevant information for this period.

53 TA, SS1195/R1468/86, J.A. Erasmus to SN, 8 March 1886. This
evidence suggests that 1886 is a more secure date for the restarting
of initiation than 1887.

54 TA, SS1721/R8578/88, G.S. van Vuuren to Landdrost,
Heidelburg, 19 Sept. 1888, and R8744/88, J.A. Erasmus to SN, 20
Sept. 1888. See also Naude, Boerdery, pp. 200-207; B.J. Kruger,
Discussies en Wetgewing rondom die Landelike Arbeidsvraagstuk
in die Suid-Afrikaanse Republiek 1885-1889, Unpublished MA
Dissertation, University of South Africa, 1965.

55 TA, KG, 139/91, Tapis, Thoeba and Muis appear before the State
President, 22 June 1891; SS3090/R14195/91, J.A. Erasmus to SN,
9 Nov. 1981.

56 TA, KG, 653/87, L.C. Janse van Rensburg to Kommandant-Generaal, 14 March 1889.

57 University of the Witwatersrand (UW), African Studies Institute (ASI), Oral History Project (OHP),Interview with E. Sibanyoni by V. Nkumane, Middelburg, 4 Sept. 1979; Interview with J. Jiyane by V. Nkumane, 3 Sept. 1979. Some of the periodisation of these accounts is not entirely clear, and it is possible that events which took place after the 1882-1883 war are merged with those that took place after the 1899-1902 war. Both resulted in heavy losses of cattle for the Ndebele. But the Swazi were key intermediaries in the trade and this strengthens the probability that these recollections have their roots in the 1880s as the Swazi were severely affected by both Rinderpest and East Coast Fever and are unlikely to have been in a position to trade cattle in the years after 1900. See J. Crush, 'Tin Mining in the Valley of Heaven', Unpublished Seminar Paper, African Studies Institute, University of the Witwatersrand, March 1987.

58 TA, SS11697/R7440/88, Petition for release of Niabel, 14 Aug. 1888; SS6545/R9652/97, Petition for release of Niabel, 6 Aug. 1897.

59 TA, SS7389/R10817/98, Speech by Commandant-General, 28 July 1898.

60 TA, SS8060/R1374/99, Two petitions with a total of 146 signatures from the Middelburg district.

61 O.J.O. Ferreira (ed.), *Geschiedenis Werken en Streven van S.P.E. Trichard*, (Pretoria, 1975), pp. 202-206; Secretary of Native Affairs (SNA), NA2204/02, E. Hogge sends minutes of meeting in Middelburg district, 6 Oct. 1902; NA226/03, Report of the Sub-Native Commissioner, Middelburg, 5 January 1903; UW, ASI, OHP, Interview with Sibanyoni; Interview with Jiyane; Interview with J. Motha by V. Nkumane, 11 September 1979.

62 For a recent comprehensive discussion, see J. Krikler, 'A Class Destroyed, a Class Restored', Unpublished African Studies Seminar Paper, University of Cape Town, 1986.

63 UW, ASI, OHP, Interview with Sibanyoni.

64 TA, SNA, NA/2204/02, E. Hogge sends minutes of meeting in Middelburg district, 6 Oct. 1902. See also TNADAR, 1903, pp. 22-25.

65 Ibid.; Krikler,'A Class Destroyed', pp. 24-30.

66 Ibid.; TA, SNA, 1459/03, E. Hogge to SNA, 9 July 1903.

67 TNADAR, 1903, pp. 22-23.

68 UG 22-14, Evidence of G.J.W. du Toit, p. 261; South African Native Affairs Commission, Vol. 4, evidence of E. Hogge, p.467.

69 Ibid.

70 UG 22-14, Evidence of H. Rose Innes, p. 273, and W. King, p. 274.

71 Ibid., Evidence of Chief Jafita, p. 410.

72 Ibid., Evidence of T. Edwards, p. 411.

73 P. Mayer, 'The Origin and Decline of Two Rural Resistance Ideologies', in P. Mayer (ed.), *Black Villagers in an Industrial Society* (Cape Town, 1980).

74 Fourie, *Amandebele*, pp. 124-39.

75 UW, ASI, OHP, Interview with Motha.

76 Ibid., Interview with Jiyane.

77 Ibid., Interview with Motha.

78 Ibid.

79 In 1919 'The Ndzundza and Manala National Association' was formed with the intention to unite the Ndzundza and Manala and to 'raise them as a nation among nations', but this remained the preserve of a small élite group, and while its history remains obscure it is unlikely that it had much wider impact. For the constitution and initial office bearers see TA, NTS, 109/1016/-19/F201, P.R. Mashiane to SNA, 11 Nov. 1919 and enclosures.

80 It would also be wrong to imagine that the 'traditionalism' of these communities prevented them from engaging in other forms of resistance to life on the farms. The Middelburg district, for example, was a key area of activity of the Industrial and Commercial Workers' Union in the Transvaal in the 1920s, and the extent to which this rural militancy was due to the particular history of defeat and dispossession of the Ndzundza deserves further investigation.

Turning Region into Narrative

English Storytelling in the Waterberg

Isabel Hofmeyr

Towards the middle of 1899 an eighteen-year-old English woman, Mary Fawssett, or Mollie as she was known, and her aunt, Edith, set sail for South Africa.[1] Disembarking at Durban, they made their way to Pretoria and then to Blaauwbank, a farm about 30 kilometres north of present day Vaalwater in the Waterberg district. Here they joined Edith's sister Katherine and her husband Arthur Peacock, a manager for the Transvaal Consolidated Land and Exploration Company.[2]

This bushveld farm world must have been somewhat strange to Mollie, not least because a war was soon to break out. When it did, Mollie felt herself to be living in a 'little world' behind a 'thick curtain dropped'.[3] To overcome her sense of isolation, she described her new experiences to an English school friend in letters which were never posted since the already tenuous postal system disappeared entirely during the war. The world that Mollie documented was one rooted in the universe of the farm divided into smaller areas of homestead, garden and *stat* around which she arranged an ordered social hierarchy.

Beyond the farm, however, events were not at all clear. Apart from the Boer commandos, there were groups of 'Masibi kaffirs' who occasionally attacked the people in the *stat*. To Mollie these various hostilities meant constant treks between the farm and Warmbaths to avoid belligerent Boers, English or 'Masibis'. Mollie had little way of understanding the events beyond the farm which were dominated by the logic of local politics that turned the war into a pretext for certain groups to pursue their own local objectives with more vigour.

The Waterberg Commando, for example, under the less than spectacular leadership of Frederick Albertus Grobler, commandant for the region, were reluctant participants to begin with, and shambled about the region spawning military chaos as they went. Frequent calls for men to be sent to the fronts in the south or to the fever-ridden Limpopo border in the north went unheeded or were tardily implemented. Instead *weglopers*, *huisblywers* and *wegskuilers* congregated on high farms where they suffered not from fever but from *verlofsiekte*. Away from military and health hazards they could increase their labour demands on the black population, while their leaders, all noted northern Transvaal figures, continued to pursue their local and divisive politicking that invariably promoted *persoonlike oorwegings* above *landsake*.[4]

Not far from this draft dodging, and not entirely unconnected to it, another two men used the war to pursue their long-standing fight for the leadership of the Langa section of the Transvaal Ndebele, a position left vacant by the suicide of Masibi, the father of the two feuding brothers, 'Hans' and 'Bakeberg' Masibi. The story of this 'unfraternal brawl' had as its most visible participants the spiteful and drunken Masibi brothers, Grobler, and various other corrupt Boer officials, a fastidious missionary, Sonntag, and subsequently a dithering Native Commissioner, Scholefield. Together they and their confusing maze of supporters acted out a set of complex and overlapping local interests involving issues of land and labour pressure, relationships of clientage between Boer and African leaders, ethnic conflict, and internal division within the Ndebele community. In fact, one of the reasons that brought 'Masibi' warriors on a punitive raid to Blaauwbank was that the people there had fled from their location with its chiefly tribute demands for the comparative quiet of company land.[5]

However, if Mollie was not in a position to appreciate the intricacies of local Waterberg politics, she had her own frameworks of complexity for interpreting the world that provided ways to 'return to a close-by exoticism via far-off detours'.[6] Some of these conventions are predictable and have to do with notions of 'Englishness', so powerful they could accommodate her uncle's (admittedly unwilling) membership of the Waterberg Boer commando. Her sense of time was also 'English', deriving as it did from the Church of England calendar which provided the dates, like 'Sunday after Epiphany Jan 7 1900', for all the letters written on a Sunday evening.

Mollie also spent a lot of time writing, reading and gardening, and from these activities she generated patterns through which she could imagine her new world and make it familiar. Gardening, for example, a cultural process of remaking the landscape, was one way of doing this. A largely 'female place' dominated by 'the aunts', Katherine and Edith, the garden represented an area of female community, craft and skill that continued to form an important theme in the lives of the women descendants of this family. One of Mollie's daughters, Elizabeth (Clarke), worked as a florist for a time, and also used her landscape skills to become a watercolourist of some note. The idea of the garden also formed an important theme in the religious life of the family and was seen as a point of outreach to black women.[7]

Writing was another central activity and, postal problems notwithstanding, Mollie resolved to 'write the war through'. Writing made the world familiar, as she explained to her friend in words whose faint biblical cadence reminds us that the act of writing could carry a meaning almost as significant as religion: 'Sundays seem strange now without these few words to you. It always does me good. It seems so nice to think that I have this to make you seem close to me, although the dark curtain is so very thick that it makes things seem very far away.'[8]

A few years earlier another colonial woman not very far away from Blaauwbank expressed similar ideas about writing:

> I used to pass my days in writing a story, without which amusement I should have collapsed under the combined heat, dullness and anxiety of that time at Rustenburg. But it is wonderful how one can forget oneself and one's own troubles in inventing the joys and woes of creatures of one's imagination.[9]

Reading and books also occupied a central place and provided a medium through which the bushveld world could be imagined. It is principally their absence which illustrates this point: '... can't imagine how funny it feels without a single almanack... and can you imagine how strange it feels without letters, like a thick curtain dropped.' 'Poor Aunt E. she has read every single book, I think, in the house.. It does seem hard for she loves reading so and to wait till war is over seems a long time if you want a nice book.'[10]

It is also through the 'texts' of her old world that the people of the new get placed: 'I do love looking at them [the people of the *stat*], of course we can't talk except by signs or unless a Dutch-speaking kaffir can translate... I think it is so nice that the women are always called "maids" and the children "piccanins". Do you remember singing, "Good night, my little piccanin". I often think of it, it was so nice.'[11]

In many ways Mollie's letters may seem unremarkable: lesser colonial documents from an obscure frontier. However, as 'everyday testimony' from a region about which very little is known, they are of considerable interest, not least because they reveal the consciousness of a young colonial woman, its 'structures of feeling', and the lines of identity by which her new place and world are imagined. In addition, as documents of a specific locality, they illustrate something of the complex and crowded world that any region always is.

The world that Mollie principally describes — a farm in the Waterberg — was a place that many others both before and after her were to document in diaries, memoirs, travel accounts, articles and books. Together these documents remember, and imaginatively 'reinvent', the same region from the preconceptions of a particular group — English-speaking settlers. In broad terms, the ways in which these people write about region are similar to Mollie's since all these texts, like colonial writing in general, follow the pattern of 'return[ing] to a close-by exoticism via far-off detours'.

This paper will attempt some preliminary observations about this literature — written mostly in the first half of this century — and the way it reconstructs a region. The investigation will involve various questions. What kind of world do these stories come from, and how do they imagine this world textually? In what sense, if any, can these stories be classified as 'regional' or, in a slightly different way, can they be said to embody a defined 'sense of place'? How, in other words, is region turned into narrative?

These are of course exceedingly difficult questions both to conceptualise and to answer. The idea of region is a slippery one, as we are told by a bewilderingly large interdisciplinary body of scholarship. To clarify it ultimately requires a saturated social history that can 'fix' the region from the outside by specifying its relationships to a broader economic and political world, while suggesting its more intimate, inside meanings which give shape to the meandering 'life paths' of its various inhabitants.[12]

Furthermore, the northern Transvaal, as one of its few scholars has said, 'is an area seldom visited by academic research'.[13] Within this neglected terrain the Waterberg is an extreme example: its most documented feature is its geology. Although against such a background this paper can offer no saturated social history, it can provide a broad taxonomy of the literature and history of the region and some of their major themes.

A place, as Williams has pointed out, is neither automatic nor self-evident.[14] Places have to be made both imaginatively and materially. They require, in other words, certain preconditions. Perhaps the most obvious of these is that for a bit of the earth to be seen as a region, it must have a shape economically, physically and imaginatively, not all of course strictly co-terminous.

The area of the north-western Transvaal which Boer settlers were to call the Waterberg has a very distinctive shape. While in some senses the term Waterberg refers to the magisterial district whose boundaries have shifted over time,[15] physically the area is dominated by a mountain range which rises suddenly to the north-west of the Springbok Flats. Comprising several smaller ranges, the whole series is known as the Waterberg (or sometimes just Waterberg), and forms part of an almost continuous mountain barrier that stretches to the east and marks the beginnings of the lowveld. 'Behind' or west of the mountains lies an uneven plateau, known variously as the Palala or Waterberg plateau or the Limpopo Highlands. It declines to the west and then drops suddenly to the Limpopo valley.[16]

When people talk about the Waterberg they often refer generally to the magisterial district, but there is as well a more specific meaning which refers to the mountain/plateau region or, as one resident put it describing her perceptions of the area: 'The mountains on that side and the Limpopo this side.'[17] This is often considered the 'true Waterberg', or as some people call it, the north Waterberg.[18] Imaginatively the shape of the area derives, too, from the mountains which divide the magisterial district into 'this side' and 'that side'. The following testimony from a resident describing how one approaches the area from Nylstroom, illustrates this imaginative organisation of space:

> The plain, and the seven sisters and then the Nek is over the hill and then this side you're in the Waterberg proper. I think the Waterberg does extend to Nylstroom but our Waterberg as such is the north Waterberg, you know, it comes from those hills. As everyone used to say, if you live north of the nek, you're mad. A man went in to get his driver's licence and they said: 'I'm not going to risk my life with you, you come from north of the nek.'[19]

This perception of a zone 'behind the mountain' has a history going back to the 1850s when early Boer settlers began trickling into the south of the region. At that time its northern parts must have seemed both alluring and dangerous. Its fevers and flies made it one of the last areas in the Transvaal to be colonised, but its vast game resources, and later its rumoured mineral deposits, made it a place of legend into which many hunters went in the middle decades of the century primarily in search of ivory.

At this time, and from a European point of view, it was an unknown region at the very edge of the familiar world. But as a place of legendary riches, it generated its own wealth of stories, tales and mythologies which gave it a powerful imaginative reality that was to influence many people, one of whom was Eugene Marais. When he was a young boy in Pretoria, the tales of hunters returning from the Waterberg captivated his attention:

> From that wonderland, the hunters' wagons used to come to Pretoria to unload their ivory and skins at the trading stores: Giraffe-skin whips; sjamboks of rhinoceros and hippopotamus hides, cured until they were quite translucent, the sheen and colour of clear amber; rhinoceros horns and dried hides of all the big animals of the wild bushveld - blue wildebeeste, sable and roan antelopes, hartebeeste, giraffes and numbers of others we boys of the civilized south could only guess at.[20]

Not surprisingly, the hunters also had tales to tell: 'hair-raising stories of midnight attacks and hair-breadth escapes... In all their tales loomed large Mapela "the black eagle" sitting on his insurmountable crags and holding the Waterberg in continual fear.'[21] To at least some further south, the Waterberg was a region constituted by narrative, a far-away place which produced not only game but storytellers, traditionally people from afar, as Benjamin has pointed out.[22] So powerful were these stories that Marais later spent a decade of his life in the Waterberg and in turn became one of its most noted storytellers.

Like Marais, other white settlers were to be attracted by its 'fictions' of being 'the ideal theatre of manly adventure, of great endeavours and the possibility of princely wealth'.[23] The area was also to provide material for a group of colonial storytellers like Vere Stent, Stuart Cloete, Gustav Preller and possibly Haggard and Buchan.[24]

Another writer, Cyril Prance, translated the Waterberg into a literary convention which he called 'Skranderberg', a 'sort of Transvaal parallel to Hardy's Wessex'.[25] Using the convention of the Afrikaner storyteller called Tante Rebella, Prance documents the social morphology of the region in stories which look back to Gibbon and Blackburn and probably acted as models for Bosman. In addition to this fiction, the Waterberg has generated documentary and travel writing, and since Sarah Heckford travelled into the Waterberg as a trader in the 1870s there have been other travellers, like Louis Leipoldt for example, who have recorded their impressions of the region.[26] While these travellers came to pass and not to stay, those who lived in the region also produced a body of testimony both published and unpublished.[27]

It is primarily this literature with which the present paper is concerned. But first we must pause to look briefly at the historical context from which it came and 'about' which it shaped itself.

This reality was of course not all magical tales and legendary experiences for by the 1880s the entire region was, from a European point of view, still considered a 'remote and pestilential corner of Africa'[28] that mostly harboured fractious chiefs, foolhardy hunters, desperate criminals on the run from the law,[29] and unfortunate officials who from the 1860s had to contend with a region that was an administrative nightmare. Tax from both black and white was mostly a theoretical issue from which the authorities in Pretoria constantly demanded practical results. And even if an official should track down a tax offender, the administration of justice was extremely patchy since many cases — mostly for stock theft, poaching and illegal liquor selling — never happened: the witness *nergens te vinden* or the accused *gevlucht en kan niet weer gevonde worden*. It was in all a rather grim frontier from which officials sent whining and self-pitying letters telling of chaotic office conditions aggravated by aggressive white ants.[30]

However, where this administrative confusion failed, the Boer settlers resorted to more violent means, particularly when it came to extending their control over the people with whom they shared their world. In their forms of conquest, the Boers were in many ways similar to Mzilikazi's raiding state that had affected the region in the 1820s and 1830s. From the 1850s, and particularly in the 1860s, when the settler population was strengthened by people retreating from concerted African resistance in the Zoutpansberg, the Boer commandos waged various campaigns against the African communi-

ties of the area, particularly the Langa Ndebele in the north and the
Bakgatla Mosetla in the south.[31] While the power of these
communities was considerably eroded by these campaigns, and in
addition many families, particularly from Bakgatla communities,[32]
were scattered on Boer farms, they remained none the less semi-
independent communities for some time, largely because effective
white settlement was so long in coming.

However, despite the realities of *de facto* occupation, from an early
date settlers imaginatively shaped the region as they wished it to be.
Hence one finds many narratives that suggest how the Waterberg
world could, should, or might be. The outlines of this world are
perhaps best seen in maps which, like stories, project or imply a
desired world.

Turn of the century maps often represented the area as
predominantly blue and pink in a ratio of roughly two to one:

> Blue showed the land held by Land Companies and Corporations
> domiciled in Johannesburg, and pink marked the 'dud' remainder
> which had been left on the hands of Paul Kruger's government —
> till conquest transferred it to Queen Victoria and her 'heirs,
> successors and assigns'.[33]

Since the area was considered so remote and pestilential, the
smattering of white on the map denoting private European ownership
would have been imperceptibly small. Equally tiny were brown areas
symbolising regions of black tenure:

> Except where exiguous areas as were marked in brown to indicate
> ownership by 'black stuff' which had learned its place in white
> South Africa, the northerly wilderness had largely been torn
> piecemeal from Bantu kings, offenders against the majesty of an
> exotic law.[34]

In the official imagination of the map, black residence existed chiefly in
the four state-established locations mainly in the north of the district.[35]
The general European attitude to the area was best captured in another
map convention which named much of the north-western Transvaal
'DBU' — 'Dense, Bushy, Unsurveyed'.[36]

Such maps, reflecting only *de jure* ownership, wished away the untidy realities of *de facto* occupation. The 'fiction' represented in this map is one shared by many other stories. They too suppress black life, removing people imaginatively beyond the borders of the farm, there to merge with the landscape and its wild life.[37]

In the 1880s the Kruger state attempted to make a white presence in the Waterberg more real through a series of occupation laws aimed to encourage settlement and 'pacification', particularly 'behind the mountain'.[38] But burghers mostly sold their allotted lands to speculators and land companies since agriculture 'over the hills' offered no great incentive. The most arable land lay in the valleys of the three major rivers of the region. These areas, however, were particularly fever ridden, while higher, healthier ground was either too mountainous or had thin, sandy, infertile soil. Running cattle, if a slightly better proposition, was still hazardous.[39] By 1902 settlement was still largely 'this side' of the hills, and there were said to be 1 500 white households virtually all settled within a 35-mile (about 55-kilometre) radius of Nylstroom, where they mostly ran cattle and farmed small amounts of wheat, tobacco and mealies.[40]

While this figure may reflect some demographic distortion as a result of the Anglo-Boer War, white settlement did in fact come late to the region. When more white settlers began arriving, they did so partly through initiatives tied up with British settlement schemes, and partly through patterns of internal Afrikaner migration that for a time at the beginning of the century filled up areas where land was cheap when other regions were emptying.[41] During the last quarter of the nineteenth century the number of British settlers to South Africa increased markedly.[42] Like the Peacocks and Edith Fawssett who arrived in the 1880s, a few of these settlers made their way to the Waterberg. However, the majority of English-speaking settlers who arrived in the Waterberg did so as part of the post-Anglo-Boer War land settlement schemes.

Propagated not only by the state, these schemes were also energetically promoted by a phalanx of organisations that generated a euphoric gospel of land settlement and anglicisation.[43] While these schemes were mostly unworkable (a 'gross scandal' as one put it), by 1902 some 700 men had seen fit to settle in the Transvaal under various programmes.[44] As the Waterberg was an area of almost entirely crown and company land which its owners were keen to offload, somewhere between 100 and 200 of these men ended up in that region, mainly on the Springbok Flats. Their numbers however soon diminished rapidly due to drought and inexperience of local farming conditions.[45]

This failure did not deter the land settlement agencies and their members. One of their number, William MacDonald from the Transvaal Land Board, was still zealously and actively advocating land settlement when the second major wave of settlers was being recruited after the First World War. As editor of the *Agricultural Journal of South Africa*, he continued to urge 'big-boned' men to take to the plough to convince 'the faint-hearted sceptics and the do-nothing critics' of the farming potentialities of South Africa.[46] A forceful and prolific writer, MacDonald worked with the almost magical sets of associations that words like farmer, farm, land and agriculture could generate — associations so powerful that a full understanding of them would go a long way towards explaining why eminent British colonial officials could readily embark on disastrous land schemes, not once but several times.

In MacDonald's idiom farming almost ceased to be a craft or profession but was instead portrayed as an inherited condition of gentility ('I could not help myself. I was born a good farmer's son').[47] Farming did not necessarily require experience or capital. Instead this cluster of ideas stressed alternative qualifications, one of which was soldiering.[48] In addition, farming was elevated to the status of a secular religion that could heal social wounds and restore social balance: 'Give the miner a comfortable home and a piece of freehold land which he may call his own and you will immediately remove the cancerous sore of continual unrest. Have you ever thought of the healing power of land — the great sympathetic, silent, Mother of Mankind?'[49]

Most of these ideas were of course 'fictions', but like the hunters' tales before them they played some part in attracting settlers. By the 1920s there were several hundred of them who had come to the Waterberg, many like Stuart Cloete from the trenches of the First World War. Shattered by his war experiences, he reverted 'to the simplest things in life, to woman... — and the land. To dig, to sow, to plant and watch things grow... It was a Garden of Eden existence.'[50] By 1920 he was employed by a land company as manager. He lived on various farms on the Springbok Flats and then moved to a farm near Hammanskraal. In many ways Cloete was the 'ideal-type' settler: his life was deeply shaped by colonial literature — Haggard, Livingstone, and Selous[51] — and his experience in the bushveld was in turn processed into further colonial stories. As he explained, the Waterberg was 'the place where I saw the Africa about which later I was to spend my life writing'.[52]

Like Cloete, very few of these English settler farmers stayed. Most moved away to towns and not a few killed themselves, worn out by the endless battle of undercapitalised farming.[53] The few with more capital and determination stayed, bringing with them new methods of agriculture and 'new cultural directions'.[54] Later the beneficiaries of increased state involvement in white agriculture, these English families who remained were to witness over the first thirty years of this century a transition in the area. Beginning with energetic post-Anglo-Boer War plans for reconstructing agriculture, the remote world of the Waterberg began to change, but only very slowly and imperceptibly. Some of the symbols of this change were things like the surveyor, the Model T Ford and the railway. The first of these appeared in the Waterberg towards the end of the century, the second after the First World War, and the third amidst great celebration when the railhead advanced to Vaalwater in 1928.

These forces, along with things like primary education, the spread of communication, and easy travel are, as one has said, 'the great solvents of local culture', and under their impact some of the rougher 'localisms of remoteness' began to disappear.[55]

In fiction, however, they started gaining new imaginative life, as much of the English literature of the Waterberg nostalgically reconstructed that which was vanishing. One writer expressed these changes through the symbol of the automobile: as a result of 'the mass production of Messrs Ford and Dodge', the region witnessed 'huge cars crowded with tourists intent on exploration in "the blue" in the hope of inflicting their experiences and observations on some London publisher or editor'.[56] In many ways, then, the fiction from this small but significant group of English settlers constitutes a literature of remembering. But in the structure of that memory itself, one can detect the historical traces of their experience which manifest themselves in certain recurrent designs in these narratives. The overarching pattern takes shape around the idea of the mountain range as a barrier-frontier which becomes the pretext for narratives of difficult journeys into a remote world. This world beyond the mountains is in turn recreated by a series of stories focusing on the social format of the settler world rooted in the universe of the farm. Let us consider each of these stages in more detail.

Like most people, Eugene Marais first entered the Waterberg from

Nylstroom. He travelled with a man called Dolf Erasmus, and they headed for the Waterberg which lay before them 'like a gapless wall'. Fortunately their journey went smoothly. Had it been raining, things would have been different, for then the black turf or 'cotton soil' of the Springbok flats 'became frightful to pull through'.[57] This specifically regional feature often becomes something which triggers stories that in turn become part of the repertoire of a 'Waterberg tale'.[58] It was a tale that carried on over the mountains. There the thin sandy soil made a journey an experience which was often translated into narrative.[59]

As Erasmus and Marais continued their journey, there loomed before [them] the massive front of a range which quite clearly had no break'. With no gorge or pass, they 'toiled up the zig-zag road— with frequent rests'.[60] The point they had reached is known as Sandrivierspoort or the Nek, one of the major entrances to the Waterberg. As a place of entry and exit, it was from an early date a node of commerce with a store and hotel.[61] It was also a repository of narrative since it was a place in which stories were told. Today it is no longer a point of commercial consequence, yet it remains none the less a place about which stories get told and through which stories get recalled. It is in other words a type of historical mnemonic in which narrative gets 'stored'. One documenter of the region describes it as 'a country store and inn, and many a story could that rambling, white-washed building tell, for after the perils of the Nek every trekker would relax there and restore his nerves with liquid refreshment'.[62]

While the store's function has largely disappeared, it remains a narrative landmark for many white residents. As one informant explained: 'As you go down you go over a steep hill and there's a bend and there's a shop... It's an antique shop now that was a hotel years ago. The big thing was to get past that hotel, that was the big challenge to all.' These remarks in turn triggered a story about the exploits of his grandfather at the Nek.[63] While in general terms these stories are variants of colonial romances which posit a frontier across which experience will be different, they have a specificity deriving from a very precise landscape which gives these 'narratives of entry and exit' an identifiable regional feel.

The pattern of these journey narratives have as well other regional variations. Take, for example, the stories of seasonal movement arranged around the winter movement of people down to bushveld territory used as hunting ground and winter pasture.[64] There are also stories revolving around the introduction of mechanised transport and communications. These include a vein of narrative whose protagonists are the Model T Ford or 'Tin Lizzie', and the steam engine whose arrival in Vaalwater in 1928 old residents recall in tremendously precise detail.[65]

The Model T stories often lampoon outsiders attempting to enter the district on roads which existed only in the fiction of a map. Faced with these conditions, the driver has to accommodate himself to the region sometimes by reconverting the car to a donkey wagon or, as Leipoldt had to do, by stuffing grass into repeatedly punctured tyres.[66] Once inside the region or behind the mountains, the specific vegetation and ecology form another morpheme of the Waterberg story.[67] In addition, storytellers appropriate smaller geographical demarcations like 'the moepel', a designation derived from the region's vegetation.[68]

However, the overriding form into which experience is cast is the classic settler narrative— the farm story.[69] Like Mollie Fawssett, most settlers imagined and organised their world through the farm, and most narratives, too, share this pattern. While narratologically these tales may appear merely as variants of the farm story, they, like the narrative of the colonial journey, have a specific regional core. Take, for example, the settler's perception of the black world. In a pattern common in much colonial writing, the farm boundary is the line of exclusion beyond which lies the wilderness, as in the following passage where a father imagines his son on a Waterberg farm:

> ... veld stretches to the skyline from the bush-clad kopjes on the borders of the farm... We shall buy you a gun... and when you have been taught how properly to handle it, you can guard the chickens from the wild cats, and the eggs from the leguvaan... and you might catch a jackal sneaking along just after sundown... or you may prevent a kaffir from stealing your uncle's crops and taking his oxen for meat, but you will have to be careful because the magistrate will fine you twenty-five pounds. For stray dogs remove the bullets and fill the cartridge with salt. It stings but does not injure, and they will never return.[70]

The farm in this passage becomes the unit whose borders are threatened by vermin, a category into which Africans have been translated. The prophecy in the passage becomes self-fulfilling. When

the boy, James Bredfield, grows up, he turns into the presaged hunter
of people not outside but inside the farm boundaries.

> James Bredfield had a battle-royal one day, for he was mobbed by
> the population of the native *stad*... which was in the farm. John
> was anxious when he heard it, for his son had walked into the
> angry crowd and seized a herd-boy whom he suspected of stealing
> cattle for meat.[71]

While this type of perception could no doubt be found in many farm
narratives, there is an element of regional particularity in these stories
which, if not precisely Waterberg, is at least bushveld or northern
Transvaal specific. This particularism has to do with the way tenants
are perceived. In Waterberg stories most black characters are seen
through the 'three-month' or 'ninety-day' system which operated on
most farms.[72] In addition, in the character of the indentured or
apprenticed worker one sees the traces of earlier, more coercive labour
systems.[73]

As this is a settler literature we get almost no glimpses from the
tenants' side. Where we do, it constitutes an interesting perspective on
the farm. On his travels, Leipoldt approached a man with legendary
clairvoyant ability. The man promised to demonstrate his skill: 'But
not here. Not on the farm. The farm [is] not the proper place to call the
spirits to.'[74]

Another variant of the farm story is the narrative of beacons,
boundaries, and the paraphernalia of surveying and land transactions,
one of the cultural forms through which the land is structured and
possessed. Again these stories have a regional shape since the issue
they deal with constitutes a major theme of the northern Transvaal
generally and the Waterberg and Zoutpansberg specifically. Here by
the end of the nineteenth century land title and tenure was, as one
commission put it, 'bordering on chaos', given the practices of land
grants to burgers, the pattern of land speculation, and the lack of
surveyors.[75] Part of Milner's reconstruction plan involved imposing a
British and surveyed order on the Transvaal landscape. This task,
however, was not always easy in remote and difficult terrain where
Boer farmers could use their local knowledge to *verneuk* Milner
experts and other 'khaki' officials who said things like 'Hah-de-doo'
and 'my good man'.[76]

Yet another regional concern of the farm story derives from the agricultural limitations of the Waterberg. As one farmer said: 'Do not put thy faith in mealies — not in the Waterberg.'[77] Probably until at least the 1920s much white farming was generally theoretical and most white settlers were transitory. The most permanent and productive farmers were mainly black tenants and peasants. This was of course hardly the situation to foster the heroic *plaasroman* (farm novel) in which farms 'become the seat to which... lineages are mystically bound, so that the loss of a farm assumes the scale of the fall of an ancient house, and the end of a dynasty'.[78] It would, in fact, have been very difficult for any storyteller to monumentalise farming in the Waterberg, and instead many narratives generate a sly humour by playing off heroic notions of farming against the everyday realities of farm practice, involving as they did 'bilious' days,

> when a farmer's life seemed but a turgid grind of worry with egg-eating hens and dogs; hen-eating hawks and cats; calves that will not suck; cows that refuse to allow suction; fence-jumping oxen; ticks, tampans, locusts, army-worm, bag-worm and cut-worm; spons-siekte, gal-siekte, nieu-siekte, vuur-siekte...[79]

In addition, Waterberg stories often comically invert the symbolic hierarchies of farming. Hence the hallowed occupation of ploughing and reaping, often believed to be superior to animal husbandry, was referred to by at least one as '*twakboerdery*' (literally 'tobacco farming', but also 'nonsense farming'). For this man, Hans van Heerden of Nooitgedacht, only cattle farmers were truly 'people' and 'farmers'.[80]

In many instances the gap between the symbolic perception of farming and the practical world was enormous, particularly since most white 'farmers' in the Waterberg hardly worked the land at all, preferring instead to 'farm' biltong and peach brandy. While this was not a cultural tradition followed by English-speaking settlers, not many of them did much farming either, preferring instead by all satirical accounts to play tennis most of the time.[81] Despite this reality, the notion of 'being a farmer' was an extremely powerful one, and writers like Prance exploit the humour implicit in the gap between principle and practice, particularly in the case of English settlers caught up as they were in the massive fiction of land settlement. From this situation issues forth a range of stories of the 'tennis-mad' English, the 'stoep ornament' farmer, and those attempting to reconstruct a 'lady novelists' perfect ranch' in 'poison plant veld at a hundred miles from rail'.[82]

Since few Europeans lived by farming alone, people cultivated a wide range of skills. Brewing, hunting, poaching, and selling animals both dead and alive were predominant. Others included trading, 'smousing', transport riding, 'doctoring', photography, teaching, charcoal production, tin mine work, blacksmith work, state and land company posts and labour agencies.[83]

In the literature these crafts translate themselves into a range of strongly typological figures like the *smous*, the wandering teacher, the state official, and so on. Some of the stories, too, probe the format of social relationships that grow around the patterns of power and profession in any community. Take the case of Oom Stoffel who has enriched himself through trading and cattle grabbing during the 'English war'. He becomes a man of prestige to whom many in the region are indebted. Hence he feels he can move a beacon to enlarge his farm with impunity, since any jury would be composed of people under his patronage. He is in the end given away by a 'Zulu policeman', a double outsider not bound by the invisible contracts of the Afrikaner community.[84]

Particular crafts seem to attract clusters of stories. In some instances these have to do with a vanishing social type like the blacksmith.[85] In other instances stories cohere around the 'hidden crafts' of the region, particularly brandy distilling. As with the farm stories, these humorously exploit the distance between the legislated reality and the regional practice. In a situation where *brandewyn-ketels* (brandy-stills) were common, attempts to outlaw distilling were of course half-hearted, not least because the law enforcers themselves were often part of the community which bound them by its codes of power and patronage.[86]

Another type of skill also hidden, but in ways very different from distilling, was that rather diffuse category, 'local knowledge', which any number of stories explore. It is also something which the protagonist of any Waterberg story is said to have and knows how to use to get ahead. The precise content of the knowledge varies, but it is generally tied up with the ability to maximise the repertoire of skills mentioned earlier. Hence, for example, the dithering Native Commissioner Scholefield, whom we met earlier, soon resigned and procured a position with the Transvaal Land Owners' Association inspecting farms on the strength of his local knowledge which obviously increased with the job and put people like him in a favourable position to acquire land.[87] This Scholefield type is one that appears often in the fiction of the area, and was of course a recognisable type in the bushveld where administrative remoteness promoted unorthodox methods. Delius's portrait of Abel Erasmus delineates the 'ideal-type' of this character.[88] In Waterberg fiction one gets fainter versions of this character of a similar fiefly bent, but in these stories they are generally more comically inefficient and blusteringly incompetent than their counterpart in the eastern Transvaal.[89]

Connected to the idea of local knowledge is the idea of storytelling. The storyteller is someone who stores this 'local knowledge' and can use it like other skills to get ahead. Consider the following example:

> Father and son arrived in Tronksdorp and put up at the hotel, where they met the agent who was handling the sale of the farm for its owners, a garrulous and plausible gentleman, who had served Her Late Majesty as a full private in several wars. Old John and young James thought that he was an excellent man and, indeed, he was a cheerful fellow with a fund of anecdotes which made you laugh as you signed in dangerous places upon which he had put his finger. He was a genius at turning away subsequent wrath with funny stories gliding from a smooth tongue.[90]

Stories in a sense, then, act as forms of social currency whereby identities are established and confirmed. However, a remote place like the Waterberg early this century was an ideal area for inventing identities as the many fugitives who hid in the area attest.[91] And around this theme of 'invented identities' a number of stories get told. One example is 'The Stockwhip', in which one man kills another and through 'making up stories' assumes his identity and inheritance. However, it is through his skilful use of a larger sign of identity — his ability to wield a whip — that he gets caught.[92]

Storytelling, then, would appear to be another of the crafts that people in the Waterberg practised.[93] The sociology of the storytelling situation is of course an extremely complex one that cannot be explored here. None the less this body of Waterberg literature opens some interesting insights into the ways in which storytelling both oral and written can function. To Mollie Fawssett, for example, writing was a crucial act of 'realigning' her identity in a new situation. Her aunt, Edith, was also an accomplished storyteller whose skill is remembered to this day.[94] Cyril Prance translated Edith and her household into a story of his own, while many of his other stories are clearly derived from major events in the region which in turn became the subject of orally circulated narrative, some of which still circulates today, quite possibly having been given a new impetus by Prance's written version.[95] Prance, too, attempted to probe some aspects of the meaning and status of a storyteller in a community through the figure of Tante Rebella, the 'stay-at-home' narrator, the exact opposite of the storyteller who brings experiences from afar.[96]

Stories get made through an intricate web of experience, perception, interaction and circulation. And while the readership and circulation of stories like Prance's are difficult to gauge, it is perhaps important to note that they occupied a 'storytelling space' that no longer really exists today. Known sometimes as 'magazinery', these stories represented a modest craft practised widely by people who depicted regional realities for local newspapers and magazines. Again not their major livelihood, it formed one of the repertoire of regional skills mentioned earlier.[97] Arguably, one aspect of this storytelling craft in turn involved learning, mastering and co-ordinating another smaller repertoire — the range of constituent parts found in Waterberg narratives. In some sense these narrative building blocks may derive from a reality similar to but wider than the Waterberg, notably that of the bushveld and northern Transvaal. None the less the skill of assembling these in dexterous combinations remains the same.

This skill of storytelling in white communities is something that also largely disappeared with the 'great solvents of local culture'. However, in the Waterberg one can still see its traces and outlines: some of Edith's descendants, for example, are still good raconteurs. However, while the performance of storytelling may largely have vanished, the memory of stories still remains and plays no small part in historical remembering, since stories continually act as one of the two most common forms of recalling the past. If one cannot remember a story in recalling times and events of which one has no direct experience, then one has to follow the second procedure that all historians use, namely deduction and speculation.[98]

If we accept Williams's assertion that a sense of place is something made, something requiring pre-conditions, then this essay has suggested that one of these prerequisites is that a region exists in narrative; that 'the places of experience' be remembered through story, and that the stories be 'about' the land, cohering around its social and physical shape. The design, texture and character of these stories are in turn structured by the region's economic and social shape which also ordains, for example, the places in which stories get made and the range of experience about which stories get told. In this web resides something that could arguably be called a Waterberg story whose grammar has been shaped by a particular regional history. A lot of theoretical narrative study goes the other way, working towards a 'pure' grammar of narrative where specific historical and regional information is somehow incidental, a type of optional extra one can take or leave. Through this preliminary case study I have attempted to suggest the opposite: like 'a Waterberg tale', stories have regional and historical shapes that run deep.

Notes

1 My thanks to Lois and Charles Baber, Rosalind King and Lex and Helen Rodger for making material and memories available to me. My thanks as well to Peter Delius, Michael du Plessis and Gordon Pirie, who suggested material for this article.

2 Paragraph and subsequent story of Mary Fawssett (later Davidson) based on Elizabeth Clarke, *Waterberg Valley* (Johannesburg, 1955); Mary Davidson, 'Merci ma tante', mimeograph; Interviews with Lois Baber and with Lois and Charles Baber, Boschdraai, Vaalwater district, August 1986; Letters entitled 'Mary Davidson's (Fawssett's) letters to her school friends in England — written during the Anglo-Boer War and never posted' (Letters), in possession of Lois Baber.

3 Letters, 'Sunday after Epiphany Jan 7 1900' and 'July 15th 1900'.

4 Paragraph drawn from Eppo Broos, Die Noordelike Hooflaer in die Distrikte Zoutpansberg, Waterberg en Rustenburg vanaf die Begin van die Tweede Vryheidsoorlog tot die Besetting van Pretoria, Unpublished MA Dissertation, University of Pretoria, 1943, pp. 18-21, 34-44, 59-67, quoted phrases from pp. 63 and 18. In translation, which here and elsewhere is my own, the phrases are as follows: 'deserters', 'stay-at-homers', 'hiders', 'personal considerations', 'national affairs'.

5 Paragraph based on Transvaal Archives (TA), SNA 95 201/03; for evidence of clientage, see letter J.H. Craig to Capt de Bertodano, 4 June 1901; Letter Chas Maggs to De Bertodano 4 June 1901; see 'The War between the Native Chiefs Hans Masebe and Bakeberg

Masebe, 1899-1901', report by Ch. Sonntag, for evidence of land and labour pressure, ethnic and internal division; see Affidavits, sub-file 135/01, for attacks on tenants on company land.

6 Phrase from Michael de Certeau, 'Practices of Space', in M. Blonsky (ed.), *On Signs* (Oxford, 1985).

7 Letter from Charlotte Parker to Mrs Davidson, 8 Jan. 1941, recommending an article 'Gardening with God' for use with the Mothers' Union. In possession of Lois Baber, Boschdraai, Vaalwater.

8 Letters, 'January 14' (1900).

9 Sarah Heckford, *A Lady Traveller in the Transvaal* (London, 1882), pp. 64-65.

10 Letters, 'Jan 7, Sunday after Epiphany' and 'Jan 14, Second Sunday after Epiphany', respectively.

11 Letters, '24 Sunday after Trinity'.

12 I have relied on Allan Pred, 'Structuration and Place: On the Becoming of Sense of Place and Structure of Feeling', *Journal for the Theory of Social Behaviour*, 13 (1983), 45-73; D.W. Meinig, 'Geography as an Art', *Transcripts of the Institute of British Geographers* NS 8 (1983) 314-28; D.C. Pocock, 'A Place and the Novelist', ibid., 6 (1981), 337-47; M.E. Eliot Hurst, 'A Sense of Place', in M.E. Eliot Hurst (ed.), *I Came to the City: Essays and Comments on the Urban Scene* (Boston, n.d.), pp. 40-45; D.N. Jeans, 'Some Literary Examples of Humanistic Descriptions of Place', *Australian Geographer* 14 (1979), 217-14; E.V. Walter, 'The Places of Experience', *Philosophical Forum*, 12 (1980-81), 159-81; Raymond Williams, *The Country and the City*, (London, 1973); Emily Toth (ed.), *Regionalism and the Female Imagination* (Pennsylvania and New York, 1985); F.W. Morgan, 'Three Aspects of Regional Consciousness', *Sociological Review*, 31 (1939), 68-88; E.W. Gilbert, 'The Idea of a Region', *Geography*, 45 (1960), 157-75.

13 R. Wagner, 'The Zoutpansberg: The Dynamics of a Hunting Frontier, 1848-1867', in S. Marks and S. Trapido (eds), *Economy and Society in Pre-Industrial South Africa* (London, 1980), pp. 313-49.

14 Raymond Williams, *The Country and the City*, p. 124.

15 TA, T34, D.J. Pieterse, *Argief Waterberg (AW)*, 'Inleiding: Landdroste, Waterberg-Zoutpansberg' (Johannesburg, 1933).

16 Drawn from J.H. Wellington, *Southern Africa: A Geographical*

Study (Cambridge, 1955), p. 85; Interview with Lex Rodger, Louwskraal, Hanglip, August 1986; Monica Cole, *South Africa* (London and New York, 1966), pp. 653-60.

17 Interview with Lois Baber.

18 Leon Rousseau, *The Dark Stream* (Johannesburg, 1982), p. 217; Interview with Lois Baber.

19 Interview with Lois Baber.

20 Eugene Marais, 'The Road to the Waterberg', in Leon Rousseau (ed.), *Versamelde Werke*, Vol. 2 (Pretoria, 1984), p. 1203.

21 Ibid.

22 Walter Benjamin, 'The Storyteller', in *Illuminations* (Glasgow, 1977), pp. 84-85.

23 Marais, 'The Road to the Waterberg', p. 1203.

24 See S. and B. Stent, *The Forthright Man* (Johannesburg, 1972); Stuart Cloete, *The Gambler: An Autobiography 1920-1939* (London, 1973); Preller based much of his prolific writing for magazines like *Huisgenoot* and *Brandwag* on his experiences in the Waterberg. For Buchan and Haggard see Lex Rodger, 'Vintage Waterberg', Unpublished typescript, n.d.

25 Cyril Prance, *Tante Rebella's Sagas* (*TRS*) (London, 1937), p. 17. Prance's other books include *Under the Blue Roof* (*UBR*) (Bloemfontein, 1944); *Dead Yesterdays* (*DY*) (Port St Johns, 1943); *The Riddle of the Veld* (*RV*) (Durban, 1941); *A Socialist Scrap Book* (Durban, 1945).

26 C. Louis Leipoldt, *Bushveld Doctor* (Cape Town, 1983).

27 This material includes Clarke, *Waterberg Valley*, and also her *Transvaal Poems* (Johannesburg, n.d.); Davidson, 'Merci ma tante', and letters, diaries and papers of this family in possession of Lois Baber and Rosalind King; Anna Havenga, *Life in the Wilds of the Northern Transvaal* (London, 1913); Amy J. Baker, *I Too Have Known* (London, 1911); sections of Francis Bancroft, *The Veldtdwellers* (London, 1938); Nancy Courtney-Acutt, *Bushveld* 1913; A.G. Bee, *Rolling Home* (London, 1936), and *A Man Should Rejoice* (London, 1938); Nancy Courtney-Acutt, *Bushveld* (Durban, 1942); W. Saunders (ed.), *The Reminiscences of a Rand Pioneer* (Johannesburg, 1977); Lex Rodger, 'Vintage Waterberg' and 'The Stockwhip', Unpublished typescripts, n.d.

28 Wagner, 'The Zoutpansberg', p. 336.

29 See details in Prance, 'A Sign-post "In the Blue"', *UBR*, p. 16, 'A "Hydro" in the Bush', *TRS*, p. 169, and 'The Old Adam in the

Veld', *TRS*, p. 75.

30 Paragraph based on documents from TA, AW: for ants, see 1, sub-file 8-53, 1880, 13/31, 5 May 1880; for tax, see 1, sub-file Jan.-Dec. 1885, LB 16/85, 13 May 1885, and 2, sub-file Jan.-Dec. 1886, 175/86, 2 Aug. 1886; for court cases, see 93, sub-file 1895, case against D. Kaiser for liquor-selling, n.no., n.d., and case against G.C. Engelbrecht, n.no., n.d. Phrases in translation: 'nowhere to be found', 'fled and cannot be found'.

31 See Wagner, 'The Zoutpansberg', pp. 316, 322-23; Transvaal Native Affairs Department, *Short History of Transvaal Native Tribes* (Pretoria, 1905), pp. 15 and 18; TA, SNA 67, 2338/02, Native Commissioner, Waterberg, Miscellaneous papers relative to his district.

32 See *Short History of Transvaal Native Tribes*, p. 28.

33 Prance, 'The Tragi-Commedy of "Little Egypt" ', *DY*, p. 105. Land figures from Transvaal (Colony) Commissioner of Land Departments Annual Report, 1901-04, Surveyor General, p. D8, 'Tables of Areas...', which states that of the 15 503 square miles that make up the Waterberg, 4 747 or about one-third was crown land. Almost the entire remaining two-thirds was company land, *Agricultural Journal of South Africa*, 11 (1915), p. 118.

34 Prance, *DY*, pp. 105-106. Figures of white ownership deduced from company and crown land figures above.

35 TA, SNA 67, 2338/02; Linda Chisholm, Proletarianization and Resistance in the Northern Transvaal, 1901-1906, Unpublished MA Dissertation, University of London, 1979, p. 23.

36 Prance, 'In the "D.B.U." ', *DY*.

37 See Bee, *Rolling Home*, for such descriptions.

38 TA, SNA 176, 2430/03, Precis of correspondence relative to the enquiries of the Zoutpansberg Land Tenure (Occupation) Commission.

39 Extrapolated from Wellington, *Southern Africa*, and Cole, *South Africa*.

40 TA, GOV 631, Report on Waterberg District by Major French, 1903.

41 J.F.W. Grosskopf, *The Poor White Problem in South Africa: Report of the Carnegie Commission: Part 1, Economic Report: Rural Impoverishment and Rural Exodus* (Stellenbosch, 1932), pp. 66 and 76. I am indebted to Andrea van Niekerk for this point.

42 W. Beinart, P. Delius and S. Trapido (eds), *Putting A Plough to the*

Ground (Johannesburg, 1986), p. 28.

43 M. Streak, Lord Milner's Immigration Policy for South Africa, 1897-1905, Unpublished MA Dissertation, Rand Afrikaans University, 1969; S. Marks and S. Trapido, 'Lord Milner and the South African State', in P. Bonner (ed.), *Working Papers in Southern African Studies* Vol. 2 (Johannesburg, 1981).

44 Figures from Transvaal (Colony) Commissioner of Lands Departments Annual Report 1905-06, which gives the Transvaal figures as 323 men under squatter settlement schemes, while the same report for 1904, p. A13, lists 309 under Settlers Ordinance and 139 under Crown Land Disposal. Quote from TA, GOV 1059, PS 17/53/07, Land William Mountjoy.

45 Streak, Lord Milner's Immigration Policy, p. 37; Interviews with Charles Baber and Lex Rodger. Figures (which are very approximate) based on Transvaal (Colony)... Annual Report 1901-04, which lists 78 people as settling in the Waterberg under Settlers' Ordinance Provisions. For the 323 under squatter settlement provisions, there are no regional figures, but they were dispersed to various areas of the Transvaal, one of which was the Springbok Flats, remembered as having a lot of soldier-settlers.

46 Phrase from W. MacDonald, *Facts from Fifty Farmers* (Johannesburg, 1914), p. 10. His other works include *The Immortal Struggle* (Johannesburg, 1918), and *Makers of Modern Agriculture* (London, 1913).

47 MacDonald, *Facts from Fifty Farmers*, p. 10.

48 See ibid., 'Introduction', for farming on 'indomitable perseverance' alone. For a range of perceptions of what constituted qualifications for settler-farmers, see Report of the Land Settlement Commission, South Africa, Part II, Documents and Evidence (Cd 627, 1901), in which people variously advanced nationality, energy, military experience, having immediate family as farmers, age, and strength as reasons for applying for land.

49 MacDonald, writing in *Agricultural Journal of South Africa*, of which he was editor, Vol. 11, No. 7 (1915) 23.

50 Cloete, *The Gambler*, p. 9.

51 Ibid., p. 72

52 Ibid., p. 107.

53 Prance, 'The Riddle Posed', *RV*, p. 4.

54 Beinart *et al.*, *Putting a Plough to the Ground*, p. 29.

55 Morgan, 'Three Aspects of Regional Consciousness', pp. 74 and 80.

56 Prance, 'A Sign-Post "In the Blue"', *UBR*, p. 166.
57 Quotes from Marais, 'The Road to the Waterberg', p. 1204, and Heckford, *A Lady Traveller*, p. 331.
58 For examples see Heckford, *A Lady Traveller*; Rodger, 'Vintage Waterberg', p. 3; Prance, 'Discoverer's Right', *UBR*.
59 See Heckford, *A Lady Traveller*; Interview with Lois Baber.
60 Marais, 'The Road to the Waterberg', p. 1205.
61 Interview with Mary Chaney, Vaalwater, August 1986.
62 Clarke, *Waterberg Valley*, p. 2.
63 Interview with Lois and Charles Baber.
64 Prance, 'The Earthly Hope Man Set Their Hearts Upon', *TRS*.
65 For Model T stories, see much of Prance and Rodger; for railway stories, see Interview with Lois Baber.
66 Leipoldt, *Bushveld Doctor*; Interview with Lois Baber.
67 See, for example, Clarke, *Transvaal Poems*, based largely on the trees and landscape of the region; Bee, *A Man Should Rejoice*, p. 290; Prance, 'Liberty Hall', *UBR*.
68 Interview with Mary Chaney.
69 Jean Marquard, 'The Farm: A Concept in the Writing of Olive Schreiner, Pauline Smith, Doris Lessing, Nadine Gordimer and Bessie Head', *Dalhousie Review* 59 (1979), 293-307.
70 Bee, *Rolling Home*, p. 3.
71 Bee, *A Man Should Rejoice*, p. 291.
72 Clarke, *Waterberg Valley*, p. 19; Grosskopf, *Carnegie Report*, p. 167; Interviews with Lois Baber; with Nancy Davidson, Klipfontein, Vaalwater district, Aug. 1986; with Enoch Magwaza, Blackhill, Witbank district, September 1986.
73 Prance, 'Father's Folly', *TRS*.
74 Leipoldt, *Bushveld Doctor*, p. 291.
75 TA, SNA 176, 2430/03.
76 Prance, 'Cursed Be He', *TRS*. Translation of expression: 'crook'.
77 Bee, *A Man Should Rejoice*, p. 293.
78 J.M. Coetzee, 'Lineal Consciousness in the Farm Novels of C.M. van den Heever', Paper presented to the AUETSA Conference, Cape Town, 1985, pp. 2-3.
79 Prance, 'A Desert Place Apart', *UBR*, p. 79.
80 Marais, 'Die Mielies van Nooitgedacht', in Rousseau, *Versamelde Werke*, Vol. 1, p. 399.
81 Interview with Rodger; Prance, 'The "Tennis Klub" at Edenhoek', *TRS*, pp. 188-91.

82 Prance, 'Strange Birds in the Bush', *TRS*.

83 Based on information drawn from Heckford, *A Lady Traveller*; Marais, *Versamelde Werke, passim*; Havenga, *Life in the Wilds of the Northern Transvaal*; Interview with Rodger; Courtney-Acutt, *Bushveld*.

84 Prance, 'Cursed Be He', *TRS*.

85 See Lex Rodger, 'The Blacksmith: From Civilization to the Bushveld', *Star*, 14 April 1948; Prance, 'In the "DBU" ', *UBR*; Grosskopf, *Carnegie Report*, p. 145.

86 Prance, 'A Fly on Fortune's Wheel', 'Dentistry in Dooidonkies-dorp', 'Our "Boys" ', *RV*, pp. 30, 192, 204; Rousseau, *The Dark Stream*, p. 214.

87 Johannesburg Public Library, Papers of the Transvaal Land-owners' Association, Minute Book, Meeting, 14 Sept. 1904.

88 Peter Delius, 'Abel Erasmus: Power and Profit in the Eastern Transvaal', Beinart *et al.* (eds), *Putting a Plough to the Ground*, pp. 176-217.

89 Prance, 'A Fly on Fortune's Wheel', *RV*.

90 Bee, *A Man Should Rejoice*, p. 289.

91 See Rousseau, *The Dark Stream*, p. 236.

92 Lex Rodger, 'The Stockwhip'.

93 This is a point that comes from conversation with Tim Couzens.

94 Interviews with Lois and Charles Baber and with Nancy Davidson.

95 The story based on 'the aunts' is 'Victorians on the Veld', *TRS*; for an example of the latter category, see 'The Tragi-comedy of "Little Egypt" ', *DY*, whose plot Lois Baber remembered as a narative of her youth.

96 Benjamin, 'The Storyteller', pp. 84-85.

97 The word 'magazinery' comes from *TRS*; Rodger, Courtney Acutt, Prance, Edith Fawssett and Elizabeth Clarke all worked as journalists or contributed to periodicals.

98 These comments are extrapolated from interviews done in the Waterberg and from *Poetics* 15 (1986), particularly W-D. Stempel, 'Everyday Narrative as a Prototype', pp. 203-16, and Charlotte Linde, 'Private Stories in Public Discourse', pp. 183-202.

'She preferred living in a cave with Harry the snake-catcher'

Towards an Oral History of Popular Leisure and Class Expression in District Six, Cape Town, c. 1920s-1950s

Bill Nasson

The area of Cape Town known as District Six officially came into existence in the nineteenth century. It was adjacent to the central business district of the city and a mere nose away from local factory production. The sweat and skills of its mostly poor inhabitants sustained the infrastructure of the Cape Town economy — retailing, services and small-scale secondary manufactures. By the twentieth century District Six was an almost exclusively working-class residential locality with relations of propinquity and community which bound petty bourgeois inhabitants to the proletariat around them. Its demographic and social context was that of a still lingering cosmopolitanism: despite the strengthening pulse of urban racial segregation, some immigrant Jews, Britons and Italians still lived cheek by jowl with the majority population of coloured Capetonians and a trickle of Africans.

Up to the time of the forced removal under apartheid of the District Six population and the final demolition of their homes in the 1970s, the area had an identity and an imagery rooted in a sense of separateness and social and cultural localism. Its shoestring terraced streets reproduced a richly varied and introverted way of life, marked by interests, traditions and values which powerfully shaped its distinctive popular sociability, culture and politics. In particular, the largely autonomous development of a throbbing popular recreational and cultural life was one of the most striking characteristics of the District Six community. The persistence and adaptations of its customs and practices through the first half of the twentieth century gave legitimacy and expression to local creativity and local impulse. Using oral evidence to illuminate levels of popular experience not usually accessible in documentary sources, this study hopes to provide, if not a window, at least a peephole into how leisure experience helped to shape the lives and consciousness of people in District Six.

Clearly, in the marketing of leisure as capitalist enterprise, it is virtually impossible to think of the District Six street or neighbourhood without considering the distribution of cinema as a popular institution. Cinema-going was unquestionably the most popular form of paid entertainment in the inter-war years, continuing to grow in attraction through the 1940s and 1950s. The local 'bioscope' occupied a very special niche in the recreational life of the community, a place to which both adults and children went in order to be cocooned in the dream world of the flickering screen. Attendance was regular and habitual, as films continually widened their audience appeal and imaginative power to transport people out of themselves and the humdrum confines of their work and domestic lives at least once a week. It is important to emphasise that 'bioscope' tended to be firmly local. Thus, the neighbourhood National, Star or City, or even the more distant West End off Somerset Road (a favourite Saturday matinee haunt for District Six children, which had a rococo downstairs milk bar to lure them during intervals), assumed a location in community life not unlike that of the English pub. The local character of cinemas extended to some establishments outside District Six; inhabitants lived within easy strolling distance of 'a lot of bioscopes in town. It was only after the War that the bioscopes became for Europeans only one side and the Coloured people the other side, and you couldn't enter in the wrong side'.[1] Pre-apartheid Cape Town had a wider range of open venues which even working-class cinema-goers could customarily regard as their own. Thus, while 'mostly we had our own bioscopes... the Colosseum and the Alhambra was close for us too'.[2]

One or two cinemas in the general area — like the City on Sir Lowry Road or Wolfram's Bioscope in nearby Woodstock — were converted shops or warehouses owned by emigré Jewish entrepreneurs who ran them as an adjunct to their retailing activities. But the beloved locals like the Star, the British Bioscope, the National, the Union, and later the Avalon, were purpose-built, independent cinemas or picture theatres. While they tended to be fairly small and unpretentious in appearance, their names — the Star, the West End, the Empire, the

British Bioscope — dripped with the promise of glamour or old Imperial splendour. The Avalon alone had an imposing structure with clean sweeping lines, decor, and accoutrements to match the glitter of its name.

There was clearly more to 'going to bioscope' than the building itself, whether spartan or comfortable. On the pavement outside there were often buskers who sang and danced in front of patrons, or other inventive street entertainers with performing animals. And in the commercially competitive 1930s and 1940s in particular, cinema attendance was surrounded by a great paraphernalia of promotion and advertising. Managers who 'were all sharp and shrewd... these people who opened bioscopes'[3] used a rich variety of methods to promote current and future showings; adept use was made of the foyer, the environs of the cinema, its staff, and even of children casually plucked from the pavement. For Alexander Korda's The Drum (with Sabu, 1938), a famous Kiplingesque potboiler, the imaginative manager of the Star kitted out the doorman in a pith helmet, had a model wooden fort complete with Union Jack erected at the entrance, and paid several children 2d. each to 'wear hats like you see on the proper Indians you get in India... turbans was what they were called, I think... they were made up from nice pink crinkle paper. They had to walk up and down in Hanover Street, to give out bioscope advertisements to the people walking there.'[4] The Jewish family which owned and ran the Union had a unique attraction in the shape of 'the first Shetland pony they had here... in the district... this pony was a star turn... really it was.' It pulled a trap 'which had a small board at the back... covered in white, and on this was written in bold print the name of the film that was being advertised.' The Union's manager 'used to drive right up to Buckingham House, Buckingham Palace, right down Zonnebloem, down Hanover Street, up Cannon Street, down William Street where the other bioscope was, give them a shot in the eye, down into Caledon Street where there was another bioscope... and down the side street back into Hanover Street'.[5] To promote The Mark of Zorro (with Tyrone Power, 1940) one cinema had a large cut-out of a horse fixed to a wall of a neighbouring shop and fitted its ushers with black eyemasks and fake silver spurs. Such novel entertainments inside and outside the auditorium provided a further rich seam of amusement and diversion for gawping patrons.

But no amount of advertising wizardry could draw and hold an intensely alert and critical working-class audience if a film was thought or found not to be to its taste. Ultimately, 'the first Saturday matinee was the important show. If the show wasn't any good, man, you would get very few people there afterwards at the night show. The children would come back and say if it was rubbish when everyone was having supper. Well, if the bioscope wasn't any good, Mónday night it would be empty. Man, word used to go round so quick. It was word of mouth, that time.'[6] A united and self-conscious audience, reflecting a stable and cohesive neighbourhood identity, possessed the power to affect the kind of entertainment put on the local screen; it could enforce its own celluloid preferences by voting with its collective backside or by barracking. In the 1940s and 1950s, for example, dire Afrikaans 'snot en trane' weepies (the Huisgenoot equivalent of British and American 'B' movies) met with derisory hooting. Such Afrikaner cultural forms never enjoyed popularity. Nervous, loan-financed cinema owners could not afford a long run of flops, and had to be quick off the mark to change dud screenings. For instance, 'there at the West End it would be off with one show and they would try something else the next day. Just like that, so quick.'[7]

The bulk of cinema-goers chose a film for its star or its story or both, and many developed a preference for the products of particular companies — Warners, MGM, Twentieth-Century Fox or RKO. Cinemas tended to be contracted to market the films of specific studios; this gave each of them a distinctive character and identity in the eyes of fans, so that 'at the Star it was always Warner Brothers and at the Avalon you knew it was Twentieth-Century Fox. To see George Raft, or James Cagney or Errol Flynn, we would always, always, go to the Star.'[8] The working-class audiences of District Six overwhelmingly chose American over more mannered British films, much as did their class counterparts in Birmingham, Cardiff, or Glasgow. For the American products were slick and technically polished. They had fast dialogue, strong acting, and plenty of narrative and visual movement; such features made them hugely popular with a mass audience which went to be entertained and not 'improved' or educated. Films with tempo and action were big draws, such as Depression gangster pieces like Little Caesar (1930), Public Enemy (1931), and Scarface (1932). So were Westerns, with cowboy actors like Gene Autry and Tom Mix, and later John Wayne and Gary Cooper. When a massively popular genre contained a massively popular star, auditoriums bulged for days. Films like They Died with their Boots On (with Errol Flynn, 1940), Vera Cruz (with Gary Cooper, 1954), and The Fastest Gun Alive (with

Glenn Ford, 1956) would 'have them pushing and pushing to get in, sometimes the doors almost broke. It was really something to see... the people would say "yup" or "pardner" when they were talking in the queues.' When the Star screened an Errol Flynn western, 'Man, the people would really go wild then. Ooo... it was such a big event. There wasn't really proper queues then, just everybody was pushing... it used to go right across the road so the buses and even the cars they just couldn't pass through. And the people wouldn't move. Not even for the bus — the driver had to go up some other street to get past.'[9] The pervading influence of westerns in the district had a marked impact on the dress styles and demeanour of the New Year carnival, with troupes like the 'Red Indians' whooping and thumping through the streets with buffalo head trappings, feathers and the Stars and Stripes.

Epics were also of marked appeal, notably the rash of stagey Italian costume sagas of the 1950s (such as Queen of Babylon, Demetrius and the Gladiators, and Goliath and the Barbarians) which made local box office stars of Victor Mature and Edmund Purdom, and predictably produced a new crop of infants named Victor or Edmund from the Peninsula Maternity Home. As part of their regular programme, cinemas would also screen weekly serials (with arresting titles like The Iron Claw), newsreels, or animated shorts. In the 1930s, for instance, 'The British was famous for serials. The Lone Ranger was always good, but Gordon of Ghost City was now really the best. As children, we never missed it. Never.'[10]

While the principal attraction was the screen, it is essential to remember that this was only part of the total recreational experience which the phrase 'going to bioscope' encapsulated. Often running through performances was the sound of live singing, which helped to invigorate celluloid diversions into a live musical event, with demonstrative mass audience participation. In the British Bioscope, as elsewhere, 'you would have cartoons, like a Tom and Jerry and newsreel. They were English. And what was really popular everywhere were songs. You know, the music would appear on the screen with the words, and there would be a choir singing the song and then the audience would join in the singing of the song... "Just a Song of Twilight" was one of those songs'.[11]

The Union and the Empire were known for staging elaborate and bizarre live variety acts. A celebrated high spot of the Union was the appearance of a dog troupe trained to perform a canine fantasy of British class society. As one informant recalled:

When my mother first had the Union Bioscope there was a stage in the old bioscope, and she had heard of a couple who had come out from England who had about forty dogs. They were all of the miniature type and there were a couple of larger dogs who were poodles. Now all of these dogs were put on an act. There was the soldier, the sailor, the tinker, the tailor, the lovers, the nursemaid, the couple who would walk behind the nursemaid pushing a pram with a little dog inside the pram, dressed up with a bonnet and everything to look like the baby and the nurse would push the pram, she in her black uniform with a white apron, and a cap on her head also. And the father and mother would walk behind, he with his long pants and a cap on his head and the mother with a dress, long dress in those days and a boater hat, and she would walk behind... And there you had the different types of life amongst the dogs.[12]

This informant also remembered that at the Empire,

when my father acquired his bioscope he wanted a stage there and he introduced all types of entertainment. He had the dancers with very wide dresses and in the operating box he had a light going with all variegated colours and as this person would intertwine her very wide skirts, it was like a fairy, red, pink, mauve, green, yellow... a heliotrope and it would go on all these colours, and the audience would go mad... And then they had a review of singing and dancing, and then he had the strong man picking up weights, different kinds of weights and dumb bells and so on, then he had a boxing match on the stage, so they could watch the boxing. This would be a special, special night... Ooh, we had such full houses when they had the boxing on.[13]

In a community in which outside recreation was mostly defined in male terms (street gambling, sports clubs, street bands and choirs), the social influence of the cinema was considerable; men and women regularly attended performances together, breaking through the strict gender separation characteristic of so many other leisure activities. At the Star in the 1940s there was one noted couple of unusually indiscriminate taste, vividly recalled by an usher: 'For many years, I don't remember how many, Row K Seats 27 and 28 were reserved on every Saturday afternoon for Mr and Mrs Lewis. It didn't matter what film there was showing. They always came. Those seats were always kept empty for them. That was their place.'[14]

The respectable culture of the skilled and settled working class saw cinema as a venue where adolescents could mix reasonably safely, preserving standards of moral behaviour and social decorum. The matinee certainly posed fewer problems of control for anxious parents than the intimacy of dances. For girls from strict homes wanting an acceptable and cosy environment for flirtations, there was 'only the bioscope, my dear. We wasn't allowed dances... We was too young to go to places like that... when you sixteen... only seventeen... we wasn't allowed to stay with a boy alone, or so. But in the bioscope it was a whole crowd. So the crowd would see you home safe, and your boyfriend too.'[15] In leisure relations, as in other dimensions of everyday life, customary codes of courtship and a complex set of expectations and obligations socialised adolescents into conforming to the standards and self-image of class respectability. Very few, it seems, attended films with outsiders. For 'in those days a boy didn't court a girl in Salt River or took a girl from Woodstock, just from our own area... We were all in the same community.'[16] Invariably, 'you couldn't have friends on the other side of town'.[17]

No less essential than a public show of standards was obedience. A girl 'wasn't allowed night shows, only matinees, and then we had to come straight home... my auntie always used to find out if it was that time.'[18] It was crucial for women's standing in a community of other women that they be seen to be rearing daughters or nieces in a chaste, respectable way; wayward behaviour thus invited swift and sharp retribution. If cinema by day was healthy, cinema at night threatened to subvert adult efforts to control leisure time and space. In the case of one informant,

once I went at night to bioscope, and Lord! I was punished for a whole month. I couldn't go out, man. Me and Mabel... we planned it. There was a western, man, a marvellous western by the Star bioscope... Ooo, the people was pushing so to get in there... Oh heena, we had a good time. But the next day! My auntie, she slapped me so hard, and Mabel got it too, on the other side. She forbid me to go to bioscope again, until after a whole month, man. We had to tell the boys that we girls couldn't come out, and they must just leave us alone. If this one can't come out, man, there's others. It was a sad month for me and Mabel.[19]

If cinema attendance crossed gender boundaries, it was acutely sensitive to social differentiation. While the practice of going to bioscope was wholeheartedly embraced by both working-class and middle-class patrons, there was both a hierarchy of cinemas and internal class differentiation within auditoriums. Cinemas were ranked by admission prices, hard or soft seating, programme content (Stewart Grainger at the Avalon, George Raft at the Star), and the degree of precariously imposed order and structured experience during screenings. At some cinemas, classes jostled together at the gates but did not mingle in the aisles, as better-off patrons sauntered upstairs for plush if faded seats. Elsewhere, in the 1940s and 1950s, it became commonplace for neighbourhood gangs like the Globe, the Reds, and the Black Cats to monopolise certain rows, roughly bundling out anyone foolhardy enough to risk occupying a seat which had been appropriated as customary territory. Or food would be the element separating the rough from the respectable, the mannerly from the unmannerly. For instance,

> you could take in anything to the Star you know, they had just wooden seats downstairs, so it was all right for fish and chips or other hot food. But not at the Avalon, no, never at the Avalon. The Avalon, you see, was a more respectable kind of bioscope. It was mostly a better class of person who went there, although it was not much more to go in there than the Star.[20]

Roy Rosenzweig, in his recent absorbing study of working-class culture in Worcester, Massachusetts, has argued that in the 1920s and 1930s cinema attendance became increasingly 'a more controlled... and anonymous experience... the movie theater lacked the sort of ominous working-class autonomy'.[21] Did the District Six proletariat experience a similar reduction in their class and cultural autonomy? In its heyday, the medium of popular cinema in District Six undoubtedly reflected a distinct and probably widening class and cultural gap between patrons. The context of this process was, naturally, differentials of wealth within the area and the process of class formation itself. We see its human expression in how the working classes of the district defined themselves against the visible and irritating respectability and snobbishness of neighbouring, more well-to-do Walmer Estate. Gritting their teeth outside the Avalon, the aspirant patricians of that suburb did battle with the pushing plebs who referred to them sneeringly as coming from 'up there' or as being 'Walmer English' or 'Black Sea Point'.[22]

But the rowdy culture of Hanover Street prevailed over the prim and the genteel. The style of the Star or of the British Bioscope did not represent the domestication or reform of working class leisure by the cultural idiom of a dominant élite. Far from the role of the bioscope audience becoming more passive during this period, the overall trend was the other way. Inside an auditorium smelling sharply of disinfectant, orange peel, chips, and samoosas, a high-spirited audience brought the jostle and open mix of the city street indoors. Patrons sought to move at will between seats, under the variously indulgent or resentful gaze of fellow-viewers. And there was high-spirited interplay between crowds and the screen. Far from turning recreation into a private and anonymous consumption activity, bioscope transmitted a boisterous and communal style of working-class relaxation which was 'such a rumpus, man, people didn't restrain themselves. They loved it, being there, waiting for it to go black.' There is no reason to doubt the rough veracity of the writer Richard Rive's autobiographical reflection in his novel, *Buckingham Palace, District Six*, about the notorious usher at the Star Bioscope who apparently 'took to riding up and down the aisle on a bicycle, lashing out with his belt at any unfortunate urchin who provoked his displeasure'.[23] Inside the auditorium of a cinema like the Star, leisure behaviour clearly became a raucous contest between order and freedom which both sets of participants — managers and ushers and patrons — were eager to wage.

Bioscope also did not represent the intrusion of an impersonal market institution into the locality. For its basic format was that of a small family business, with the owner well known and personally involved in operations. It was penny capitalism with a chubby face. Impresarios had an engaging personal presence, like 'Mr Goldberg... he always wore a brown suit and he smoked a cigarette, and the ash always used to fall on his waistcoat, and when he used to sit down the buttons on his waistcoat used to always come together because he was so fat.' Ruben of the City 'had a cast in one eye', while a competitor, Hertzberg, is remembered by 'heavy tweed suits... and a trilby hat'. Another characteristically conspicuous figure was the owner of the Empire, who 'was getting bald, they called my father Bailey Bless Bioscope, and when they saw him they used to say, "Good morning Bailey Bless", or "Good afternoon Bailey Bless", they never called him anything else'.[24] The local cinema owner, like the small shopkeeper, 'took his class identity from his customers rather than from his relationship with capital and property'.[25] Work and residential identification pulled such small managers towards a working-class way of life.

Families who owned and controlled cinemas were distinguished not by any grand manner but by a common touch. Relations were often marked by an easy-going sociability and shrewd cultural identification with audiences. Sometimes proprietors indulged in a coarse, barnstorming style as they waded through their crowded auditoriums. The impresario of the Union 'would walk along the aisle to see if everything was in order, and as she passed she would smell the dagga and she would say in Afrikaans, "Wie rook da?", and she would go and call this manager of hers and she walked along with a stick... they were dead scared of her.' As a full house meant a full till, the Union's hardboiled owner 'would say "Stay op, stay op", and she would get another two or three people on to the benches, the benches she could do it with... with the benches she could move them up, that was where she got some advantage if it was a packed house.'[26]

Undoubtedly audiences went to bioscope to be entertained and distracted. But bioscope in District Six was more than just the people's picture palace. It appealed because it was both escapist yet strongly rooted in the everyday realities of working-class life. In a community riven by the division of labour, the cinema was marked by a division of distribution. Its importance went beyond the commercial marketing of mass entertainment. Some owners hired out their venues for school concerts. Others granted the use of their cinemas for workers' meetings during strikes and political protest rallies. During World War II, 'when almost everyone was living from hand to mouth, there was rationing you see, and then suddenly there was no rice. Just mealie rice. There was terrible anger then, and people would go to the British Bioscope for a protest meeting, sometimes in the darkness, when Cape Town was blacked out.'[27] Proprietors with professed ideals of public service gave benefit performances for the poor and unemployed during the inter-war depression years. Particularly striking was the use of the Empire and the Union 'during the weekends for meetings and for council meetings as well, and amongst the councillors was Dr Abdurahman and Isaac Persel. Well, Dr Abdurahman always wore a black fez with a tassel hanging down... he always looked spick and span and immaculate.' For converts of revivalist religious denominations, the bioscope stage was sometimes the improbable spot to celebrate rites of passage. On one remembered occasion, 'it was a church meeting or something, they had one of the African children anointed and he was called Empire after the bioscope'.[28]

The largest area of recreational space was the street. Living, working, shopping, learning and leisure all interacted with the dense collective traditions and way of life of the street. If the separate, amorphous, and mushrooming popular culture of District Six was open to all, it was most open and most energetic on the streets in which so much of it was constructed and reproduced. Derived from old and distinctly local oral and cultural traditions, the street theatre of District Six settled into a form of 'folkloric' and customary adaptation to a life of general poverty and hardship.

Almost every day would see some excitement taking place in the street, for it was home to constantly absorbing sights and entertaining spectacle. Its vibrant communal life drew people like a magnet, for 'outside, you could feel the life, man. We were an outdoor people, then.'[29] The sounds of its high spirits and horseplay bubbled across pavements, alleyways, and yards. The social historian Jerry White, in his study of the street culture of the Campbell Bunk community in North London, has called it, 'a theatre which never closed; its audience and actors were never all asleep at once'.[30] In District Six, as in lumpenproletarian Islington, the rough culture of the street ran through life like a brightly coloured thread. There were unstaged entertainments which onlookers could stand back and enjoy, like noisy squabbles between neighbours over shared street washing lines, pavement fights, swaying and toppling drunks, or the sorry sight of a hawker's fruit and vegetable barrow upending, scattering and mashing its contents. 'And then, you know, everyone would run over. It's like a lot of locusts swarming down and just absorbing whatever there is.'[31]

The hubbub of shebeens also spilled over into the street; drawing curious onlookers to peep and speculate; their lure was particularly strong if they were linked to strangers or foreigners: 'There was a house in Java Street where there used to live whatchacallits... Swahilis. They just used to make merry, man. You know how those Swahilis are... during the weekend it used to be a bit rowdy, especially on a Saturday night when they used to give a Bop. It was a shebeen too. We used to come out and see what's going on. They used to say "You'd pay your shilling, your bob, by the door, to go into the bob Bop, then you find it's a shebeen, so you got to hop!" That's what they used to call it'.[32] There would be catcalling after well-known 'stock' street characters, like rag-and-bone men, beady-eyed gamblers, fah-fee runners, or individuals who bore abnormalities like hare lips or hunched backs. The style, identification, and image of widely recognised 'characters' was frequently fixed by street nicknames which unerringly singled out an individual's defect, aberration or mannerism and magnified it to a satirical, mocking, or endearing label of distinction. Thus, typical of conspicuous street figures in the 1930s was a pimply debt collector labelled 'Knopies' Campbell and a deaf Afrikaner rag-and-bone man known cruelly as 'Ore' du Toit.

In the predominantly Jewish area around Harrington, Albertus, and Buitenkant Streets, there was 'Jood Brood', who ran a small corner bakery for many years, opening up at six every morning to sell hot bread rolls. A man with 'a white apron which always looked black', a 'high hat' and an eyepatch, he also produced toffee apples: 'We used to come over from Constitution Street and then he came out when he saw us and he waved and he shouted "Apples!"'. Then we always ran to him and we made a ring and danced. They said he buried his eye in one of the apples. So we always used to shout, "Sell us your eye today, Jood" '.[33] Hanover Street contained a 'fat Jew, a man with reddish hair... Ou Rooikop Jood'. His 'very cheap watermelon konfyt' and 'such polony' captured the pockets and palates of children and his Russian-Jewish origin their popular imagination: 'Ou Rooikop couldn't talk proper English and when sailors would come up from the docks, they were Russians like him, he would sit outside with them, and they would talk, talk, talk. It was all in their own language and people would stand there to listen. They were just so excited. Sometimes they would dance, and everybody would go congregate around them... Ou Rooikop was nice, man! He would get a big brown paper bag and throw out black liquorice.'[34]

The evolution of galleries of popularly nicknamed characters formed an integral part of the popular culture of the street and represented one of its most enduring continuities. In the early 1920s, there was 'Oogies Chingy', a one-eyed Chinese who illegally peddled sixpenny fah-fee tickets from a waterlogged basement pumphouse at the upper end of Hanover Street. His cocky presence always attracted an inquisitive, bantering crowd. Three decades later, around Springfield Street, there was much gaping and hooting at 'Motjie Tetlip', an Indian woman who ran a corner cafe and whose 'hare lip was like a woman's tit, that's how it looked... that was an old joke there for many years'.[35] Such open public fascination with human curiosities reflects something of the uniquely freakish quality of immediate, felt, community life. It testifies to the florid diversity of the district and to the burly and boisterous character of relations in streets and open spaces. The content and expression of popular amusement made no allowance for the sensitive. But for nicknamed individuals involved in shopkeeping, hawking, betting or other exchange activities, the crowd attraction of physical abnormality could have a positive side. Being an object of popular ridicule may have been hurtful and humiliating, but it often aided earnings; the visibility of red hair or an eyepatch was invaluable in building up and keeping a neighbourhood network of 'regulars', helping to transmute onlookers into customers.

Rituals of name-calling also reflected social animosities and tensions. Direct encounters across the double barriers of class and respectability produced mocking laughter, sometimes light-hearted, but often curling into derision. For instance, the sobriety, discipline and reforming zeal of some petty bourgeois professionals who worked in District Six but lived elsewhere, did not necessarily earn them the respect and deference of poorer children. In the 1930s and 1940s, the headmaster of Albertus Street Methodist Primary School, 'it was a school for the poor... we called it "die stye skooltjie" ', was a Mr Joshua, a man who affected a patronising and authoritarian manner. In the locality 'he was not popular... he was not of our kind. He was full of himself because he lived in Walmer Estate. "Black Sea Point" as we used to call it. Mr Joshua used to say, "Ek is die Hoof van die Albertus Street Primêre Skool", but people used to say that if he was in charge of "die stye skooltjie" he must just be a ou "stye" principal! He had very long ears, and children used to run behind him and shout "Donkie, donkie" '.[36]

The streets of District Six provided a range of stamping grounds for a variety of bizarre and bewildering street entertainments. Whether settled or nomadic like Raphael Samuel's showmen 'comers and goers' of Victorian London,[37] eccentric and odd individuals were readily accepted into the rough-and-tumble libertarian mode of life of the district and made part of the community. People would gather to stare at the antics of professional fit-throwers and bogus epileptics who tried to scrape a living off the sympathy and charity of visiting outside professionals like midwives and public health visitors. The more inventive of these casual drifters would fake elaborate injuries or gory wounds, their capacity for variation a constant source of awe for wide-eyed children. In the early 1920s, for example, there was 'Pox Hendrik'

who (some said) came from the Knysna forests and whose afflictions
'were made just like a magician with always some new thing'. Later,
there was 'Stokkies' Jacobs who tapped the streets for many years as an
amputee victim of a score of grisly industrial accidents and both World
Wars: 'Now he was a real stalwart... now it would be a arm then it
would be a leg. We would tell him if there was a real status person
coming. Especially if they were in a real status symbol car, like a
Daimler, that time. Then afterwards we would shout, "Luck today,
Stokkies?" '38

Conspicuous beggars, chance performers, and those involved in the
perambulating circuits of organ-grinding and kerbstone draughts,
domino and gaming displays kept a casual foothold in the social
economy and cultural world of District Six. Finding a place in the
underlife of the area, they lived in the precarious gulf between the
settled working class of District Six and propertied and professional
Cape Town. Such street entertainers were accepted with glee by a lively
and sharp-eyed community which offered not only a sanctuary to the
displaced, but an arena for their cunning and talents. And while local
residents were not themselves duped by the street guile of performing
wanderers, they clearly relished the spectacle of quick wits and even
faster hands being turned upon the purses of middle-class visitors and
other strangers.

Strange lifestyles or outlandish behaviour were clearly among the
most celebrated and joyous features of working-class neighbourhood experience. The activities of some 'entertainers' magnified the
positive, communal features of working-class life; one vivid example
can be drawn from Bligh Street in the 1930s in the shape of 'Mrs
Perrins... a spiritualist'. A 'white woman' whose 'hair was dyed flaming
red', Mrs Perrins was a widow whose income was derived from 'one or
two houses which she let.' She provided a clairvoyancy service for 'if
anybody in the area wanted to know anything they would go to her'.
Rumour attributed her visionary powers to reported sightings that
'she had a skeleton there in the cupboard'. As 'most of the people in the
area grew up with her', there was friendship and a sense of common
identity and interest between Mrs Perrins and her clients: she kept an
open house and was known never to charge for her services. Her
clairvoyance, in which 'she used to sort of go into a trance', attracted so
many goggling and shoving neighbours that 'it was like going into a
scrum to get into there'. Typically the staple needs met by Mrs Perrins
revolved around the troubles, misfortunes and grief of families. Thus,

'when my uncle was missing and my auntie went to her — and she said they will find his body on the rocks because he drowned hisself. Which was quite true. They found his body on the rocks. And when my mother's washing went missing she went to her first, and she told my mother too, you'll find your things.'[39]

As the historian Keith Thomas has noted, laughter at improvised public amusement is at its most forceful when it springs from a common sense of paradox and from contexts and meanings which involve anomalies or conflicts of values and ideas.[40] It may thereby reflect popular perceptions of strange and surprising incongruities in social structure and the organisation of class relations. Popular cultural expression of inversions of the 'natural' order reveals something of the grainy social fabric and brash class incoherence which existed in parts of District Six society. Between the wars amongst the mostly destitute cave-dwelling 'bergies' of the Woodstock caves on the lower slopes of Table Mountain could be found a scattering of freethinking and flamboyant men and women. Their entry into District Six life was through its popular street culture which provided them with a flash identity:

> Some looked very nice, I remember one — she had a white man and he used to catch snakes with a snake stick. His name was Harry. And if this woman walked down that road — you would never say she comes out of a cave. She used to work and she used to come out all dressed up. She was very well dressed... with gloves and a hat and everything on. She was a Standard Eight teacher. A better class person... I don't know what made her stay like that. But she preferred living in a cave with Harry the snake catcher. He used to come down, past our road, with all those snakes on his back — in a bag. We used to touch the things you know, and they can wriggle.[41]

Music in District Six occupied an important place in popular social life. The area enjoyed particularly well-developed band, dancing and choral traditions which had their own distinct province of expression and meaning. Music was not a minority leisure experience, and the relationship between popular music and popular culture was striking. For the area had, at virtually every level, an extremely vigorous popular musical culture which represented a compound of custom and modernity.

It was, for example, commonplace for people to group together to make music in their own homes; this was often not an inward, exclusive activity, but one which was neighbourly and shared, helping to foster street loyalties and solidarities. One family 'had a little old piano — we could sing ourselves, and bring other children in. We couldn't play so well but we'd go ting tong ting and just make our own music... My uncle could play piano so my auntie could sing, and I would sing and the next door neighbours — we were like one big family... They had a lot of children. There were lots of them there and ma and oupa, they would all come around.'[42] In another, 'granny had an organ — she couldn't play but my mother could play some hymns and so on. We would put it on the stoep on Sundays and our neighbours would come. At that time it was all mixed, you know, whites and coloureds all lived in the same street, sort of neighbours, and going into one another's houses. It was my mother they came out to appreciate. My mother had a beautiful voice — she sang in the choir in St Augustine's Church and I also sang in that choir.'[43] There were instances when the arrival of a brass tramping band or choir would spur a local singing bird into giving an impromptu performance. One popular family brass band was comprised of 'German people and very fat. We would follow them down Muir Street. People would bring out chairs to sit on the pavement and listen. Sometimes my uncle, he was in a choir, he would stand at his gate and sing out to this band. He had such a wonderful voice.'[44]

Those musicians who worked in cinema in the earlier silent movie period enjoyed an opportunity to extend their capabilities and repertoire. Working children and adults from very different class and ethnic backgrounds had the chance of making pleasurable new music or even of enjoying the thrill of being lionised by local audiences as popular performers in their own right. One gifted, self-taught instrumentalist was a taxi driver called Tommy Thomas, who 'was the pianist in the Empire Bioscope... he was Coloured and he played by ear, didn't have any music, just had an ear for music, and he saw the film, it was a classic or sad, or something stupid with Laurel and Hardy, he had to play sort of ragtime music.'[45]

Evenings and afternoons were also whiled away at commercial venues in Cape Town which staged orchestras, bands and singers. Cabaret at the Tivoli and Palm Court bands at Delmonico's provided intimacy of atmosphere for courting couples. Attendance at opera and at classical music concerts in the City Hall was one of the small pleasures of 'respectable' working-class life. The provision of low seat prices, and their stability across the inter-war decades did much to extend audience potential: 'On my father's old gramophone I remember the spring used to break and a new one cost seven-and-six. And you should know how hard it is to collect up seven-and-six. It takes weeks. But there was always money for him to go to the opera, it was cheap.'[46] What is striking is that in households in which there was a continuous tradition of attendance at live music venues, the taste for 'high' musical culture coexisted with more popular strains. Here entertainment was not seen as being class-bound or class-specific.

Street choral music and the Christmas and New Year band movement naturally had a close and often direct association with organised religion, and perhaps best epitomised the theme of what the social history of leisure defines as 'rational' or 'improving' popular recreation. Under the rubric of social control, a popular musical culture related to church, chapel or mosque can be seen as aiding the formation of a religious, respectful and dutiful working-class population. If the industrial wage labour of local factories, small workshops and sweatshops provided its own disciplines and controls, here was a complementary form of male leisure for harmonising men and boys: beneficent, healthy, well-structured, and in a different moral league from the popular revelry and fiesta disorderliness of the Coon Carnival. The crisply-flannelled artisanry of Cape Malay Choirs such as the Sweetheart Maids, the Red Roses and the Royal Coronations could generate enormous levels of commitment and enthusiasm. The clothing needs of their leisure activities brought seasonal prosperity for tailors and gave groups such as the Malay Tailors' Association a special role in the making of recreational life in the community. By the 1940s and 1950s these choirs had also come to enjoy the patronage of Stellenbosch University Afrikaner academics with cloudy and obsessive pseudo-anthropological interests in singing Asiatics; some of them adjudicated choir competitions and actually helped to mould the folk-song repertoire.[47]

It could therefore be argued that street choir and band institutions, subject to the purposeful interpenetration of religion and patronage, can be seen as an expression of some form of social control. Yet there is also a sense in which they were undeniably independent working-class institutions, worker-organised and worker-led; their strength and depth of popularity lay in the mass support they received from the District Six community: 'I tell you, when we were little we would follow them to wherever they went... we would try to get near to them and walk with them. They sang close up to us, when we were on the pavement there... I wanted to touch those smart red blazers and their white tackies. They was something really beautiful. They wasn't faraway on the radio. They was here, they was our choirs, singing for us.'[48] What this suggests is that, instead of viewing organised popular street music as either an expression of social control or as class expression, the reality is that it was perhaps both. Significantly, there was always a tension between the two, with the balance shifting first one way, then the other.

If the cultural forms and idioms of District Six life had a central conduit for their production, preservation and transmission into consciousness, it was without doubt the annual Coon Carnival. Demonstrating the resilience and continuity of custom, it formed the ritual climax of the popular recreational year. It was also a particularly clear example of leisure as a productive practice: the sale of clothing material and associated adornments boomed, tailors worked flat out, and in expenditure on food and drink people celebrated to the limit of their means, and beyond that if they could. For carnival time 'we always saved a little every month. But we saved it to spend it, and the shops in Hanover Street were open for us, man, many of them for twenty-four hours.'[49]

Carnival was a potent affirmation and celebration of local community identity, in which the working-class population expressed itself through uninhibited pleasure-seeking and indulgence. It brought not only colourful costumed procession and an opportunity for the display of dancing, musical skills and high jinks in the street, but a concentrated expression of family and neighbourhood identity through conviviality and hospitality. Neighbours who stood aloof from the spontaneity and demonstrative behaviour of the New Year carnival atmosphere were sneeringly dubbed 'Kenilworth coloureds', or accused of 'being white' or 'mense wat hulle wit hou'.[50] Clearly, in embodying the image of a common local humanity and a common culture, carnival also tested the limits of class harmony and intermingling.

District Six had a deservedly long-standing reputation as a place of rough, independent and robust character, free of irksome petty restrictions on boisterous public enjoyment and open-air amusements. The traditional annual spree of the Coon Carnival, whose many and complex ingredients can only be hinted at here, demonstrated that identity most emphatically. Its ebullient festivity remains most vigorously alive in the collective memory of those who celebrated it in its peak years. On the first of January, 'die eerste Nuwejaar', with a massive local audience swelled with visiting crowds, 'you'd find a hub of people in Hanover Street. You couldn't even find a place to walk, you know, the way people were milling around.' Pavements along the procession circuit were in a state of perpetual bustle, and along 'daai hele route' spectators camping and sleeping out to secure a favourable viewing spot were 'gepak soos sardiens'.[51]

Costumes changed every year, 'die colours change elke jaar. Elke jaar different outfits.' And the choice of plumage was cloaked in secrecy until carnival day, for 'die een troep mag nie weet wat die ander troep gaan dra nie... dit was 'n baie groot secret'. Participation in troupes was open to men of widely varying backgrounds. Thus Coon membership drew both 'die meer respectable mense' as well as notorious criminals like the Globe Gang, 'die Globe Gang, hulle het ook 'n Coons gehad. Hulle was die Pennsylvanian Darkies. Die Pennsylvanian Darkies het elke jaar clean sweep gemaak met die trophies.' Their most celebrated drum-major, Tommy Julies, sported "n tamaai groot Globe op sy kop, gemaak soos 'n globe'.[52]

One remarkably immediate and imaginative recreation of festivity at this time draws on a full range of experiences, ideas and relationships which structured the meaning of carnival in popular consciousness. What counted was immersion in the spontaneity of street life and its porous folk enthusiasms, free of killjoys and external interference:

> We had a lot of pleasure, man. Now tonight, it's Old Year's Eve, then my auntie would make all ready, food and everything, then she would send me down, me and Mabel my friend. She would say we must go down and keep our places. Then we would sit on the shop steps. All the shops in Hanover Street were right next to one another. Then when my auntie got everything finish, they would come down, with baskets and blankets so that we could stay the whole night there. We didn't sleep hey, because the place is alive... Things was different then, man, I'm speaking about over forty years ago when the United Party was still in. Now it comes to midnight. And the midnight teams come out... And then, later in the day, the Coons come up... And — oooh! — when they come up Hanover Street! I thought it was too small that street for the

people... The Coons come marching through some on stilts, and some were Redskins, they were dancing and prancing. And they also rode horses, just like the old days... Just like a Mardi Gras, like they have overseas, just like that... There was not a policeman in sight — and the people would be happy. That was the grandest time of our lives — the New Year. All year we looked forward to that day.[53]

The experience of schooling did little to reform working-class recreational behaviour. Organised games or informal play could not be held inside most school grounds through lack of adequate space and facilities: the result was that during breaks pupils swarmed out to reclaim their common tarmac or snatch of turf, creating their own unstructured play space for games and fun. Many 'just used the roads as a playground, soccer, rugby, cricket, whatever we wanted to play'.[54] At one primary school in the early years of this century, 'at 11 o'clock we used to break and we used to go to the park, Trafalgar Park. We used to play in the park until the bell would ring. Then, one day, we wore aprons to school, not gyms... And we went to the park and it was also spring, it was lovely with dew. And we'd take our aprons off for when the wind blows, and sail down the hill.'[55]

Already at this early life-cycle stage it becomes possible to see the inhabitants of District Six inheriting and reproducing a customary kind of popular leisure of their own making. It also becomes possible to glimpse the material roots of that cultural experience, grounded in an identifiable locale and inadequate housing. For it was overcrowding which drove play into the street, 'we didn't have games in the house, we made our own games.' Territorial pressure meant 'that we were too occupied in the houses, there was nowhere to hide. To enjoy ourselfs we would go to the street'.[56]

Like adults, children sought to preserve their own realms. The few accessible local parks were regarded as their own. And their sense of leisure 'freedom' contained an ever-active and ever-conscious awareness of living under the reality of external white concession or white enclosure. The relationship between leisure and class was also a relationship between leisure and race: 'We had a nice park we could play in. The name was Greenhaven. It's up there by Roeland Street. We named it ourselves, and that was our park. We'd go to that park and we'd play in that park — no European people ever chased us away.' The newly prohibitory brutalities of Nationalist apartheid after 1948 sent children scuttling back to the streets of District Six, shocked and bemused at being hounded out of outside recreational areas they had traditionally appropriated as their own: 'They even marked the benches! There was me and another girl and we just flopped down on the bench and ooo... God, those people. It was all boere. "GET UP, bladdy Hotnots, look you where you sit, STAAN OP, STAAN OP!" I just ran. It wasn't far from our home... I just ran up Darling Street and I go home. Apartheid — we just got to know that. "Hey — weet jy, watch waarom jy speel!" '57

For the District Six population, an awareness of living a culturally defined way of life outside and below dominant and élite society was a matter of distancing and security. There is special historical force in the reflection of one of the fictional characters in Rive's *Buckingham Palace*, that 'it's only in the District that I feel safe'.58 For it was within the shell of the District that people felt able to snuggle into a broadly 'corporate' class culture which, for the bulk of the community, had some internal coherence. The construction of that popular leisure, on their terms, was a crucial element in a defensive local world. That world, with its creative and 'free' popular cultural nexus, was one very largely impervious to bland rational recreation and the reform of manners.

The life of District Six workers was oppressive and hard, with poor housing, low pay, cyclical and seasonal unemployment, and chronic instability. But that community also imbued its popular life and practices with the indigenous resources of the locality. It did so in a manner which at once reaffirmed its peculiarly cosmopolitan heritage and identity, and invested it with a rolling tolerance and libertarianism to be found perhaps nowhere else in South Africa, with the possible single exception of the black Johannesburg suburb of Sophiatown until that area's Group Areas obliteration in the 1950s.59 In this sense popular cultural life in District Six may be regarded as the maintenance of a separate identity, an urban subculture as a response to an overwhelmingly subordinate social position. And of particular importance to it was the penetration and diffusion of the bonds and ties of 'community' as expressed through the recreational hub of cinema or street carnival.

With self-awareness of community went the reality of traditions whereby groups and classes in District Six lived and let live. In relationships and differences within their community they knew that there were some dainty boundaries which could not be crossed: 'Our neighbours opposite were the Carelses, nice people. They had a Rover car. When my father was out of work once, he washed it for them for ten months and my mother took in Mrs Carelse's washing. They could give us a hand... We all used to go to the Circus and to the Coons together, but we always walked down and met them there. I think they didn't want our bare feet in their nice car'.[60]

While the District Six community held together, while it could fuse creativity and hard-headed ideals of independence, morality and a shared way of life, there was relatively little to challenge what Gareth Stedman Jones has termed in another context a chosen 'culture of consolation' in the teeth of subordination.[61] That culture of consolation was rooted in the mean material realities of economic life.

Unemployment, low and irregular earnings, and casual employment bred a local labour process with a recreational life which was by habit and instinct a mercurial grabbing of experience or opportunity, with a style which was often bewilderingly picaresque. Against it, capital from the municipality of Cape Town did not come flooding in to endow the over thirty thousand inhabitants of this run-down neighbourhood with their own recreational grounds, libraries, sports fields or swimming baths. Yet, plainly put, one cannot but be left to wonder how any civic merchants of efficient, 'rationally' consumed leisure could have competed with the lure of the realm of Harry the snake catcher. For snake-catching was a world of fun somewhat distanced from the production and consumption of leisure as a commodity of bourgeois society.

Notes

This contribution to Holding their Ground *is dedicated to the memory of Richard Rive, 1931-1989.*

Oral evidence presented here is drawn from the collection of District Six life histories currently being collected by the Western Cape Oral History Project in the Department of History at the University of Cape Town. These recordings and transcripts are being preserved as an archive. Most of the respondents quoted in the text were born before 1920, and the oldest in 1901. In order to preserve customary conventions of confidentiality, informants remain anonymous. Names have been altered here and there, but the quotations are otherwise literal transcriptions, except for the elimination of some hesitations and repetitions.

1 Mrs G.D., b. 1913. Factory worker.
2 Mrs B.K., b. 1912. Home seamstress.
3 Mrs Z.A., b. 1906. Daughter of cinema owner.
4 Mr S.E., b. 1919. Mechanic.
5 Mrs Z.A.
6 Mrs E.W., b. 1918. Washerwoman.
7 Mr B.S., b. 1919. Market stallholder.
8 Ibid.
9 Ibid.
10 Mrs E.W.
11 Mr S.C., b. 1930. Teacher.
12 Mrs Z.A.
13 Ibid.
14 Mr S.C.
15 Mrs V.A., b. 1917. Factory worker.
16 Mrs B.K.
17 Mrs E.W.
18 Mrs B.J., b. 1918. Domestic worker.
19 Mrs V.A.
20 Mr S.C.
21 R. Rosenzweig, *Eight Hours for What We Will: Workers and Leisure in an Industrial City, 1870-1920* (Cambridge, 1983), pp. 217-18. See also J. Richards, *The Age of the Dream Palace: Cinema and Society in Britain, 1930-1939* (London, 1984), p. 24.
22 Mr I.W., b. 1918. Transport driver.
23 R. Rive, *Buckingham Palace, District Six* (Cape Town, 1986), p. 8.
24 Mrs Z.A.
25 G. Crossick, 'The Petite Bourgeoisie in Nineteenth-Century Britain', in P. Thane and A. Sutcliffe (eds), *Essays in Social History*, Vol. 2 (Oxford, 1986), p. 178.
26 Mrs Z.A. ('Who's smoking there?', 'Shift up, shift up.')
27 Mrs J.J., b. 1917. Factory worker.
28 Mrs Z.A.
29 Mr W.S., b. 1915. Carpenter.
30 J. White, 'Campbell Bunk, a Lumpen Community in London between the Wars', *History Workshop Journal*, 8 (1979), 25.
31 Mr W.S., b. 1920. Stevedore.
32 Mrs E.W.
33 Mrs N.O., b. 1906. Stallholder.
34 Mrs R.D., b. 1911. Hatmaker.

35 Mr S.C.

36 Ibid. ('the little sixpenny school', 'I am the Head of the Albertus Street Primary School'.)

37 R. Samuel, 'Comers and Goers', in H.J. Dyos and M. Wolff (eds), *The Victorian City: Images and Realities*, Vol. 1 (London, 1973), p. 123.

38 Mr S.C.

39 Mrs G.A., b. 1920. Domestic worker.

40 Cited by M. Ingram, 'Ridings, Rough Music and Mocking Rhymes in Early Modern England', in B. Reay (ed.), *Popular Culture in Seventeenth Century England* (Croom Helm, 1985), p. 175.

41 Mrs G.D.

42 Mrs A.A., b. 1916. Factory worker.

43 Mrs N.O.

44 Ibid.

45 Mrs Z.A.

46 Mrs G.A.

47 See M.S. Jeppie, Historical Process and the Constitution of Subjects: I.D. du Plessis and the Reinvention of the 'Malay', BA Hons Dissertation, University of Cape Town, 1987, esp. Chs 1-3.

48 Mr S.D., b. 1910. Fruit hawker. ('Tackies' are tennis shoes.)

49 Mr S.A., b. 1920. Plumber.

50 Mrs R.D.; Mr I.W.

51 Mr D.M., b. 1922. Labourer. ('that whole route', 'packed like sardines'.)

52 Ibid. ('new colours and new outfits every year', 'one troop was not to know what another was planning to wear... it was a great secret', 'the more respectable type', 'the Globe Gang also had a troupe. They were the Pennsylvanian Darkies. The Pennsylvanian Darkies used to make a clean sweep of the trophies every year', 'an enormous sphere on his head, made like a globe'.)

53 Mrs F.M., b. 1901. Shop worker.

54 Mr D.M.

55 Mrs H.S., b. 1903. Factory box maker.

56 Mrs A.A.

57 Mrs G.J., b. 1937. Domestic worker. ('Stand up, stand up!', 'Hey, watch out, be careful where you play!'.)

58 Rive, *Buckingham Palace*, p. 67.

59 See A. Proctor, 'Class Struggle, Segregation and the City: A History of Sophiatown, 1905-1940', in B. Bozzoli (ed.), *Labour, Townships*

and Protest: Studies in the Social History of the Witwatersrand (Johannesburg, 1979), pp. 49-89; D.M. Hart and G.H. Pirie, 'The Sight and Soul of Sophiatown', *Geographical Review*, 74 (1984), pp. 38-47.

60 Mrs R.L., b. 1928. Factory worker.

61 G. Stedman Jones, 'Working Class Culture and Working Class Politics in London, 1870-1900: Notes on the Remaking of a Working Class', *Journal of Social History* 7 (1974), 499.

Index

318